Graphics Programming in Turbo Pascal® 5.5

An Object-Oriented Approach

Graphics Programming in Turbo Pascal® 5.5

An Object-Oriented Approach

BEN EZZELL

Addison-Wesley Publishing Company, Inc.

Reading, Massachusetts   Menlo Park, California   New York
Don Mills, Ontario   Wokingham, England   Amsterdam   Bonn
Sydney   Singapore   Tokyo   Madrid   San Juan

Many of the designations used by manufacturers and sellers to distinguish their products are claimed as trademarks. Where those designations appear in this book and Addison-Wesley was aware of a trademark claim, the designations have been printed in initial capital letters.

ISBN: 0-201-55076-8

Copyright © 1990 by Ben Ezzell

All rights reserved. No part of this publication may be reproduced, stored in a retrieval system, or transmitted, in any form or by any means, electronic, mechanical, photocopying, recording, or otherwise, without the prior written permission of the publisher. Printed in the United States of America. Published simultaneously in Canada.

Production Editor: Amorette Pedersen
Cover Design by: Doliber Skeffington Design
Set in 11-point Times by Benchmark Productions

ABCDEFGHIJ-MW-943210
First Printing, May 1990

Dedicated, with respect, to the memory and vision of
Georges Pierre Seurat
1859-1891

Nearly a century before computers and a half-century before television, Georges Seurat broke with the French Impressionists to become the pioneer artist of the Pointillist (or Neo-Impressionist) school of painting. The principal difference was that instead of strokes and broad areas of paint blended to the desired hue, the Pointillist school of painting employed regular touches of pure color—points of color—which mixed optically, creating the shimmering effects of colored light.

Seurat's style was later adopted by other, better known painters such as Van Gogh, Pissarro, and Matisse. In due course it appeared in electronic form as pixel graphics (which in the hands of an artist remains, as always, Art).

Table of Contents

INTRODUCTION   xiii

PART 1
LEARNING GRAPHICS   1

CHAPTER 1
Introduction To Video Graphics   3
  Why use graphics displays?   4
  Video Adapter Types   5
  Video Modes   6
  Disadvantages   6
  Using Units   7
  Knock, Knock! What's There?   8
  Graphics Error Functions   11
  Other Graphics Mode Functions   13

CHAPTER 2
Viewport, Screen, and Page Functions   23
  Multiple Graphics Pages   25

Chapter 3
Color and Palette Functions — 29
   IBM-8514 Video Graphics Card — 34

Chapter 4
Screen Position Functions — 37
   GetMaxX and GetMaxY — 37
   GetX and GetY — 38

Chapter 5
Pixel Drawing and Image Functions — 39
   Pixel Functions — 39
   Line Drawing Functions — 40
   Line Styles — 41
   Rectangles, Bar Graphs, and Polygons — 43
   Video Aspect Ratio — 46
   Circles, Curves, and Arcs — 47
   FillEllipse — 50
   Fill Patterns and Fill Colors — 52
   The Internal Graphics Buffer — 54
   Image Manipulation — 55

Chapter 6
Graphics Text Functions — 59
   Text Functions — 60
   Graphics Text Styles, Justification, and Sizing — 61
   Text Settings Information — 64

Chapter 7
Advanced Graphics Pascal — 67
   Smart Linking — 67
   Linking Graphics Drivers and Fonts — 68
   Using Linked Drivers and Fonts — 69
   User-Designed Drivers and Fonts — 72

Part 2
Using Turbo Pascal Graphics — 75

Chapter 8
Combining Text With Graphics — 77
   Caveat — 77

Combining Text With Graphics	79
Functions for Variable Output	79
Concatenating Strings for Output	80
Other Output Utilities	81
Alternative Applications	84
Automatic Erasure	85
Summary	86

CHAPTER 9
Business Graphic Displays — 89

A Cautionary Note	89
Business Graph Demos	90
The Pie Graph Displays	90
Exploded Pie Graphs	95
Bar Graphs	96
Multiple Bar Graphs	99
Improving The Monochrome Display	102
Three-Dimensional Graphs	103
The Line Graph Display	112
Summary	117

CHAPTER 10
Simple Animation Techniques — 133

Image Animation	134
Morphological Animation	151
Summary	161

CHAPTER 11
Image Manipulation and Image Files — 177

Image Files: Storage and Retrieval	178
Files With Multiple Images	182
More Image Manipulation	183
Vector Calculations	190
Other Image Rotation Options	195
Summary	195

CHAPTER 12
Colors and Color Selection — 205

Video Signal Cues	207
CGA Colors	206
The IBM8514 and VGA Video Adapters	208

EGA/VGA Color	209
The Color Relations Cube	211
Summary	217

CHAPTER 13
Using A Mouse With Graphics Displays — 225

Reading Mouse Events as Cursor Keys	225
A Direct Mouse Interface	226
The Mouse Unit	226
The Object Mouse Unit	228
The GenMouse Object Type	234
The GraphicMouse Object Type	234
The Implementation Section	235
GenMouse Implementation	236
The GraphicMouse Methods	244
Other Object Mouse Methods	245
The LightPen Methods	247
The MousePtr Utility	247
Summary	248

CHAPTER 14
Buttons, Scrollbars, and Control Objects — 271

Graphic Control Objects	272
The Point Object Type	273
Mouse Access	276
The Button Object Type	277
The RadioButton Object Type	286
The ScrollBar Object Type	290
The VueMeter Object Type	298
Other Meter Objects	300
The CtrlTest Demonstration	301
Summary	306

CHAPTER 15
Creating Icons — 329

Creating Icon Images	330
The Icon Object	333

CHAPTER 16
Turtle Graphics — 353

The Turtle Graphic Commands	355

Turtle Movements	356
Turtle Drawing	361
Turtle Information	362
Turtle Graphics Demo (TUR-DEMO.PAS)	362
Summary	369

CHAPTER 17
Graphics Printer Output — 383

Using the Epson Dot-Matrix Printers	384
Using The LaserJet Printer Utility	391
Writing Graphics Characters to the LaserJet	395
Sixteen and Four Tone Grayscale Palettes	395
LJGraph Unit	396
More on Colors and Color Mapping	407

CHAPTER 18
Graphics Plotter Output — 417

Color Printers	417
Color Plotters	418
Selecting The Plotter Serial Interface	421
Using The PLOTTER Utility	422
Plotting The Screen	424

CHAPTER 19
The Turbo Font Editor — 435

Introduction to Stroked Fonts	436
General Capabilities	438
Font Editor Display	439
Editing Tools	442
Font Editor Command Reference	444
Beginning a New Font from Scratch	449
Using Custom Fonts	450
BGI Stroke File Format	452

CHAPTER 20
On The Shores of Fractal Seas — 455

The Fractal Universe	456
The Mandelbrot Set	456
The Henon Curve	461
The Malthusian Curve	462

Hic Draconis	465
Summary	466

APPENDIX A
The BGI Driver Toolkit — 477

Creating Device Drivers for the Borland Graphics Interface	477
The BGI Driver Toolkit	477
Introduction	478
BGI Run-time Architecture	478
BGI Graphics Model	479
Device Driver Construction Particulars	496

APPENDIX B
A VGA 256-color .BGI Driver — 499

APPENDIX C
The Graphic Character Fonts — 501

INDEX — 513

Introduction

Many years ago, my first introduction to Turbo Pascal was the venerable version 1.0—by current standards a veritable dinosaur—but, at the time, a wonderful compiler with a truly marvelous support library.

Of course, this early version did not provide any support for graphics, but that was all right because neither did anyone else, including most computer manufacturers. I was using a Heath/Zenith All-In-One H/Z-100 which, while monochrome, did provide three banks of addressable video RAM—three separate 64K banks for the red, green, and blue guns that appeared on a monochrome (well, amber) video as "shades of gray" (ok, "shades of amber") with a resolution of 640x225 pixels.

I didn't have any convenient way to address the video, which did not differentiate between character and graphics modes. Text modes were bit-addressible. BASIC offered a few options for direct pixel addressing, but BASIC was exactly what I was trying to get away from.

Happily, the world is full of hackers and one such inventive soul—whose name I do not now remember—quickly devised and published a brief assembly language routine called POINT that could be called as an external procedure from Turbo Pascal and, addressed with coordinate and color parameters, would write a pixel directly to the video memory.

Naturally, POINT was not transferable to the IBM compatibles. But since IBM graphics were rare, there wasn't a great deal of incentive to simplify programs to the point where they could run on IBM compatibles. Therefore, many of us had a lot of fun devising our own graphics routines, including everything from line- and circle-drawing algorithms to image-capture methods.

Pixel graphics were an idea that held wide appeal and graphics video cards were an increasingly popular add-on for everyone's systems. Borland wasn't slow to follow suit because all of these graphics routines which I and other hackers had laboriously hand-crafted for our own use were suddenly standard routines in Turbo Pascal, along with other graphics routines that either hadn't occurred to us or hadn't been important enough to warrant development.

In what we have come to consider and expect as typical Borland fashion, Turbo Pascal graphics quickly grew from convenient utilities to essential and comprehensive routines providing full graphics capabilities including graphics windows, video hardware recognition, custom graphics drivers, and graphics character fonts.

Of course, there are still a few features which would be nice to have, such as a convenient method to scroll a graphics window or methods to extend the graphics image beyond the display limits. Overall, the Borland Graphics Interface (BGI) provides a complete and flexible graphics package without unnecessarily restricting how we use these features.

With object-oriented Turbo Pascal, graphics have become more than convenient—now they're simple. However, with the inertia typical of human nature, the myth still persists that Turbo Pascal is not a serious graphics language.

In the world of C programming, it was no great surprise to anyone that graphics should become convenient, and since it was Turbo C providing the graphics features, it was obvious that these would be excellent graphics capabilities and well worth the programmer's investment in time and development. This is a rather narrow view because it was Turbo Pascal—not Turbo C—which first introduced the graphics features and *precisely the same* graphics features are found in both languages!

So, welcome to the wonderful world of graphics. They are anything you wish them to be, from serious business applications to frivolous entertainment, or anything in between. Have fun and, graphically speaking, happy hacking.

Part One

Learning Graphics

CHAPTER 1

Introduction To Video Graphics

There is a myth prevalent in the computer industry which holds that Pascal is not a graphics-oriented language and is not capable of graphics applications. Perhaps, in some past computer age, this myth may have been justified because there was a time when computers were not graphics-oriented (excepting the early Apple systems, which were graphics-oriented but not application-oriented).

But yesterday's myths are not today's realities. Video systems have expanded greatly from the original CGA systems which were only vaguely graphics capable. And the early 2-MHz, 16K systems, which lacked both the speed and memory for graphics applications, are effectively obsolete, supplanted by 20/30+ MHz systems with a megabyte and larger memories.

At the same time, graphics interfaces and applications such as Microsoft Windows, OS/2, and Ventura Publisher are both popular and common.

And, most importantly, Turbo Pascal has emerged as not only a graphics-oriented compiler, but, using the Borland Graphics Interface, as a graphics superstar. It provides the procedures and functions that support graphic applications and the speed of execution necessary to make graphic applications practical—as well as desirable.

Graphics are no longer just elaborations used to fancily dress otherwise conventional programs or to provide color and imagery for arcade games. Instead, graphics have become not only a new standard, but a standard against which many—if not most—future applications will be judged. This is hardly a temporary trend. Even portable computers, though most still lack color capabilities, are hurrying to match or emulate high-resolution graphics displays. My newest system, for example, has VGA video in the form of a back-lit, super-twist liquid crystal screen and, while color is emulated as 16 levels of gray, a total weight of 14 pounds, superb clarity, and go-anywhere operation are more than a fair trade-off. In fact, much of the typesetting and illustrations (both of which are impossible without excellent graphics capabilities) for this book have been executed on—you guessed it—my lap top portable.

When even portable computers can support great graphics, doesn't it seem likely that graphics are here to stay?

Why use graphics displays?

While a program's general appearance is an important factor, particularly in the competitive commercial environment, graphic displays have advantages far more important than the merely cosmetic.

Today, the term *Graphic User Interface*, or GUI, is used as a generic reference for any application or system that employs graphic screen elements and mouse selection rather than relying solely on keyboard input controls. In general, GUI elements are designed for ready recognition without requiring explanations or documentation and provide for more human-oriented interactions than the familiar **C:>** prompt. In some cases, such as the aggressively icon-oriented Macintosh, this is taken to extremes which many find annoying.

Extremes aside, a balanced combination of graphics and text elements permits the presentation of information in forms that are easily and rapidly understandable. For example, scrollbars that show location within long lists or page orientations and also provide both a mouse control for changing display position and mouse-operated pushbuttons (which change state to show selections), are marvelous graphic elements that operate without requiring explanation.

In the same fashion, business graphs are often easier to understand and compare than columns of figures and, for many mathematical applications, a good three-dimensional graph reveals a whole world of understanding which raw data or formulas do not. For typesetting software, there is simply no substitute for graphics—witness the popular WordPerfect 5.0, which provides both the standard text displays and a graphics typeset view of a page output (including images).

On the other hand, elaborate folder and trashcan icons that must be dragged around the screen to accomplish anything at all can be an annoyance. Obviously, a balance is required.

But, before worrying about what to use, the first requirement is simply to be able to create graphics displays.

Which Graphics Display

The current proliferation of video hardware (now including at least 10 standard video adapters) has presented its own problems for the programmer. Each design of video hardware supports a different set of capabilities, may use different memory addresses, may or may not support multiple graphics pages (and/or multiple text pages), and may support video modes ranging from 320x200 to 1024x768 pixel displays and ranging from monochrome to 256-color displays.

Of course, the initial problem facing every graphics programmer is simply the question of identifying which video adapter is installed in what machine. One option has always been to ask end-users, allowing them to select the video mode that will be used. This is also a poor choice because even professional programmers are not always certain with what hardware they are working and the average end-user may not know if he or she has a graphics adapter at all, much less what type it is. The alternate choice is to have your software query the hardware to determine the present configuration.

Assuming that some standard for hardware identification existed, this would be a simple matter. But, unfortunately for programmers, the proliferation of video adapter hardware has occurred without any formalized provisions for identification. In a previous book, *Programming The IBM User Interface*, I discussed several methods to test for the presence or absence of CGA/EGA video adapters and some of the problems inherent in correctly identifying hardware.

Happily, the release of Turbo Pascal version 4.0 (and Turbo C 1.5) has relieved much of the indecision of identifying, supporting, and using the various video adapter cards currently available. Also, judging by Borland's past performance, it seems fairly safe to assume that new video adapters will be similarly supported.

Unhappily, this welcome support for diverse video capabilities has resulted in creating its own confusion over how to use these new tools, what is possible and, in general, what to do with a plethora of new capabilities.

This confusion is precisely the subject of this book.

Video Adapter Types

Turbo Pascal (version 4.0 or later) and Turbo C (version 1.5 or later) each provide comprehensive support for all major video card types currently in use. At this time, I will be discussing and illustrating graphics in Turbo Pascal only.

If you are using Turbo C, corresponding functions are provided, using essentially the same function and procedure names and operating in effectively the same manner.

Contemporary video cards range from the text-only original video systems to the ultra-high resolution IBM-8514 (popular with typesetting and CAD software applications), with a variety of resolutions lying between the two. The higher resolution video cards must be matched with monitors of corresponding pixel resolution, but this is a hardware matter and, for all practical purposes as a programmer, you may simply assume the hardware present corresponds to the identification returned by Turbo Pascal's DetectGraph function. Any discrepancies in matching between video cards and monitors are the end-user's responsibility and should not be the programmer's concern.

Most, if not all, multisync and higher resolution graphics video cards offer some recognition of the actual monitor type.

Video Modes

Every PC, XT, or AT is equipped with some type of video adapter card. Beginning with the very basic video card, you may have the Monochrome Display Adapter (MDA), which supports text-only display. If this is the case, you will not be able to program or use graphics without upgrading your system.

The first step up is the popular Color Graphics Adapter (CGA) card, while higher resolutions and wider options are provided by the Hercules Monochrome Graphics Adapters, Multi Color Graphics Array (MCGA), and Enhanced Graphics Adapter (EGA) video adapters. For more advanced graphics capabilities, as for typesetting or CAD applications, the AT&T 400-Line Graphic Adapter, Variable or Video Graphics Array (VGA), sometimes called Multi-Sync video, PC-3270, and IBM-8514 video adapters all offer even higher pixel resolutions.

In Turbo Pascal, graphics support for all of these types is provided in the form of six graphics interface (.BGI) units (ATT, CGA, EGAVGA, HERC, IBM8514, and PC3270) and four graphics fonts (GOTH.CHR, LITT.CHR, SANS.CHR, and TRIP.CHR). As new video graphics cards appear, new .BGI units may be included for support—while new .CHR fonts may be user-created or purchased from commercial sources. (See also Chapter 17, Appendix D, and Appendix E.)

The graphics support units, however, are not included in the standard memory models as distributed—an omission made for the express purpose of speeding compilation time when graphics are not needed.

Disadvantages

Once a program has been compiled the .EXE program can be distributed with external .BGI and .CHR files required for operation. Together, these files require approximately 60K of disk space. Granted, this isn't an excessive requirement in terms of storage, but relying on external files for execution can create difficulties.

First, a call to InitGraph must include the drive and path specification of where the .BGI (and .CHR) modules are located. If no path is specified, then the current directory is assumed. Normally, this routing information is supplied by the programmer and, if the required files are not found (a problem which can occur for a variety of reasons no matter how well designed a program is), your program will terminate!

Second, if the default (current) path is assumed and all external files are present but the program is called from another directory or drive, this will also cause a crash!

Third, never depend on the end-user to be aware of the importance of external files. They may love your program and guard it jealously but, as soon as space becomes a problem, may erase necessary external files. It happens, be prepared. Alternatively, you can link the .BGI and .CHR files directly into the graphics library, increasing your .EXE program in size by about 30K (see Chapter 9, *Advanced Graphics Management Functions*), while making the drivers and fonts a part of your .EXE program rather than external files.

One other option: if linking these files results in too large a program, you might try flagging the external files as **R**ead-Only, **S**ystem, and/or **H**idden.

Using Units

Turbo Pascal provides several units—supplementary function libraries providing extended support for special applications—which currently include the DOS, GRAPH, GRAPH3, OVERLAY, PRINTER, SYSTEM, and TURBO3 units. Also, custom units can be created to provide new functions and procedures. Custom units are used as conveniently as the distribution units.

To use a unit—choosing the GRAPH unit as an example since it will be essential to all of the programs in this book—is simplicity itself and requires very little except the statement.

    uses GRAPH;

in the program header.

When functions from several units are required, multiple units can be referenced in a single line, thus:

    uses CRT, DOS, GRAPH, TURTLE;

The order in which the units are called is immaterial and any number of units can be included. The preceding example also includes one custom unit, TURTLE, which will be created in this book.

The Include Directories Option

If the unit files are not included in your Turbo Pascal root directory, Turbo's Integrated Development Environment includes a provision for specifying directory paths for the Turbo, EXE & TPU, Include, Unit, and Object files. (See "Directory Options" in the *Turbo Pascal User's Guide*.)

To specify the unit directory path, select the **Options**, **Directory**, and **Unit** entries from the menu and enter the full path specification where the unit (.TPU) files are located. Multiple paths may be specified by separating the paths with a semicolon (;), as in the following:

```
\TP\UNITS;\TP\EXE;\TP\OBJECT
```

This example specifies three subdirectories where units may be found, the \TP\UNITS directory, the \TP\EXE directory—where a newly compiled .TPU file would appear since this is the directory specified under the **EXE** option—and the \TP\OBJECT directory. The Pascal root directory, \TP, is included by default.

Knock, Knock! What's There?

The first step in your graphics program is to initialize the appropriate graphics driver. For a list of supported graphics video cards, drivers, and graphics modes, see Table 1-1.

Table 1-1: Video Modes Supported By Turbo Pascal

GRAPHICS DRIVER[1]	VALUE	GRAPHICS MODES	KEY VALUE[2]	COLUMN X ROW	PALETTE OR COLORS[3]	VIDEO PAGES
DETECT	0	requests **InitGraph** to execute autodetection				
CGA	1	CGAC0	0	320x200	C0	1
		CGAC1	1	320x200	C1	1
		CGAC2	2	320x200	C2	1
		CGAC3	3	320x200	C3	1
		CGAHI	4	640x200	2 colors	1
MCGA	2	MCGAC0	0	320x200	C0	1
		MCGAC1	1	320x200	C1	1
		MCGAC2	2	320x200	C2	1
		MCGAC3	3	320x200	C3	1
		MCGAMED	4	640x200	2 colors	1
		MCGAHI	5	640x48	2 colors	1

GRAPHICS DRIVER[1]	VALUE	GRAPHICS MODES	KEY VALUE[2]	COLUMN X ROW	PALETTE OR COLORS[3]	VIDEO PAGES
EGA	3	EGALO	0	640x200	16 colors	4
		EGAHI	1	640x350	16 colors	2
EGA64	4	EGA64LO	0	640x200	16 colors	1
		EGA64HI	1	640x350	4 colors	1
EGAMONO	5	EGAMONOHI	3	640x350	2 colors	1 - 2[4]
IBM8514[5]	6	IBM8514LO	0	640x480	256 colors	1
		IBM8514HI	1	1024x768	256 colors	1
HERC	7	HERCMONOHI	0	720x348	2 colors	4
ATT400	8	ATT400C0	0	320x200	C0	1
		ATT400C1	1	320x200	C1	1
		ATT400C2	2	320x200	C2	1
		ATT400C3	3	320x200	C3	1
		ATT400MED	4	640x200	2 colors	1
		ATT400HI	5	640x200	2 colors	1
VGA	9	VGALO	0	640x200	16 colors	4
		VGAMED	1	640x350	16 colors	2
		VGAHI	2	640x480	16 colors	1
PC3270	10	PC3270HI	0	720x350	2 colors	1

1. The *GraphicDriver* and *GraphicMode* names are constants defined in GRAPHICS.H, as are the corresponding numerical and mode values (see note 2).
2. Mode settings returned by InitGraph, DetectGraph, or GetGraphMode.
3. C0..C3 refer to the predefined 4-color palettes—see SetPalette.
4. With 64K on an EGAMONO card, only one video page is supported; with 256K, two video pages are supported.
5. Autodetection will not correctly recognize the IBM-8514 graphics card. Instead, InitGraph or DetectGraph will identify the IBM-8514 card as a VGA graphics card which the IBM-8514 will emulate correctly (IBM8514LO is equivalent to VGAHI). To use the higher resolution mode (IBM8514HI, which is 1024x768 pixels), assign the value IBM8514 (numerical value 6—defined in GRAPHICS.H) to the graphdriver variable before calling InitGraph. Do not use DetectGraph or DETECT with InitGraph. See also the text notes on IBM-8514 and SetRBGPalette.

DetectGraph

Normally, the DetectGraph function is called by InitGraph, but it can also be called independently in order to determine the current graphics driver and graphics mode.

Example:
```
uses GRAPH;
var
    GraphDriver, GraphMode: integer;
begin
    GraphDriver := DETECT;
    DetectGraph( GraphDriver, GraphMode );
    ...
end;
```

If a problem occurs, *GraphDriver* returns an error code; otherwise, *GraphDriver* identifies the appropriate driver type and *GraphMode* returns the highest valid video mode for this driver. For DetectGraph, no driver path is required (see InitGraph).

The DetectGraph function does not initialize any graphics settings. The principal reason for calling DetectGraph directly would be to subsequently use InitGraph to call a specific graphics driver or to select a graphics mode which InitGraph would not call by default. Alternatively, a different mode can be called after initialization by using the SetGraphMode function.

Value returned: *GraphDriver* returns a driver type or error code; *GraphMode* returns the highest valid video mode.

Portability: IBM PCs and compatibles only, corresponding functions exist in Turbo C.

InitGraph

Using Turbo Pascal, the InitGraph function is provided to set the initial graphics parameter values, load the proper graphics driver, and set the system to the desired graphics mode.

Example:
```
uses GRAPH;
const
    DriverPath = '';
var
    GraphDriver, GraphMode : integer;
begin
    GraphDriver := DETECT;
    InitGraph( GraphDriver, GraphMode,
               DriverPath );
    ...
end.
```

Setting *GraphDriver* as zero (DETECT) instructs InitGraph to call *DetectGraph(GraphDriver, GraphMode)* to determine the type (and settings) of the installed video graphics adapter. If an error occurs, *GraphDriver* returns an error code indicating the type of error. Table 1-2 lists the graphic error codes.

Table 1-2: Initialization Graphic Error Codes

CODE	MESSAGE
−2	Cannot detect graphics card
−3	Cannot locate graphics driver file(s)
−4	Invalid driver (or not recognized)
−5	Insufficient memory to load graphics driver

The DetectGraph and GraphResult functions return the same error codes shown in Table 1-2.

If no error occurs, then the internal error code is set to zero and InitGraph allocates memory for the appropriate graphics driver, loads the required .BGI file from disk, and sets the default graphics parameter values. Also, *GraphDriver* returns the driver type while *GraphMode* returns the mode setting.

GraphDriver and *GraphMode* can also be specified (either by using the appropriate numerical constants or by using the driver and mode names as defined in the GRAPH.TPU unit). In either case, *DriverPath* shows the drive and path where the .BGI graphics drivers are located. If *DriverPath* is null then these files must be located in the default directory. If they are located in a different directory, then the complete path specification should be shown as:

```
DriverPath = '\TP\BGI';
```

Since the *DriverPath* set by InitGraph is also used by SetTextStyle to search for the character font (.CHR) files, both .BGI and .CHR files must be located in the same directory.

Value returned: *GraphDriver* returns a driver type or error code; *GraphMode* returns the highest valid video mode.

Portability: IBM PCs and compatibles only, corresponding functions exist in Turbo C.

GetDriverName

The GetDriverName function returns a string with the name of the current graphics driver.

Example: `uses GRAPH;`

`OutTextXY( 50, 50, 'Using driver ' + GetDriverName );`

GetDriverName can only be used after InitGraph has established a graphics driver and mode. See GetModeName for related information.

Portability: IBM PCs and compatibles only, corresponding functions exist in Turbo C.

Graphics Error Functions

As mentioned, if a graphics video card is not present, if the graphics drivers are not found, or if some other error occurs during the detection of initialization, an error code is returned by DetectGraph or InitGraph. There are, however, other conditions where a graphics error can occur and the functions GraphResult and GraphErrorMsg are provided to test and display appropriate error results and messages.

GraphResult

The GraphResult function returns a numerical error code set by the last graphics operation that reported an error. This will be an integer value in the range −15..0. Since the error condition is reset to zero when GraphResult is called, the returned value should be stored in a local variable and then tested for further action.

Example:
```
uses GRAPH;
var
    ErrorNumber;

ErrorNumber = GraphResult;
```

Value returned: Graph Result returns an error code (−15..0), see Table 1-3 for interpretation.

Portability: IBM PCs and compatibles only, corresponding functions exist in Turbo C.

Table 1-3: Graphics Error Messages

ERROR CODE	GRAPHICS_ERROR CONSTANT	ERROR MESSAGE STRING
0	grOk	No error
−1	grNoInitGraph	.BGI graphics not installed (use InitGraph)
−2	grNotDetected	Graphics hardware not detected
−3	grFileNotFound	Device driver file not found (.BGI file)
−4	grInvalidDriver	Invalid device driver file
−5	grNoLoadMem	Not enough memory to load driver
−6	grNoScanMem	Out of memory in scan fill
−7	grNoFloodMem	Out of memory in flood fill
−8	grFontNotFound	Font file not found (.CHR file)
−9	grNoFontMem	Not enough memory to load font
−10	grInvalidMode	Invalid graphics mode for selected driver
−11	grError	Graphics error (*generic error*)
−12	grIOerror	Graphics I/O error
−13	grInvalidFont	Invalid font file
−14	grInvalidFontNum	Invalid font number
−15	grInvalidDeviceNum	Invalid device number

The *GraphicsErrors* constants and error messages are defined in the GRAPH unit.

GraphErrorMsg

The GraphErrorMsg function returns a pointer to the appropriate error message string. These strings are defined in the graphics library (GRAPHICS.LIB) but a separate error message routine can be created to display a more complete or more informative error message if desired.

Example: `uses GRAPH;`
          `var`
              `ErrorNumber;`

          `ErrorNumber = GraphResult;`
          `writeln( GraphErrorMsg( ErrorNumber ) );`

Value returned: none.

Portability: IBM PCs and compatibles only, corresponding functions exist in Turbo C.

Other Graphics Mode Functions

With the exceptions of the EGAMONO, HERC, and PC3270 video drivers, each video driver supports two or more video modes that offer varying pixel resolutions or different color palettes. To handle mode inquiries and to change operating modes, Turbo Pascal provides several functions:

GetGraphMode

The GetGraphMode function returns an integer value showing the current (operational) graphics mode which was set by InitGraph or SetGraphMode.

Example: `uses GRAPH;`
          `var`
              `CurrentMode : integer;`

          `CurrentMode = GetGraphMode;`

Value returned: current graphics mode.

Portability: IBM PCs and compatibles only, corresponding functions exist in Turbo C.

GetModeRange

The GetModeRange function is called with an integer value specifying the graphics driver (which may be an integer variable or one of the constants defined in the GRAPH unit) and returns two values defining the minimum and maximum valid modes supported by the indicated driver.

Example: `uses GRAPH;`
          `var`
              `LoMode, HiMode : integer;`

          `GetModeRange( GraphDriver, LoMode, HiMode );`

If the value passed as *GraphDriver* is invalid, then both *LoMode* and *HiMode* return −1.

Value returned: minimum and maximum valid modes or −1 error code.

Portability: IBM PCs and compatibles only, corresponding functions exist in Turbo C.

GetMaxMode

The GetMaxMode function returns the highest mode number valid for the currently loaded driver, returning the value directly from the driver. The GetModeRange function is still supported but is valid for the BGI (Borland-supplied) drivers only.

Example:
```
uses GRAPH;
var
    MaxMode : integer;
MaxMode := GetMaxMode;
```

All drivers support modes *0..GetMaxModes* and the value returned is the maximum value that can be passed to the SetGraphMode procedure.

Portability: IBM PCs and compatibles only, corresponding functions exist in Turbo C.

GetModeName

The GetModeName function is called with a mode value and returns the appropriate mode name for the current graphics driver.

Example:
```
uses GRAPH;
var
   i : integer;
OutTextXY( 50, 50, 'Valid modes are: ' );
for i := 0 to GetMaxMode do
   OutTextXY( 60, 65 + 10 * i,
              GetModeName( i ) );
```

Mode names are embedded in each graphics driver and can be used as menus, to display status, or to report system capabilities.

Portability: IBM PCs and compatibles only, corresponding functions exist in Turbo C.

GraphDefaults

The GraphDefaults function resets all graphic settings to their default values (the values originally set by InitGraph and defined in the GRAPH unit). This includes resetting the viewport (graphics window) to the entire screen; moving the current position to (0,0); resetting default palette colors, background color, and drawing color; resetting the default file and pattern styles; and resetting the default text font and justification modes.

Example: `uses GRAPH;`

          `GraphDefaults;`

Value returned: none.

Portability: IBM PCs and compatibles only, corresponding functions exist in Turbo C.

SetGraphMode

The graphics mode must have been previously initialized by InitGraph. The SetGraphMode function must be called with a graphics mode that is valid for the current device driver (use GetGraphMode to find the current mode value or GetModeRange to check permissible values). When called, SetGraphMode selects a new graphics mode, clearing the screen and resetting all graphics variables to their default values (see GraphDefaults).

Example:
```
uses GRAPH;
var
    ModeNumber : integer;
SetGraphMode( ModeNumber );
```

The SetGraphMode function can also be used with the RestoreCrt function to switch back and forth between text and graphics displays. *InitGraph must have been called before either of these functions can be used.*

Example:
```
uses GRAPH;
var
    CurrentMode : integer;
CurrentMode = GetGraphMode;
RestoreCrtMode;                          /* text mode    */
SetGraphMode( CurrentMode );    /* graphics mode*/
```

If SetGraphMode is called with a value that is invalid for the current device driver, GraphResult will return a value of −10 (grInvalidMode).

Value returned: none, see GraphResult for error codes.

Portability: IBM PCs and compatibles only, corresponding functions exist in Turbo C.

RestoreCrtMode

The RestoreCrtMode function resets the system video to the original text mode detected by the call to InitGraph. This can be used with SetGraphMode to alternate between text and graphics displays.

Example: `uses GRAPH;`

        `RestoreCrtMode;`

Value returned: none, see GraphResult for error codes.

Portability: IBM PCs and compatibles only, corresponding functions exist in Turbo C.

CloseGraph

The CloseGraph function restores the system to the normal text mode originally detected by InitGraph. This also deallocates the memory used by the graphics system for drivers, fonts, and internal buffer.

Example: `uses GRAPH;`

        `CloseGraph;`

If you wish to switch back and forth between text and graphics, use the RestoreCrtMode and SetGraphMode functions.

Value returned: none, see GraphResult for error codes.

Portability: IBM PCs and compatibles only, corresponding functions exist in Turbo C.

FIRSTGRP.PAS

```
{=====================================}
{            FIRSTGRP.PAS             }
{   demo for initializing graphics    }
{   mode in Turbo Pascal version 5.5  }
{=====================================}

uses GRAPH, CRT;

type
   Str10 = string[10];    Str20 = string[20];
const
   DriverNames : array[ 0..10 ] of Str10 =
      ( 'Detect', 'CGA', 'MCGA', 'EGA', 'EGA64',
        'EGAMono', 'IBM8514', 'HercMono', 'ATT400',
        'VGA', 'PC3270' );
   Fonts : array[ 0..4 ] of Str10 =
      ( 'Default', 'Triplex', 'Small', 'SansSerif',
```

```pascal
            'Gothic' );
   LineStyles : array[ 0..4 ] of Str20 =
      ( 'Solid', 'Dotted', 'Center', 'Dashed',
        'User Defined' );
   FillStyles : array[ 0..11 ] of Str20 =
      ( 'Empty', 'Solid', 'Line Fill', 'Light Slash',
        'Slash', 'Back Slash', 'Light Back Slash',
        'Hatch', 'XHatch', 'Interleave', 'Wide Dot',
        'Close Dot' );
   TextDirect : array[ 0..1 ] of Str10 =
      ( 'Horizontal', 'Vertical' );
   HorizJust : array[ 0..2 ] of Str20 =
      ( 'Flush Left', 'Centered', 'Flush Right' );
   VertJust : array[ 0..2 ] of Str10 =
      ( 'Bottom', 'Centered', 'Top' );
var
   GraphDriver,                  { graphics driver value    }
   GraphMode,                    { graphics mode value      }
   AspectRatio,                  { screen pixel aspect ratio }
   MaxX, MaxY,                   { maximum screen resolution }
   MaxColors  : integer;         { maximum colors available }
   xasp, yasp : word;            { factors for aspect ratio }
   Palette    : PaletteType;
function N2S( Val, Digit : integer ): string;
   var                           { converts integer to string }
      Buffer : string;
   begin
      str( Val:Digit, Buffer );
      N2S := Buffer;
   end;
function R2S( Val : real; Digit, Decimal : integer ):
string;
   var                           { converts real to string }
      Buffer : string;
   begin
      str( Val: Digit: Decimal, Buffer );
      R2S := Buffer;
   end;
procedure TestGraphicError;
   var
      ErrorCode : integer;
   begin
      ErrorCode := GraphResult;        { check the result    }
      if ErrorCode  grOk then          { if an error occurs  }
      begin                            { reset to text mode  }
         CloseGraph;                   { report the error    }
         writeln(' Graphics System Error: '
```

```pascal
                          GraphErrorMsg( ErrorCode ) );
         halt( 1 );                         { and halt program   }
      end;
   end;
procedure ChangeTextStyle( fnt, dir, chrsz : integer );
   var
      ErrorCode : integer;
   begin
      ErrorCode := GraphResult;            { clear error code }
      SetTextStyle( fnt, dir, chrsz );
      TestGraphicError;                    { check for errors }
   end;
procedure StatusLine( msg : string );
   var                       { display status line at bottom }
      Height : integer;
   begin
      SetViewPort( 0, 0, MaxX, MaxY, True );
      SetColor( MaxColors-1 );     { start with max color   }
      ChangeTextStyle( DefaultFont, HorizDir, 1 );
      SetTextJustify( CenterText, TopText );
      SetLineStyle( SolidLn, 0, NormWidth );
      SetFillStyle( EmptyFill, 0 );
      Height := TextHeight( msg );     { get char height    }
      Bar( 0, MaxY-(Height+4), MaxX, MaxY );
      Rectangle( 0, MaxY-(Height+4), MaxX, MaxY );
      OutTextXY( MaxX div 2, MaxY-(Height+2), msg );
      SetViewPort( 1, Height+5,
                   MaxX-1, MaxY-(Height+5), True );
   end;
procedure DrawBorder;
   var          { draw solid line around current viewport }
      vp : ViewPortType;
   begin
      SetColor( MaxColors - 1 );           { set draw color }
      SetLineStyle( SolidLn, 0, NormWidth );
      GetViewSettings( vp );
      Rectangle( 0, 0, vp.x2-vp.x1, vp.y2-vp.y1 );
   end;
procedure ReportWindow( header : string );
   var
      Height : integer;
   begin
      ClearDevice;                    { clear graphics screen }
      SetColor( MaxColors - 1 );
      SetViewPort( 0, 0, MaxX, MaxY, True );
      Height := TextHeight( header );        { char height }
```

```pascal
         ChangeTextStyle( DefaultFont, HorizDir, 1 );
         SetTextJustify( CenterText, TopText );
         OutTextXY( MaxX div 2, 2, header );
         SetViewPort( 0, Height+4,
                      MaxX, MaxY-(Height+4), True );
         DrawBorder;
         SetViewPort( 1, Height+5,
                      MaxX-1, MaxY-(Height+5), True );
      end;
procedure Pause;
   var
      Ch : char;
   begin
      StatusLine( 'Press any key...' );
                                        { put msg on screen    }
      while KeyPressed do Ch := ReadKey;
      Ch := ReadKey;                    { wait for a key entry }
      ClearDevice;                      { clear the screen     }
   end;
procedure StepDisplay( var y : integer );
   var                                  { steps display & color }
      Color : integer;
   begin
      inc( y, TextHeight( 'W' ) + 2 );
      Color := GetColor - 1;
      if Color = 0 then Color := GetMaxColor;
      SetColor( Color );
   end;
procedure ReportStatus;
   var                   { report current system configuration }
      ViewInfo : ViewPortType;
      LineInfo : LineSettingsType;
      FillInfo : FillSettingsType;
      TextInfo : TextSettingsType;
      Driver, Mode, Buffer : string;
      x, y, GraphHi, GraphLo : integer;
   begin
      x := 10;
      y :=  4;
      ReportWindow( 'Graphic Status Report' );
      GetViewSettings( ViewInfo );
      GetLineSettings( LineInfo );
      GetFillSettings( FillInfo );
      GetTextSettings( TextInfo );
      GetPalette( Palette );
      SetTextJustify( LeftText, TopText );
```

```
          OutTextXY( x, y, 'Graphics driver        : ' +
                     GetDriverName + '.BGI');
          StepDisplay( y );
          OutTextXY( x, y, 'Graphics device        : (' +
                     N2S( GraphDriver, 1 ) + ')' +
                     DriverNames[GraphDriver] );
          StepDisplay( y );
          OutTextXY( x, y, 'Graphics mode          : (' +
                     N2S( GraphMode, 1 ) + ')' +
                     GetModeName( GraphMode ) );
          StepDisplay( y );
          GetModeRange( GraphDriver, GraphHi, GraphLo );
          OutTextXY( x, y, 'Valid mode range       : Low = ' +
                     N2S( GraphHi, 1 ) + ', High = ' +
                     N2S( GraphLo, 1 ) );
          StepDisplay( y );
          OutTextXY( x, y, 'Screen resolution      : ' +
                     '( 0, 0, ' +
                     N2S( GetMaxX, 2 ) + ', ' +
                     N2S( GetMaxY, 2 ) + ')' );
          StepDisplay( y );
          OutTextXY( x, y, 'Current viewport       : (' +
                     N2S( ViewInfo.x1, 2 ) + ', ' +
                     N2S( ViewInfo.y1, 2 ) + ', ' +
                     N2S( ViewInfo.x2, 2 ) + ', ' +
                     N2S( ViewInfo.y2, 2 ) + ')' );
          StepDisplay( y );
          if ViewInfo.Clip then Buffer := 'ON'
                           else Buffer := 'OFF';
          OutTextXY( x, y, 'Clipping               : ' +
                     Buffer );
          StepDisplay( y );
          OutTextXY( x, y, 'Current position (CP) : (' +
                     N2S( GetX, 2 ) + ', ' +
                     N2S( GetY, 2 ) + ')' );
          StepDisplay( y );
          OutTextXY( x, y, 'Max / this color       : ' +
                     N2S( MaxColors, 2 ) + ' / ' +
                     N2S( GetColor, 2 ) );
          StepDisplay( y );
          OutTextXY( x, y, 'Line thick / style     : ' +
                    N2S( LineInfo.Thickness, 2 ) + ' / ' +
                    LineStyles[ LineInfo.LineStyle ] );
          StepDisplay( y );
          OutTextXY( x, y, 'Fill color / style     : ' +
                     N2S( FillInfo.Color, 2 ) + ' / ' +
                     FillStyles[ FillInfo.Pattern ] );
          StepDisplay( y );
          OutTextXY( x, y, 'Character size / font : ' +
```

```pascal
                    N2S( TextInfo.CharSize, 2 ) + ' / ' +
                    Fonts[ TextInfo.Font ] );
      StepDisplay( y );
      OutTextXY( x, y, 'Text direction          : ' +
                    TextDirect[ TextInfo.Direction ] );
      StepDisplay( y );
      OutTextXY( x, y, 'Horizontal justify      : ' +
                    HorizJust[ TextInfo.Horiz ] );
      StepDisplay( y );
      OutTextXY( x, y, 'Vertical justify        : ' +
                    VertJust[ TextInfo.Vert ] );
      StepDisplay( y );
      OutTextXY( x, y, 'Aspect Ratio   ( x/y ) : ' +
                    N2S( xasp, 4 ) + ' / ' +
                    N2S( yasp, 4 ) + ' = ' +
                    R2S( AspectRatio, 5, 3 ) );
      Pause;
   end;
procedure Initialize;
   begin  { initialize graphics system and report errors  }
      GraphDriver := DETECT;    { Request auto-detection  }
      InitGraph( GraphDriver, GraphMode, '\TP\BGI' );
      TestGraphicError;         { check graphics errors   }
      GetPalette( Palette );    { read palette parameters }
      MaxColors := GetMaxColor + 1;
      MaxX := 380;                       { set viewport size }
      MaxY := 194;
      GetAspectRatio( xasp, yasp );      { hardware aspect }
      AspectRatio := xasp div yasp;
   end;                            { calculate aspect ratio }

begin
   Initialize;                   { set graphics mode       }
   ReportStatus;                 { show graphics settings  }
   CloseGraph;                   { set text mode           }
end.
```

CHAPTER 2

Viewport, Screen, and Page Functions

Just as windowing and screen management routines are provided for text display modes, similar control features are provided for graphics display modes. These include the ClearDevice and ClearViewPort functions (graphics equivalents of ClrScr), SetViewPort (equivalent to Window), GetViewSettings, and the SetActivePage and SetVisualPage functions.

Not all of these graphics functions have text mode equivalents and there are several text mode functions that are not provided with graphics mode equivalents. Even when a graphics function appears similar to the text mode equivalent, it may not operate identically to the text function.

The first of these screen management functions is Clear Device.

ClearDevice

The ClearDevice function erases the entire graphics screen—regardless of viewport settings—and moves the current position (CP) to the screen home position (0,0). This does not affect the active viewport (if any is in effect). The viewport settings remain unchanged, but the entire screen is cleared, not merely the viewport. No values are returned and no error condition should be generated.

Example: `uses GRAPH;`
              `ClearDevice;`

While ClearDevice is similar to the text command ClrScr, where the text function is window sensitive (it can be used to clear only the currently active window), the ClearDevice command resets the entire active graphics screen but does not affect alternate graphics screens (if any are supported by the graphics hardware present). Remember that text functions such as ClrScr do not work in graphics modes and vice versa. See ClearViewPort, SetActivePage, and SetVisualPage for more information.

ClearViewPort

The ClearViewPort function erases the current viewport (graphics window), moving the current position (CP) to home (0,0) within the viewport setting. Unlike the ClearDevice function, ClearViewPort is limited to a specific area of the screen and operates similarly to the text command ClrScr with an active window setting.

Example:
```
uses GRAPH;
ClearViewPort;
```

See also GetViewSettings and SetViewPort.

SetViewPort

The SetViewPort function is roughly equivalent to the text function Window and is used to set an active viewport. The coordinates *XLeft*, *YTop*, *XRight*, and *YBottom* are absolute screen coordinates and affect only the active graphics page (see SetActivePage).

Example:
```
uses GRAPH;
var
    XLeft, YTop, XRight, YBottom : integer;
    ClipFlag : boolean;

SetViewPort( XLeft, YTop, XRight, YBottom,
             ClipFlag );
```

The fifth argument passed to SetViewPort is the *ClipFlag*. If *ClipFlag* is true, clipping will be in effect and all drawings will be restricted to the current viewport. If *ClipFlag* is false, then drawings may extend beyond the viewport perimeters without limitation.

Please note that the viewport limits do not affect the GetImage or PutImage commands and a pixel image being written to the screen will not be truncated at the viewport perimeter, regardless of the *ClipFlag* setting.

If invalid coordinates are passed to SetViewPort, GraphResult will return a value of −11 (graphics error or generic error) and the previous viewport settings (if any) will remain in effect. Both the InitGraph and SetGraphMode functions initialize the current viewport to the entire graphics screen as defined by the current mode setting. See also ClearViewPort and GetViewSettings.

GetViewSettings

The GetViewSettings function uses the record variable *ViewPort* to return the current graphics window coordinates and the *ClipFlag* setting. The coordinates returned are absolute screen coordinates.

Example:
```
uses GRAPH;
var
    ViewPort : ViewPortType;
GetViewSettings( ViewPort );
```

If *ClipFlag* is true, drawings are truncated at the current viewport margins. See SetViewPort for further details. See also ClearViewPort, InitGraph, and SetGraphMode.

The *ViewPortType* record structure is predefined (in the Graph unit) as:

```
type
   ViewPortType = record
                     x1, y1, x2, y2 : integer;
                     clip : boolean;
                  end;
```

Multiple Graphics Pages

Several graphics video cards offer support for two to four pages of graphics display (most without restricting color or resolution). To allow use of these capabilities, Turbo Pascal provides two functions: SetActivePage, which selects the active graphics output page and SetVisualPage, which selects the graphics page that actually appears on the screen (monitor). These are most often used for graphics animation. These commands are valid only with the drivers and modes shown in Table 2-1:

Table 2-1: Graphics Modes Supporting Multiple Pages

GRAPHICS DRIVER	DRIVER VALUE	GRAPHICS MODE	MODE VALUE	RESOLUTION XAXIS x YAXIS	COLORS AVAILABLE	GRAPHICS PAGES
EGA	3	EGALO	0	640x200	16	4
		EGAHI	1	640x350	16	2
EGAMONO	5	EGA-MONOHI	3	640x350	2	4[1]
HERC	7	HERC-MONOHI	0	720x348	2	2

GRAPHICS DRIVER	DRIVER VALUE	GRAPHICS MODE	MODE VALUE	RESOLUTION XAXIS x YAXIS	COLORS AVAILABLE	GRAPHICS PAGES
VGA	9	VGALO	0	640x200	16	4
		VGAMED	1	640x350	16	2[2]

1. The EGAMono card must have 256K RAM to support multiple video pages—some EGAMono cards have only 64K RAM.
2. Originally, the VGAHI mode (640x480) supported only one graphics page, but many VGA-capable video cards (i.e., multi-sync cards) support two to four pages. No standards to determine page support capabilities currently exist.

Remember, where multiple graphics pages are supported, the graphics pages are numbered from zero and page zero is active by default.

Where multiple graphics pages are not supported, the SetActivePage and SetVisualPage commands will simply not operate. By default, page zero will remain as the active output page and the active visual page.

But, relying on this default behavior is not necessarily the best approach to handling multiple video pages. In many cases, it might be better to know how many—if any—video pages are available and have your program respond accordingly. The following sample procedure, VideoPages, returns zero if no alternate video pages are available or an integer value if more than one video page is supported:

```pascal
uses GRAPH;
var
   GraphDriver, GraphMode : integer;
function VideoPages : integer;
var
   Result : integer;
begin
   Result := 0;
   case GraphDriver of
      EGA : case GetGraphMode of
               EGALO : Result := 3;
               EGAHI : Result := 1;
            end; { case }
      EGAMONO : Result := 0;
      HERC : Result := 1;
      VGA : case GetGraphMode of
               VGALO : Result := 3;
               VGAMED : Result := 1;
               VGAHI : Result := 0;
            end; { case }
   end; { case }
   VideoPages := Result;
end;
```

Some EGAMono cards support four video pages, but mode and driver settings do not identify which cards have 256K RAM and which have only 64K RAM. Thus, the best default value returned is 0, however, this can be changed if your application requires a different response.

All remaining drivers and modes identify themselves as supporting single video pages, but newer video cards may require modification of this selection table. As mentioned previously, no standards for determining the number of supported video pages exist.

SetActivePage

The SetActivePage function selects which graphics page (*PageNum*) will be used for output by all graphics functions. This does not affect the graphics page currently being displayed (see SetVisualPage), but does allow graphics operations to be directed to an invisible page. It is then displayed either by using the GetImage or the PutImage function (use the PutImage function after changing the active page to match the visual page) or by changing the displayed page.

Example:
```
uses GRAPH;
var
    PageNum : integer;
SetActivePage( PageNum );
```

SetVisualPage

The SetVisualPage function selects the specified graphics page (*PageNum*) for active display. This is not necessarily the same as the active output graphics page (see SetActivePage) but it is used to switch the video display between different graphics pages. The change is effective immediately (certainly too fast for the eye to follow), requiring only one screen refresh cycle for a complete display change.

Example:
```
uses GRAPH;
var
    PageNum : integer;
SetVisualPage( PageNum );
```

The SetActivePage and SetVisualPage functions are demonstrated in Chapter 10.

CHAPTER 3

Color and Palette Functions

In addition to knowing which graphics card and which graphics driver to use, you also need to know what palettes or colors are supported.

With the CGA, MCGA, and ATT400 drivers in 320x200 pixel modes, color selections are limited to the four-color predefined color palettes (C0, C1, C2, and C3). With higher resolutions, some graphics cards offer 16 colors; others offer two or four colors, but with color selection independent of the predefined palettes.

Lastly, with the IBM8514, a palette of 256 colors becomes possible with a tint selection from a total of 262,144 shades. The following color and palette functions are not compatible with the IBM8514 driver—see *IBM-8514 Video Graphics Card*.

GetMaxColor

The GetMaxColor function returns the maximum valid color number (or palette size – 1) for the current graphics mode. This is valid in both high and low resolution modes. Thus, in a low resolution (320x200) mode, GetMax-Color will return a value of 3, one less than the number of colors in the predefined palettes. In high resolution modes such as EGAHI, the value returned will be 15 and, in monochrome modes such as ATT400HI, a value of 1 will be returned.

Example: uses GRAPH;
          var
              MaxColors : integer;
          MaxColors := GetMaxColor + 1;

Please note that normally the value indicates only the number of separate palette colors which can be used, not the maximum color values. Also, this function is not valid in the IBM8514 mode. See also SetColor.

SetColor

The SetColor function selects the current drawing color or foreground color.

Example: uses GRAPH;
          var
              ForeColor : integer;
          ForeColor := GetMaxColors;
          SetColor(ForeColor);

In low resolution CGA modes (320x200 pixel), the color selected is the palette color number, not the actual color value. In CGAC2 mode, SetColor(0) selects the background color (see SetPalette), SetColor(1) selects GREEN (color value 2), SetColor(2) selects RED (color value 4), and SetColor(3) selects BROWN (color value 6).

In high resolution modes, the color values can be either the symbolic names (which are defined in the GRAPH unit) or the numerical values. If the SetPalette or SetAllPalette functions have been used to change the palette color values, the symbolic color names may not produce the expected results.

The current color selected is used for drawing and for graphics text output. The current FillColor, however, may be different from the current drawing color (see Chapter 5).

The colors selected are retrieved from a record of *PaletteType* as *Palette.Color[ColorNumber]*. The *PaletteType* structure is defined in the GRAPH unit as:

```
const
   MaxColors = 15;
type
   PaletteType = record
      Size : byte;
      Colors : array[1..MaxColors] of shortint;
   end;
```

See SetPalette for predefined color palettes. See also GetColor and SetBkColor.

GetColor

The GetColor function returns the current drawing (foreground) color. In low resolution modes using color palettes, the value returned will be the palette number, not the actual color value.

Example: `uses GRAPH;`
  `var`
    `ForeColor : integer;`
  `ForeColor := GetColor;`

In high resolution (16 color) modes, the value returned will correspond to the color values unless the SetPalette and SetAllPalette functions have been used to change the palette values.

See SetColor for color values, and SetPalette for palette colors. See also GetBkColor.

SetBkColor

The SetBkColor function selects the background color values by changing the first entry in the active color palette (*Palette.Color[0] := BackColor*) to the specified color value (see also SetPalette).

Example: `uses GRAPH;`
  `var`
    `BackColor : integer;`
  `BackColor := 0;`
  `SetBkColor( BackColor );`

When SetBkColor is called with a new value, the background color on the entire screen is changed. If this new background color corresponds to the color of an image *already on the screen*, the image will be invisible, though the image information will not be lost. When the background color is changed to a contrasting color, the invisible image will again become clear.

The argument *BackColor* can be either the symbolic color name or the color value. Table 3-1 shows how color names are predefined in the GRAPH unit.

Table 3-1: Background Color Values

NAME	VALUE	NAME	VALUE
Black	0	DarkGray	8
Blue	1	LightBlue	9
Green	2	LightGreen	10
Cyan	3	LightCyan	11
Red	4	LightRed	12
Magenta	5	LightMagenta	13

NAME	VALUE	NAME	VALUE
Brown	6	Yellow	14
LightGray	7	White	15

In low resolution (320x200) color palette modes, only the first entry in the palette (*Palette.Color[0]*) can be changed (see SetPalette).

In high resolution 16-color modes (EGA/VGA/etc.), all palette colors can be changed using the SetPalette or SetAllPalette function. However, if this is done, the symbolic color names may not provide the expected results.

GetBkColor

The GetBkColor function returns the current background color value, not the palette entry number since the background color is always *Palette.Color[0]*.

Example:
```
uses GRAPH;
var
    BackColor : integer;
BackColor := GetBkColor;
```

See also GetColor and SetBkColor.

GetPalette

The GetPalette function fills the *Palette* structure with current palette information (settings).

Example:
```
uses GRAPH;
var
    Palette : PaletteType;
GetPalette( Palette );
```

Here is the *PaletteType* structure:

```
const
    MaxColors = 15;
type
    PaletteType : record
        Size : byte;
        Colors : array[1..MaxColors] of shortint;
    end;
```

Palette.Size gives the number of colors valid for the current graphics driver and mode. *Palette.Color* is an array of *Size* of bytes containing the color values for each entry in the palette. These color values are shown in Table 3-2.

Table 3-2: Color Values

CGA		EGA/VGA	
NAME	VALUE	NAME	VALUE
Black	0	EGABlack	0
Blue	1	EGABlue	1
Green	2	EGAGreen	2
Cyan	3	EGACyan	3
Red	4	EGARed	4
Magenta	5	EGAMagenta	5
Brown	6	EGABrown	20
LightGray	7	EGALightGray	7
DarkGray	8	EGADarkGray	56
LightBlue	9	EGALightBlue	57
LightGreen	10	EGALightGreen	58
LightCyan	11	EGALightCyan	59
LightRed	12	EGALightRed	60
LightMagenta	13	EGALightMagenta	61
Yellow	14	EGAYellow	62
White	15	EGAWhite	63

Most (if not all) EGA/VGA graphics cards will accept either the CGA or the EGA/VGA symbolic color names and color values appearing in Table 3-2. CGA graphics cards, however, may respond unexpectedly to the EGA/VGA color values.

See also GetPaletteSize, GetDefaultPalette, SetAllPalette, and SetPalette.

GetDefaultPalette

The GetDefaultPalette function returns a palette definition record containing the palette information as it was initialized by the driver during InitGraph.

Example: `uses GRAPH;`
```
       type
           OrgPalette : PaletteType;
       GetDefaultPalette( OrgPalette );
```

See also GetPalette and GetPaletteSize.

GetPaletteSize

The GetPaletteSize function returns the size of the palette color look-up table, indicating how many palette entries can be set in the current graphics mode.

Example: `uses GRAPH;`
```
       var
           PaletteSize : integer;
       PaletteSize := GetPaletteSize;
```

SetPalette

With any of the 320x200 pixel video graphics modes (CGA, MCGA, or AT&T), color selections are limited to predefined 4-color palettes: C0, C1, C2, and C3. In each palette, the background color (*Palette.Color[0]*) can be user-defined, but colors 1..3 cannot be changed. In every other graphics mode, all colors can be redefined. Table 3-3 lists these predefined palettes.

Example:
```
    uses GRAPH;
  int palette_index, color;
  SetPalette( palette_index, color );
```

Table 3-3: Predefined Palettes and Colors

PALETTE	COLOR0	COLOR1	COLOR2	COLOR3
C0	Black	LightGreen	LightRed	Yellow
C1	Black	LightCyan	LightMagenta	White
C2	Black	Green	Red	Brown
C3	Black	Cyan	Magenta	LightGray

SetAllPalette

The SetAllPalette function assigns *NewPalette* as the current palette with all new color assignment affected immediately. The color values for *NewPalette* must be assigned using SetPalette.

Example:
```
      uses GRAPH;
      type
         NewPalette : PaletteType;
      SetAllPalette( NewPalette );
```

In low resolution (320x200) graphics modes using the predefined color palettes, the SetAllPalette command is not valid since only the background palette color is assignable. Changing graphics modes—as from CGAC0 to CGAC2—to change color palettes also erases (resets) the graphics screen. See also GetPalette.

IBM-8514 Video Graphics Card

The IBM-8514 video graphics card provides high-resolution color from an extended selection of color values. But the palette assignment tools used for more common resolution do not work for the IBM-8514 and; therefore, special functions are provided.

The IBM-8514 graphics card and IBM8514 driver supports a color palette of 256 colors chosen from a total of 262,144 (256K) color values. No symbolic constants are defined for this driver but the IBM-8514 card can also emulate VGA modes.

SetRBGPalette

The SetRBGPalette routine is provided for use with the IBM-8514 graphics card and IBM8514 driver, supporting a color palette of 256 colors chosen from a total of 262,144 (256K) color values.

Example:
```
uses GRAPH;
var
    ColorNum, RedVal,
    BlueVal, GreenVal : integer;
SetRBGPalette( ColorNum, RedVal,
               BlueVal, GreenVal );
```

The DetectGraph function will not identify the IBM-8514 card correctly but will instead identify this hardware configuration as VGA compatible. The VGA driver is recommended for maximum compatibility (see InitGraph) when the extended resolution of the IBM8514HI mode is not required.

Also, no symbolic constants are defined for this driver. Instead, each color is defined by three six-bit values for the Red, Green, and Blue components.

The *ColorNum* argument sets the palette color (0..255) to be defined by the *RedVal*, *BlueVal*, and *GreenVal* arguments. Only the six most significant bits of the low byte of each color argument are used (values from 0 to 252 in steps of 4—for example, arguments of 252, 253, 254, and 255 are treated identically since the 6 most significant bits are the same).

The other palette manipulation routines in the graphics library are invalid with the IBM8514 driver in the IBM8514HI (1023x768 pixel) mode. This includes SetAllPalette, SetPalette, and GetPalette. Also, the FloodFill routine is not valid with this driver and mode.

CHAPTER 4

Screen Position Functions

In graphics modes, the familiar 80 by 25 screen coordinates are replaced by pixel coordinates which, depending on the video hardware, may vary from 320 horizontal by 200 vertical to as high as 1,024 horizontal by 768 vertical (with newer and higher resolutions appearing almost daily).

Because of the variety of screen resolutions, most graphics programs begin by checking the hardware for the appropriate drivers (see Detector.Pas in Chapter 1), and then using functions such as GetMaxX and GetMaxY to determine the screen size, adjusting subsequent operations to fit within these screen limits.

GetMaxX and GetMaxY

The GetMaxX and GetMaxY functions return the maximum x-axis and y-axis screen coordinate (maximum CP) for the current graphics driver and mode. For example, in EGAHI mode (640x350), GetMaxX returns 639 (0..639) and GetMaxY returns 349 (0..349). Both are independent of viewport settings.

Example:
```
         uses GRAPH;
         var
             MaxX, MaxY : integer;

         MaxX = GetMaxX;
         MaxY = GetMaxY;
```

See also GetViewSettings, GetX, and GetY. Similar information is available in text modes using the GetTextInfo function.

GetX and GetY

The GetX and GetY functions return the current position in horizontal and vertical pixel coordinates. The returned coordinates are relative to the active viewport; if no viewport is set, the default viewport includes the entire screen.

Example:
```
uses GRAPH;
var
    XPos, YPos : integer;

XPos = GetX;
YPos = GetY;
```

See also GetY, GetViewSettings, MoveRel, and MoveTo. Similar information is available in text modes using WhereX and WhereY.

MoveTo

The MoveTo function moves the current position (CP) to the absolute screen pixel coordinates specified by (x,y), relative to the current viewport settings where (0,0) is the upper-left corner. The resulting CP is *not* limited by the current viewport settings or by the minimum and maximum screen coordinates.

Example:
```
uses GRAPH;
var
    x, y : integer;

MoveTo( x, y );
```

If no viewport settings have been made, the default settings include the entire screen. See also MoveRel.

In text modes, GotoXY provides the equivalent function.

MoveRel

For graphics application, a relative move is often handier than an absolute move. For this, the MoveRel function shifts the new current position a relative distance from the old current position using the offset specified by (dX, dY).

Example:
```
uses GRAPH;
var
    dX, dY : integer;

MoveRel( dX, dY );
```

The resulting CP is not limited by the current viewport settings or by the minimum and maximum screen coordinates. See also MoveTo.

CHAPTER 5

Pixel Drawing and Image Functions

While lines and curves are useful for many drawing applications, some images can only be created by manipulating individual pixels. Of course, the line and curve functions could hardly operate without pixel write procedures. Also, by using pixel functions on a macro scale, entire images can be saved, rewritten, erased, or combined with existing screen images.

Pixel Functions

First are the pixel functions that provide the means to write individual screen pixels and to read the color values of existing screen pixels.

PutPixel

The PutPixel function sets the pixel specified by (*xpos,ypos*) to the indicated color. In graphics modes using predefined palettes, *color* must be in the range 0..3, where 0 provides the background color value. In full palette color modes, either the predefined color names from the GRAPH unit or the integer color values may be used.

```
Example:   uses GRAPH;
           var
               XPos, YPos, Color : integer;
           PutPixel( XPos, YPos, Color );
```

GetPixel

The GetPixel function returns the color palette index of the indicated pixel at (*x*,*y*).

Example:
```
uses GRAPH;
var
    X, Y : integer;
    Color : word;
Color = GetPixel( X, Y );
```

The returned values may not correspond to the actual color value, depending on palette reassignments. See also GetImage and PutPixel.

Line Drawing Functions

Turbo Pascal provides three drawing functions—Line, LineTo, and LineRel—for making straight lines. The coordinate points used for these lines are integer coordinates (positive or negative) that are plotted relative to the current viewport coordinates, but which need not be restricted to the viewport limits. However, if the viewport *ClipFlag* is true, the lines drawn will be truncated at the viewport borders.

If *ClipFlag* is false, lines are truncated only at the limits of the screen, even though the endpoint coordinates and the resulting current position may still lie outside the viewport and/or the screen limits.

Two drawing modes are also supported: CopyPut and XOrPut. See SetWriteMode for details.

Line

The Line function draws a line beginning at the first coordinate pair (*XStart, YStart*) and ending at the second coordinate pair (*XEnd, YEnd*), using the current drawing color, line style, and thickness. The CP is not changed.

Example:
```
uses GRAPH;
var
    XStart, YStart, XEnd, YEnd : integer;
Line( XStart, YStart, XEnd, YEnd );
```

See also LineRel and LineTo.

LineTo

The LineTo function draws a line beginning at the CP and ending at the specified coordinates (*XPos, YPos*). The current drawing color, line style, and thickness are used and CP is reset to (*XPos, YPos*).

Example: uses GRAPH;
          var
              XPos, YPos : integer;
          LineTo(XPos, YPos);

See also Line and LineRel.

LineRel

The LineRel function draws a line from CP to a point offset from CP by the horizontal and vertical distances specified by (*dX, dY*). The line is drawn using the current color, line style, and thickness. CP is updated to (*cpX + dX* , *cpY + dY*).

Example: uses GRAPH;
          var
              dX, dY : integer;
          LineRel(dX, dY);

See also Line and LineTo.

Line Styles

For graphics drawing, two line thicknesses and several line styles are provided. You can also define a custom line style using a 16-pixel pattern. The line thickness and pattern settings are used by the Arc, Bar, Bar3D, Circle, DrawPoly, Ellipse, Line, LineRel, LineTo, PieSlice, and Rectangle functions.

SetLineStyle

The SetLineStyle procedure accepts three arguments setting the current line style, pattern, and width.

Example: uses GRAPH;
          var
              LinePattern : word;
              Style, Width : integer;
          SetLineStyle(Style, LinePattern, Width);

Unless Style is specified as UserBitLn (value 4), which sets a custom, user-defined pattern, the LinePattern parameter is ignored and can be passed as zero.

Tables 5-1 and 5-2 show how the constants for the style and width parameters are enumerated in the GRAPH unit.

Table 5-1: Line Styles

NAME	VALUE	DESCRIPTION
SolidLn	0	Solid line (*default*)
DottedLn	1	Dotted line
CenterLn	2	Centered dash line
DashedLn	3	Dashed line
UserBitLn	4	User-defined style

Table 5-2: Line Widths

NAME	VALUE	DESCRIPTION
NormWidth	1	1-pixel width (*default*)
ThickWidth	3	3-pixel width

A line width of 2 can be assigned, but any value greater than 3 will result in a graphics error, causing the line style and width to be set to the default settings.

The remaining argument, *LinePattern*, is a 16-bit word defining a custom bit pattern to be used for drawing the line. The *LinePattern* argument is applicable only if *Style = UserBitLn* (numerical value 4). If *Style <> UserBitLn*, then a *LinePattern* must still be supplied even though it is ignored. A zero entry is acceptable.

When a user-defined pattern is used, each pixel corresponding to a one-bit in the pattern is turned on, pixels corresponding to a zero-bit are left off. Thus, if *LinePattern = $FFFF*, a solid line is drawn and, if *LinePattern = $9999*, a dashed line alternating two pixels on, two pixels off will result. For a long-dashed line, *LinePattern = $FF00* or *$F00F* might be used. If invalid parameters are passed to SetLineStyle, GraphResult will return a value of −11 (graphics error or generic error) and the current line style will remain in effect.

See also GetLineSettings.

GetLineSettings

The GetLineSettings function returns *LineInfo* with the current line style, pattern (*upattern*), and thickness.

Example:
```
uses GRAPH;
var
    LineInfo : LineSettingsType;
GetLineSettings( LineInfo );
```

The record structure *LineSettingsType* is defined in the GRAPH unit as:

```
type
  LineSettingsType : record
                       LineStyle : integer;
```

```
            UPattern : word;
            Thickness : word;
         end;
```

See SetLineStyle for predefined styles and thicknesses.

SetWriteMode

The SetWriteMode function sets the write mode for drawing operations. Two constants are defined in the GRAPH unit as:

```
   const
      CopyPut = 0;       { default }
      XOrPut  = 1;
```

The *CopyPut* mode is the default. It uses the MOV instruction to write pixels directly to the screen during drawing operations, thus overwriting the existing screen image.

The *XOrPut* mode setting uses the XOR instruction to combine the drawn image with the existing screen image. Using the *XOrPut* mode, drawing a figure a second time erases the image.

Example: `uses GRAPH;`

   `SetWriteMode( XOrPut );`

   `SetWriteMode( CopyPut );`

The SetWriteMode options affect only the DrawPoly, Line, LineRel, LineTo, and Rectangle routines.

Rectangles, Bar Graphs, and Polygons

While any of the following geometric forms can be created using the line drawing function, it is certainly more convenient to have functions that provide faster handling for common shapes.

Rectangle

The Rectangle function draws a square or rectangle as defined by the corner coordinates passed as arguments. The figure is drawn using the current line style, thickness, and color. If one or more corners do not fall within the current viewport limits and the *ClipFlag* is set, then only the portion of the figure that fits within the viewport will be created.

Example: `uses GRAPH;`
   `var`
      `XLeft, YTop, XRight, YBottom : integer;`

   `Rectangle( XLeft, YTop, XRight, YBottom );`

Bar

The Bar function draws a square or rectangle as defined by the corner coordinates passed as arguments. However, unlike the figure created by the Rectangle function, the Bar figure is not outlined but, instead, uses the current fill pattern and fill color (not the drawing color) to create a solid rectangle. For an outlined Bar, use Bar3D with a depth setting of zero.

Example: `uses GRAPH;`
`var`
`    XLeft, YTop, XRight, YBottom : integer;`
`Bar( XLeft, YTop, XRight, YBottom );`

See also GetColor, GetFillSettings, GetLineStyle, Rectangle, and SetFill-Pattern.

Bar3D

The Bar3D function outlines a three-dimensional rectangular bar using the current line style and drawing color, then fills in the faces of the figure using the current fill pattern and fill color.

Example: `uses GRAPH;`
`var`
`    XLeft, YTop, XRight, YBottom : integer;`
`    Depth : word;`
`    TopFlag : boolean;`
`Bar3D( XLeft, YTop, XRight, YBottom,`
`       Depth, TopFlag );`

The bar's depth is given in pixels (normally about 25 percent of width) and is set back at an x/y ratio of 1:1 (approximately 45 degrees adjusted by the screen aspect ratio). Since negative depths are not accepted, *Depth* is a (unsigned) word value rather than a (signed) integer value.

If the *TopFlag* parameter is passed as false, no top is added to the bar, allowing bars to be stacked.

If desired, a more elaborate figure can be created with each face of the figure filled with a different color and/or pattern using the FloodFill function. If this is desired, use the SetFillPattern function to select EmptyFill before calling Bar3D.

See also Bar, GetColor, GetFillSettings, GetLineStyle, and Rectangle.

DrawPoly

The DrawPoly function draws the outline of a polygon using current color settings and line style.

Example: uses GRAPH;
```
  const
    Figure1 : array[1..18] of integer =
    ( 100, 100, 110, 120, 100, 130, 120, 125, 140,
      140, 130, 120, 140, 110, 120, 115, 100, 100 );
    Figure2 : array[1..18] of integer =
    ( 180, 100, 210, 120, 200, 130, 220, 125, 240,
      140, 230, 120, 240, 110, 220, 115, 220, 100 );
  var
    Points : word;

Points = SizeOf( Figure1 ) /
         ( 2 * SizeOf( integer ) );
DrawPoly( Points, Figure1 );
DrawPoly( SizeOf( Figure2 ) /
         ( 2 * SizeOf( integer ) ), Figure2 );
```

The *Points* argument gives the number of vertices for the polygon, while *Poly* points to a sequence of integer pairs, each pair defining the x/y coordinates for a vertex of the polygon. In order to draw a closed figure with *N* vertices, *Points* must equal *N+1* and the final *(Nth+1)* coordinate pair must be equal to the first coordinate pair.

In the example, *Figure1* defines a four-pointed star. Instead of assigning a constant to *Points*, the number of points in the figure is calculated from *SizeOf(Figure)* divided by two times *SizeOf(integer)* since each point requires two integer coordinates.

The second figure, *Figure2*, changes the four-pointed star into an open line figure but is still created in the same manner. The vertex coordinates can also be assigned as pairs of PointType, thus:

```
  const
    Figure1 : array[1..9] of PointType =
       ((x:100;y:100), (x:110;y:120), (x:100;y:130),
        (x:120;y:125), (x:140;y:140), (x:130;y:120),
        (x:140,y:110), (x:120;y:115), (x:100;y:100));
    Figure2 : array[1..9] of PointType =
       ((x:100;y:100), (x:210;y:120), (x:200;y:130),
        (x:220;y:125), (x:240;y:140), (x:230;y:120),
        (x:240,y:110), (x:220;y:115), (x:220;y:100));
  var
    Points : word;

Points = SizeOf( Figure1 ) / SizeOf( PointType);
DrawPoly( Points, Figure1 );
DrawPoly( SizeOf( Figure2 ) / SizeOf( PointType ),
          Figure2 );
```

This second example is functionally the same as the first; both draw identical figures.

See also GetLineSettings, GetColor, FillPoly, SetGraphBufSize, and SetWriteMode.

FillPoly

The FillPoly function draws the outline of a polygon using the current color settings and line style, and then fills the polygon using the current fill pattern and fill color.

Example:
```
      uses GRAPH;
  const
    Figure1 : array[1..18] of integer =
        (  75,   0, 100,  50, 150,  75, 100, 100,  75,
          150,  50, 100,   0,  75,  50,  50,  75,   0 );
    Figure2 : array[1..8] of integer =
        (  75,  50, 100,  75,  75, 100,  50,  75 );
  FillPoly( SizeOf ( Figure1 ) /
          ( 2 * SizeOf( integer ) ), Figure1 );
  FillPoly( SizeOf ( Figure2 ) /
          ( 2 * SizeOf( integer ) ), Figure2 );
```

The FillPoly function is called in the same fashion as the *Poly* function.

In the example, *Figure1* defines a four-pointed star. Instead of assigning a constant to *Points*, the number of points in the figure is calculated from *SizeOf(Figure1)* divided by two times *SizeOf(integer)* since each point requires two integer coordinates.

The second figure, *Figure2*, creates an open square. Note, however, that FillPoly will close the figure by connecting the start and end points, then fill the enclosed region.

Unlike FloodFill, the fill algorithm used by FillPoly does not depend on a continuous outline to define the area, thus broken line styles are acceptable, and will simply fill the area defined by the polygon, which includes overwriting any other figure within the new boundary.

If an error occurs, GraphResult returns –6 (*out of memory in scan fill*).

See also DrawPoly, GetFillSettings, SetFillPattern, GetColor, and SetGraphBufSize.

Video Aspect Ratio

Each graphics driver and graphics mode has an associated *aspect ratio*, the ratio between vertical and horizontal pixel sizes and spacing. A figure which appears round on one screen (and graphics card/mode) may appear squashed or elongated using different graphics hardware.

In order to ensure that geometric figures appear—more or less as intended—on the screen, the screen aspect ratio is used to calculate and correct the distortions created by differences in hardware and graphics cards.

GetAspectRatio

The GetAspectRatio function returns two word values that can be used to calculate the AspectRatio for a particular graphics driver and graphics mode.

Example:
```
uses GRAPH;
var
    xasp, yasp : word;
    AspectRatio : real;

GetAspectRatio( xasp, yasp );
AspectRatio = xasp / yasp;
```

For example, using an EGA graphics card (*EGAHi*), an aspect ratio of 0.775 is found (*xasp = 7750, yasp = 10000*) since the EGA pixels are roughly 1/3 taller than they are wide. On the other hand, when using a VGA graphics card, the aspect ratio is found to be 1.000 (*xasp = 10000, yasp = 10000*) and the pixels are basically square. As you can see, there is a considerable difference between the two screen presentations.

GetAspectRatio returns integer values for the x- and y-axis aspects with the aspect ratio calculated as *xasp/yasp*.

This device aspect ratio is used automatically as a scaling factor with the Arc, Circle, and PieSlice routines to normalize the appearance of circles and circular arcs on the screen.

With the Ellipse routine, the aspect scaling ratio must be specifically included; otherwise, no adjustment is applied. The aspect ratio can also be used with other geometric figures in order to correct scaling and appearance.

The y-axis aspect factor is normalized to 10,000 and, in general, *xasp* <= 10,000 (most screens' pixels are taller than they are wide).

Circles, Curves, and Arcs

Curves are the hardest figures to create, requiring relatively complex calculations to determine the points composing them. Thus, the functions Circle, Ellipse, and Arc offer no small convenience in creating curved figures.

The Circle function creates a complete circle, while Arc and Ellipse are called with start and end angles and may produce complete (closed) curves or only partial arcs.

Also, the GetArcCoords function returns the start and end coordinates of the last call to Arc or Ellipse, allowing lines to be joined to the ends of arcs. The PieSlice function uses a combination of these capabilities to create an arc with lines drawn from the end points to the center.

The start and end angles for Arc, Ellipse, and PieSlice are given in degrees, with 0 degrees and 360 degrees at the right, 90 degrees at the top, 180 degrees at the right, and 270 degrees at the bottom. (See Figure 5-1.)

To draw a closed arc or ellipse, simply specify a start angle of 0 degrees and an end angle of 360 degrees. Angles greater than 360 degrees can be used as arguments, but will be reduced to 0..360. For example, a starting angle of 300 degrees and an end angle of 450 degrees will draw an Arc from the 300 degrees point to the 90 degrees point.

Of course, the same Arc can be drawn by simply specifying 300 degrees and 90 degrees as the start and end points. There is no inherent requirement for the end angle to be greater than the start angle, but allowing angles greater than 360 degrees can simplify many programming procedures.

Figure 5-1: Drawing Arc Angles

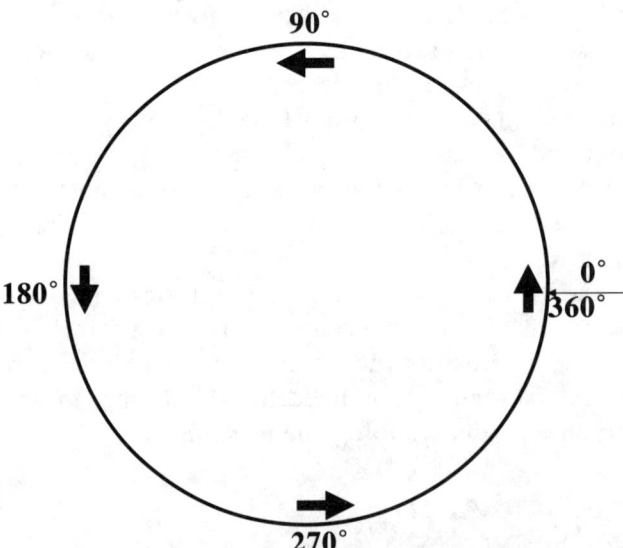

The angles for arc, ellipse and pieslice run counter-clockwise (widershins) beginning with 0°/360° at the right, 90° at the top, 180° at the left, and 270° at the bottom.

The Arc, Circle, Ellipse, and PieSlice functions do not use the current line style. All curves are drawn as solid lines using the current drawing color.

Circle

The Circle function draws a complete Arc from 0 degrees to 360 degrees. The circle is drawn using the current drawing color, centered at the given screen coordinates, and using the radius specified (in pixels).

Example:
```
uses GRAPH;
var
    XCenter, YCenter, Radius : integer;
Circle( XCenter, YCenter, Radius );
```

Since, unlike Ellipse, Circle is called with a single radius argument, the screen aspect ratio is automatically applied to adjust the results to produce a correct (circular) appearance.

See also Arc, Ellipse, GetAspectRatio, and PieSlice.

Arc

The Arc function draws a circular curve with the specified radius between the angles specified and centered at the given x and y coordinates. The start and end angles are in degrees (0..360). The center coordinates and radius are in pixels. The current drawing color and line style are used and correction for the screen aspect ratio is handled automatically.

Example:
```
uses GRAPH;
var
  XCenter, YCenter,
  StartAngle, EndAngle, Radius : integer;
Arc( XCenter, YCenter,
     StartAngle, EndAngle, Radius );
```

See also Circle, Ellipse, GetAspectRatio, and PieSlice.

Ellipse

The Ellipse function is similar to Arc except that separate radii are specified for the x and y axis. The elliptic arc is centered at the given x and y coordinates, beginning and terminating at the specified start and end angles and using the current drawing color. For a complete (closed) ellipse, use a start angle of 0 degrees and an end angle of 360 degrees.

Example:
```
uses GRAPH;
var
    XCenter, YCenter, StartAngle,
    EndAngle, XRadius, YRadius : integer;
Ellipse( XCenter, YCenter, StartAngle, EndAngle,
         XRadius, YRadius );
```

or:

```
Ellipse( XCenter, YCenter, StartAngle, EndAngle,
         XRadius, YRadius * AspectRatio );
```

Unlike Arc and Circle, correction for the screen aspect ratio is not applied automatically. If proportional radii, rather than specific pixel distances, are required, the y-axis distance should be adjusted as *YRadius * AspectRatio*.

See also Arc, Circle, FillEllipse, PieSlice, and Sector.

FillEllipse

The FillEllipse procedure operates similarly to the Ellipse procedure, but fills the drawn ellipse using the current fill color and style. The ellipse is outlined in the current drawing color.

Example:
```
uses GRAPH;
var
    XCenter, YCenter, StartAngle,
    EndAngle, XRadius, YRadius : integer;

FillEllipse( XCenter, YCenter,
             StartAngle, EndAngle,
             XRadius, YRadius );
```

or:

```
FillEllipse( XCenter, YCenter,
             StartAngle, EndAngle,
             XRadius, YRadius * AspectRatio );
```

See also Ellipse and Sector for more information.

GetArcCoords

The GetArcCoords function returns the end points and center coordinates of the last call to Arc or Ellipse.

Example:
```
uses GRAPH;
var
    ArcInfo : ArcCoordsType;

GetArcCoords( ArcInfo );
```

The structure *ArcCoordsType* is defined in the GRAPH unit as:

```
type
   ArcCoordsType : record
                     X, Y : integer;
                     XStart, YStart,
                     XEnd, YEnd : integer;
                   end;
```

The info structure defines the center point (*X, Y*) coordinates of the arc, the starting point coordinates (*XStart, YStart*, which are pixel coordinates, not the angle), and the end point (*XEnd, YEnd*) of the arc. These values can be used to draw chords, radii, or other lines meeting the ends of the arc and are also used by the PieSlice function.

If the Circle function was the last curve function called, then GetArcCoords will return the center coordinates of the Circle while the (*XStart, YStart*) and (*XEnd, YEnd*) coordinates will be the 0 degree position on the Circle.

PieSlice

The PieSlice function creates an arc, draws lines from the end points to the center point, and then fills in the completed PieSlice.

Example:
```
uses GRAPH;
var
    XCenter, YCenter,
    StartAngle, EndAngle, Radius : integer;
PieSlice( XCenter, YCenter,
          StartAngle, EndAngle, Radius );
```

The figure outline is drawn using the current drawing color and the current line style for the radius lines, then filled using the current fill pattern and fill color (see FloodFill). Screen aspect ratio adjustment is automatic.

See also Arc, Circle, Ellipse, and GetAspectRatio.

Sector

The Sector procedure draws and fills an elliptical sector similar to the PieSlice procedure.

Example:
```
uses GRAPH;
var
    XCenter, YCenter,
    StartAngle, EndAngle,
    XRadius, YRadius : integer;
Sector( XCenter, YCenter,
        StartAngle, EndAngle,
        XRadius, YRadius );
```

The figure outline is drawn using the current drawing color, using the current line style for the radius lines, then filled using the current fill pattern and fill color (see FloodFill). No screen aspect ratio adjustment is applied.

See also Arc, Circle, Ellipse and PieSlice.

Fill Patterns and Fill Colors

Several functions, including FloodFill, GetFillPattern, GetFillSettings, SetFillPattern, and SetFillStyle, are provided to handle fill patterns, to fill enclosed areas, and to create custom fill patterns.

FloodFill

The FloodFill function fills a bounded (enclosed) region that was defined by the specified border color (normally this will be the current drawing color). The (*XPoint, YPoint*) coordinates specify some point within the area to be filled, using the current fill pattern and fill color.

```
Example:   uses GRAPH;
           var
               XPoint, YPoint, BorderColor : integer;
           FloodFill( XPoint, YPoint, BorderColor );
```

If the start point is outside a bounded region, the exterior region (limited by the borders set by ViewPort) will be filled. If any break occurs in the line defining the region, the fill will leak. (Even a very small break will cause a leak.)

For future compatibility, FillPoly is recommended wherever possible instead of FloodFill. If an error occurs, GraphResult will return a value of −7 (*out of memory in flood fill*).

See also FillPoly, GetFillSettings, GetLineSettings, and SetGraphBufSize.

SetFillPattern

The SetFillPattern selects an 8x8 user-defined fill pattern in the specified color. In the following example, *Diamond* is a sequence of 8 bytes, each byte corresponding to 8 pixels in the pattern. One bit turns on pixels, zero bits turn off pixels. The *Diamond* example pattern creates a small 7x7 diamond pattern with a one-pixel border at the right and bottom.

```
Example:   uses GRAPH;
           const
              Diamond : array[1..8] of byte =
                         ( $10, $38, $7C, $FE,
                           $7C, $38, $10, $00 );
           var
              Color : integer;
           SetFillPattern( Diamond, Color );
```

After SetFillPattern is called to establish the user-defined pattern, SetFillStyle must be called to make UserFill (12) the current pattern. A few other possible patterns are:

```
const
   checker : array[1..8] of byte =
             ( $AA, $55, $AA, $55, $AA, $55, $AA, $55 );
   chains1 : array[1..8] of byte =
             ( $6F, $40, $A0, $A0, $A0, $40, $6F, $00 );
   chains2 : array[1..8] of byte =
             ( $3C, $C3, $A0, $90, $90, $A0, $3C, $C3 );
```

See also GetFillPattern, GetFillStyle, and SetFillStyle.

SetFillStyle

The SetFillStyle function sets the current fill pattern and fill color. Fill and drawing colors are separate and may have different values.

Example: `uses GRAPH;`

   `SetFillStyle( SolidFill, GREEN );`

Table 5-3 shows how fill patterns are defined in the GRAPH unit.

Table 5-3: Fill Patterns

PATTERN NAME	VALUE	DESCRIPTION
EmptyFill	0	Background color
SolidFill	1	Solid fill
LineFill	2	Fill with ———
LtSlashFill	3	Fill with ////
SlashFill	4	Fill with ////, thick
BkSlashFill	5	Fill with \\\\, thick
LtBkSlashFill	6	Fill with \\\\
HatchFill	7	Light crosshatch
XHatchFill	8	Heavy crosshatch
InterleaveFill	9	Interleaving lines
WideDotFill	10	Wide-spaced dots
CloseDotFill	11	Close-spaced dots
UserFill	12	User-defined pattern

All patterns except EmptyFill use the current fill color. Pattern 12 (UserFill) can only be called *after* SetFillPattern has established a user-defined fill pattern.

See also FillPoly, FloodFill, GetFillPattern, and GetFillStyle.

GetFillPattern

The GetFillPattern function returns the last fill pattern set by a previous call to SetFillPattern.

Example: `uses GRAPH;`
`var`
`    FillPatternInfo : FillPatternType;`

`GetFillPattern( FillPatternInfo );`

If no user-defined fill pattern has been set by a call to SetFillPattern, the *FillPatternInfo* array is returned filled with $FF. FillPatternType is defined in the GRAPH unit as:

`type`
`    FillPatternType = array[1..8] of byte;`

See SetFillPattern.

GetFillSettings

The GetFillSettings function returns information in *FillInfo* about the current fillpattern settings.

Example: `uses GRAPH;`
`var`
`    FillInfo : FillSettingType;`

`GetFillSettings( FillInfo );`

The structure *FillSettingType* is defined in the GRAPH unit as:

`type`
`    FillSettingType : record`
`                         Pattern : word;`
`                         Color : word;`
`                      end;`

The pattern record element returns a number value indicating a predefined pattern number only, not the pattern elements.

See also GetFillPattern, SetFillPattern, and SetFillStyle.

The Internal Graphics Buffer

As noted, several of the graphics functions can return error messages that indicate there is insufficient buffer memory to accomplish their tasks. When this happens, the SetGraphBufSize function can be used to allocate additional buffer memory.

SetGraphBufSize

Several of the graphics routines use a memory buffer created by InitGraph with a default buffer size of 4K (4,096 bytes), sufficient to fill a polygon with roughly 650 vertices. The buffer size can be decreased to save space or increased if more buffer memory is required.

Example:
```
        uses GRAPH;
        var
            BufSize : word;
        SetGraphBufSize( BufSize );
```

The SetGraphBufSize function must be called before calling InitGraph. In Turbo C (only) SetGraphBufSize returns the original buffer size.

Image Manipulation

In addition to drawing functions, procedures are supplied for copying, erasing, duplicating and manipulating screen images. These are essential for any type of animation and, even for less elaborate applications, are useful in image replication.

ImageSize

The ImageSize function returns the byte size required to store the bit image specified by the screen coordinates. If the size required for the image is greater than 64K, a value of $FFFF (unsigned 65535 or signed –1) is returned.

Example:
```
        uses GRAPH;
        var
            Size : word;
        Size = ImageSize( ulx, uly, lrx, lry );
```

See also GetImage and PutImage.

GetImage

The GetImage function saves the pixel image from the screen area which is specified by the four parameters. The InitSize function is used to calculate the required memory and the GetMem function allocates memory for image storage (memory allocation must be less than 64K).

Example:
```
        uses GRAPH;
        var
            BitImage : pointer;
            XLeft, YTop, XRight, YBottom : integer;
            Size : word;
```

```
        Size = ImageSize( XLeft, YTop,
                          XRight, YBottom );
        GetMem( BitImage, Size );
        GetImage( XLeft, YTop, XRight, YBottom,
                  BitImage^ );
```

Notice the caret (^) appended to the *BitImage* parameter in the call to GetImage, indicating that the parameter is a pointer address rather than an array of bytes or a static variable. A similar notation is used with the PutImage procedure.

See also ImageSize and PutImage.

PutImage

The PutImage function writes a previously saved bit image to the screen with the upper-left corner of the image appearing at (*XLeft, YTop*). The *Ops* parameter controls how each image pixel (color) is combined with the existing screen pixels.

Example:
```
          uses GRAPH;
          var
              BitImage : pointer;
              XLeft, YTop : integer;
              Ops : word;

          PutImage( XLeft, YTop, BitImage, Ops );
```

Table 5-4 shows how the *Ops* options are defined in the GRAPH unit.

Table 5-4: Image Options

NAME	VALUE	DESCRIPTION
CopyPut	0	Image is copied to screen, replacing existing pixels
XOrPut	1	Image is eXclusive-OR'd with existing pixels
OrPut	2	Image is inclusive-OR'd with existing pixels
AndPut	3	Image is ANDed with existing pixels
NotPut	4	Copies the inverse bit-image to the screen

The PutDemo.Pas program will demonstrate how the various PutImage options operate. PutDemo is written for color monitors, EGA or VGA is preferred, but can be adapted to run on monochrome systems though the color overlay effects will not be markedly different. I suggest running the program as it stands, then experimenting with different color values, fill patterns, and copy options.

The Image Copy Options

CopyPut   Each pixel in the image is mapped directly to the screen, replacing any existing image pixels. This includes image pixels that are blank (background). An entirely blank image can be used to "erase" other images or portions of the screen. More often, however, the *XOrPut* option is used to "unmap" an existing image.

XOrPut   Each existing screen pixel's value is eXclusively OR'd with the corresponding image byte and the result is written back to the screen. When an image is XOR'd with a existing screen image, the result is a composite of the two.

In PutDemo.Pas, notice how the LightCyan pixels (1011) XOR'd with the Blue (0001) background become LightGreen (1010) while LightRed XOR'd with Blue (0001) becomes LightCyan (1011) with the results appearing cleanly against the background image.

If the same image is then XOR'd a second time, it effectively cancels itself bit by bit, leaving the original screen restored. This option is particularly useful for animation where an image needs to be written over an existing screen, then erased again to leave the original screen in place. This put-option will be used heavily in the ANIMATE1.PAS demo (see Chapter 10).

OrPut   This could also be called "Either/Or" since each image byte is OR'd with corresponding screen pixels and the result is then written back to the screen. Remember, each bit in each pixel is OR'd with the bits in the image so the result is a color composite of the background and the image.

Notice how, in PutDemo.Pas, LightCyan (1011) OR'd with Blue (0001) remains LightCyan (1011), while LightRed (1100) OR'd with the Blue (0001) background becomes LightMagenta (1101).

AndPut   With AndPut, the bits which are on in both the screen pixel and the image byte are also on in the result. The blank background in the Star image wipes out both the Box outline and the fill color except where the Star image actually overlies the Box. Also, the LightRed (1100) AND'd with LightBlue (1001) becomes DarkGray (1000).

NotPut   This is the same as CopyPut except that the image is bit inverted—all Black (0000) pixels in the image become White (1111). The background image is overwritten and lost.

See also ImageSize and GetImage.

CHAPTER 6

Graphics Text Functions

Once a graphics mode has been set, the conventional text displays are no longer available and labels and text information can only be displayed using graphics text displays. In the graphics modes, however, graphics text display operates quite differently from conventional text display.

For example, the conventional character screen positions (column and row coordinates) no longer apply and an individual character can appear almost anywhere on the screen, special provisions are required in order to track the screen display position and decide where the next display Line should appear, as well as to write graphics text to the screen. These include the OutText and OutTextXY functions.

Also, since character sizes can be varied, different vertical and horizontal justifications are offered, and text can be displayed in both horizontal and vertical orientations, the Line offset and display positions become more than a little confusing. These variable settings are controlled by SetTextStyle, SetTextJustify, and SetUserCharSize. Because of these variables and complications, several functions have been provided to make it easier to keep track of display positions, font sizes, and string widths. These include GetText-Settings, TextHeight, and TextWidth.

Text Functions

Because of the elaborations of graphics string output, you should be able to write a string to the screen while in graphics mode before venturing into the esoterica of fonts, sizing, and orientation.

Unfortunately Pascal does not currently permit the creation of functions that accept a variable parameter list (as do the familiar Write and WriteLn procedures). Therefore, when program variables and other changing data are required to be written, alternatives which produce concatenated strings must be used—they will be demonstrated shortly. At the moment, the OutText and OutTextXY procedures provide the principal text output.

OutText

The OutText function displays a string in the viewport (graphics window) beginning at CP. The current font selection, drawing color, character size, text orientation (direction), and justification are used.

Example: `uses GRAPH;`

       `OutText( 'Display string for viewport' );`

If horizontal justification is LeftText and direction is HorizDir (default settings for graphics text display), CP's x-axis coordinate is advanced by *TextWidth(textstring)*, otherwise the CP is not altered.

See GetTextSettings, OutTextXY, SetColor, SetTextSettings, TextHeight, and TextWidth for related information.

OutTextXY

The OutTextXY function displays a string in the viewport beginning at the coordinates specified by (*x, y*), which are relative to the viewport settings. The current font selection, drawing color, character size, text orientation (direction), and justification are used.

Example: `uses GRAPH;`
      `var`
          `x, y : integer;`
      `OutTextXY( x, y, 'Display string in viewport' );`

The current position's coordinates are not affected. See also GetTextSettings, OutText, SetColor, SetTextSettings, TextHeight, and TextWidth.

Graphics Text Styles, Justification, and Sizing

Where conventional text modes offer the display equivalent of a typewritten page, graphics text modes come closer to providing a typeset display. And part and parcel of this enhancement are the capabilities to change fonts, select different horizontal and vertical justifications, to change character sizes, and even to run text displays vertically instead of horizontally.

SetTextStyle

The SetTextStyle function sets the current graphics text font, the direction for the text display (horizontal or vertical), and the character size.

Example:
```
uses GRAPH;
var
    CharSize : integer;
SetTextStyle( Font, Direction, CharSize );
```

Table 6-1 shows how the standard fonts are defined in the GRAPH unit.

Table 6-1: Graphics Text Fonts

NAME	VALUE	DESCRIPTION
DefaultFont	0	Bit-mapped 8x8 font
TriplexFont	1	Stroked triplex font
SmallFont	2	Stroked small font
SansSerifFont	3	Stroked sans-serif font
GothicFont	4	Stroked gothic font

The DefaultFont is built into the graphics system. Of the other fonts, only one is normally kept in memory at any time. Also the .CHR files for the selected font must be located in the directory or subdirectory indicated by InitGraph as *DriverPath* before the font can be loaded.

Multiple fonts, however, can be linked to your program using the BGIOBJ utility (see BGIOBJ Linking in Chapter 7). In this case, the RegisterBGIFont function is used to select the font required.

By default, graphics text direction is horizontal, but can be set to vertical (rotated 90 degrees counterclockwise). The two graphics text directions are defined in GRAPHICS.H as shown in Table 6-2.

Table 6-2: Graphics Text Direction

NAME	VALUE	DESCRIPTION
HorizDir	0	Left to right (*default*)
VertDir	1	Bottom to top

In vertical orientation, the text string begins at the bottom, and runs upward. No provisions currently exist for a string display running down the page or for an inverted string (upside down, running right to left), but these can be created if desired.

For bit-mapped font(s), *charsize* may be 0..10. Values zero and one display 8x8 pixel rectangles, value 2 displays a 16x16 pixel rectangle, continuing up to 10 times normal size. For stroked fonts, *charsize = 0* magnifies the stroked font by the default factor of four or by the user-defined size factors set by SetUserCharSize. The maximum valid *charsize* is 10.

If invalid values are passed to SetTextJustify, GraphResult will return −11 (*general error*) and the current text settings will remain unchanged.

See also SetTextJustify, TextHeight, and TextWidth.

SetTextJustify

The SetTextJustify function selects horizontal and vertical text justification. The default values are LeftText, TopText (0,2).

Example:
```
uses GRAPH;
var
    hJustify, vJustify : word;

SetTextJustify( hJustify, vJustify );
```

Constants for text justification are defined in the GRAPH unit as shown in Table 6-3.

Table 6-3: Graphics Text Justification

HORIZONTAL JUSTIFY		VERTICAL JUSTIFY	
NAME	VALUE	NAME	VALUE
LeftText	0	BottomText	0
CenterText	1	CenterText	1
RightText	2	TopText	2

For horizontal justification, *LeftText* displays the text string to the right, starting at CP; *CenterText* displays the text string, centered at CP; and *RightText* displays the text string to the left, ending at CP. For vertical justification, *BottomText* aligns the bottom of the character string with CP, *CenterText* aligns the center of the display string at CP, and *TopText* aligns the top of the string with CP.

When justification is set as *LeftText* and direction as *HorizDir*, the current position's *x* setting is advanced after a call to OutText by TextWidth(string).

See SetTextStyle for related information.

Figure 6-1: Graphic Text Justification

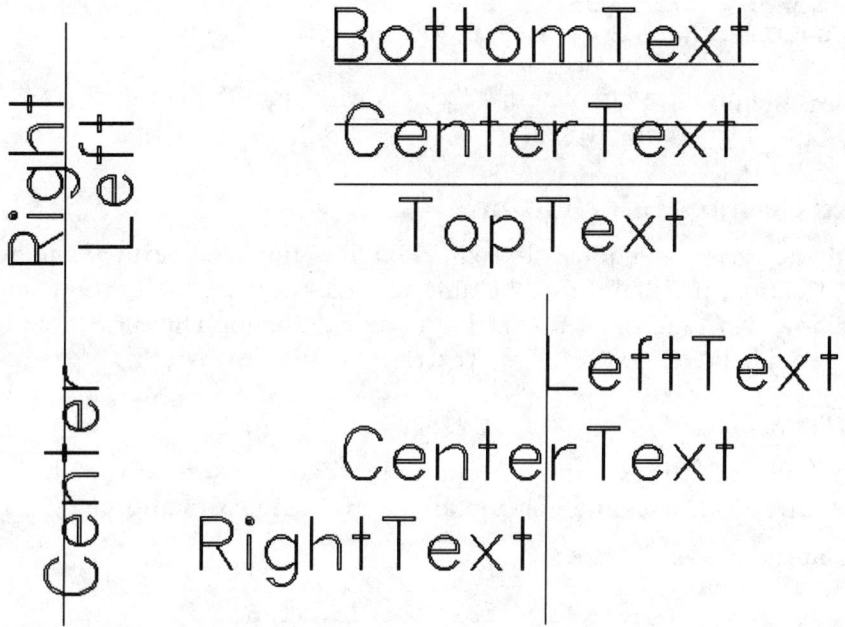

SetUserCharSize

The SetUserCharSize function provides user-defined character magnification for stroked fonts only! This does not function with the DefaultFont characters and the font adjustment parameters are active only if SetTextStyle has been called to set *charsize = 0*.

Example:
```
          uses GRAPH;
          var
              xMult, xDiv, yMult, yDiv : integer;
          SetUserCharSize( xMult, xDiv, yMult, yDiv );
```

When SetUserCharSize is called to select custom character scaling, the resulting width is defined as *xMult/xDiv*, while the resulting height is defined as *yMult/yDiv*. For example, to create a display with characters scaled to a height of 3 (24 pixels) and twice as wide as they are tall (48 pixels), SetUserCharSize would be called with the following:

```
   xMult = 6;    xDiv = 1;
   yMult = 3;    yDiv = 1;
   SetUserCharSize( xMult, xDiv, yMult, yDiv );
```

For tall, narrow characters the following call would be used:

```
xMult = 3;   xDiv = 2;
yMult = 6;   yDiv = 1;
SetUserCharSize( xMult, xDiv, yMult, yDiv );
```

and would produce characters 12 pixels wide and 48 pixels tall.

See also GetTextSettings.

Text Settings Information

With the variety of choices in fonts, text direction, and vertical and horizontal justification, it is helpful to be able to find out what the current settings are and how wide and tall a text string is. For these applications, three functions are provided: GetTextSettings, TextHeight, and TextWidth.

GetTextSettings

The GetTextSettings function returns the *TextInfo* structure with the current font, direction, size, and horizontal and vertical justification.

```
Example:   uses GRAPH;
           var
               TextInfo : TextSettingsType;

           GetTextSettings( TextInfo );
```

The structure *TextSettingsType* is defined in the GRAPH unit as in the following:

```
TextSettingsType : record
                       Font : word;
                       Direction : word;
                       CharSize : word;
                       Horiz : word;
                       Vert : word;
                   end;
```

See also OutText, TextHeight, TextWidth, and SetTextStyle for further information.

TextHeight and TextWidth

The TextHeight and TextWidth functions return the vertical and horizontal sizes of a string.

```
Example:   uses GRAPH;
           var
               charheight, charwidth : integer;
```

```
charheight = TextHeight( 'Text String' );
charwidth  = TextWidth( 'Text String' );
```

The TextHeight function returns the height of a string in pixels, using the current font size, scaling factors, and text direction. This may be the height of a single character or the height of an entire string. When a single character is used, an uppercase character is customary even though the returned information is based on calculated size and not the actual display size (for example, a "u" will return the same size as "U").

The TextWidth function returns the width of a string in pixels, using the current font size, scaling factors, and text direction. This may be the width of a single character or, more often, the width of an entire string.

CHAPTER 7

Advanced Graphics Pascal

Beginning with version 4.0 of Turbo Pascal, a graphics unit has been supplied (GRAPH.TPU) as a supplement to the standard function libraries. Unlike C compilers, Turbo Pascal does not require separate libraries for different memory models and the single instruction *uses GRAPH;* makes the graphics functions and definitions available to your program.

And, because Turbo Pascal uses a smart linker, no penalties in memory requirements, program size, or execution speed are incurred by including function units.

Smart Linking

In earlier versions of Turbo Pascal—and historically with other compilers—including special libraries imposed penalties in program size and memory usage because the entire library became part of the compiled program. This was true even when only one or two functions within the library were used or even if the library was not referenced at all.

With smart linking, however, only those elements specifically needed by the program are included in the .EXE program. Likewise, data elements and constants that are provided by the library unit are included only if they are needed (and most constants, such as color names, are compiled as integer or word values in the first place). The savings realized by a smart compiler are not limited to the external libraries. These same criteria are applied to the program's source code as well.

For example, suppose you have written a program and, during development and testing, you included a variety of special functions and procedures to report on what is taking place while the program is being tested. At the same time, in the program header, a large block of constants, string variables, and several data arrays are declared, again for use during testing and development.

Of course, once the program is finished, these additions are not required and the obvious response would be to go through the program deleting these addenda.

With smart linking, these special programming features can be left in place—in case of future need—and all that needs to be removed are the references which call the features. These can actually be commented out and left in place rather than deleted. When the program is compiled, all of these unreferenced blocks of source code will not be included and the constants, string variables, and data arrays—even though they appear globally in the program's header—are also omitted.

When compiling to memory instead of to disk, keep in mind that the smart linker is not enabled. Ergo, programs may be smaller when compiled to disk.

Linking Graphics Drivers and Fonts

By default, both Turbo Pascal and Turbo C use dynamically linked graphics drivers (*.BGI files) and graphics fonts (*.CHR files). While the use of external drivers and fonts offers advantages in limiting compiled program size and flexibility in adding new drivers and fonts at later dates, there are two disadvantages in depending on external files for operation.

First, when using external drivers and fonts, the drive and directory path where the external utilities are located must be specified by the programmer at compile time (see InitGraph in Chapter 1). If the specified path or drive is changed later, the program must be recompiled with the new information.

Second, while the .BGI and .CHR files can be distributed with your compiled program, these extra files are subject to accidental erasure and to other hazards, which can result in a dissatisfied end-user.

But there is an alternative: linking the drivers and fonts directly as a part of the graphics library so no external files are required. After this is done, the drivers and fonts will be a part of the .EXE code produced by the compiler.

The first step in linking driver and font files requires calling the BINOBJ utility to convert the .BGI and .CHR files into .OBJ files. The BINOBJ utility is distributed with Turbo Pascal and is described in the *Turbo Pascal User's Guide*. A sample MAKE source program, BGILINK.MAK, is included in the

BGIEXAMP.ARC archive along with the demo programs, DRIVERS.PAS, FONTS.PAS, and BGILINK.PAS.

Creating Driver and Font Units

Turbo Pascal provides a stand-alone Make utility that is described in the *Turbo Pascal User's Guide*, but which is essentially a utility accepting a series of macro instructions for creating a program or a group of programs.

The source file, BGILINK.MAK, which is included in the BGIEXAMP.ARC archive, contains instructions. These instructions create a series of .OBJ files from the .CHR and .BGI units and link these .OBJ files into two units: FONTS.TPU and DRIVERS.TPU. To use the BGILINK.MAK instructions, the MAKE.EXE and BINOBJ.EXE utilities (both distributed with Turbo Pascal) must be available either in the current directory or in a directory available through the DOS PATH definition.

The BGILINK.PAS, DRIVERS.PAS, and FONTS.PAS source codes (all included in the BGIEXAMP.ARC archive) must be in the current drive or directory together with all of the *.CHR font files and *.BGI driver files and, of course, the BGILINK.MAK file.

Make is invoked from any DOS prompt using the instruction

```
make -fBGILINK.MAK
```

and interprets the instructions in the .MAK file, calling on Turbo Pascal to compile the DRIVERS.PAS and FONTS.PAS source programs and the BINOBJ utility to convert files into .OBJ files. After this is done, the DRIVERS.TPU and FONTS.TPU units may be included by any program in the uses statement, thus:

```
uses GRAPH, DRIVERS, FONTS;
```

As desired, the BGILINK.MAK source can be amended to include new fonts (see Chapter 17 and Appendix F) or to include new or custom drivers (see Appendices D and E). Old fonts and drivers can be commented out if not needed but this is not necessary since only the fonts and drivers requested by the application program will be linked in the final .EXE program.

Using Linked Drivers and Fonts

Before the staticly linked graphics drivers and fonts can be used by a program, there is one other requirement that does not occur when using external drivers and fonts: the driver(s) and font(s) must be registered before calling InitGraph.

RegisterBGIDriver

The RegisterBGIDriver function is used to register a statically linked graphics driver. If the specified graphics driver is not found, a negative error code is returned; otherwise, the internal driver number is returned. Table 7-1 lists the graphics drivers and their corresponding symbolic names.

Example: `uses GRAPH;`

```
        if RegisterBGIDriver( @NameDriverProc ) < 0 )
           then halt( 1 );
```

Table 7-1: Graphics Drivers

DRIVER	SYMBOLIC NAME[1]
CGA.BGI	CGADriverProc
EGAVGA.BGI	EGAVGADriverProc
HERC.BGI	HercDriverProc
ATT.BGI	ATTDriverProc
PC3270.BGI	PC3270DriverProc
IBM8514.BGI	IBM8514DriverProc[2]

1. The driver symbolic names were assigned by instructions in the BGILINK.MAK file.
2. The IBM8514 driver is not included in the BGILINK.MAK instructions as distributed.

DRIVER.INC

```
           {=====================================}
           { DRIVER.INC — call RegisterDrivers }
           {=====================================}
   uses GRAPH, DRIVERS;

   procedure AbortDriver( FontName : string );
      begin
          writeln( FontName, ': ',
                   GraphErrorMsg( GraphResult ) );
          halt( 1 );
      end;

   procedure RegisterDrivers;
   begin
      if( RegisterBGIDriver( @CGADriverProc ) < 0 )
         then AbortDriver( 'CGA' );
      if( RegisterBGIDriver( @EGAVGADriverProc ) < 0 )
         then AbortDriver( 'EGA/VGA' );
      if( RegisterBGIDriver( @HercDriverProc ) < 0 )
         then AbortDriver( 'Herc' );
      if RegisterBGIDriver( @ATTDriverProc ) < 0
         then AbortDriver( 'ATT' );
```

```
      if RegisterBGIDriver( @PC3270DriverProc ) < 0
         then AbortDriver( 'PC3270' );
      if RegisterBGIDriver( @IBM8514DriverProc ) < 0
         then AbortDriver( 'IBM8514' );
   end;

begin
   RegisterDrivers;
   Initialize;
   ....
   CloseGraph;
end;
```

Portability: IBM PCs and compatibles only, corresponding functions exist in Turbo C. See preceding for information on creating linked-in graphics drivers.

RegisterBGIFont

The RegisterBGIFont function is used to register a linked stroked font character set. If the specified font is not found, a negative error code is returned; otherwise, the registered font number is returned. See Table 7-2 for a list of the graphics fonts.

Example:
```
uses GRAPH;

if RegisterBGIFont( NameFontProc ) < 0
   then halt(1);
```

Table 7-2: Graphics Fonts

FONT FILE	SYMBOLIC NAME
TRIP.CHR	TriplexFontProc
LITT.CHR	SmallFontProc
SANS.CHR	SanSerifFontProc
GOTH.CHR	GothicFontProc

Note: The symbolic font names were assigned by instructions in the BGILINK.MAK source file.

FONTS.INC

```
{=================================}
{ FONTS.INC — call RegisterFonts  }
{=================================}

uses GRAPH, FONTS;

procedure AbortFont( FontName : string );
   begin
      writeln( FontName, ': ',
```

```
                    GraphErrorMsg( GraphResult ) );
        halt( 1 );
     end;
  procedure RegisterFonts
  begin
     if RegisterBGIFont( TriplexFontProc ) < 0
        then AbortFont( 'Triplex' );
     if RegisterBGIFont( SmallFontProc ) < 0
        then AbortFont( 'Small' );
     if RegisterBGIFont( SanSerifFontProc ) < 0
        then AbortFont( 'Sans Serif' );
     if RegisterBGIFont( GothicFontProc ) < 0
        then AbortFont( 'Gothic' );
  end;
  begin
     RegisterDrivers;
     RegisterFonts;
     Initialize;
     ....
     CloseGraph;
  end;
```

Portability: IBM PCs and compatibles only, corresponding functions exist in Turbo C. See preceding for information on creating statically linked graphics fonts.

User-Designed Drivers and Fonts

Two procedures are supplied to permit the installation of user-defined or vendor-supplied device drivers or graphics fonts. Both of these procedures are described in extensive detail in the *Turbo Pascal Reference Guide* and are given a brief mention here because of limited applicability.

See also Appendixes D, E, and F for related information.

InstallUserDriver

The InstallUserDriver function is used to register a vendor-supplied graphics driver.

Example: uses GRAPH;

```
           var
              Driver : integer;
           Driver := InstallUserDriver( 'XGA', nil );
```

The *Name* parameter is the filename of the external device driver and *AutoDetect* (*nil* in the example) is a pointer to an optional autodetect function which may not be included within the driver.

The InstallUserDriver function returns an integer value for the default video mode for the new driver or, if an installation error occurs, an error value.

InstallUserFont

The InstallUserFont function is used to register a user-defined or vendor-supplied stroked font.

Example: `uses GRAPH;`

```
var
    FontName : string;
    FontNum  : integer;

FontNum := InstallUserFont( FontName );
```

The InstallUserFont function is used to register any stroked font not included in the BGI graphics system. If the specified font is not found, a negative error code is returned; otherwise, the registered font number is returned. If the internal font table is full, a value of 0 (default font) will be reported.

Part Two

Using Turbo Pascal Graphics

CHAPTER 8

Combining Text With Graphics

In the first section of this book, I discussed the various Turbo Pascal graphics commands and briefly illustrated many of them. In this section, these commands will be used to create graphics and utilities and to demonstrate how various procedures and applications can be created.

These demonstrations will include combining text and graphics, creating two- and three-dimensional graph displays for business applications, simple animation techniques, turtle graphics, image manipulation and rotation, image file storage, and using a mouse with graphics displays. Since programs must operate on a variety of hardware with varying resolutions and color capabilities, techniques for adapting to various hardware will also be demonstrated.

Also, with the release of Turbo Pascal 5.5, Pascal has become object-oriented; therefore object-oriented programming techniques will be incorporated in graphics applications. But object-oriented programming is not the primary topic of this book and will not be covered in comprehensive detail—for further information refer to my companion volume: *Object-Oriented Programming in Turbo Pascal 5.5*, available from Addison-Wesley Publishing Company.

Caveat

Most of these demonstrations have been created specifically for use with EGA or higher resolution graphics hardware using a color monitor. When practical, additional code has been included for adaptation to CGA or monographic equipment but, in many cases, some modification of the source codes may be necessary for lower resolution modes.

While lower resolution and monochrome equipment is graphics capable, 640x350 color provides a good minimum standard for demonstrating graphics applications. If these applications and demonstrations were written to operate only under the restraints and limitations of the lowest common resolutions and color capabilities, a great deal of real capability would simply be ignored.

Thus, the EGA vertical resolution of 350 pixels and the VGA vertical resolution of 480 pixels provide space to show far more detail than is possible with CGA's 200 pixels (though the 1,024 vertical resolution of the IBM-8514 would be nice). At the same time, a palette of 16 colors certainly shows more visual information than monochrome. Therefore, the utilities demonstrated will make use of these capabilities whenever possible—even though such resolutions may not be universally available.

While some earlier computer designs did not differentiate between text and graphics, contemporary MS-DOS systems do not permit mapping the ROM-based character set(s) directly into a graphics display. To overcome this limitation, both Turbo Pascal and Turbo C provide a default bit-mapped graphics character set that is a replacement for the ROM character set, including the extended ASCII characters (ASCII $80..$FF) which provide foreign characters such as the English pound sign, the Japanese yen, the accented vowels, and the graphics and math characters.

These extended ASCII characters may not be included in all stroked fonts and attempts to print extended character codes using stroked fonts may be ignored or may draw garbage. See Appendix F for details on all graphics fonts.

The graphics character fonts are not merely a replacement for the ROM-based characters and, in graphics modes, text displays can be much more elaborate than is possible under text modes.

Four "fancy" stroked typefaces—Gothic, Sans Serif, Triplex (Roman), and Small—are supplied as standard fonts and string character positions can be adjusted by pixel instead of character positions; both the default and the stroked typefaces can be enlarged up to 10 times their normal sizes; the stroked typefaces can be proportioned to be taller or wider; strings may be set flush left, centered, or flush right and displayed vertically as well as horizontally.

Combining Text With Graphics

While the default font is a fixed-width font (all characters are the same basic width), the stroked fonts are proportional (for example, a capital "W" is proportionally wider than a lowercase "i") and character placement and string spacing reflect these, providing a better appearance than typewriter style text.

But there are also a few limitations. The two principal output functions OutText and OutTextXY (discussed in Chapter 6) each write a string to the screen; OutText using the default CP and OutTextXY accepting screen position coordinates for the text output. But both of these functions accept only a single string for output and there is no direct provision for printing variables or building strings for output as supported in text modes by the Write and WriteLn functions.

Unfortunately, Turbo Pascal does not currently permit creating analogous functions accepting variable parameter lists to serve these same purposes. But there are other ways to produce similar results.

Functions for Variable Output

Since the OutText and OutTextXY functions will accept only a single string argument for output, the simplest method of displaying variables is to create functions that accept variable arguments and return formatted strings which can be handled.

Only two number-to-string functions are used here for illustration, but similar functions can be created to handle any type of special format.

Integer-to-String Conversion

The simplest case of a formatted output string is converting an integer value, which is done by the I2S function:

```
function I2S( Val : integer ): string;
   var
      Buffer : string[10];
begin
      str( Val, Buffer );
      I2S := Buffer;
end;
```

Since no width argument is used in the str procedure, the string result is unpadded and the returned string consists only of the integer characters representing the value.

Real-to-String Conversion

Converting real values to strings requires a bit more information than converting an integer value. Therefore, the R2S function is called with two additional arguments for the number of digits (overall width of the resulting string) and the number of requested decimal places.

```
function R2S( Val : real;
              Digit, Decimal : integer ): string;
   var
      Buffer : string[20];
   begin
      str( Val:Digit:Decimal, Buffer );
      R2S := Buffer;
   end;
```

Calling *R2S(517.2345, 7, 3)* returns the string 517.234, with the value in the fourth decimal place rounded to display only three decimals. A value of 517.2346 would be rounded up to return the string 517.235.

Unlike the I2S function, however, the results returned by R2S will be left-padded with blanks to the requested digit width and right-padded with zeros to the requested decimal places. If the calling value is larger than the indicated digits, additional digits will be left-appended to display the string result. For example, calling *R2S(543217.2, 7, 3)* returns the string 543217.200, with a total width of 10 places even though a width of only seven places was requested. (A buffer width of 20 characters has been used to provide ample space for most values.)

Additional information on string formatting by the str procedure can be found in the *Turbo Pascal Reference Guide* under the write procedure.

Concatenating Strings for Output

With the two string conversion functions, writing variables using OutText and OutTextXY becomes almost as convenient as it is in text modes with the Write and WriteLn functions. For example,

```
Write(    'Pi is: ', Pi:11:9, '!' );
```

and

```
OutText( 'Pi is: '+R2S(Pi,11,9)+'!' );
```

produce the result

```
Pi is:  3.141592653!
```

The only real difference between the two is that where the Write procedure accepts a variable parameter list, the OutText procedure was called with a single string produced by using the concatenation operator (+) and the R2S function.

More complex output strings can be built in this same fashion, concatenating string references, elements from arrays of strings, products of formulas used as the arguments of the I2S and R2S functions—a bit more complicated than using Write and WriteLn perhaps, but with moderate care, not that difficult.

Other Output Utilities

Writing material to a graphics screen is only half of the task and it also helps to be able to erase material that is no longer desired or part of the screen where something new is about to be written.

When a new string is written to the screen in conventional text modes, the existing material is simply written over, vanishing automatically as the new characters are assigned to each row/column position. In graphics modes, however, text output is drawn rather than written. New text written over existing text results, not in the new replacing the old, but in an overlapping combination of characters—a result which is usually more confusing than helpful.

Occasionally, this overwriting could be useful, if only in a frivolous sense. One programmer, who is partially color-blind, found that he could use graphics mode to write two or three different texts to the same area of the screen resulting in a graphics mishmash that nobody else could read. And, by changing the palette assignments (see Chapters 3 and 12), each layer of text became plainly visible ... if only to color-blind individuals. But it is most often undesirable to overwrite characters; therefore, the EraseStr function is provided.

The EraseStr Function

The EraseStr function is provided to erase the appropriate area of the screen before writing a string to the screen. It is intended to remove a block of graphics background that would interfere with the string image. However, this function can also be used to erase a string or portion of a string if necessary.

To clear a space for an output string, EraseStr is called with the x-axis and y-axis coordinates that will be used to position the output string and with a copy of the output string itself.

```
procedure EraseStr( xLoc, yLoc : integer;
                    Txt : string );
```

The first things EraseStr needs to know are the current text settings. This is information that may be available elsewhere, but rather than having to pass a great deal of information when EraseStr is called, it is much easier to let the procedure ask for its own copy of the data. Therefore, a local variable *TextInfo* is declared.

```
var
   TextInfo : TextSettingsType;
   XDim, YDim : integer;
   TextImage : pointer;
```

The local variables *XDim* and *YDim* will be used for the string dimensions while the *TextImage* pointer will be the key to rapid and effective erasure of a selected portion of the screen.

EraseStr begins by checking the text justfication settings that are in effect, which assumes they will not be changed before the new string is written to the screen.

```
begin
   GetTextSettings( TextInfo );
```

According to the text output direction, the x and y dimensions of the output string are assigned to the appropriate variables. Also, for horizontal output, the *XLoc* variable is decremented to provide a one-pixel offset for the erase area. For vertical output, the *YLoc* variable is incremented for the same reason.

```
case TextInfo.Direction of
   HorizDir : begin
                 XDim := TextWidth( Txt );
                 YDim := TextHeight( Txt );
                 dec( XLoc );
              end;
   VertDir  : begin
                 YDim = TextWidth( Txt );
                 XDim = TextHeight( Txt );
                 inc( YLoc );
              end;
end;   { case }
```

In the next steps, *XLoc* is adjusted according to the horizontal justification setting.

```
case TextInfo.Horiz of
   LeftText   : { no adjustment } ;
   CenterText : dec( XLoc, XDim div 2 );
   RightText  : dec( XLoc, XDim );
end; { case }
```

And *YLoc* is adjusted using the vertical justification setting.

```
case TextInfo.Vert of
   BottomText : dec( YLoc, YDim );
   CenterText : dec( YLoc, YDim div 2 );
      TopText : { no adjustment } ;
end; { case }
```

Before any attempt is made to erase a screen area, two tests are needed to ensure that the *XLoc* and *YLoc* coordinates fall within the valid screen area. If either *XLoc* or *YLoc* falls outside the screen area, then nothing would be erased from the screen because subsequent calls to the GetImage and PutImage functions would attempt to use coordinates that did not exist in video memory. Thus, if necessary, *XLoc* and *YLoc* are adjusted to lie within the screen limits and, at the same time, the *XDim* and *YDim* offsets are changed to compensate.

```
while xloc < 0 do
begin
   inc( XLoc );
   dec( XDim );
end;
while yloc < 0 do
begin
   inc( YLoc );
   dec( YDim );
end;
```

Now it's time to actually erase a block of screen. Begin by allocating memory for *TextImage* according to the screen area that will be cleared. The function ImageSize uses the *XLoc*, *YLoc*, *XDim*, and *YDim* variables to return an unsigned integer indicating the number of bytes required for the selected image.

```
GetMem( TextImage,
        ImageSize( XLoc, YLoc, XDim, YDim ) );
```

Next, GetImage is called, storing the screen image in the memory area indicated by TextImage before PutImage returns the image using the XOrPut option, leaving the desired screen area blank.

```
GetImage( XLoc, YLoc, XLoc + XDim, YLoc + YDim,
          TextImage^ );
PutImage( XLoc, YLoc, TextImage^, XOrPut );
```

Lastly, Dispose is used to release the memory allocated for *TextImage*. The *TextImage* pointer variable cannot be referenced outside of the EraseStr function. However, memory that has been allocated locally does remain allocated until it is released—and it must be released while the *TextImage* pointer is still available—specifically, before exiting EraseStr.

```
    Dispose( TextImage );
end;
```

When EraseStr is called again, a new block of memory will be allocated and a new *TextImage* pointer assigned. If memory were repeatedly allocated without being released, the system memory could be quickly exhausted and subsequent calls to this or other functions would produce error results.

EraseBlock

As an alternative to the image functions, the necessary screen area could have been erased by rewriting the individual pixels using the background color, for example:

```
procedure EraseBlock( Left, Top,
                      Right, Bottom : integer );
   var
      i, j, k : integer;
begin
   k := GetBkColor;
   for i := Left to Right do
      for j := Top to Bottom do
         PutPixel( i, j, k );
end;
```

This second option does save the small amount of memory that is allocated in the preceding EraseStr function but, as a trade-off, it is considerably slower in execution than the GetImage and PutImage functions.

Alternative Applications

Earlier, I mentioned that the EraseStr function could also be used to erase a string or portion of a string. This statement was only half true: it can certainly be used to erase an existing string. The second application, erasing a portion of a string is slightly less practical since EraseStr was not specifically designed for this purpose.

Still, both of these functions can be accomplished but there are a couple of prerequisites which must be recognized.

First, the text style, fonts, and justification must be the same as when the string was originally written. Second, the original drawing color must be in effect. Third, the screen coordinates where the original string was written must be known. And, fourth, the string itself must be known.

If any of the first three items have changed, an attempt to erase an existing string or a portion of an existing string will have unexpected results. And, in graphics modes, there is no convenient method of reading a text string back from the screen as can be done in text modes.

Now, assuming that the text settings and color are correct and that the original screen coordinates are known, the first question is erasing an existing string. This is a simple operation—just call EraseStr directly using the x and y screen coordinates and the string, and the appropriate area of the screen will be XOR'd with itself. This leaves the screen blank and ready for a rewrite.

In the second application, erasing a portion of a string, the easiest method is to begin by erasing the entire string and then rewriting the portion of the string which is desired. While several elaborate schemes could be constructed for selectively erasing specific graphics characters or substrings, all of them would require far more processing and time; the preceding can accomplish the task quite promptly.

Word processing, per se, is not the topic of this book and using graphics fonts and text display is hardly the simplest method of programming a word processor or similar application. However, you may find it necessary to employ text editing procedures along with a graphics application. If so, here are a few hints:

The best probable approach would be to treat the screen image as a mapped copy of the actual text array in memory, using some indexing scheme to identify a correspondence between a "line" of text in memory and its graphics position on the screen.

If the bitmapped DefaultFont is used, the screen position for any character is relatively easy to calculate since all characters are fixed width. If the stroked fonts are being used, then the TextWidth function is the optimum method for deciding where a particular string ends.

Also, the screen cannot be scrolled up or down in the usual manner. While it is possible to use GetImage and PutImage to move a major portion of the screen image, the memory requirements can be excessive. If so, a simpler method is to move some smaller portion of the screen, using multiple moves to shift as much of the screen as necessary.

A similar technique can be used for left and right scrolling.

Automatic Erasure

As a final provision, two simple procedures are created as analogs to OutText and OutTextXY: GWrite and GWriteXY. Both procedures require single string arguments and produce the same display output as OutText and OutTextXY, but have the added advantage of erasing the underlying screen before drawing the new text string.

Since the GWrite procedure is called without position parameters, the current position coordinates are retrieved as arguments for the EraseStr procedure using the GetX and GetY functions.

```pascal
procedure GWrite( TxtStr : string );
   begin
      EraseStr( GetX, GetY, TxtStr );
      OutText( TxtStr );
   end;
```

Since the GWriteXY procedure is called with position coordinates, these are passed directly to EraseStr and then OutTextXY is called instead of OutText.

```pascal
procedure GWriteXY( XLoc, YLoc ; integer; TxtStr : string );
   begin
      EraseStr( XLoc, YLoc, TxtStr );
      OutTextXY( XLoc, YLoc, TxtStr );
   end;
```

These are two simple enhancements that can be revised and improved in several fashions.

For example, you might prefer to have the GWrite procedure update the current position to the end of the text line and create a new version, called GWriteLn, which resets the current position to begin a new line of text below the last.

Of course, which position coordinate to update—the x-axis or y-axis—would depend on whether the text orientation is horizontal or vertical (but these are easily-implemented decisions and are left as an exercise according to your preferences).

Summary

So far, you've seen the basic elements necessary for formatted graphics text output, including provisions to erase background images as necessary. While they are lacking fancy elaborations, these basic tools can be extended and improved in a variety of fashions including, if you are so inclined, creating a full-fledged graphics editor.

The next chapter will use text labels together with business graph displays. While the EraseStr provisions demonstrated here are not used, text positioning techniques will be an important element, particularly in the pie graph demonstration.

GWRITE.INC

```
{ ========================================= }
{                 GWRITE.INC                }
{   utilities for graphics text output      }
{ ========================================= }
```

```pascal
procedure EraseStr( xLoc, yLoc : integer; Txt : string );
   var
      TextInfo : TextSettingsType;
      XDim, YDim : integer;
      TextImage : pointer;
   begin
      GetTextSettings( TextInfo );
      case TextInfo.Direction of
         HorizDir : begin
                       XDim := TextWidth( Txt );
                       YDim := TextHeight( Txt );
                       dec( XLoc );
                    end;
         VertDir : begin
                      YDim = TextWidth( Txt );
                      XDim = TextHeight( Txt );
                      inc( YLoc );
                   end;
      end;  { case }
      case TextInfo.Horiz of
         LeftText : { no adjustment } ;
         CenterText : dec( XLoc, XDim div 2 );
         RightText : dec( XLoc, XDim );
      end; { case }
      case TextInfo.Vert of
         BottomText : dec( YLoc, YDim );
         CenterText : dec( YLoc, YDim div 2 );
         TopText : { no adjustment } ;
      end; { case }
      while xloc < 0 do
      begin
         inc( XLoc );
         dec( XDim );
      end;
      while yloc < 0 do
      begin
         inc( YLoc );
         dec( YDim );
      end;
      GetMem( TextImage,
              ImageSize( XLoc, YLoc, XDim, YDim ) );
      GetImage( XLoc, YLoc, XLoc + XDim, YLoc + YDim,
               TextImage^ );
      PutImage( XLoc, YLoc, TextImage^, XOrPut );
      Dispose( TextImage );
   end;
procedure GWrite( TxtStr : string );
```

```
   begin
      EraseStr( GetX, GetY, TxtStr );
      OutText( TxtStr );
   end;

procedure GWriteXY( XLoc, YLoc ; integer;
                    TxtStr : string );
   begin
      EraseStr( XLoc, YLoc, TxtStr );
      OutTextXY( XLoc, YLoc, TxtStr );
   end;
```

CHAPTER 9

Business Graphic Displays

Business applications often require graphic displays to show sales figures, financial information, stock price fluctuations, and almost any other type of numerical data. The reasons for this demand of graphic displays are simple: first, a graph display makes information easier to understand than a column of figures; second, a graph offers convenient visual comparisons making trends, irregularities and shifts much more obvious than the numbers themselves and; third, graph displays are more impressive than alphanumerical displays.

The business graphs demonstrated here have been created with visual appeal in mind, using colors and fill patterns where possible and, in some cases, have been designed more to be visually impressive than to be visually informative. Granted, this is a purely subjective distinction but it is also one which you will need to be aware of when creating graphs and selecting the styles of display, patterns, and colors to be used.

A Cautionary Note

When creating a graph display, restraint is the best virtue. It is not only possible to include too much information in a graph, but it is common for the resulting graphic display be rendered unintelligible by virtue of an excess of artistic style, information, and cross-correlation.

Remember, the first purpose of a graph is to present information in a manner and style that shows convenient correlations between different figures. This primary function—information—should not be overshadowed and defeated by colors, patterns, labels, logos, or other elements intended to make the informative eye-catching. Concentrate on information first, entertainment second.

Business Graph Demos

While there are at least several hundred styles of business graphs, five basic graph displays will be illustrated in this chapter: pie graphs, bar graphs, multiple bar graphs, 3-D bar graphs, and line graphs. (To print graph displays, see Chapter 17.)

The first four graph types—pie, bar, multiple bar, and 3-D bar—have been combined in a single demo program, while the line graph demo is created separately for reasons that will be discussed later. Each of these first four graph styles will present the same data, but in a different format. The demo program will pause after each graph, waiting for a key stroke. The last graph demo (3-D) will show several displays with different depths, pausing after each display.

The data used for the demo has been written as two arrays, one of integer and one of char. In actual practice, this information would normally be read from external sources such as spread sheet data, database files, internally created data arrays, or from data files specifically created by your own program(s).

```
Accounts : array[1..4,1..9] of integer =
          ( ( 1986, 133, 35, 33, 17, 29, 15, 17, 32 ),
            ( 1987, 122, 41, 30, 25, 18, 24, 43, 21 ),
            ( 1988, 111, 65, 57, 14, 17, 39, 32, 17 ),
            ( 1989, 100, 60, 70, 12, 16, 13, 17, 12 ) );
AccTypes : array[1..9] of STR5 =
          ( '      ', 'Motor', 'Acsry', 'Reprs', 'Govmt',
            'Lease', 'Tires', 'Paint', 'Misc' );
```

The dummy data sets shown are figures for four years income for an anonymous corporation, broken down by eight categories. This data was selected simply for simulation and you can experiment with the graph displays by changing the figures.

The Pie Graph Displays

Four separate pie graphs are created, one for each year's data using the function DrawPieGraphs to position these four displays—see Figure 9-1. Three parameters are used, the first specifying the array index for the year, the second and third specifying the x and y screen positions where the pie graph will be centered.

```
procedure DrawPieGraphs;
   var
      i : integer;
   begin
      ClearDevice;
      GraphDefaults;
      Rectangle( 0, 0, MaxX, MaxY );
      PieGraph( 1,   GetMaxX div 4,   GetMaxY div 4 );
      PieGraph( 2,   GetMaxX div 4, 3*GetMaxY div 4 );
      PieGraph( 3, 3*GetMaxX div 4,   GetMaxY div 4 );
      PieGraph( 4, 3*GetMaxX div 4, 3*GetMaxY div 4 );
   end;
```

For CGA systems, a separate set of screen coordinates has been provided, but EGA or higher resolution with color is recommended.

Figure 9-1: Pie Graphs

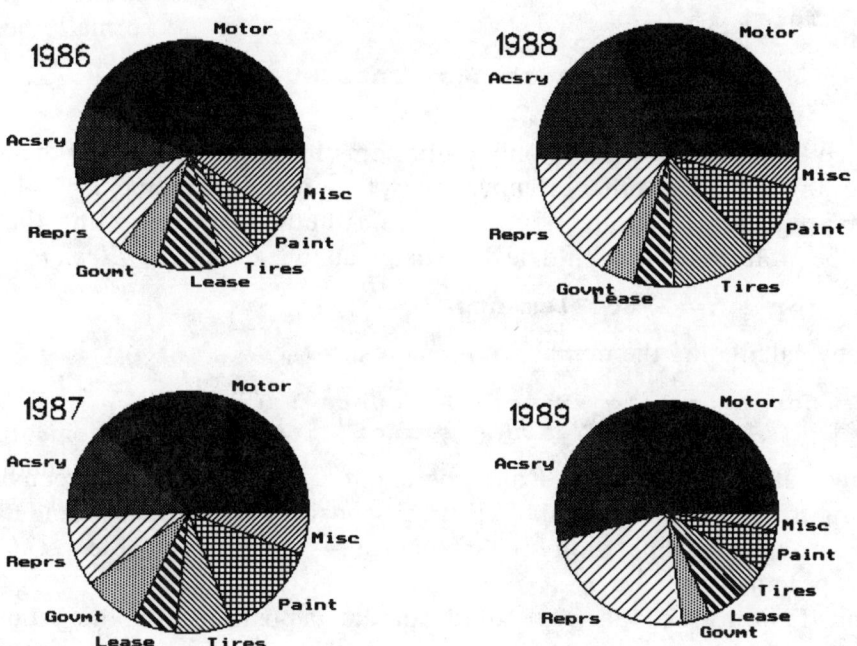

When the PieGraph function is called, several local variables are established: *Total* is initialized as zero and will be used to determine the total value of all of the data elements so that the slices can be apportioned correctly; *m* is initialized as 135 and will be used to position the year label; *s* and *t* are initialized as zero and will be used for start and terminate angles for each slice.

```
procedure PieGraph( DataSet, x, y : integer );
   const
      BlankLine = $0000;
   var
      i, m, r, s, t, HJust, VJust,
      Total, CapColor : integer;
      ArcRec : ArcCoordsType;
```

The *BlankLine* variable is also initialized as zero and will be used to draw an invisible line for positioning labels around the pie graph. The elaboration of $0000 is not actually necessary, a simple 0 would suffice, but to define a less empty line style, a four-digit hexadecimal specification is necessary and this form has been followed here.

In the first step, all of the items for the current year (dataset) are totalled and the radius, *r*, is set to $^1/4$ of the total.

```
m := 135;
Total := 0;
for i := 2 to 9 do
   inc( Total, Accounts[ DataSet, i ] );
r := Total div 4;
```

Since I know that there are only eight items for each year, I used the actual integer in the loop. In other circumstances, the number of elements might vary from application to application, a different method of controlling the loop might be preferred. This could be done using an index element, *Elements*, thus:

```
for i := 1 to Elements do
```

Or by calculating the number of elements:

```
for i := 1 to sizeof( Accounts ) /
             Years * sizeof( integer ) do
```

Now that I have the radius, I'm going to put a year label on the screen before drawing the pie graph. Instead of arbitrarily positioning the label—and having to create a new label position for each data set—I prefer to be able to calculate the proper position.

Since I know the radius (*r*), I could calculate a position from this bit of data but I have a more elegant method in mind. When PieGraph was called, the variable *m* was initialized at 135, an angle that will be toward the top left of the eventual pie graph.

The line style is set to *BlankLine*, previously defined as $0000, and the fill style is set to 0 (EmptyFill) and fill color to 0 (Black).

```
    SetLineStyle( UserBitLn, BlankLine, NormWidth );
    SetFillStyle( 0, 0 );
```

Next, the PieSlice function is called with the x and y center coordinates in order to draw a pie slice beginning at the angle *m* and ending at the angle *m+1* with a radius of *r+10*. A minimum angle width of one degree is required or PieSlice will simply do nothing. Also, using a radius 10 pixels greater than will be used for the pie graph yields a position outside the eventual graph image.

```
    PieSlice( x, y, m, m+1, r+10 );        { min width 1° }
    GetArcCoords( ArcRec );
```

The pie slice drawn in this case will be invisible, but it does yield a screen position which can be retrieved by calling GetArcCoords. Before doing anything with this information, however, the current color, text style, direction, and justification need to be set.

```
    if MaxColors > 4 then SetColor( White );
    SetTextStyle( SansSerifFont, HorizDir, 2 );
    SetTextJustify( RightText, BottomText );
```

Now the OutTextXY function can be called with the *xEnd* and *yEnd* coordinates in *ArcRec*, and the year data, which is the 0th element in each *Accounts[DataSet]*, is written to the screen.

```
    OutTextXY( ArcRec.xEnd, ArcRec.yEnd,
               I2S( Accounts[ DataSet, 1 ] ) );
```

Remember, GetArcCoords returns a data record which contains the start and end x and y screen coordinates for the last call to any of the Arc, Circle, Ellipse, or PieSlice functions.

This particular method of calculation to determine an appropriate screen position for a label will be used several times while the pie graph is being drawn in order to position a label correctly for each pie slice. Before proceeding, the default text style is selected and, if practical, the drawing color is reset.

```
    SetTextStyle( DefaultFont, HorizDir, 1 );
    if MaxColors > 4 then SetColor( EGAYellow );
```

At this point, the actual pie slices are drawn, again using a loop for a known number of data elements:

```
    s := 0;
    t := 0;
    for i := 2 to 9 do
    begin
```

The fill style and color are arbitrarily changed for each slice. In this application, on a monochrome system, the fill color setting can be ignored, though the drawing color is not so inconsequential. Also, the line settings are reset to a solid line before a new pie slice is created.

```
SetFillStyle( i-1, i-1 );
if MaxColors > 4 then SetColor( White );
SetLineStyle( SolidLn, 0, NormWidth );
```

The end angle for the pie slice is calculated as the proportional angle. As you will notice, all of the calculations are being carried out as double values for accuracy, with the final result being returned to an integer value since the PieSlice function does not accept float or double. Also, the calculated value has been incremented by 0.5 before truncation in order to round the results to the nearest integer instead of the next lower integer.

```
inc( t, round( 360 * ( Accounts[ DataSet, i ]
               / Total ) + 0.5 ) );
```

If any angle is returned greater than 360 degrees, an unlikely error except on the final slice, then the value is arbitrarily fixed at 360 to prevent a confusing display. Likewise, if the last pie slice does not complete the Circle (if *t* is less than 360), then a correction is made to keep the pie graph neatly finished. This type of error is *not* unlikely when a number of angles are calculated, each being rounded to the nearest integer value—but the cumulative error should not exceed one degree per slice. In this example, a maximum error of 8 degrees would be possible.

```
if t > 360 then t := 360;
if( i = 9 ) AND ( t < 360 ) then t := 360;
```

Depending on your application, you may wish to arrange matters so the correction is added to the largest individual slice or to apportion the error among the various slices.

Next, the actual pie slice is created using the x and y center coordinates, the start angle *s*, the end angle *t* and the radius *r*.

```
PieSlice( x, y, s, t, r );
```

Now it is time to reset the line style to *BlankLine* and reset the fill style and fill color to *EmptyFill* and *Black*. Also, the working *CapColor* is set to the bright equivalent of the fill color used for the last pie slice (i+8) and, if practical, the drawing color is set to *CapColor*.

```
SetLineStyle( UserBitLn, BlankLine, NormWidth );
SetFillStyle( 0, 0 );
CapColor := i+8;
if CapColor > 15 then CapColor := 7;
if MaxColors > 4 then SetColor( CapColor );
```

At this point, the program is repeating the same operation that was used to position the year number before this pie graph was started. There is, however, a slight difference. The angle *m* becomes the mid-angle between the start and end angles (*s* and *t*) of the current pie slice and an invisible pie slice is drawn. GetArcCoords returns the screen coordinates for the endpoints of this invisible slice.

```
m := round( ( t - s ) / 2 + s );
PieSlice( x, y, m, m+1, r+5 );
          { must have a minimum width of one degree }
GetArcCoords( ArcRec );
```

The next step arranges the vertical and horizontal text justification settings so that the label for the current pie slice will be positioned appropriately outside the pie graph and OutTextXY is called to write the label *AccTypes[i]* to the screen.

```
if ArcRec.xEnd > x then HJust := LeftText
                   else HJust := RightText;
if ArcRec.yEnd > y then VJust := TopText
                   else VJust := BottomText;
SetTextJustify( HJust, VJust );
OutTextXY( ArcRec.xEnd, ArcRec.yEnd,
           AccTypes[i] );
```

Last, the current end angle becomes the start angle for the next pie slice and the loop continues.

```
    s := t;
  end;
end;
```

Exploded Pie Graphs

The technique used to position the labels for the pie graph can also be used to produce an exploded pie graph, a pie graph in which one or more segments are offset from the center to emphasize a specific segment. In order to keep the symmetry of the overall pie graph, the offset must be at the correct angle, the mid-angle of the slice. The following example code will provide a five-pixel radius offset by first creating an invisible pie slice:

```
SetLineStyle( UserBitLn, BlankLine, NormWidth );
SetFillStyle( 0, 0 );
m := ( t - s ) / 2 + s;
PieSlice( x, y, m, m+1, 5 );
GetArcCoords( ArcRec );
```

Then the fill style and drawing colors are reset:

```
        SetFillStyle( i, i );
        if( MaxColors > 4 ) SetColor( WHITE );
        SetLineStyle( SolidLn, 0, NormWidth );
```

And the offset pie slice is created centered on the *Arcrec* coordinates of the invisible slice:

```
        PieSlice( ArcRec.XEnd, ArcRec.YEnd, s, t, r );
```

Naturally, the label for this slice will also require its position to be calculated with the additional 5 units radius in order to be proportionally located.

Bar Graphs

While pie graphs are visually more impressive, bar graphs offer a clearer visual comparison of magnitude. Most often, bar graphs are drawn vertically, as in the demonstration program, but they may also be presented horizontally—see Figure 9-2.

While the PieGraph function does not compensate for horizontal resolutions less than 640 pixels, the BarGraph function does adjust the graphic presentation to fit both the vertical and horizontal resolutions of the screen and graphics mode in use, beginning by setting width to *MaxX* and height to *MaxY*.

```
procedure BarGraph;
   var
      i, j, x, y, hStep, vStep, Top, Bottom,
      BarHeight, Width, Height, Left : integer;
```

Now a viewport (window) is created, leaving a margin at the top which is necessary for the labels that later will be written along the side. Next, width is decremented by 30 to leave space for amount labels, the horizontal graph step (*hStep*) is calculated from the width variable to provide for 32 columns and the vertical step (*vStep*) is calculated from the height variable. Finally, bottom variable is set to six times the vertical step (*vStep*).

```
   begin
      Width  := MaxX;
      Height := MaxY;
      Left   := 0;
      Top    := 0;
      ClearDevice;
      GraphDefaults;

      SetViewPort( Left,         Top+5,
                   Left+Width, Top+Height+5, False );
```

In this particular instance, the graph is being vertically divided into six increments, each increment to be 25 units (which might be dollars, pounds, or yen in hundreds, thousands, or similar units). In an application where the range of values is not known in advance, you might prefer your program to test for the highest value, which would be displayed and then create graph increments accordingly, numbering the vertical scale marks as appropriate. (See the LineGraph function for an example.)

Figure 9-2: Bar Graphs

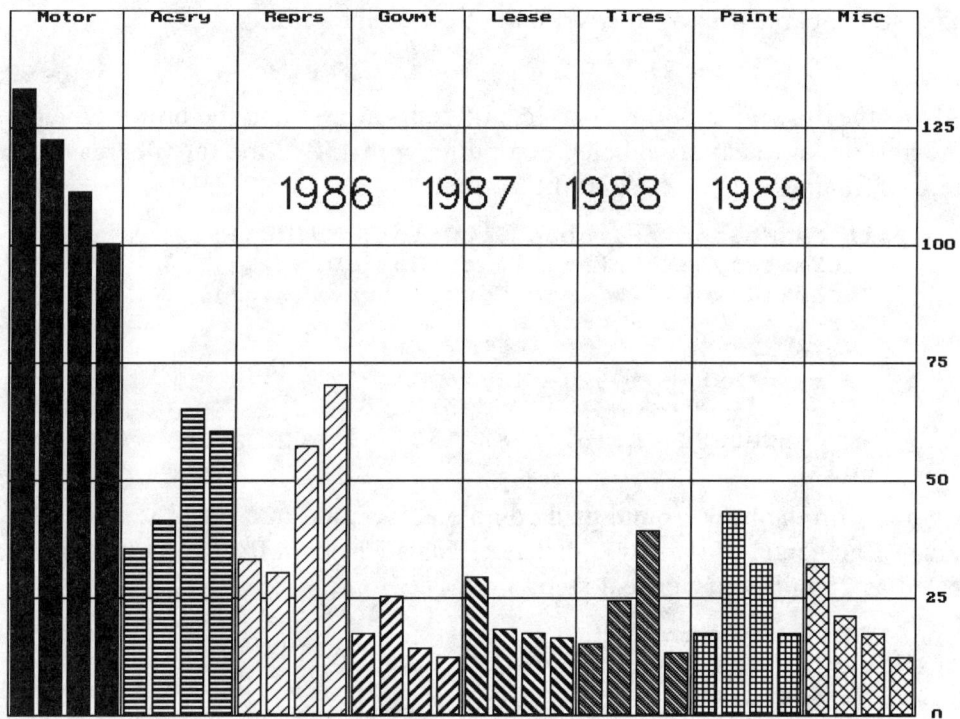

Horizontally, the bars will be grouped in units of four, placing each type of entry from each of the four year's data together. Thus, vertical markers are drawn every fourth *hStep*:

```
dec( Width, 30 );
hStep := Width div 32;
vStep := Height div 6;
Bottom := vStep * 6;
if MaxColors > 4 then SetColor( GREEN );
i := 0;
repeat
   Line( i, 0, i, vStep * 6 );
   inc( i, hStep * 4 );
until i > hStep * 32;
```

Horizontal scale lines are drawn for each *vStep*:

```
if MaxColors > 4 then SetColor( CYAN );
i := 0;
repeat
   Line( 0, i, hStep * 32, i );
   inc( i, vStep );
until i > Bottom;
```

And, with the scaling grid completed, the bottom variable is moved up one pixel so the bars will not overwrite the base of the grid:

```
dec( Bottom );
```

Now the drawing color, text style, and fonts are set and the unit increments (the horizontal lines) are labeled beginning with 150 at the top, decreasing in steps of 25 until 0 is reached at the bottom.

```
if MaxColors > 4 then SetColor( WHITE );
SetTextStyle( DefaultFont, HorizDir, 1 );
SetTextJustify( CenterText, CenterText );
for i := 0 to 6 do
begin
   x := hStep * 32 + 15;
   y := i * vStep;
   OutTextXY( x, y, I2S( 150 - i * 25 ) );
end;
```

Now, with the background grid complete, it's time to create the bars themselves. The height of the bar is calculated as a vertical offset from bottom and scaled as 25 units per vertical step.

```
for i := 2 to 9 do
begin
   for j := 1 to 4 do
   begin
      BarHeight := Bottom -
         round( Accounts[j][i] * vStep / 25 );
```

If the current video system is color capable in high resolution, then a new outline color (drawing color) and fill color are used for each year's bar. Otherwise, only the fill style is changed and the draw and fill colors are kept as White (*MaxColors–1*).

```
if MaxColors > 4 then SetColor( j+1 );
if MaxColors > 4
   then SetFillStyle( i-1, j+9 )
   else SetFillStyle( i-1, MaxColors-1 );
```

Even though a two-dimensional graph is being created, the Bar3D function is used, but with a depth of 0 specified. The Bar function does not draw an outline, but creates a bar using the fill style and color. Using the Bar3D function provides an outline in the current drawing color and creates a better appearance.

```
      Bar3D( (i-2)*hStep*4 + (j-1)*hStep+2,
             BarHeight,
             (i-2)*hStep*4 + (j-1)*hStep+hStep-2,
             Bottom, 0, False );
   end;                                    { end of loop for j }
```

As the last step within this loop, after each bar for the four years' data have been drawn, the drawing color is reset to White and a label is written at the top of the bar graph column.

```
      if MaxColors > 4 then SetColor( WHITE );
      OutTextXY( (i-1)*hStep*4-hStep*2, 5,
                 AccTypes[i] );
   end;                                    { end of loop for i }
```

Finally, if high resolution and color are supported, then the four years (year numbers) are added to the screen, and colors corresponding to the drawing color and fill color are used for each year's bars. If the system is monochrome, then there is relatively little purpose in this unless you simply want to show the years. You might, however, modify the code to draw a small block by each year number using the corresponding year's fill style.

```
      x := MaxX div 3;
      y := MaxY div 4;
      SetTextStyle( SansSerifFont, HorizDir, 4 );
      for i := 1 to 4 do
      begin
         if MaxColors > 4 then SetColor( i+1 );
         OutTextXY( x, y, I2S( Accounts[ i, 1 ] ) );
         inc( x , TextWidth('     ') );
      end;
   end;
```

Multiple Bar Graphs

While combining several years' data in a single bar graph allows for convenient comparison between different years, it also makes the comparison between different categories within each year difficult. There are times when separate graphs for each year are more useful (and sometimes more impressive) than a single combined graph and the DrawMultiGraphs function creates four graphs on a single screen, one for each year's data.

```pascal
procedure DrawMultiGraphs;
begin
   ClearDevice;
   GraphDefaults;
   MultiBarGraph( 1, 0,           0           );
   MultiBarGraph( 2, MaxX div 2, 0            );
   MultiBarGraph( 3, 0,           MaxY div 2 );
   MultiBarGraph( 4, MaxX div 2, MaxY div 2 );
end;
```

Like BarGraph, MultiBarGraph adjusts the graphic presentation to fit both the vertical and horizontal resolutions of the screen and graphics mode in use, beginning by setting width to *MaxX div 2* and height to *MaxY div 2–13*. The height setting includes a 13-pixel margin and the width includes a 30-pixel margin so that the several graphs do not butt against each other.

```pascal
procedure MultiBarGraph( DataSet, Left, Top : integer );
   var
      Width, Height, i, hStep, vStep,
      Bottom, x, y : integer;
      Scale : real;
```

The viewport (window) and scaling factors are set up the same as in the BarGraph function, except that only eight bars will be arranged horizontally and a vertical scaling factor is calculated as the variable scale instead of executing a separate scaling calculation each time.

```pascal
begin
   Width  := MaxX div 2;
   Height := MaxY div 2 - 13;
   SetViewPort( Left,        Top+5,
                Left+Width, Top+Height+5, False );
   dec( Width, 30 );
   hStep := Width div 8;
   vStep := Height div 6;
   Bottom := vStep * 6;
   Scale := vStep / 25;
```

Then a background grid is written with scale factors along the right margin.

```pascal
   if MaxColors > 4 then SetColor( GREEN );
   for i := 0 to 8 do
      Line( i * hStep, 0, i * hStep, vStep * 6 );
   if MaxColors > 4 then SetColor( CYAN );
   i := 0;
   repeat
      Line( 0, i, hStep * 8, i );
      inc( i, vStep );
   until i > Bottom;
```

And the graph is created for the selected year's data, similar to BarGraph but with one principal difference. Since single bars will need to be labeled and these will not be wide enough for horizontal text labels, the vertical text direction is selected. The labels will be written centered horizontally over each bar and flush against a point five pixels below the top of the viewport.

If you are using an EGA or higher resolution system, you should notice that the labels appear clearly in white even though some partially overlie a colored bar. This was also the reason why the Bar function, instead of the Bar3D function, was used—because an outline might have made the overlying captions more difficult to read. In monochrome modes, however, this becomes a major problem.

```
      if MaxColors > 4 then SetColor( WHITE );
      SetTextStyle( DefaultFont, HorizDir, 1 );
      SetTextJustify( CenterText, CenterText );
      for i := 0 to 6 do
      begin
         x := hStep * 8 + 15;
         y := i * vStep;
         OutTextXY( x, y, I2S( 150 - i * 25 ) );
      end;
      SetTextStyle( DefaultFont, VertDir, 1 );
      SetTextJustify( CenterText, TopText );
      for i := 1 to 8 do
      begin
         if MaxColors > 4
            then SetFillStyle( i, i+7 )
            else SetFillStyle( i+1, MaxColors-1 );
         Bar( ( i - 1 ) * hStep + 2,
              Bottom -
              round( Scale*Accounts[DataSet,i+1]-1 ),
              i * hStep - 2,
              Bottom-1 );
         OutTextXY( (i-1)*hStep + hStep div 2, 5,
                    AccTypes[i+1] );
      end;
```

As a last step, the year data are written to each graph:

```
   SetTextStyle( SansSerifFont, HorizDir, 2 );
   SetTextJustify( CenterText, BottomText );
   x := Width div 2;
   y := Height div 2 - 4;
   OutTextXY( x, y, I2S( Accounts[ DataSet, 1 ] ) );
end;
```

Improving The Monochrome Display

There is a problem with monochrome display modes where a label overwrites a bar and is not legible. However, there is a simple method you can use with a monochrome display that cures this problem.

First, in MultiBarGraph, add a variable declaration for an image pointer.

```
Caption : pointer;
```

The viewport, text, and color settings are made as before and the background grid lines are drawn. Then, in the loop before drawing the bar, EraseStr (defined in Chapter 8) is called to erase the area where the label will be written and the label is sent to the screen.

```
for i := 0 to 7 do
begin
   x := i * hStep + hStep / 2;
   y := 5;
   EraseStr( x, y, AccTypes[i+1] );
   OutTextXY( x, y, AccTypes[i+1] );
```

Next, memory space is allocated for the caption image:

```
GetMem( Caption, ImageSize( x, y,
                  TextHeight( AccTypes[i+1] ),
                  TextWidth( AccTypes[i+1] ) ) );
```

And, because horizontal justification was set to *CenterText*, *x* is offset by half the string height of *AccTypes[i+1]* to ensure that the correct image area is read.

```
dec( x, TextHeight( AccTypes[i+1] ) div 2 );
```

Now the GetImage function reads the label image from the screen as Caption before PutImage uses the *XOrPut* option to erase the label momentarily.

```
GetImage( x, y,
          x+TextHeight( AccTypes[i+1] ),
          y+TextWidth( AccTypes[i+1] ),
          Caption^ );
PutImage( x, y, Caption^, XOrPut );
```

The bar is draw as before:

```
if MaxColors > 4
   then SetFillStyle( i+1, i+1 );
   else SetFillStyle( i+1, MaxColors-1 );
Bar( i*hStep+2,
     bottom-scale*Accounts[dataset,i+1]-1,
     (i+1)*hStep-2, bottom-1 );
```

And then PutImage is called again with the *XOrPut* option to eXclusively-OR the caption image with the screen image—with the result that the portion of the label which overlies a bar is now a visible black on white instead of an invisible white on white.

```
PutImage( x, y, Caption^, XOrPut );
```

Finally, the memory allocated to *Caption* is released.

```
        dispose( Caption );
    end;
```

This same modification can be used with color displays, but the effects may not be precisely what you expect. Remember, eXclusively-ORing White with White produces Black, but eXclusively-ORing White with Blue produces Yellow. Incidentally, if you are using an EGA/VGA system, delete the line in the Initialize function in the GRAPHALL.PAS demo which reads:

```
GraphDriver := DETECT;
```

and add the instructions:

```
GraphDriver := CGA;
GraphMode   := CGAHI;
```

This will force your system to emulate a CGA system and demonstrate the difficulties in a monochrome display. This is also a good way to test your programs to see how they will execute on a CGA system without having to move them to another computer.

Three-Dimensional Graphs

While Turbo Pascal provides the Bar3D function to make a three-dimensional bar graph, actually creating a 3-D graph display can be slightly more complicated. In its simplest form, a 3-D bar graph would simply be a flat bar graph. Its bars are drawn with the illusion of depth using Bar3D, but with only a single horizontal row of bars.

If you are going to use the three-dimensional effect, however, at some point you will want to display several rows of bars with the illusion of depth in the rows as well as the individual bars themselves; this creates further complexity. Figure 9-3 shows these multiple bar graphs.

First, the 3-D bars created by Bar3D can be generated with different depths. Second, for best appearance, a three-dimensional graph requires a three-dimensional setting with scaling lines and an overall appearance of depth corresponding to the depth aspect of the individual bars. Third, everything must be tied together in a consistent whole rather than appearing to be merely an assemblage of scattered parts.

In a purely rational sense, a 3-D bar graph is not as informative as a series of flat bar graphs. Visually, it is difficult to discern clearly the relative heights of the various bars and precisely how a specific bar aligns with the background scale lines but the three-dimensional graph is visually very impressive—see Figure 9-4.

Figure 9-3: Multiple Bar Graphs

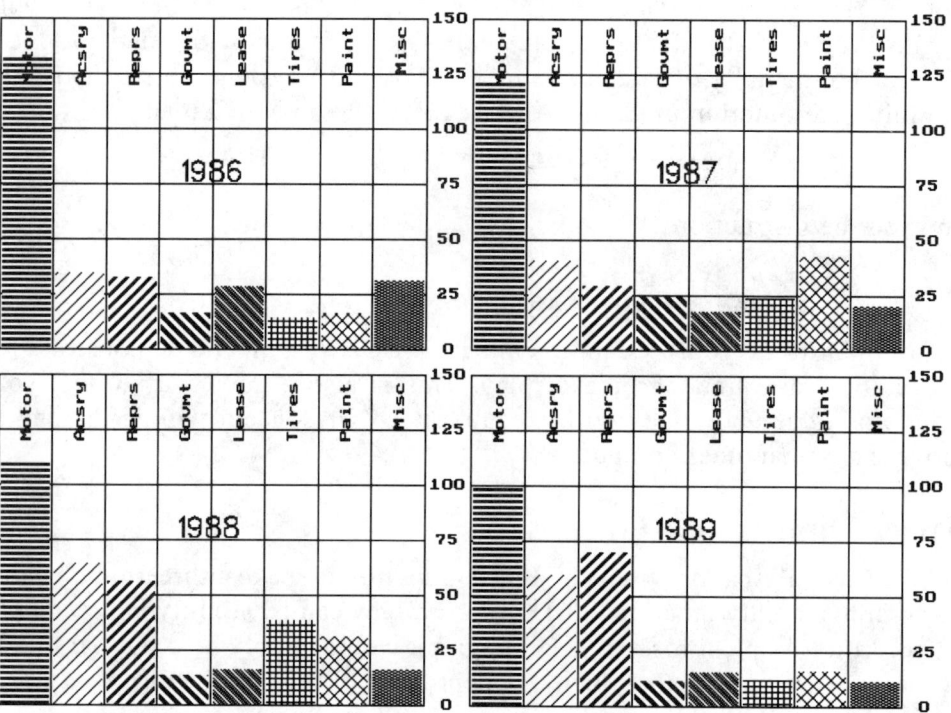

Therefore, the same data that has been presented in the form of pie and bar graphs will now be displayed in the form of four rows and eight ranks of three-dimensional columns against a scaled three-dimensional field. Also, for purposes of demonstration, Graphs_3D will show the same graph data using a series of *ZAxis* depths in steps of 5, from 15 to 40 pixels (assuming adequate vertical resolution).

The variables *XAxis* and *YAxis*, which are the horizontal and vertical scale increments, are assigned values scaled to fit within the current screen size limits. *XOrg* and *YOrd* provide the screen origin point for all three axes. The graph width (*XWidth*) and height (*YHeight*) are now set to multiples of *XAxis* and *YAxis*, which will remain constant, while *ZDepth* will be recalculated for each graph display as the *ZAxis* increment size is changed.

Figure 9-4: Three-Dimensional Bar Graphs

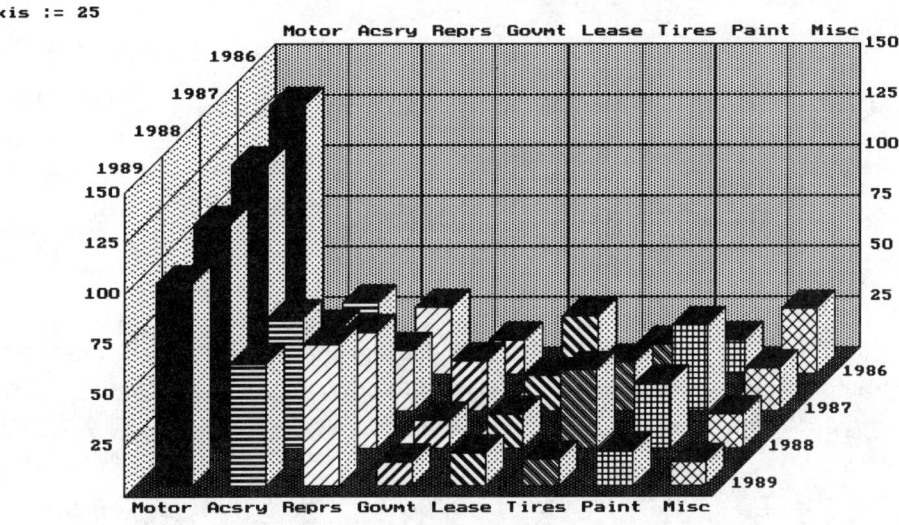

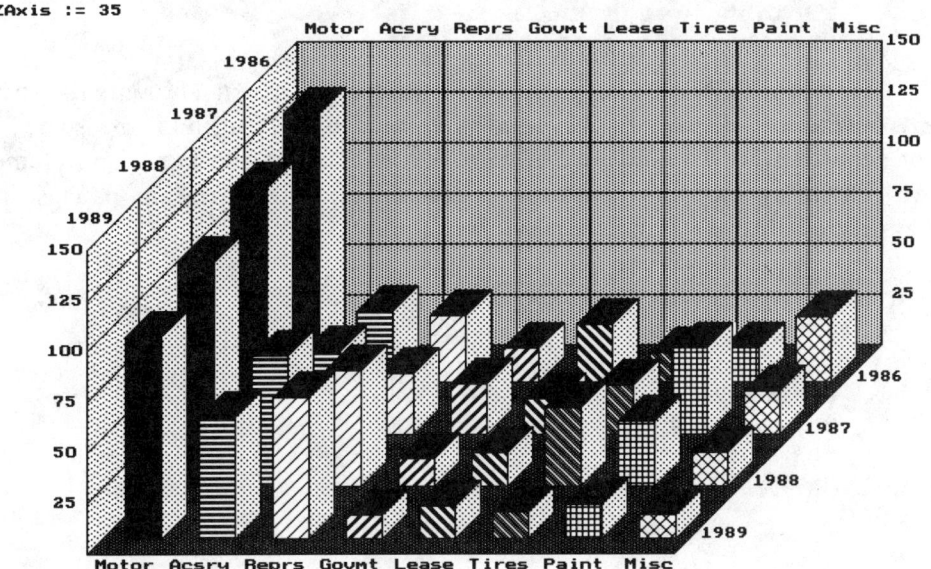

```pascal
procedure Graphs3D;
   begin
      ClearDevice;
      GraphDefaults;
      XAxis := MaxX div 13;
      YAxis := MaxY div 14;
      ZAxis := 10;
      XOrg  := MaxX div 3;
      YOrg  := MaxY div 2;
      Scale := YAxis / 25;
      ZAxis := 15;
```

Graphs_3D loops as long as the display produced by the *ZAxis* value does not exceed the screen limits.

```pascal
      repeat
         ThreeDGraph;
         inc( ZAxis, 10 );
      until YOrg+4*ZAxis > MaxY;
   end;
```

The ThreeDGraph function creates each graph display, beginning by clearing the screen and setting the z-axis depth (*ZDepth*) for the current *ZAxis*.

```pascal
procedure ThreeDGraph;
  var
     x, y : integer;
  begin
     ClearDevice;
     XWidth  := 8 * XAxis;
     YHeight := 6 * YAxis;
     ZDepth  := 4 * ZAxis;
```

A caption is displayed in the upper-left corner of screen, showing the current *ZAxis* size, the display background is created by GraphField, the scale lines for each axis are labeled by ShowLabels and, lastly, the bar graph elements are drawn by the ShowAccounts function and the program pauses for a keystroke before creating the next graph display.

```pascal
     SetTextJustify( LeftText, TopText );
     SetColor( GetMaxColor );
     x := 10;    y := 10;
     OutTextXY( x, y, 'ZAxis := ' + I2S( ZAxis ) );
     GraphField;
     ShowLabels;
     ShowAccounts;
     Pause;
  end;
```

The several elements of the overall graph display have been broken into separate tasks in order to reduce a complex program to manageable proportions.

The GraphField Function

The first of these tasks is the GraphField function which creates a three-dimensional backdrop for the graph, complete with grid lines for all three axes. If color is supported, then the FillPlane function is used to create three solid planes in blue, red, and yellow—rather like three sides of a box—which will form the background for the display. FillPlane is simply a convenient enhancement of the FillPoly function.

```
procedure GraphField;
   var
      i : integer;
   begin
      if MaxColors > 4 then
      begin
         FillPlane( XOrg, YOrg,
                    XOrg+XWidth, YOrg,
                    XOrg+XWidth, YOrg-YHeight,
                    XOrg, YOrg-YHeight,
                    SolidFill, LightBlue );
         FillPlane( XOrg, YOrg,
                    XOrg-round(ZDepth/AspR),
                    YOrg+ZDepth,
                    XOrg-round(ZDepth/AspR),
                    YOrg+ZDepth-YHeight,
                    XOrg, YOrg-YHeight,
                    SolidFill, LightRed );
         FillPlane( XOrg, YOrg, XOrg+XWidth, YOrg,
                    XOrg+XWidth-round(ZDepth/AspR),
                    YOrg+ZDepth,
                    XOrg-round(ZDepth/AspR),
                    YOrg+ZDepth,
                    SolidFill, Yellow );
      end;
```

Next, three lines are drawn from the screen origin point at *XOrg/YOrg*. If the background planes were created, these lines delineate the planes. If the system is using monochrome display, then these axis lines and the following grid lines will serve to create the backdrop.

```
      Line( XOrg, YOrg,                      { major X axis }
            XOrg+XWidth, YOrg );
      Line( XOrg, YOrg,                      { major Y axis }
```

```
                  XOrg, YOrg-YHeight );
      Line( XOrg, YOrg,                         { major Z axis }
            XOrg-round(ZDepth/AspR), YOrg+ZDepth    );
```

If you will notice, the z-axis line (above) is adjusted for the screen aspect ratio, *AspR*. This same adjustment will appear in all "positioning" calculations involving the z-axis in order to keep the z-axis angle effectively constant (approximately 45 degrees) for all screen resolutions.

```
      if MaxColors > 4 then SetColor(GREEN);
      i := XOrg + XAxis;            { X-axis position lines }
      repeat
         Line( i, YOrg, i, YOrg-YHeight );
         Line( i, YOrg,
                i-round(ZDepth/AspR), YOrg+ZDepth );
         inc( i, XAxis );
      until i > XOrg + XWidth;

      if MaxColors > 4 then SetColor( CYAN );
      i := YOrg - YAxis;            { Y-axis position lines }
      repeat
         Line( XOrg, i, XOrg+XWidth, i );
         Line( XOrg, i,
                XOrg-round(ZDepth/AspR), i+ZDepth );
         dec( i, YAxis );
      until i < YOrg - YHeight;

      if MaxColors > 4 then SetColor( RED );
      i := ZAxis;                   { Z-axis position lines }
      repeat
         Line( XOrg-round(i/AspR), YOrg+i,
               XOrg-round(i/AspR)+XWidth,  YOrg+i );
         Line( XOrg-round(i/AspR), YOrg+i,
               XOrg-round(i/AspR), YOrg-YHeight+i );
         inc( i, ZAxis );
      until i > ZDepth;
   end;
```

The FillPlane Function

The FillPlane function is simply a convenient method of passing a set of calculated points to be assigned to an integer array (*polygon*) before calling the FillPoly function. This is faster than using the FloodFill function and will be used several times in this demonstration program to fill large or small areas with either solid colors or patterns. The color value passed (*FColor*) is tested for validity and defaults to White if monochrome graphics are being used.

```
procedure FillPlane( X1, Y1, X2, Y2,
                     X3, Y3, X4, Y4,
```

```
                           FStyle, FColor : integer );
   var
      Polygon : array[1..10] of integer;
   begin
      Polygon[1] := X1;            Polygon[2] := Y1;
      Polygon[3] := X2;            Polygon[4] := Y2;
      Polygon[5] := X3;            Polygon[6] := Y3;
      Polygon[7] := X4;            Polygon[8] := Y4;
      Polygon[9] := Polygon[1];
      Polygon[10]:= Polygon[2];
      if MaxColors < 4 then FColor := MaxColors - 1;
      SetFillStyle( FStyle, FColor );
      FillPoly( 5, Polygon );
   end;
```

The ShowLabels Function

The ShowLabels function displays labels for all three axes of the display, beginning with the vertical (y-axis) magnitude scales along both the right and left sides of the display. The right side positions are relatively easy to calculate since they are stepped from the *YOrg* position with an x-axis offset equal to *XOrg + XWidth + 15*.

The left side, however, requires both a y-axis offset, which is easily calculated as *ZDepth – i * YAxis* and an x-axis offset (left from *XOrg*), which is slightly more complicated but is calculated as *XOrg – ZDepth / AspR – 15*. Remember, the *ZDepth* variable is plotted at an angle so the actual screen offset must be calculated using the screen aspect ratio *AspR* to maintain the 45-degree screen angle for the z-axis.

```
procedure ShowLabels;
   var
      i, j, k, l, m : integer;
   begin
      SetTextJustify( CenterText, CenterText );
      j := XOrg + XWidth + 15;
      l := XOrg - round( ZDepth / AspR ) - 15;

      for i := 1 to 6 do
      begin
         k := YOrg - i * YAxis;
         OutTextXY( j, k, I2S( i*25 ) );
         m := YOrg + ZDepth - i * YAxis;
         OutTextXY( l, m, I2S( i*25 ) );
      end;
```

The *AccTypes* labels are written horizontally across the top and bottom of the graph:

```pascal
        if MaxColors > 4 then SetColor( LightBlue );
        j := XOrg + 25;
        l := j - round( ZDepth / AspR );
        m := YOrg + ZDepth + 8;
        k := YOrg - YHeight - 8;
        for i := 1 to 8 do
        begin
           OutTextXY( j, k, AccTypes[i+1] );
           OutTextXY( l, m, AccTypes[i+1] );
           inc( j, 50 );
           inc( l, 50 );
        end;
```

And the year dates are written at an angle along the z-axis:

```pascal
        if MaxColors > 4 then SetColor( LightGreen );
        for i := 0 to 3 do
        begin
           j := XOrg -
                round( ( i*ZAxis + ZAxis/2 ) / AspR ) + 2;
           m := YOrg + round( i*ZAxis + ZAxis/2 );
           k := m - YHeight;
           l := j + XWidth;
           SetTextJustify( LeftText, TopText );
           OutTextXY( l, m, I2S( Accounts[ i+1, 1 ] ) );
           SetTextJustify( RightText, BottomText );
           OutTextXY( j, k, I2S( Accounts[ i+1, 1 ] ) );
        end;
     end;
```

The ShowAccounts Function

The bars for each year could have been drawn using a double loop and incrementing the colors for each year. Instead, four separate loops are used here permitting the assignment of specific colors for each year's bars.

```pascal
procedure ShowAccounts;
   var
      i : integer;
   begin
      if MaxColors > 4 then SetColor( EGAYellow );
      for i := 2 to 9 do
      begin
         AddBar( i-2, 0, round( Accounts[1,i] * Scale ),
                 LightCyan, Cyan );
         AddBar( i-2, 1, round( Accounts[2,i] * Scale ),
                 LightRed, Red );
         AddBar( i-2, 2, round( Accounts[3,i] * Scale ),
                 LightBlue, Blue );
```

```
        AddBar( i-2, 3, round( Accounts[4,i] * Scale ),
                LightGreen, Green );
      end;
   end;
```

The AddBar Function

The AddBar function is used to create and position the three-dimensional graph bars. The *BarWidth* and *BarDepth* variables, which set the size of the bar, are initialized as half the x-axis and z-axis step sizes. Making each bar smaller than the spacing between the bars offers a better visual effect and permits seeing "between" bars so that taller bars do not completely hide the smaller bars behind them.

```
procedure AddBar( Left, Bottom, Height,
                  Color1, Color2 : integer );
   var
      Top, Right, BarWidth, BarDepth : integer;
   begin
      BarWidth := XAxis div 2;
      BarDepth := ZAxis div 2;
      if MaxColors < 4 then
      begin
         Color1 := MaxColors - 1;
         Color2 := MaxColors - 1;
      end;
```

The fill style for each bar is incremented from left to right. If the display is in monochrome, this helps to make the several bars easier to distinguish.

```
      SetFillStyle( Left+1, Color1 );
```

The left and bottom variables began as integers in the 1..8 and 1..4 ranges and describe step positions but are now converted to the actual screen offset positions. *Right* and *top* provide the remaining corner parameters.

```
      Left     := XOrg + ( Left * XAxis ) -
         round( ( ( Bottom + ( 0.35 * ZAxis ) / XAxis )
            * ZAxis ) / AspR );
      Bottom := YOrg + round( ( Bottom+0.70 ) * ZAxis );
      Right  := Left + BarWidth;
      Top    := Bottom - Height;
```

At this point, Bar3D could be used to create the display bars for this graph. However, there is one flaw in this: the z-axis angle produced by Bar3D does not always match the z-axis angle produced by the screen aspect. For this reason, Bar3D is called with a 0 depth and the FillPlane function is called to create each bar's side and top.

```
         Bar3D( Left, Top, Right, Bottom, 0, False );
         FillPlane( Right, Top,
                    Right+round( BarDepth/AspR ),
                    Top-BarDepth,
                    Right+round( BarDepth/AspR ),
                    Bottom-BarDepth,
                    Right, Bottom,
                    CloseDotFill, Color1 );
         FillPlane( Left, Top, Right, Top,
                    Right+round( BarDepth/AspR ),
                    Top-BarDepth,
                    Left +round( BarDepth/AspR ),
                    Top-BarDepth,
                    SolidFill, Color2 );
   end;
```

If you would like to experiment, simply comment out the two FillPlane calls, set Bar3D's depth as *BarDepth/AspR*, and change the final parameter from 0 to 1 to put a top on the bar.

The Line Graph Display

The previous demos used the same data set for each graph form. Line graphs, however, are normally used to show a half-dozen or fewer data sets with each containing a large number of sequential data points. For demonstration, four data sets will be used, each containing 20 sequential data points. As with the previous demo, for convenience, the data points are contained in a 4 by 20 matrix. In actual practice though, the graph data would probably be read from some external source or generated within the program.

```
const
   Accounts : array[1..4,1..20] of integer =
            ( ( 119, 121, 132, 140, 141, 139, 142,
                135, 133, 123, 121, 120, 124, 111,
                109, 119, 122, 132, 140, 142 ),
              (  97,  99, 100, 107, 119, 123, 137,
                148, 159, 160, 168, 172, 167, 155,
                159, 163, 165, 155, 151, 148 ),
              (  59,  73,  66,  49,  40,  39,  41,
                 45,  46,  52,  56,  59,  60,  56,
                 51,  54,  55,  53,  72,  75 ),
              (  13,  15,  16,  19,  22,  20,  17,
                 18,  19,  21,  24,  26,  28,  27,
                 22,  20,  19,  23,  25,  24 ) );
   Years : array[1..5] of integer =
            ( 1985, 1986, 1987, 1988, 1989 );
   AccTypes : array[1..4] of STR5 =
            ( 'GenMec', 'UnvEle', 'StrOil', 'NrtMfr' );
```

Again, to make the graph visually impressive, a set of four graphic images will be used in the plot and CreateImages is used to construct these. In other circumstances, you might prefer to create a series of images separately—as by using the EditIcon utility demonstrated in Chapter 15—loading various images from disk as required. Figure 9-5 shows the completed line graph display.

Figure 9-5: Line Graphs

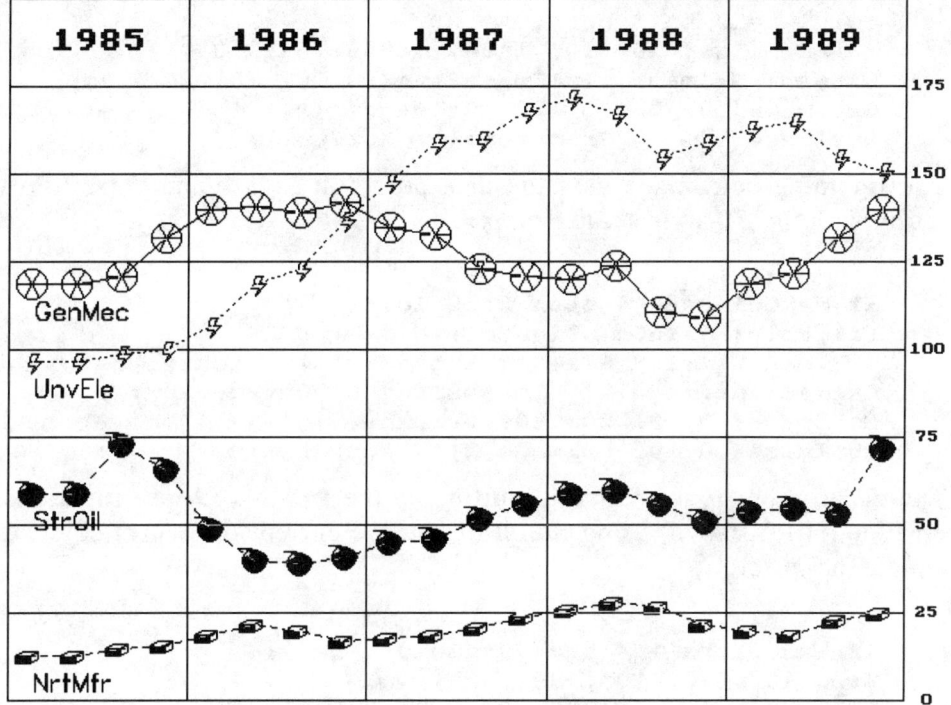

The CreateImages Function

This function is used to generate and save a series of graphic images that will be used to emphasize points on the line graph. The array figure is a set of points describing a small stylized lightning bolt.

```
procedure Create_Images;
   const
      Figure : array[1..16] of integer =
         ( 10,  5, 15,  5, 12, 10, 17, 10,
           10, 18, 12, 13,  8, 13, 10,  5 );
   var
      i : integer;
```

The wheel or gear image is created from a series of small pie segments. Please realize that any small arc figure will be grainy. For a small detailed figure, the IconEdit utility can be used to create either a disk bit-image or a program listing that can be included in your application source code.

```
begin
                         { wheel / gear }
   SetFillStyle( EmptyFill, 0 );
   if MaxColors > 4 then SetColor( 10 );
   for i := 0 to 5 do
      PieSlice( 10, 10, i*60, (i*60)+60, 10 );
   GetMem( GrImage[1], ImageSize( 0, 0, 20, 20 ) );
   GetImage( 0, 0, 20, 20, GrImage[1]^ );
   PutImage( 0, 0, GrImage[1]^, XOrPut );
```

The lightning bolt image uses the data points in *Figure* and the FillPoly function with the fill style set to EmptyFill.

```
                       { lightning bolt }
   if MaxColors > 4 then SetColor( 11 );
   FillPoly( SizeOf( Figure ) div
             ( 2 * SizeOf( integer ) ), Figure );
   GetMem( GrImage[2], ImageSize( 0, 0, 20, 20 ) );
   GetImage( 0, 0, 20, 20, GrImage[2]^ );
   PutImage( 0, 0, GrImage[2]^, XOrPut );
```

The oil drop image is created in outline by the Arc and Ellipse functions. Then FloodFill is called, using SolidFill and the current (drawing) color, to complete the image.

```
                         { oil drop }
   if MaxColors > 4 then SetColor( 12 );
   Arc( 10,  10, 105, 360, 8 );
   Ellipse(  0,  5, 300, 90,  8, 3 );
   Ellipse(  3, 10,   0, 90, 16, 8 );
   SetFillStyle( SolidFill, GetColor );
   FloodFill( 10, 10, GetColor );
   GetMem( GrImage[3], ImageSize( 0, 0, 20, 20 ) );
   GetImage( 0, 0, 20, 20, GrImage[3]^ );
   PutImage( 0, 0, grimage[3]^, XOrPut );
```

The box image is the simplest of the four, using the Bar3D function to create a small cube.

```
                           { box }
   if MaxColors > 4 then SetColor( 13 );
   Bar3D( 0, 10, 10, 15, 5, True );
   GetMem( GrImage[4], ImageSize( 0, 0, 20, 20 ) );
   GetImage( 0, 0, 20, 20, GrImage[4]^ );
```

```
      PutImage( 0, 0, GrImage[4]^, XOrPut );
   end;
```

In each case, memory is allocated for the image using GetMem and ImageSize, then GetImage stores the screen image and PutImage uses the *XOrPut* option to erase the screen for the next drawing. (See Chapter 10 for further details on image manipulation.)

The LineGraph Function

The LineGraph function begins by testing the data to find the highest value that requires plotting (*MaxVal*) and the viewport (window) is set to provide a top margin to allow space for labels.

```
procedure LineGraph;
   var
      width, height, left, top,
      i, j, hStep, vStep, vSteps,
      bottom, x, y, MaxVal : integer;
      scale : real;
   begin
      width := GetMaxX;
      height := GetMaxY;
      left := 0;
      top := 0;
      MaxVal := 0;
      for i := 1 to 4 do
         for j := 1 to 20 do
            if Accounts[i,j] > MaxVal
               then MaxVal := Accounts[i,j];
      SetViewPort( left, top+5,
                   left+width, top+height+5, False );
```

Next, vertical and horizontal steps are set to fit with the current screen resolution and with *MaxVal*.

```
         dec( width, 30 );
         hStep  := width div 20;
         vSteps := ( MaxVal div 25 ) + 2;
         vStep  := height div vSteps;
         bottom := vStep * vSteps;
         scale  := vStep / 25;
```

A series of vertical bars are drawn to mark off the years.

```
         if MaxColors > 4 then SetColor( GREEN );
         i := 0;
         repeat
            Line( i, 1, i, vStep * vSteps );
```

```
      inc( i, hStep * 4 );
until i > hStep * 32;
```

Then a set of horizontal bars are drawn and labeled with amounts in steps of 25 to complete the graph background grid.

```
SetTextJustify( CenterText, CenterText );
i := 0;
repeat
   if MaxColors > 4 then SetColor( BLUE );
   Line( 0, i, hStep * 20, i );
   if MaxColors > 4 then SetColor( WHITE );
   x := hStep * 20 + 15;
   y := i;
   str( round( ( bottom-i )/vStep )*25, Buffer );
   OutTextXY( x, y, Buffer );
   inc( i, vStep );
until i > bottom;
```

Each set of data is plotted separately, using a different color and line style. This plot begins by setting the CP relative to the first horizontal graph position (*hStep/2+3*) and the adjusted vertical position (*bottom − scale*Accounts[i,0]+8*) and calling OutText to put a label on the screen. Then the CP is set to the actual first plot position.

```
SetTextStyle( SansSerifFont, HorizDir, 1 );
SetTextJustify( LeftText, TopText );
for i := 1 to 4 do
begin
   SetLineStyle( i-1, 0, 1 );
   if MaxColors > 4 then SetColor( i+1 );
   MoveTo( hStep div 2 + 3,
      bottom - trunc( scale*Accounts[i,1] ) + 8 );
   OutText( AccTypes[i] );
   MoveTo( hStep div 2,
      bottom - trunc( scale*Accounts[i,1] ) );
```

The data plot begins with the appropriate image (symbol) centered on the plot position, then a line is drawn to the next graph position.

When the loop is finished, a final symbol is added at the end plot position.

```
   for j := 1 to 19 do
   begin
      PutImage( GetX-10, GetY-10,
               GrImage[i]^, XOrPut );
      LineTo( hStep div 2 + j * hStep,
         Bottom - trunc( Scale*Accounts[i,j] ) );
   end;
   PutImage( GetX-10, GetY-10,
```

```
            GrImage[i]^, XOrPut );
    end;
```
If you would prefer a simpler display, instead of the PutImage functions, a three by three dot could also be used to show the plot position.
```
    for x := -1 to 1 do
        for y := -1 to 1 do
            PutPixel( hStep / 2 + x,
                      bottom - scale*Accounts[i,0]+y,
                      GetColor );
```
One final step is required to list the years against the graph display.
```
    if MaxColors > 4 then SetColor( White );
    SetTextJustify( CenterText, CenterText );
    SetTextStyle( DefaultFont, HorizDir, 2 );
    for i := 1 to 5 do
    begin
        x := i * hStep * 4 - hStep * 2;
        y := vStep div 2;
        str( Years[i], Buffer );
        OutTextXY( x, y, Buffer );
    end;
end;
```

Summary

Business graphs are one of the most important graphics applications if only because boardroom executives from the old-school can appreciate the value of financial graphs, even if only to use the graphic presentation to impress others. Cynicism aside, it is simply a recognized fact that business applications are judged, at least in part, by the quality and variety of their graphics. In real-world programming, presentation and impressions are important if only to grab the customer's initial attention.

So, be as cynical as you like but don't let cynicism get in the way of success—here are the tools for making an impression, use them and have fun.

GRAPHALL.PAS — multiple graph demos

```
uses GRAPH, CRT;

type
   STR5 = string[5];
const
   Accounts : array[1..4,1..9] of integer =
           ( ( 1986, 133, 35, 33, 17, 29, 15, 17, 32 ),
             ( 1987, 122, 41, 30, 25, 18, 24, 43, 21 ),
```

```
                    ( 1988, 111, 65, 57, 14, 17, 39, 32, 17 ),
                    ( 1989, 100, 60, 70, 12, 16, 13, 17, 12 ) );
   AccTypes : array[1..9] of STR5 =
            ( '     ', 'Motor', 'Acsry', 'Reprs', 'Govmt',
              'Lease', 'Tires', 'Paint', 'Misc'  );
var
   GraphDriver, GraphMode, MaxColors, ErrorCode,
   XWidth, YHeight, ZDepth,
   XAxis,  YAxis,   ZAxis,
   XOrg,   YOrg,
   MaxX,   MaxY : integer;
   Scale,  AspR : real;
procedure Initialize;
   var        { initialize graphics system and report errors }
      xasp, yasp : word;
   begin
      GraphDriver := DETECT;
      InitGraph( GraphDriver, GraphMode, '\TP\BGI' );
      ErrorCode := GraphResult;
      if ErrorCode <> grOk then
      begin
         writeln(' Graphics System Error: ',
                   GraphErrorMsg( ErrorCode ) );
         halt( 1 );
      end;
      MaxColors := GetMaxColor + 1;
      GetAspectRatio( xasp, yasp );
      AspR := xasp / yasp;
      MaxX := GetMaxX;
      MaxY := GetMaxY;
   end;

procedure Pause;
   var
      Ch : char;
   begin
      while KeyPressed do Ch := ReadKey;
      Ch := ReadKey;
   end;
function I2S( Value : integer ): string;
   var
      Buffer : string[10];
   begin
      str( Value, Buffer );
      I2S := Buffer;
   end;
```

```
{******************** PIE GRAPH ********************}
procedure PieGraph( DataSet, x, y : integer );
   const
      BlankLine = $0000;
   var
      i, m, r, s, t, HJust, VJust,
      Total, CapColor : integer;
      ArcRec : ArcCoordsType;
   begin
      m := 135;
      Total := 0;
      for i := 2 to 9 do
         inc( Total, Accounts[ DataSet, i ] );
      r := Total div 4;
      SetLineStyle( UserBitLn, BlankLine, NormWidth );
      SetFillStyle( 0, 0 );
      PieSlice( x, y, m, m+1, r+10 );
            { one degree minimum Width required }
      GetArcCoords( ArcRec );
      if MaxColors > 4 then SetColor( White );
      SetTextStyle( SansSerifFont, HorizDir, 2 );
      SetTextJustify( RightText, BottomText );
      OutTextXY( ArcRec.xEnd, ArcRec.yEnd,
               I2S( Accounts[ DataSet, 1 ] ) );
      SetTextStyle( DefaultFont, HorizDir, 1 );
      if MaxColors > 4 then SetColor( EGAYellow );

      s := 0;
      t := 0;
      for i := 2 to 9 do
      begin
         SetFillStyle( i-1, i-1 );
         if MaxColors > 4 then SetColor( White );
         SetLineStyle( SolidLn, 0, NormWidth );
         inc( t, round( 360 * ( Accounts[ DataSet, i ]
                     / Total ) + 0.5 ) );
         if t > 360 then t := 360;
         if( i = 9 ) AND ( t < 360 ) then t := 360;
         PieSlice( x, y, s, t, r );
         SetLineStyle( UserBitLn, BlankLine, NormWidth );
         SetFillStyle( 0, 0 );
         CapColor := i+8;
         if CapColor > 15 then CapColor := 7;
         if MaxColors > 4 then SetColor( CapColor );
         m := round( ( t - s ) / 2 + s );
         PieSlice( x, y, m, m+1, r+5 );
               { must have a minimum Width of one degree }
         GetArcCoords( ArcRec );
```

```pascal
            if ArcRec.xEnd > x then HJust := LeftText
                                else HJust := RightText;
            if ArcRec.yEnd > y then VJust := TopText
                                else VJust := BottomText;
            SetTextJustify( HJust, VJust );
            OutTextXY( ArcRec.xEnd, ArcRec.yEnd,
                       AccTypes[i] );
            s := t;
         end;
      end;
procedure DrawPieGraphs;
   var
      i : integer;
   begin
      ClearDevice;
      GraphDefaults;
      Rectangle( 0, 0, MaxX, MaxY );
      PieGraph( 1,   GetMaxX div 4,   GetMaxY div 4 );
      PieGraph( 2,   GetMaxX div 4, 3*GetMaxY div 4 );
      PieGraph( 3, 3*GetMaxX div 4,   GetMaxY div 4 );
      PieGraph( 4, 3*GetMaxX div 4, 3*GetMaxY div 4 );
   end;

   {****************** BAR GRAPH ********************}
procedure BarGraph;
   var
      i, j, x, y, hStep, vStep, Top, Bottom,
      BarHeight, Width, Height, Left : integer;
   begin
      Width := MaxX;
      Height := MaxY;
      Left := 0;
      Top := 0;
      ClearDevice;
      GraphDefaults;

      SetViewPort( Left,         Top+5,
                   Left+Width, Top+Height+5, False );
      dec( Width, 30 );
      hStep := Width div 32;
      vStep := Height div 6;
      Bottom := vStep * 6;
      if MaxColors > 4 then SetColor( GREEN );

      i := 0;
      repeat
         Line( i, 0, i, vStep * 6 );
         inc( i, hStep * 4 );
      until i > hStep * 32;
```

```
      if MaxColors > 4 then SetColor( CYAN );
      i := 0;
      repeat
         Line( 0, i, hStep * 32, i );
         inc( i, vStep );
      until i > Bottom;

      dec( Bottom );
      if MaxColors > 4 then SetColor( WHITE );

      SetTextStyle( DefaultFont, HorizDir, 1 );
      SetTextJustify( CenterText, CenterText );
      for i := 0 to 6 do
      begin
         x := hStep * 32 + 15;
         y := i * vStep;
         OutTextXY( x, y, I2S( 150 - i * 25 ) );
      end;
      for i := 2 to 9 do
      begin
         for j := 1 to 4 do
         begin
            BarHeight := Bottom -
               round( Accounts[j][i] * vStep / 25 );
            if MaxColors > 4 then SetColor( j+1 );
            if MaxColors > 4
               then SetFillStyle( i-1, j+9 )
               else SetFillStyle( i-1, MaxColors-1 );
            Bar3D( (i-2)*hStep*4 + (j-1)*hStep+2,
                   BarHeight,
                   (i-2)*hStep*4 + (j-1)*hStep+hStep-2,
                   Bottom, 0, False );
         end;
         if MaxColors > 4 then SetColor( WHITE );
         OutTextXY( (i-1)*hStep*4-hStep*2, 5,
                    AccTypes[i] );
      end;
      x := MaxX div 3;
      y := MaxY div 4;
      SetTextStyle( SansSerifFont, HorizDir, 4 );
      for i := 1 to 4 do
      begin
         if MaxColors > 4 then SetColor( i+1 );
         OutTextXY( x, y, I2S( Accounts[ i, 1 ] ) );
         inc( x , TextWidth('        ') );
      end;
end;
```

```pascal
{*************** MULTIPLE BAR GRAPHS *****************}
procedure MultiBarGraph( DataSet, Left, Top : integer );
   var
      Width, Height, i, hStep, vStep,
      Bottom, x, y : integer;
      Scale : real;
   begin
      Width  := MaxX div 2;
      Height := MaxY div 2 - 13;
      SetViewPort( Left,        Top+5,
                   Left+Width, Top+Height+5, False );
      dec( Width, 30 );
      hStep := Width div 8;
      vStep := Height div 6;
      Bottom := vStep * 6;
      Scale := vStep / 25;
      if MaxColors > 4 then SetColor( GREEN );

      for i := 0 to 8 do
         Line( i * hStep, 0, i * hStep, vStep * 6 );
      if MaxColors > 4 then SetColor( CYAN );
      i := 0;
      repeat
         Line( 0, i, hStep * 8, i );
         inc( i, vStep );
      until i > Bottom;

      if MaxColors > 4 then SetColor( WHITE );
      SetTextStyle( DefaultFont, HorizDir, 1 );
      SetTextJustify( CenterText, CenterText );
      for i := 0 to 6 do
      begin
         x := hStep * 8 + 15;
         y := i * vStep;
         OutTextXY( x, y, I2S( 150 - i * 25 ) );
      end;
      SetTextStyle( DefaultFont, VertDir, 1 );
      SetTextJustify( CenterText, TopText );
      for i := 1 to 8 do
      begin
         if MaxColors > 4
            then SetFillStyle( i, i+7 )
            else SetFillStyle( i+1, MaxColors-1 );
         Bar( ( i - 1 ) * hStep + 2,
              Bottom -
              round( Scale*Accounts[DataSet,i+1]-1 ),
              i * hStep - 2,
              Bottom-1 );
         OutTextXY( (i-1)*hStep + hStep div 2, 5,
```

```
                         AccTypes[i+1] );
        end;
        SetTextStyle( SansSerifFont, HorizDir, 2 );
        SetTextJustify( CenterText, BottomText );
        x := Width div 2;
        y := Height div 2 - 4;
        OutTextXY( x, y, I2S( Accounts[ DataSet, 1 ] ) );
    end;
procedure DrawMultiGraphs;
    begin
        ClearDevice;
        GraphDefaults;
        MultiBarGraph( 1, 0,              0              );
        MultiBarGraph( 2, MaxX div 2, 0              );
        MultiBarGraph( 3, 0,              MaxY div 2 );
        MultiBarGraph( 4, MaxX div 2, MaxY div 2 );
    end;
{***************** 3-D GRAPH DEMO ********************}
procedure FillPlane( X1, Y1, X2, Y2,
                     X3, Y3, X4, Y4,
                     FStyle, FColor : integer );
    var
        Polygon : array[1..10] of integer;
    begin
        Polygon[1] := X1;           Polygon[2]  := Y1;
        Polygon[3] := X2;           Polygon[4]  := Y2;
        Polygon[5] := X3;           Polygon[6]  := Y3;
        Polygon[7] := X4;           Polygon[8]  := Y4;
        Polygon[9] := Polygon[1];
        Polygon[10]:= Polygon[2];
        if MaxColors < 4 then FColor := MaxColors - 1;
        SetFillStyle( FStyle, FColor );
        FillPoly( 5, Polygon );
    end;
procedure GraphField;
    var
        i : integer;
    begin
        if MaxColors > 4 then
        begin
            FillPlane( XOrg, YOrg,
                       XOrg+XWidth, YOrg,
                       XOrg+XWidth, YOrg-YHeight,
                       XOrg, YOrg-YHeight,
                       SolidFill, LIGHTBLUE );

            FillPlane( XOrg, YOrg,
```

```pascal
                       XOrg-round(ZDepth/AspR),
                       YOrg+ZDepth,
                       XOrg-round(ZDepth/AspR),
                       YOrg+ZDepth-YHeight,
                       XOrg, YOrg-YHeight,
                       SolidFill, LIGHTRED );
       FillPlane( XOrg, YOrg, XOrg+XWidth, YOrg,
                  XOrg+XWidth-round(ZDepth/AspR),
                  YOrg+ZDepth,
                  XOrg-round(ZDepth/AspR),
                  YOrg+ZDepth,
                  SolidFill, YELLOW );
end;
Line( XOrg, YOrg,                          { major X axis }
      XOrg+XWidth, YOrg );
Line( XOrg, YOrg,                          { major Y axis }
      XOrg, YOrg-YHeight );
Line( XOrg, YOrg,                          { major Z axis }
      XOrg-round(ZDepth/AspR), YOrg+ZDepth   );

if MaxColors > 4 then SetColor(GREEN);
                                   { X axis position Lines }
i := XOrg + XAxis;
repeat
   Line( i, YOrg, i, YOrg-YHeight );
   Line( i, YOrg,
         i-round(ZDepth/AspR), YOrg+ZDepth   );
   inc( i, XAxis );
until i > XOrg + XWidth;

if MaxColors > 4 then SetColor( CYAN );
                                   { Y axis position Lines }
i := YOrg - YAxis;
repeat
   Line( XOrg, i, XOrg+XWidth, i );
   Line( XOrg, i,
         XOrg-round(ZDepth/AspR), i+ZDepth );
   dec( i, YAxis );
until i < YOrg - YHeight;

if MaxColors > 4 then SetColor( RED );
                                   { Z axis position Lines }
i := ZAxis;
repeat
   Line( XOrg-round(i/AspR), YOrg+i,
         XOrg-round(i/AspR)+XWidth,  YOrg+i );
   Line( XOrg-round(i/AspR), YOrg+i,
         XOrg-round(i/AspR), YOrg-YHeight+i );
   inc( i, ZAxis );
```

```
            until i > ZDepth;
    end;
procedure ShowLabels;
    var
        i, j, k, l, m : integer;
    begin
        SetTextJustify( CenterText, CenterText );
        j := XOrg + XWidth + 15;
        l := XOrg - round( ZDepth / AspR ) - 15;
        for i := 1 to 6 do
        begin
            k := YOrg - i * YAxis;
            OutTextXY( j, k, I2S( i*25 ) );
            m := YOrg + ZDepth - i * YAxis;
            OutTextXY( l, m, I2S( i*25 ) );
        end;

        if MaxColors > 4 then SetColor( LightBlue );
        j := XOrg + 25;
        l := j - round( ZDepth / AspR );
        m := YOrg + ZDepth + 8;
        k := YOrg - YHeight - 8;
        for i := 1 to 8 do
        begin
            OutTextXY( j, k, AccTypes[i+1] );
            OutTextXY( l, m, AccTypes[i+1] );
            inc( j, 50 );
            inc( l, 50 );
        end;

        if MaxColors > 4 then SetColor( LightGreen );
        for i := 0 to 3 do
        begin
            j := XOrg -
                round( ( i*ZAxis + ZAxis/2 ) / AspR ) + 2;
            m := YOrg + round( i*ZAxis + ZAxis/2 );
            k := m - YHeight;
            l := j + XWidth;
            SetTextJustify( LeftText, TopText );
            OutTextXY( l, m, I2S( Accounts[ i+1, 1 ] ) );
            SetTextJustify( RightText, BottomText );
            OutTextXY( j, k, I2S( Accounts[ i+1, 1 ] ) );
        end;
    end;
procedure AddBar( Left, Bottom, Height,
                  Color1, Color2 : integer );
    var
        Top, Right, BarWidth, BarDepth : integer;
```

```pascal
   begin
      BarWidth := XAxis div 2;
      BarDepth := ZAxis div 2;

      if MaxColors < 4 then
      begin
         Color1 := MaxColors - 1;
         Color2 := MaxColors - 1;
      end;

      SetFillStyle( Left+1, Color1 );
      Left    := XOrg + ( Left * XAxis ) -
         round( ( ( Bottom + ( 0.35 * ZAxis ) / XAxis )
                 * ZAxis ) / AspR );
      Bottom := YOrg +
         round( ( Bottom + 0.70 ) * ZAxis );
      Right   := Left + BarWidth;
      Top     := Bottom - Height;
      Bar3D( Left, Top, Right, Bottom, 0, False );
      FillPlane( Right, Top,
                 Right+round( BarDepth/AspR ),
                 Top-BarDepth,
                 Right+round( BarDepth/AspR ),
                 Bottom-BarDepth,
                 Right, Bottom,
                 CloseDotFill, Color1 );
      FillPlane( Left, Top, Right, Top,
                 Right+round( BarDepth/AspR ),
                 Top-BarDepth,
                 Left +round( BarDepth/AspR ),
                 Top-BarDepth,
                 SolidFill, Color2 );
   end;
procedure ShowAccounts;
   var
      i : integer;
   begin
      if MaxColors > 4 then SetColor( EGAYellow );
      for i := 2 to 9 do
      begin
         AddBar( i-2, 0, round( Accounts[1,i] * Scale ),
                 LightCyan, Cyan );
         AddBar( i-2, 1, round( Accounts[2,i] * Scale ),
                 LightRed, Red );
         AddBar( i-2, 2, round( Accounts[3,i] * Scale ),
                 LightBlue, Blue );
         AddBar( i-2, 3, round( Accounts[4,i] * Scale ),
                 LightGreen, Green );
      end;
```

```
      end;
procedure ThreeDGraph;
   var
      x, y : integer;
   begin
      ClearDevice;
      XWidth  := 8 * XAxis;
      YHeight := 6 * YAxis;
      ZDepth  := 4 * ZAxis;
      SetTextJustify( LeftText, TopText );
      SetColor( GetMaxColor );
      x := 10; y := 10;
      OutTextXY( x, y, 'ZAxis := ' + I2S( ZAxis ) );
      GraphField;
      ShowLabels;
      ShowAccounts;
      Pause;
   end;
procedure Graphs3D;
   begin
      ClearDevice;
      GraphDefaults;
      XAxis := MaxX div 13;
      YAxis := MaxY div 14;
      ZAxis := 10;
      XOrg  := MaxX div 3;
      YOrg  := MaxY div 2;
      Scale := YAxis / 25;
      ZAxis := 15;
      repeat
         ThreeDGraph;
         inc( ZAxis, 10 );
      until YOrg+4*ZAxis > MaxY;
   end;
{******************* MAIN GRAPH *********************}
begin
   Initialize;                    { set graphics mode        }
   DrawPieGraphs;
   Pause;
   BarGraph;
   Pause;
   DrawMultiGraphs;
   Pause;
   Graphs3D;
   CloseGraph;                    { restore text mode        }
end.
```

LINEGRAF.PAS — sample Line-Graph

```pascal
uses GRAPH, CRT;
type
   STR5 = string[6];
const
   Accounts : array[1..4,1..20] of integer =
              (  ( 119, 121, 132, 140, 141, 139, 142,
                   135, 133, 123, 121, 120, 124, 111,
                   109, 119, 122, 132, 140, 142 ),
                 (  97,  99, 100, 107, 119, 123, 137,
                   148, 159, 160, 168, 172, 167, 155,
                   159, 163, 165, 155, 151, 148 ),
                 (  59,  73,  66,  49,  40,  39,  41,
                    45,  46,  52,  56,  59,  60,  56,
                    51,  54,  55,  53,  72,  75 ),
                 (  13,  15,  16,  19,  22,  20,  17,
                    18,  19,  21,  24,  26,  28,  27,
                    22,  20,  19,  23,  25,  24 )  );
   Years : array[1..5] of integer =
              ( 1985, 1986, 1987, 1988, 1989 );
   AccTypes : array[1..4] of STR5 =
              ( 'GenMec', 'UnvEle', 'StrOil', 'NrtMfr' );
var
   GraphDriver, GraphMode,
   MaxColors, ErrorCode : integer;
   GrImage : array[1..4] of pointer;
   Buffer  : STR5;
procedure Initialize;
   begin
      GraphDriver := DETECT;
      InitGraph( GraphDriver, GraphMode, '\TP\BGI' );
      ErrorCode := GraphResult;
      if ErrorCode <> grOk then
      begin
         writeln(' Graphics System Error: ',
                 GraphErrorMsg( ErrorCode ) );
         halt( 1 );
      end;
      MaxColors := GetMaxColor + 1;
   end;
procedure Pause;
   var
      Ch : char;
   begin
      while KeyPressed do Ch := ReadKey;
      Ch := ReadKey;
   end;
```

```
procedure LineGraph;
   var
       width, height, left, top,
       i, j, hStep, vStep, vSteps,
       bottom, x, y, MaxVal : integer;
       scale : real;
   begin
       width := GetMaxX;
       height := GetMaxY;
       left := 0;
       top := 0;
       MaxVal := 0;
       for i := 1 to 4 do
          for j := 1 to 20 do
             if Accounts[i,j] > MaxVal
                then MaxVal := Accounts[i,j];
       SetViewPort( left, top+5,
                    left+width, top+height+5, False );
       dec( width, 30 );
       hStep  := width div 20;
       vSteps := ( MaxVal div 25 ) + 2;
       vStep  := height div vSteps;
       bottom := vStep * vSteps;
       scale  := vStep / 25;
       if MaxColors > 4 then SetColor( GREEN );
       i := 0;
       repeat
          Line( i, 1, i, vStep * vSteps );
          inc( i, hStep * 4 );
       until i > hStep * 32;
       SetTextJustify( CenterText, CenterText );

       i := 0;
       repeat
          if MaxColors > 4 then SetColor( BLUE );
          Line( 0, i, hStep * 20, i );
          if MaxColors > 4 then SetColor( WHITE );
          x := hStep * 20 + 15;
          y := i;
          str( round( ( bottom-i )/vStep )*25, Buffer );
          OutTextXY( x, y, Buffer );
          inc( i, vStep );
       until i > bottom;

       SetTextStyle( SansSerifFont, HorizDir, 1 );
       SetTextJustify( LeftText, TopText );
       for i := 1 to 4 do
       begin
          SetLineStyle( i-1, 0, 1 );
```

```pascal
            if MaxColors > 4 then SetColor( i+1 );
            MoveTo( hStep div 2 + 3,
                bottom - trunc( scale*Accounts[i,1] ) + 8 );
            OutText( AccTypes[i] );
            MoveTo( hStep div 2,
                bottom - trunc( scale*Accounts[i,1] ) );
         {     Creates a 'dot' around the plot position     }
         {   for x := -1 to 1 do                            }
         {   for y := -1 to 1 do                            }
         {     PutPixel( hStep / 2 + x,                     }
         {               bottom - scale*Accounts[i,0]+y,    }
         {               GetColor );                        }

            for j := 1 to 19 do
            begin
               PutImage( GetX-10, GetY-10,
                         GrImage[i]^, XOrPut );
               LineTo( hStep div 2 + j * hStep,
                   Bottom - trunc( Scale*Accounts[i,j] ) );
            end;
            PutImage( GetX-10, GetY-10,
                      GrImage[i]^, XOrPut );
         end;
         if MaxColors > 4 then SetColor( White );
         SetTextJustify( CenterText, CenterText );
         SetTextStyle( DefaultFont, HorizDir, 2 );
         for i := 1 to 5 do
         begin
            x := i * hStep * 4 - hStep * 2;
            y := vStep div 2;
            str( Years[i], Buffer );
            OutTextXY( x, y, Buffer );
         end;
      end;

procedure Create_Images;
   const
      Figure : array[1..16] of integer =
         ( 10,  5, 15,  5, 12, 10, 17, 10,
           10, 18, 12, 13,  8, 13, 10,  5 );
   var
      i : integer;
   begin
                        { wheel / gear }
      SetFillStyle( EmptyFill, 0 );
      if MaxColors > 4 then SetColor( 10 );
      for i := 0 to 5 do
         PieSlice( 10, 10, i*60, (i*60)+60, 10 );
```

```pascal
      GetMem( GrImage[1], ImageSize( 0, 0, 20, 20 ) );
      GetImage( 0, 0, 20, 20, GrImage[1]^ );
      PutImage( 0, 0, GrImage[1]^, XOrPut );
                { lightning bolt }
      if MaxColors > 4 then SetColor( 11 );
      FillPoly( SizeOf( Figure ) div
               ( 2 * SizeOf( integer ) ), Figure );
      GetMem( GrImage[2], ImageSize( 0, 0, 20, 20 ) );
      GetImage( 0, 0, 20, 20, GrImage[2]^ );
      PutImage( 0, 0, GrImage[2]^, XOrPut );
                  { oil drop }
      if MaxColors > 4 then SetColor( 12 );
      Arc( 10,  10, 105, 360,  8 );
      Ellipse(  0,  5, 300, 90,  8, 3 );
      Ellipse(  3, 10,   0, 90, 16, 8 );
      SetFillStyle( SolidFill, GetColor );
      FloodFill( 10, 10, GetColor );
      GetMem( GrImage[3], ImageSize( 0, 0, 20, 20 ) );
      GetImage( 0, 0, 20, 20, GrImage[3]^ );
      PutImage( 0, 0, grimage[3]^, XOrPut );
                    { box }
      if MaxColors > 4 then SetColor( 13 );
      Bar3D( 0, 10, 10, 15, 5, True );
      GetMem( GrImage[4], ImageSize( 0, 0, 20, 20 ) );
      GetImage( 0, 0, 20, 20, GrImage[4]^ );
      PutImage( 0, 0, GrImage[4]^, XOrPut );
   end;
begin
   Initialize;
   Create_Images;
   LineGraph;
   Pause;
   CloseGraph;
end.
```

CHAPTER 10

Simple Animation Techniques

Talk of animation might first bring to mind cartoon images from Saturday morning T.V. Or you might settle on advertising animation where a computer is able to eat a stick of gum or to drink a soda by plugging into the bottle. Or you may be an aficionado of the Arcade graphic animations where swarms of saucers or ninja present themselves for electronic combat.

These are all animations and are each computer generated in whole or in part. Graphic animation, however, is not a product of the computer age. Over a century ago, the zeoscope combined a series of pictures to create moving animation and graphic images appeared in the margins of books where the pages could be riffled to create a moving picture. Decades of cartoons have been created by combining carefully hand-drawn images to create masterpieces ranging from Wylie Coyote and Roadrunner to Fantasia.

Today, much of the drudgery of cartoon animation is handled by computer graphics programs, but the animation processes used may be categorized as two types: combined images and morphological images.

Combined images are images built up from a stockpile or library of image parts as used in the demo program ANIMATE1.PAS. In this very simple demo, "George" is created first as a head and torso image, this initial image is saved, then additions are made to create a second image with one arm swinging forward and the other back. And, by combining these simple images, George is able to saunter through the maze, swinging his arms as he walks in a moderately convincing graphic animation.

More complex actions; such as picking up an object or doing a broadjump, would require a different set of images and the program which allows George to walk has only a very simple set of rules and responses.

The second type of animation is the morphological image: the image created in response to a set of programming rules instead of being selected from a series of stored images. In the second animation demo, ANIMATE2.PAS, a simple stick figure (in this case limited to a head and two legs) will walk along a cluttered plane. However, instead of a series of images, each figure is created from a simple set of links describing a basic skeleton with hinge points and following a limited set of response rules.

Unlike the series of prewritten images, however, the robot image can be programmed to respond to a variety of situations and to create images to adapt to different circumstances. But there are drawbacks as well. The programmer must create decision trees and loops to adapt to the varying circumstances and the calculations required for each image are more extensive than those required to simply place the appropriate image in the correct screen position.

Image Animation

Depending on your hardware graphics card, your system may support two or more pages of graphics video memory with the zero page as the default both for visual display and for graphics mode operations. In Turbo Pascal, the SetVisualPage and SetActivePage functions provide access to the alternate video pages *if* the pages are supported by the hardware. The SetActivePage function selects the video graphics page that all graphics operations will write to. The SetVisualPage function selects which graphics video page is actually displayed.

Remember, the active page and the visual page are not necessarily the same page. Graphics operations can be carried out on any supported page whether it is visible or not and any supported page can be switched to active, or visible, display instantly. The actual time required to switch visual pages is less than 1/50 of a second (varying according to hardware capabilities).

The demo program ANIMATE1.PAS will begin by switching the active graphics page—assuming your graphics card supports alternate video pages—to go "back stage" in order to create a series of images out of sight. Once this is finished and our actor is ready, the active graphics page will be reset to match the active visual page and a maze will be drawn on screen with George appearing at the upper left of the maze. At this point, the cursor controls (or a mouse) can be used to walk George through the maze.

This is *not* a case of dragging an image across the screen. As George moves in different directions, the image is animated using a series of three poses to create the appearance of a man walking, as seen from above. Since these operations can be carried out very quickly, the screen action is slowed, using the delay function, to correspond to a realistic walking pace.

Before anything else, the program begins with a few definitions that will control the movement directions:

```
const
   Right = 0;    Left = 1;    Up   = 2;    Down = 3;
```

And a second set that controls George's poses as he moves:

```
   NStep = 0;    LStep = 1;    RStep = 2;
```

And two arrays of pointers for the graphics images that will be used:

```
var
   Flash : array[0..2] of pointer;
   Man   : array[0..3,0..2] of pointer;
```

The first array (Flash) will be used to provide a visual response whenever George runs into something while the second array (Man) provides three different poses of George facing in four directions.

The program begins by using the Initialize function to set up the graphics screen mode, then—because creating the images will require a few seconds—writes a message to the active screen display before calling SetActivePage to switch to an alternate video page as the active graphics page.

```
begin
   XPos := 3;   YPos := 3;     { initial position for maze  }
   ErrorCode := 0;              { reports any graphics errors }
   Initialize;                           { set graphics mode }
   OutTextXY(10,10,' One Moment Please ');
   SetActivePage( 1 );                    { switch video page }
```

If your hardware does not support alternate video pages, this selection command will simply be ignored and the graphics images will be visible during their construction. The time required is the same in either case, of course it is a bit more elegant to keep the nuts and bolts assembly work out of sight. If you are curious, this selection can be remarked out to allow the image creation process to proceed in plain view.

The CreateImages function constructs the graphics images that will be used, then the active video graphics page is reset to the default page and the screen is cleared. The SetVisualPage function could have been used to change the visual (displayed) graphics video page to match the active video page. The results would be the same.

```
    CreateImages;                          { create and save images }
    SetActivePage( 0 );
    ClearViewPort;
```

Now the maze for the game is created on screen and the game proceeds.

```
    CreateMaze;                            {   build the maze     }
    StartGame;                             {   now run the demo   }
```

Before exiting, the ClearImages function is used to release the memory allocated to store the several graphics images. In this particular application, memory release is not absolutely necessary since exiting the program will take care of this, however, it is still good practice to provide for proper memory management.

```
    ClearImages;                           {  free memory used  }
    CloseGraph;                            {  restore text mode }
end.
```

CreateImages

The CreateImages function creates and saves a series of graphic images, beginning with a series of integer arrays (*pflash#* and *##arm#*) that describe elements used in the images.

```
procedure CreateImages;
   const
      pflash1 : array[ 1..18 ] of integer =
         ( 100, 40, 110, 60, 100, 70, 120, 65, 140, 80,
           130, 60, 140, 50, 120, 65, 100, 40 );
      pflash2 : array[ 1..18 ] of integer =
         ( 120, 40, 110, 55,  90, 60, 110, 65, 120, 80,
           130, 65, 150, 60, 130, 65, 120, 40 );
      pflash3 : array[ 1..18 ] of integer =
         ( 140, 40, 130, 60, 140, 70, 120, 65, 100, 80,
           110, 60, 100, 50, 120, 55, 140, 40 );
      bkarm_u : array[ 1..10 ] of integer =
         ( 100, 62, 102, 68, 105,
            70, 108, 69, 109, 65 );
      ftarm_u : array[ 1..8 ] of integer =
         ( 140, 62, 143, 52, 130, 47, 125, 52 );
      bkarm_r : array[ 1..10 ] of integer =
         ( 121, 145, 128, 147, 130,
           150, 129, 153, 125, 154 );
      ftarm_r : array[ 1..8 ] of integer =
         ( 117, 176, 106, 176, 100, 165, 107, 160 );
```

These constants could also be defined as arrays of PointType, but the PointType declaration is also somewhat verbose and tedious (in the source code) without providing any real advantages in either execution or memory.

```
pflash1 : array[ 1..9 ] of PointType =
            ( ( x:100; y:40 ), ( x:110; y:60 ),
              ( x:100; y:70 ), ( x:120; y:65 ),
              ( x:140; y:80 ), ( x:130; y:60 ),
              ( x:140; y:50 ), ( x:120; y:65 ),
              ( x:100; y:40 ) );
```

The randomize function is used to seed the random number generator, then the drawing color, fill style, and fill color are selected randomly for each of the *pflash#* images.

```
MaxColor := GetMaxColor;
PtSz := SizeOf( PointType );
Randomize;
SetColor( random( MaxColor ) + 1 );
SetFillStyle( random(11) + 1, random(MaxColor)+1 );
```

When calling the FillPoly function, the size passed to FillPoly is calculated as *sizeof(pflash#)* divided by two times *sizeof(int)* since two integer values are required for each polygon point.

```
FillPoly( SizeOf( pflash1 ) div PtSz, pflash1 );
```

The SaveImage function returns a pointer to a memory image. The four parameters describe the screen coordinates for the image to be saved.

```
Flash[0] := SaveImage( 100, 40, 140, 80 );
```

Essentially the same sequence of operations is repeated for the *pflash2* and *pflash3* arrays.

George's images begin with a series of ellipses to create two heads with noses and shoulders; one head with the long axis horizontal, the other vertical. The FloodFill function fills in the images using SolidFill for the heads and HatchFill for the shoulders. Figure 10-1 shows the preliminary image.

```
SetColor( random(MaxColor)+1 );
SetFillStyle( random(11)+1, random(MaxColor)+1 );
FillPoly( SizeOf( pflash2 ) div PtSz, pflash2 );
Flash[1] := SaveImage(  90, 40, 150, 80 );

SetColor( random(MaxColor)+1 );
SetFillStyle( random(11)+1, random(MaxColor)+1 );
FillPoly( SizeOf( pflash3 ) div PtSz, pflash3 );
Flash[2] := SaveImage( 100, 40, 140, 80 );

SetColor( MaxColor );
```

```
SetFillStyle( SolidFill, MaxColor );
Ellipse(    120,   60,   0, 360, 10, 10 );
                                   { draw and fill heads }
FloodFill( 120,   60, MaxColor );
Ellipse(    220,  160,   0, 360, 13,  7 );
FloodFill( 220,  160, MaxColor );
Ellipse(    120,   51,   0, 180,  3,  3 );
                                   { now tack on noses   }
Ellipse(    207,  160,  90, 270,  3,  2 );
SetFillStyle( HatchFill, MaxColor );
                                   { change fill style   }
Ellipse(    128,   60, 270,  90, 12,  6 );
                                   { and add shoulders   }
FloodFill( 135,   60, MaxColor );
Ellipse(    112,   60,  90, 270, 12,  6 );
FloodFill( 105,   60, MaxColor );
Ellipse(    220,  154,   0, 180,  8,  9 );
FloodFill( 220,  150, MaxColor );
Ellipse(    220,  166, 180, 360,  8,  9 );
FloodFill( 220,  170, MaxColor );
```

In lieu of duplicating efforts to draw separate heads facing left, right, up, and down, two of the existing images are mapped pixel by pixel to create matching reversed images.

```
for i := 100 to 145 do
   for j := 45  to  70 do
      PutPixel( 345-i, 120-j, GetPixel( i, j ) );

for i := 204 to 235 do
   for j := 145 to 175 do
      PutPixel( 345-i, j, GetPixel( i, j ) );
```

The four end products are saved as individual images.

```
Man[Up,    NStep] := SaveImage( 100,  45, 140,  70 );
Man[Down,  NStep] := SaveImage( 205,  50, 245,  75 );
Man[Left,  NStep] := SaveImage( 203, 140, 234, 180 );
Man[Right, NStep] := SaveImage( 111, 140, 142, 180 );
```

So far, four stationary images have been created. Now two of these will be used as the basis for future images by adding arms to the bodies (see Figure 10-2). The fill style is set to CloseDotFill and FillPoly is called to add the two arms to the image.

```
SetFillStyle( CloseDotFill, MaxColor );
PutImage( 100, 45, Man[ Up, NStep ]^, CopyPut );
FillPoly( SizeOf( bkarm_u ) div PtSz, bkarm_u );
FillPoly( SizeOf( ftarm_u ) div PtSz, ftarm_u );
PutImage( 100, 45, Man[ Up, NStep ]^, OrPut );
```

Figure 10-1: Basic Figure Animation—Initial Image

The initial image consists of four ellipses. The head is an ellipse with a vertical radius of 12 and a horizontal radius of 8. Each shoulder is an ellipse with a vertical radius of 8 and a horizontal radius of 12 with centers offset 4 pixels right and left. Last, the nose is a smaller ellipse with a vertical radius of four and a horizontal radius of two.

Note that PutImage has been called twice, first with the CopyPut option and then with OrPut. With the first call, the image is written to the screen, replacing any existing pixels at the image location. Next, the FillPoly function is used to add arms as new elements to this screen image.

There is a minor problem with FillPoly, however (see Figure 10-3). The integer arrays describing each "arm" are open; that is, the integer pairs do not describe a closed figure but, since the open Line figures begin and end within the existing image, this isn't a problem. The "problem" is that FillPoly does not follow the existing outlines when adding the fill pattern. Instead, FillPoly calculates the area to fill by assuming a line between the first and last points plotted and fills everything within the polygon area. This overwrites a portion of the original image.

Figure 10-2: Creating the Secondary Image

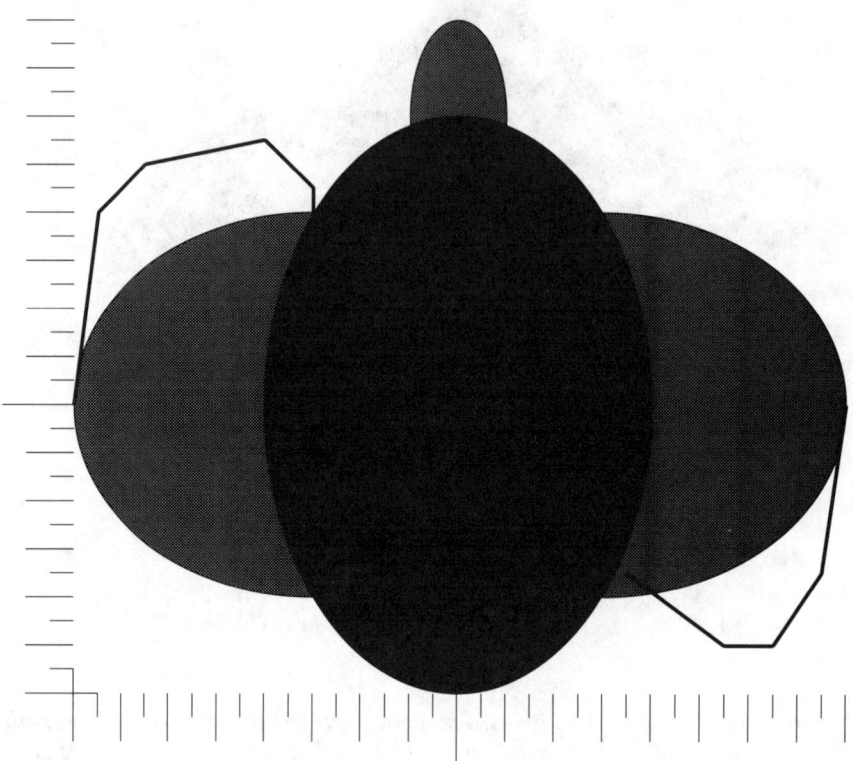

The secondary image adds definitions for two arms, drawn as if the right arm were swung slightly back (mostly elbow and upper arm) and the left arm swung slightly forward across the chest. Granted, George isn't the most animated figure in the cartoon world ... but, as you will see, he can still get around.

   Instead of trying to close the polygon in a way that avoids this overwrite, the PutImage function is called a second time, using OrPut, to restore the overwritten pixels, leaving the final image as desired.
   The first call to PutImage could be omitted since it has no effect on the operations carried out by FillPoly; the final call to PutImage will insert the head and body image. The first call, however, was used simply as a conve-

nience to line up the arms correctly and was left in the code to allow you to examine the results produced by the interaction with FillPoly.

Figure 10-3: The FillPoly Problem

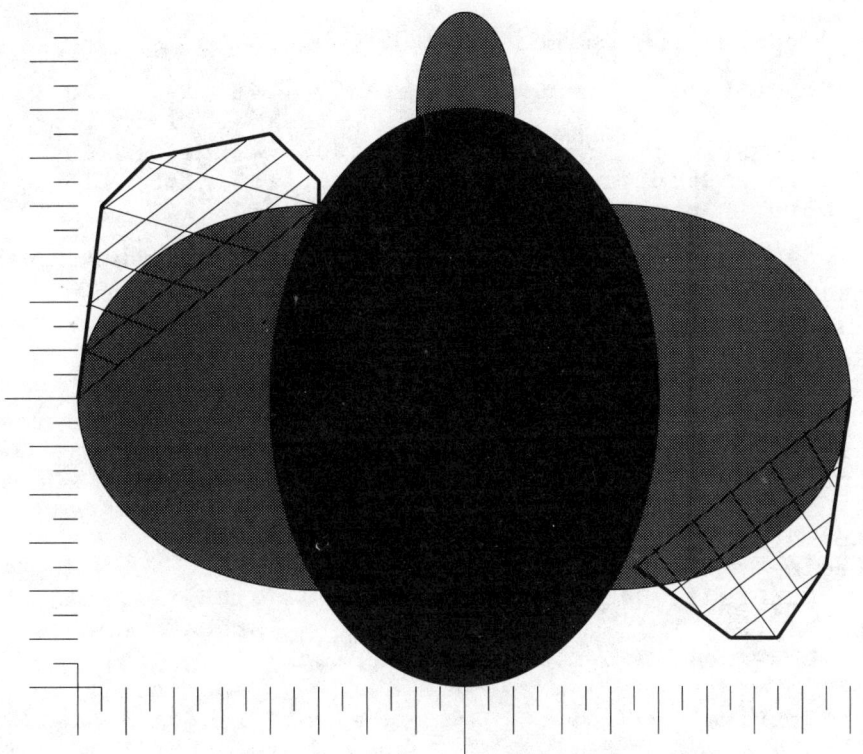

Using FillPoly with an open outline creates one minor problem—FillPoly does not follow the existing outlines but calculates the area bounded by the line elements. It assumes a line between the two end points and fills everything within the polygon area and, incidentally, overwrites a portion of the existing image (as shown).

At this point, the image has one arm in front of the body and the other swung back. Now, this image will be transposed to create three other images; one facing up, but with the arms reversed; the other two facing down with the left and right arms alternately in front and in back.

```
for i := 100 to 145 do
   for j := 45 to 70 do
   begin
```

```
            PutPixel( 345-i,      j, GetPixel( i, j ) );
                                           { rotate left/right }
            PutPixel( 345-i, 220-j, GetPixel( i, j ) );
                                           { and invert to     }
            PutPixel(        i, 220-j, GetPixel( i, j ) );
                                           { face down ...     }
         end;
```

The final four images are saved individually.

```
   Man[ Up,   LStep ]   := SaveImage( 100,  45, 145,  70 );
                                           { save all images   }
   Man[ Up,   RStep ]   := SaveImage( 200,  45, 245,  70 );
   Man[ Down, LStep ]   := SaveImage( 100, 150, 145, 175 );
   Man[ Down, RStep ]   := SaveImage( 200, 150, 245, 175 );
```

Next, using the original left-facing image, the same process is repeated, arms are added, and the result is transposed three ways, to create the final set of four images.

```
   PutImage( 100, 140, Man[ Left, NStep ]^, CopyPut );
   FillPoly( SizeOf( bkarm_r ) div PtSz, bkarm_r );
                                           { add arms }
   FillPoly( SizeOf( ftarm_r ) div PtSz, ftarm_r );
   PutImage( 100, 140, Man[ Left, NStep ]^, OrPut );
   for i := 100 to 132 do
      for j := 144 to 177 do
         begin
            PutPixel( 345-i,      j, GetPixel( i, j ) );
                                           { rotate up/down    }
            PutPixel( 345-i, 220-j, GetPixel( i, j ) );
                                           { and invert to     }
            PutPixel(        i, 220-j, GetPixel( i, j ) );
                                           { face right ...    }
         end;
   Man[ Left, RStep ]   := SaveImage( 100, 144, 132, 177 );
   Man[ Left, LStep ]   := SaveImage( 100,  43, 132,  76 );
   Man[ Right,LStep ]   := SaveImage( 213,  43, 245,  76 );
   Man[ Right,RStep ]   := SaveImage( 213, 144, 245, 177 );
end;
```

SaveImage

The SaveImage function is called with four parameters that specify the corners of a Rectangle on the screen. SaveImage uses the ImageSize function to calculate the necessary memory and GetMem to allocate memory for the specified image area, assigning a local pointer called *Image* to the memory location.

```
function SaveImage( left, top,
                    right, bottom : integer ): pointer;
   var
      Image : pointer;
      Size  : word;
   begin
      GetMem( Image, ImageSize( left, top,
                                right, bottom ) );
```

The GetImage function transfers the screen image to the memory area pointed at by *Image*, then PutImage uses the XOrPut option to erase the screen image and, finally, the image pointer is returned to the calling function.

```
      GetImage( left, top, right, bottom, Image^ );
      PutImage( left, top, Image^, XOrPut );
      SaveImage := Image;
   end;
```

At this point, memory has been allocated for the graphic image, the screen image information has been written to this memory location, and the pointer to the location has been returned to be assigned to the appropriated pointer variable so the local pointer *Image* can be forgotten.

CreateMaze

The CreateMaze function draws a maze on the screen with the maze elements described as arrays of integers specifying point pairs.

```
procedure CreateMaze;
const
   maze1 : array[0..7]  of integer =
       ( 200,  40,  50,  40,  50, 160, 100, 160 );
   maze2 : array[0..7]  of integer =
       ( 100,  80, 100, 120, 200, 120, 200, 240 );
   ...
   maze17: array[0..3]  of integer =
       ( 500, 240, 600, 240 );
var
   i, j, PtSz : integer;
   vp : ViewPortType;
```

This maze data could be retrieved from an external file or even generated by an appropriate algorithm.

The viewport (window) is set to the entire screen; in this case, EGA or higher resolution is assumed, and a brief instruction is written at the bottom.

```
begin
   SetColor( MaxColors - 1 );    { Set draw color to white }
   SetViewPort( 0, 0, 639, 349, True );
```

```pascal
SetTextStyle( DefaultFont, HorizDir, 1 );
OutTextXY(  20, 330,
            'Use Arrow Keys to move ''George'' ' + 
            '<Q>uit to exit program' );
```

Now the viewport is reduced in size and a border is drawn around the area.

```pascal
SetViewPort( 0, 0, 600, 320, True );
SetLineStyle( SolidLn, 0, NormWidth );
GetViewSettings( vp );
Rectangle( 0, 0, vp.x2 - vp.x1, vp.y2 - vp.y1 );
```

The final step is to draw the walls of the maze and to add labels for the start and finish points.

```pascal
   PtSz := SizeOf( PointType );
   OutTextXY( 10, 20, 'START' );
   DrawPoly( SizeOf( maze1 ) div PtSz, maze1 );
   DrawPoly( SizeOf( maze2 ) div PtSz, maze2 );
   ...
   DrawPoly( SizeOf( maze17 ) div PtSz, maze17 );
   OutTextXY( 550, 300, 'FINISH' );
end;
```

In this case, the DrawPoly function is used instead of FillPoly because I want lines drawn without fill added; otherwise, the operation is precisely the same as described in the CreateImages function.

No record of the maze construction, nor of the position of the walls is necessary. The program will not depend on any such record for operation. Instead, the screen image itself will be tested to decided if movements are valid or not.

StartGame

Now, it is time for the actual game control, which begins with the StartGame function. Initially, StartGame calls the PositionImage function to put George on the screen at the start coordinates, and then it reads the keyboard (or a mouse) to direct George's movements on the screen. Only five keys will be accepted as input: the Up, Down, Right, and Left arrow keys and "Q" for quit.

```pascal
procedure StartGame;
   var
      Ch   : char;
      Quit : boolean;
begin
   Quit := False;
   Move := Right;
   LastMove := Right;
   PositionImage( NStep );
```

The *Quit* variable was initialized as false. Until *Quit* is true, the *while* loop will continue.

```
while not Quit do
begin
   Ch := ReadKey;
   case upcase( Ch ) of
      #$00 : begin
```

If the first key read is a NULL, presumably one of the function keys was pressed and a second character code is read to decide which key. The four arrow keys (cursor keys) control George's movements, each calling the Move-Image function with the appropriate direction as a parameter.

```
            Ch := ReadKey;
            case Ch of
               'M' : Move_Image( Right );
               'K' : Move_Image( Left );
               'H' : Move_Image( Up );
               'P' : Move_Image( Down );
            end; {case}
         end;
```

Note that both Q and q are accepted as valid inputs since the UpCase function has been used.

```
         'Q' : Quit := True;                       { exit! }
      end; { case }
   end;
end;
```

MoveImage

The MoveImage function is called with the *NextStep* argument, which specifies the direction in which George should move. First, PutImage is called to erase the current screen image, the *Move* variable—which controls direction and selects the set of images used—takes the value *NextStep*, and PutImage is called again to put George back on the screen (but facing in the correct direction).

```
procedure MoveImage( NextStep : integer );
   var
      i, XFake, YFake, XStep, YStep, XFlash, YFlash : integer;
   begin
      PositionImage( NStep );
      Move := NextStep;
      PositionImage( NStep );
```

Before the two calls to PutImage, George may have been facing the same direction as he will be afterwards, but rather than writing a test for direction, it is simple enough to erase the existing image and restore the desired image.

Depending on the direction of movement, several variables *XFake*, *YFake*, *XStep*, *YStep*, *XFlash*, and *YFlash* are assigned values which may not be needed. It's simplest, however, to use one *switch* statement to set all six for the proper directions and then you don't have to worry about them.

```
case Move of
    Right: begin XFake  :=  5;   YFake  :=  0;
                 XStep  :=  5;   YStep  :=  0;
                 XFlash :=  5;   YFlash :=  0;   end;
    Left:  begin XFake  := -5;   YFake  :=  0;
                 XStep  := -5;   YStep  :=  0;
                 XFlash :=  2;   YFlash :=  0;   end;
    Up:    begin XFake  :=  0;   YFake  := -5;
                 XStep  :=  0;   YStep  := -4;
                 XFlash :=  0;   YFlash :=  2;   end;
    Down:  begin XFake  :=  0;   YFake  :=  5;
                 XStep  :=  0;   YStep  :=  4;
                 XFlash :=  0;   YFlash :=  0;   end;
end; { case }
```

The call to the TestMove function decides if George can move in the requested direction.

```
if not TestMove then
begin
```

If TestMove returns a Boolean false, then PutImage erases the stationary image, increments the position by *XFake* or *YFake* (one of these is always zero), places the stepping image (LSTEP) on the screen, and calls FlashImage.

```
PositionImage( NStep );
inc( XPos, XFake );
inc( YPos, YFake );
PositionImage( LStep );
FlashImage( XPos+XFlash, YPos+YFlash );
```

Now, the LSTEP image is erased, the position coordinates are returned to their previous values, and the NSTEP image is restored.

```
PositionImage( LStep );
dec( XPos, XFake );
dec( YPos, YFake );
PositionImage( NStep );
end else
```

In this manner, George takes a half-step forward, bumps into the wall of the maze, flashing stars are superimposed cartoon style and, finally, George steps back and waits for the next instruction. If TestMove returns true, then George is free to move forward. This movement begins by erasing the stationary image (NSTEP) and incrementing the position coordinates.

```
begin
   PositionImage( NStep );
   inc( XPos, XStep );
   inc( YPos, YStep );
```

In order to make the movement illusion as smooth as possible, George's *LastMove* is tested to decide with which foot he should be leading now. Actually, George's feet are never seen—only his arms swinging as he walks—but if the sequence of his movements was not coordinated, the results would look very awkward. Since *LastMove* will be either 1 or 2 (LSTEP or RSTEP), only a Boolean test is required.

```
if LastMove <> 0 then
begin
```

Each time an arrow key is pressed (or a mouse sends the equivalent signal), George is going to take several steps on the screen. Instead of writing all the individual instructions necessary for each step and each position adjustment, a loop will run through calls to the TakeStep function to make George walk forward. His last step will be the same as his first in this sequence and will end in the NSTEP (stationary) position.

```
         for i := 1 to 2 do
         begin
            Take_Step( XStep, YStep, LStep );
            Take_Step( XStep, YStep, NStep );
            Take_Step( XStep, YStep, RStep );
            Take_Step( XStep, YStep, NStep );
         end;
         Take_Step( XStep, YStep, LStep );
         PositionImage( NStep );
         delay( TimeOut );
      end else
```

The *XStep* and *YStep* variables have already been assigned the appropriate offsets for the movement direction (*Move*) and each call to TakeStep places the appropriate image on the screen, waits momentarily, erases the image, and increments the position coordinates.

If *LastMove* is LSTEP, then George starts off with RSTEP, running though the same sequences.

```
         begin
            for i := 1 to 2 do
            begin
               Take_Step( XStep, YStep, RStep );
               Take_Step( XStep, YStep, NStep );
               Take_Step( XStep, YStep, LStep );
               Take_Step( XStep, YStep, NStep );
            end;
            Take_Step( XStep, YStep, RStep );
            PositionImage( NStep );
            delay( TimeOut );
         end;
      end;
   end;
```

The TestMove function is the key decision mechanism for this game; it reads the screen pixels in the requested direction to decide if George is free to move. The *switch(Move)* directive decides which test is appropriate for the selected direction.

```
function TestMove : boolean;
var
   i : integer;    Result : boolean;
```

Since the *XPos/YPos* coordinates are the upper-left corner of the image, different offsets and ranges need to be tested for each direction. The test itself is very simple: if any pixel tested is not zero (BLACK), a zero value (FALSE) is immediately returned. This indicates the end of the test and the function exits immediately, returning a false result.

```
begin
   Result := True;
   case Move of
     Right: for i := XPos+47 to XPos+96 do
               if GetPixel( i, YPos+5 ) <> 0
                  then Result := False;
      Left: for i := XPos downto XPos-50 do
               if GetPixel( i, YPos+5 ) <> 0
                  then Result := False;
        Up: for i := YPos downto YPos-40 do
               if GetPixel( XPos+5, i ) <> 0
                  then Result := False;
      Down: for i := YPos+37 to YPos+76 do
               if GetPixel( XPos+5, i ) <> 0
                  then Result := False;
   end; { case }
```

If no non-BLACK pixels were encountered by the selected test, then a 1 (TRUE) is returned and George is free to move forward.

```
        TestMove := Result;
end;
```

In other applications, different test types might be required. This is merely the simplest test and it serves nicely in our current application. In other situations, however, you might find you need to test for a specific color value, test several pixels for a condition or test against a separate "map" for responses based on information that is not visible on the screen—or you might use a combination of all of these.

TakeStep

The TakeStep function is the principal movement function in this demo program and it is called with three parameters. The *x* and *y* arguments are the horizontal and vertical movement increments that will determine the next screen image position. The *Step* argument is passed to PositionImage to control which image (NSTEP, LSTEP, or RSTEP) will be used and also to set the value for *LastMove*.

```
procedure TakeStep( x, y, Step : integer );
   begin
      PositionImage( Step );
      delay( TimeOut );
      PositionImage( Step );
      inc( XPos, x );
      inc( YPos, y );
      if Step <> NStep then LastMove := Step;
   end;
```

The first call to PositionImage places the appropriate image on the screen; after a time delay, the second call erases the image. Note also that the position is incremented only after the image is erased.

PositionImage

The PositionImage function places the desired image on the screen using the *XOrPut* option. If the image indicated by *Move* and *Step* is already on the screen, *XOrPut* erases the image. If there is another image on the screen already, then the new image overlies the existing image without erasing it or, if the current image is being XOR'ed with itself, the original image is restored.

```
procedure PositionImage( Step : integer );
var
   x, y : integer;
begin
   x := XPos; y := YPos;
   case Move of
```

```
        Right, Left : inc( x, 8 );
        Up,    Down : inc( y, 5 );
     end;
     PutImage( x, y, Man[ Move, Step ]^, XOrPut );
  end;
```

For left and right facing images, the x-axis position is offset by 8 pixels, for up and down, the y-axis is offset by 5 pixels. This does not affect the *XPos* and *YPos* screen coordinates, but improves positioning of the images within the maze walls.

FlashImage

The FlashImage function is called—following the finest cartoon traditions—when George runs into a wall. This function overwrites George's image with a series of irregular colored "stars" while adding random sound effects. Each flash is popped onto the screen, the sound effect is activated, and the flash is then XOR'ed with itself and a new sound effect is generated.

The three flash images are cycled three times, but no time delay is used so the resulting screen image is a very brief multi-colored star or series of stars which vanish before they can be completely seen.

```
procedure FlashImage( x, y : integer );
var
   i, j, k : integer;
begin
   for i := 1 to 3 do
      for j := 0 to 3 do
         for k := 0 to 1 do
         begin
            PutImage( x, y, Flash[j]^, XOrPut );
            Sound( random(100) + 100 );
         end;
   NoSound;
end;
```

Finally, before the function exits, the NoSound function is called to cancel the last sound generated. Remember: each sound generated continues until a new Sound command is called or until the NoSound function is called to explicitly terminate the sound effects.

ClearImages

The final function used in this demonstration is the ClearImages function, which uses the dispose function to release the memory allocated for the various images.

```
procedure ClearImages;
   var
      i, j : integer;
   begin
      for i := 0 to 2 do dispose( Flash[i] );
      for i := 0 to 3 do
         for j := 0 to 2 do dispose( Man[ i, j ] );
   end;
```

Once your program exits, these memory allocations should be automatically released by the call to CloseGraph, but it is better practice to explicitly release the memory allocated to the images.

Also, in other applications, it may be advantageous to use the dispose function to release memory which was used for one application and make it available for another without waiting until the program exits.

Morphological Animation

While conventional animation techniques that use precreated images are fine for Arcade games and simple applications, the programmer is required to provide for all contingencies and to individually create each of the images required. Instead of creating individual images, the alternative is to create rules for the construction of an image and then have the computer draw each image as needed, altering and rearranging it according to the requirements.

In the second animation demo, ANIMATE2.PAS "Elmer" is a stylized stick figure consisting of a triangular body and two legs. This is not a precreated image, but is drawn and erased according to a moderately simple series of program rules. The "legs" are links with defined limits of freedom and fixed lengths—literally, a skeleton much like your own.

In the demo, Elmer will stand up, and walk across the screen from left to right. To accomplish this, a total of more than 5,000 images will be written and erased. The "standing up" requires as many as 242 images and each "step" requires up to 243 images (using 1-degree increments).

The disadvantage inherent in this approach is, first, that Elmer requires a great deal of calculation; second, the rules for Elmer's motion and position are complex; and, third, the more complex the image, the greater the processing time. These disadvantages can be overcome by various methods: movement rules can be simplified to minimize calculation; math coprocessors can cut the time required for calculations; and the calculated image can be combined in part with stored images to reduce the complexity of calculations.

The big advantage, is that the programmer can create rules and decision trees to govern the images and positions and can design these in a manner to provide flexibility that fixed images cannot emulate. The present demo does not have a complex set of responses, but the basic requirements are here and you are invited to try your hand at expanding this program to create a more complex set of adaptations.

Warning: if you don't enjoy math, you are going to hate morphological animation! There are no easy solutions or answers here; you will have to look at writing rules that require serious number crunching. Thus warned, it's time to take a look at how image morphology is handled.

ANIMATE2.PAS begins with two constants: BRIEF, which will provide a time delay constant and can be increased or decreased according to the speed of your system; and ASTEP, which controls the angle between subsequent movements.

```
BRIEF = 100;              { change value to slow images }
ASTEP = 5;                    { degrees for movement }
```

A series of global variables will be used for the action points and to define the relations between the several portions of Elmer's anatomy.

```
var
   rcolor,   lcolor,          { right and left leg colors }
   urangle,  ulangle,      { upper right & left leg angles }
   lxknee,   lyknee, rxknee, ryknee,
                              { coordinates for knees      }
   lrangle,  llangle,      { lower right & left leg angles }
   lxfoot,   lyfoot, rxfoot, ryfoot,
                              { coordinates for feet       }
   ujoint,   ljoint,          { length of leg joints       }
   xpos,     ypos,            { body coordinates (center)  }
   xoffset,  Count, i : integer;
                              { number of images written   }
```

Before getting into the special functions used here, let's take a brief digression. In Pascal, the conventional trigonometry functions accept angle arguments in radians, while Turbo Pascal's graphics functions are configured to use arguments in degrees. Since, for this application, it is more convenient to use angles in degrees (even though the conventional trigonometric functions will be used), the rad function is created to convert an angle expressed in degrees to an angle expressed in radians.

```
function Rad( degrees: integer ): real;
   begin
      Rad := PI * degrees / 180;
   end;
```

For convenience, the RSin and RCos functions are provided in order to calculate the sin and cos values for angles in degrees. An integer argument (degrees) returns a real (decimal fraction) result.

```
function RSin( degrees: integer ): real;
  begin
     RSin := sin( Rad( degrees ) );
  end;
function RCos( degrees: integer ): real;
  begin
     RCos := cos( Rad( degrees ) );
  end;
```

The main program begins by using the same Initialize function as previous programs, then it sets initial values for the variables that describe Elmer's structure and beginning position.

```
begin
   Initialize;                              {  set graphics mode  }
   urangle := 30;    ulangle := 30;         {  initial values for }
   lrangle := 0;     llangle := 0;          {  charlie (walker)   }
   ujoint  := 30;    ljoint  := 30;
   lxfoot  := 30;    lyfoot  := 150;   ryfoot := 150;
   rcolor  := BLUE;  lcolor  := RED;
   OutTextXY( 1, 1, ' Count := ' );
   xoffset := TextWidth(' Count := ');
```

The CreateField function draws a plane for Elmer to walk on and provides a few background structures for demonstration; StartWalker puts Elmer on the screen in his beginning configuration (a folded squat); RaiseWalker allows Elmer to stand up; and WalkRight is looped for the 20 steps necessary for Elmer to cross the screen.

```
   CreateField;
   StartWalker;
   Raise_Walker;
   for i := 1 to 20 do WalkRight;
   Pause;
   CloseGraph;                         {  restore text mode           }
end.
```

As standard procedure, initial values were assigned to several of Elmer's variable definitions. These, however, may not be correct and some are better established by calculation than by a programmer's entry—which is another way of saying I find it easier to let the computer figure out how Elmer fits together than to run out the angles and formulas on my pocket calculator and type them in. Why do it the hard way?

To begin, the position of the left foot is predefined and the left knee is considered to be directly above the foot (as per the defined length of the lower leg).

```pascal
procedure StartWalker;
  begin
     lxknee := lxfoot;
     lyknee := lyfoot - ljoint;
```

With the lower left leg and knee in position, the body coordinates are calculated according to the angle from vertical (*ulangle*) and the length of the upper joint (*ujoint*).

```pascal
     xpos    := round( RSin( ulangle )
                       * ujoint ) + lxfoot;
     ypos    := round( RCos( ulangle )
                       * ujoint ) + lyfoot - ljoint;
```

The calculations continue down the right leg until the right knee and, last, the right foot are positioned.

```pascal
     rxfoot := round( RSin( urangle )
                       * ujoint ) + xpos;
     rxknee := rxfoot;
     ryknee := ryfoot - ljoint;
     Body_Image( MaxColors-1 );
  end;
```

The last step is to put Elmer on the screen by calling BodyImage. The BodyImage function is called both to draw Elmer on the screen and, with a color value of 0, to erase Elmer again.

```pascal
procedure BodyImage( color : integer );
  var
     i, j, left, right, top, bottom, x, y : integer;
  begin
     SetColor( color );
     if color <> 0 then SetColor( lcolor );
```

Beginning with the left leg, CP is set to the proper coordinates and a knot is drawn for Elmer's foot, then a Line is drawn up to the knee, and another knot is added for the knee itself.

```pascal
     MoveTo( lxfoot, lyfoot );
     PlotKnot;
     LineTo( lxknee, lyknee );
     PlotKnot;
```

The Line continues up to the hip, changes color for the right leg, and works back down to the right foot.

```
            LineTo( xpos, ypos );
            PlotKnot;
            if color <> 0 then SetColor( rcolor );
            LineTo( rxknee, ryknee );
            PlotKnot;
            LineTo( rxfoot, ryfoot );
            PlotKnot;
```

The last task is drawing the body. Since Elmer's body does not bend or shift orientation, a simple set of Line commands are sufficient for this portion of his anatomy.

```
            if color <> 0 then SetColor( MaxColors-1 );
            bottom := ypos + 10;
            top    := ypos - 5;
            left   := xpos - 11;
            right  := xpos + 11;
            Line( xpos,  ypos,  left,   top    );
            Line( xpos,  ypos,  right,  top    );
            Line( xpos,  ypos,  xpos,   bottom );
            Line( left,  top,   right,  top    );
            Line( left,  top,   xpos,   bottom );
            Line( right, top,   xpos,   bottom );
            y := 1;
            OutTextXY( xoffset, y, N2S( Count, 3 ) );
            inc( Count );
         end;
```

The BodyImage function will be called more than 1,000 times (using 5-degree steps) to draw Elmer in different configurations as he moves on the screen. One alternative, to speed operations, might be to draw this portion of the body once, save the screen image, and use the putimage function with the *XOrPut* option.

The PlotKnot function draws a three-by-three pixel knot to define Elmer's feet and knees.

```
procedure PlotKnot;
   var
      i, j, k : integer;
   begin
      k := GetColor;
      for i := -1 to 1 do
         for j := -1 to 1 do
            PutPixel( GetX+i, GetY+j, k );
   end;
```

The RaiseWalker function takes Elmer from his initial squatting position to an erect posture. When Elmer was first set up, his upper leg angle (*ulangle*) was initialized at 30 degrees. Now, he'll straighten up in one-degree steps, with new knee and hip positions calculated for each one-degree change, until he is fully erect with an upper leg angle of 150 degrees. Since both legs are assumed to be moving equally and at the same time, calculations are greatly simplified.

```pascal
procedure RaiseWalker;
   var
      xknee, yknee : integer;
begin
   while( ulangle <= 150 ) do
   begin
      inc( ulangle, ASTEP );
      xknee := xpos -
               trunc( RSin( ulangle ) * ujoint );
      yknee := ypos -
               trunc( RCos( ulangle ) * ujoint );
      BodyImage( 0 );
      lxknee := xknee;
      lyknee := yknee;
      lrangle := trunc( 180 / PI *
                 ArcTan( ( lxfoot - lxknee ) /
                         ( lyfoot - lyknee ) ) );
      llangle := lrangle;
      lxknee := trunc( lxfoot -
                RSin( llangle ) * ljoint );
      rxknee := trunc( rxfoot +
                RSin( lrangle ) * ljoint );
      ryknee := trunc( lyfoot -
                RCos( llangle ) * ljoint );
      lyknee := ryknee;
      ypos := trunc( lyknee +
              RCos( ulangle ) * ujoint );
      BodyImage( 15 );
   end;
```

Finally, the right and left angles are equalized and, just in case of remaining error, the lower angles (*lrangle* and *llangle*) are set to zero.

```pascal
      urangle := ulangle;
      lrangle := 0;
      llangle := 0;
end;
```

Now that Elmer is standing, the WalkRight function will be used to move him across the screen. When you try complicating Elmer's responses, you may wish to break this function into a series of functions for calculating each movement element independently.

```
procedure WalkRight;
   var
      i : integer;
   begin
```

The first element here involves swinging the right foot (the lower right leg) up thirty degrees.

```
         for i := 1 to ( 30 div ASTEP ) do
         begin                 { swing right foot up 30 degrees }
            BodyImage( 0 );
            inc( lrangle, ASTEP );
            rxfoot := trunc( rxknee +
                     RSin( lrangle ) * ljoint );
            ryfoot := trunc( ryknee +
                     RCos( lrangle ) * ljoint );
            BodyImage( MaxColors-1 );
            delay( BRIEF );
         end;
```

Now that Elmer has his foot up, the left leg is ready to bend down until the right foot is back on the ground (or approximately so). Since Elmer doesn't weigh anything, he doesn't have to worry about falling over and can balance without adjustments. In other applications, it might be advisable to provide for a counter movement to simulate natural motion, but to keep this demo program simple, gravity is replaced by levity.

Again, the calculations begin with one foot (the left), go up to the hip, and then down to the right foot.

```
         for i := 1 to ( 30 div ASTEP ) do
         begin                 { adjust left leg to advance foot }
            BodyImage( 0 );
            inc( llangle, ASTEP );
            lxknee := lxfoot +
                     trunc( RSin( llangle ) * ljoint );
            lyknee := lyfoot -
                     trunc( RCos( llangle ) * ljoint );
            xpos   := lxknee +
                     trunc( RSin( ulangle ) * ujoint );
            ypos   := lyknee +
                     trunc( RCos( ulangle ) * ujoint );
            rxknee := xpos +
                     trunc( RSin( urangle ) * ujoint );
            ryknee := ypos -
                     trunc( RCos( urangle ) * ujoint );
            rxfoot := rxknee +
                     trunc( RSin( lrangle ) * ljoint );
            ryfoot := ryknee +
```

```
                          trunc( RCos( lrangle ) * ljoint );
          BodyImage( MaxColors-1 );
          delay( BRIEF );
        end;
```

Now it's time to straighten up the right leg—with the left leg moving to compensate:

```
        for i := 1 to ( 30 div ASTEP ) do
        begin              { bring right leg back to standing }
          BodyImage( 0 );
          dec( lrangle, ASTEP );
          rxknee := rxfoot -
                          trunc( RSin( lrangle ) * ljoint );
          ryknee := ryfoot -
                          trunc( RCos( lrangle ) * ljoint );
          xpos   := rxknee -
                          trunc( RSin( urangle ) * ujoint );
          ypos   := ryknee +
                          trunc( RCos( urangle ) * ujoint );
          lxknee := xpos -
                          trunc( RSin( ulangle ) * ujoint );
          lyknee := ypos -
                          trunc( RCos( ulangle ) * ujoint );
          lxfoot := lxknee -
                          trunc( RSin( llangle ) * ljoint );
          lyfoot := lyknee +
                          trunc( RCos( llangle ) * ljoint );
          BodyImage( MaxColors-1 );
          delay( BRIEF );
        end;
```

Finally, the left leg swings back to the standing position to complete Elmer's step:

```
        for i := 1 to ( 30 div ASTEP ) do
        begin              { bring left leg back to standing  }
          BodyImage( 0 );
          dec( llangle, ASTEP );
          lxfoot := lxknee -
                          trunc( RSin( llangle ) * ljoint );
          lyfoot := lyknee +
                          trunc( RCos( llangle ) * ljoint );
          BodyImage( MaxColors-1 );
          delay( BRIEF );
        end;
```

At this point, the coordinates and angles of each foot have been recalculated about 120 times and, inevitably, a certain amount of error has accumulated in the process. If you observe the resulting figure carefully, you may note that Elmer's right foot is slightly above the ground plane where he started and the left leg is approximately one pixel further off the ground than the right. As he continues across the screen, if no correction is made, he will slowly walk up the screen as well as to the right.

If these positions were critical, the optimum choice would be to redesign the calculation path—specifically, redesign the loop conditions—but for this application, a simple corrective function, GroundImage, is quite sufficient to keep Elmer's feet firmly on the ground.

```
      GroundImage;
   end;
```

The GroundImage function allows gravity to take charge for a moment and pulls Elmer back down to the ground by adjusting the five critical vertical coordinates.

```
procedure GroundImage;
   begin
      while GetPixel( lxfoot, lyfoot+3 ) <> 0 do
      begin
         BodyImage( 0 );
         inc( lyknee );   inc( ryknee );
         inc( lyfoot );   inc( ryfoot );
         inc( ypos );
         BodyImage( MaxColors-1 );
      end;
   end;
```

This completes the initial task of taking Elmer for a walk.

Retaining A Background Image

When you run this demo, you will notice that Elmer walks across a plane cluttered by a set of boxes. Given the simplicity of the program, Elmer is quite oblivious to this clutter and, as Elmer's image is successively redrawn, the boxes are erased by the image of his leg.

Without going into the question of having Elmer sense these obstacles and climb over them (though this is a good place for you to experiment with decision and response rules), there are two ways around having the background image erased.

One approach is to save an image of the background and, instead of using the BodyImage function with a BLACK color value to erase Elmer, use the PutImage function with the *CopyPut* option to restore the background, erase Elmer at the same time, and draw Elmer's new image for the next step. To do this, you will need three new global variables:

```pascal
var
   PositionTop, PositionLeft : integer;
   Background : pointer;
```

And, for an example, the WalkRight function would be changed like this:

```pascal
procedure WalkRight;
var
   i : integer;
begin
   for i := 1 to 30 do
   begin
      EraseImage;                { replaces BodyImage( 0 ); }
      inc( lrangle, ASTEP );
      rxfoot := rxknee + RSin( lrangle ) * ljoint;
      ryfoot := ryknee + RCos( lrangle ) * ljoint;
      GetBackground;             { add to restore background }
      BodyImage( MaxColors-1 );
      delay( BRIEF );
   end;
   ...
end;
```

The key to the operation is the GetBackground function which would be written as follows:

```pascal
procedure GetBackground;
var
   left, top, right, bottom : integer;
begin
   bottom := 150;
   if lxfoot < lxknee
      then left := lxfoot-5
      else left := lxknee-5;
   if rxfoot > rxknee
      then right := rxfoot+5
      else right := rxknee+5;
   if lyknee < ypos
      then top := ypos-7
      else top := lyknee-5;
   PositionTop := top;
   PositionLeft := left;
   GetMem( Background,
           ImageSize( left, top, right, bottom ) );
   GetImage( left, top, right, bottom, Background^ );
end;
```

The *left* and *right* variables are tested for the maximum extent of Elmer's image and *top* for the height. Of course, a slight margin has been added on all sides and, for simplicity, *bottom* is fixed. *PositionTop* and *PositionLeft* are global variables for saving the corner coordinates.

The EraseImage function uses PutImage to restore the background using *CopyPut*, then releases the memory allocated to *Background*. Remember, if memory is allocated repeatedly without being released, you will quickly run out of memory!

```
procedure EraseImage
begin
   PutImage( PositionLeft, PositionTop,
             Background^, CopyPut );
   dispose( Background );
end;
```

Also remember, the GetBackground function must be called for the first time before Elmer is placed on the screen, but *after* Elmer's feet and knees have been calculated (see the StartWalker function).

SetWriteMove

A second option to prevent Elmer from erasing the background is to use the SetWriteMode function, selecting the *XOrPut* line drawing option. The *CopyPut* option is active by default for all line drawing operations, and uses the MOV instruction to write line pixels to the screen. When the *XOrPut* option is selected, the XOR instruction replaces the MOV instruction in order to combine line pixels with existing screen pixels.

Also, when the *XOrPut* option is selected, instead of erasing an existing image using the background color, the image is redrawn with the same colors used for the original image.

Remember, the SetWriteMode options apply only with the DrawPoly, Line, LineRel, LineTo, and Rectangle functions.

Summary

The animation techniques shown in this chapter are relatively unsophisticated. Image animation requires multiple bit images and is capable of only pre-planned responses. At the same time, calculated animation can be programmed to respond to a wider variety of circumstances, but complex images require considerable processing time with results that are frequently unacceptable in real-time applications.

Still, there are circumstances where animation of one type or another is useful. But there are also many types of image handling besides cartoon animation and, in Chapter 14, icon images will be created and animated.

First, there are other image techniques which are also important, beginning with image manipulation and image files.

ANIMATE1.PAS

```pascal
program Animate1;
uses Graph, Crt;
const
    Right = 0;    Left  = 1;    Up    = 2;    Down  = 3;
    NStep = 0;    LStep = 1;    RStep = 2;
    TimeOut = 100;
var
    GraphDriver, GraphMode, MaxColors,
    Move, LastMove, XPos, YPos, ErrorCode : integer;
    Flash : array[0..2] of pointer;
    Man   : array[0..3,0..2] of pointer;
procedure Initialize;
begin
    GraphDriver := DETECT;
    InitGraph( GraphDriver, GraphMode, '\TP\BGI' );
    ErrorCode := GraphResult;
    if ErrorCode <> grOk then
    begin
        writeln(' Graphics System Error: ',
                GraphErrorMsg( ErrorCode ) );
        halt( 1 );
    end;
    MaxColors := GetMaxColor + 1;
end;
function SaveImage( left, top,
                    right, bottom : integer ) : pointer;
    var
        Image : pointer;
        Size  : word;
    begin
        GetMem( Image, ImageSize( left, top,
                                  right, bottom ) );
        GetImage( left, top, right, bottom, Image^ );
        PutImage( left, top, Image^, XOrPut );
        SaveImage := Image;
    end;
procedure CreateImages;
    const
    {===================================================}
    {   pflash1 : array[ 1..9 ] of PointType =          }
```

```
     {                ( ( x:100; y:40 ), ( x:110; y:60 ), }
     {                  ( x:100; y:70 ), ( x:120; y:65 ), }
     {                  ( x:140; y:80 ), ( x:130; y:60 ), }
     {                  ( x:140; y:50 ), ( x:120; y:65 ), }
     {                  ( x:100; y:40 ) );                }
     {================================================}
       pflash1 : array[ 1..18 ] of integer =
           ( 100, 40, 110, 60, 100, 70, 120, 65, 140, 80,
             130, 60, 140, 50, 120, 65, 100, 40 );
       pflash2 : array[ 1..18 ] of integer =
           ( 120, 40, 110, 55,  90, 60, 110, 65, 120, 80,
             130, 65, 150, 60, 130, 65, 120, 40 );
       pflash3 : array[ 1..18 ] of integer =
           ( 140, 40, 130, 60, 140, 70, 120, 65, 100, 80,
             110, 60, 100, 50, 120, 55, 140, 40 );
       bkarm_u : array[ 1..10 ] of integer =
           ( 100, 62, 102, 68, 105, 70, 108, 69, 109, 65 );
       ftarm_u : array[ 1..8 ] of integer =
           ( 140, 62, 143, 52, 130, 47, 125, 52 );
       bkarm_r : array[ 1..10 ] of integer =
           ( 121, 145, 128, 147, 130,
             150, 129, 153, 125, 154 );
       ftarm_r : array[ 1..8 ] of integer =
           ( 117, 176, 106, 176, 100, 165, 107, 160 );
var
    i, j, MaxColor, PtSz : integer;
begin
    MaxColor := GetMaxColor;
    PtSz := SizeOf( PointType );
    Randomize;
    SetColor( random( MaxColor ) + 1 );
    SetFillStyle( random(11) + 1, random(MaxColor)+1 );
    FillPoly( SizeOf( pflash1 ) div PtSz, pflash1 );
    Flash[0] := SaveImage( 100, 40, 140, 80 );

    SetColor( random( MaxColor ) + 1 );
    SetFillStyle( random(11) + 1, random(MaxColor)+1 );
    FillPoly( SizeOf( pflash2 ) div PtSz, pflash2 );
    Flash[1] := SaveImage(  90, 40, 150, 80 );

    SetColor( random( MaxColor ) + 1 );
    SetFillStyle( random(11) + 1, random(MaxColor)+1 );
    FillPoly( SizeOf( pflash3 ) div PtSz, pflash3 );
    Flash[2] := SaveImage( 100, 40, 140, 80 );

    SetColor( MaxColor );
    SetFillStyle( SolidFill, MaxColor );
    Ellipse(   120,    60,    0, 360, 10, 10 );
                                          { draw and fill heads }
    FloodFill( 120,   60, MaxColor );
```

```pascal
Ellipse(     220, 160,   0, 360, 13,   7 );
FloodFill( 220, 160, MaxColor );
Ellipse(     120,  51,   0, 180,  3,   3 );
                                    { now tack on noses     }
Ellipse(     207, 160,  90, 270,  3,   2 );
SetFillStyle( HatchFill, MaxColor );
                                    { change fill style     }
Ellipse(     128,  60, 270,  90, 12,   6 );
                                    { and add shoulders     }
FloodFill( 135,  60, MaxColor );
Ellipse(     112,  60,  90, 270, 12,   6 );
FloodFill( 105,  60, MaxColor );
Ellipse(     220, 154,   0, 180,  8,   9 );
FloodFill( 220, 150, MaxColor );
Ellipse(     220, 166, 180, 360,  8,   9 );
FloodFill( 220, 170, MaxColor );

for i := 100 to 145 do
   for j := 45 to  70 do
      PutPixel( 345-i, 120-j, GetPixel( i, j ) );

for i := 204 to 235 do
   for j := 145 to 175 do
      PutPixel( 345-i, j, GetPixel( i, j ) );

Man[ Up,NStep    ]    := SaveImage( 100,  45, 140,  70 );
Man[ Down,NStep  ]    := SaveImage( 205,  50, 245,  75 );
Man[ Left,NStep  ]    := SaveImage( 203, 140, 234, 180 );
Man[ Right,NStep ]    := SaveImage( 111, 140, 142, 180 );

SetFillStyle( CloseDotFill, MaxColor );
                                    { change fill style }
PutImage( 100, 45, Man[ Up, NStep ]^, CopyPut );
FillPoly( SizeOf( bkarm_u ) div PtSz, bkarm_u );
                                    { and add arms }
FillPoly( SizeOf( ftarm_u ) div PtSz, ftarm_u );

{ FillPoly fills calculated outLine between end points }
{ may overwrite part of original image and boundary -  }
{ restore original using OrPut                         }

PutImage( 100, 45, Man[ Up, NStep ]^, OrPut );

for i := 100 to 145 do
   for j := 45 to 70 do
   begin
      PutPixel( 345-i,       j, GetPixel( i, j ) );
                                    { rotate left/right }
      PutPixel( 345-i, 220-j, GetPixel( i, j ) );
                                    { and invert to     }
```

```pascal
            PutPixel(      i, 220-j, GetPixel( i, j ) );
                                            { face down ...        }
      end;
   Man[ Up, LStep ]    := SaveImage( 100,  45, 145,  70 );
                                            { save all images   }
   Man[ Up, RStep ]    := SaveImage( 200,  45, 245,  70 );
   Man[ Down, LStep ]  := SaveImage( 100, 150, 145, 175 );
   Man[ Down, RStep ]  := SaveImage( 200, 150, 245, 175 );

   PutImage( 100, 140, Man[ Left, NStep ]^, CopyPut );
   FillPoly( SizeOf( bkarm_r ) div PtSz, bkarm_r );
                                            { add arms }
   FillPoly( SizeOf( ftarm_r ) div PtSz, ftarm_r );
   PutImage( 100, 140, Man[ Left, NStep ]^, OrPut );

   for i := 100 to 132 do
      for j := 144 to 177 do
      begin
         PutPixel( 345-i,      j, GetPixel( i, j ) );
                                            { rotate up/down }
         PutPixel( 345-i, 220-j, GetPixel( i, j ) );
                                            { and invert to   }
         PutPixel(      i, 220-j, GetPixel( i, j ) );
                                            { face right ... }
      end;
   Man[ Left, RStep ]  := SaveImage( 100, 144, 132, 177 );
   Man[ Left, LStep ]  := SaveImage( 100,  43, 132,  76 );
   Man[ Right, LStep ] := SaveImage( 213,  43, 245,  76 );
   Man[ Right, RStep ] := SaveImage( 213, 144, 245, 177 );
end;
procedure CreateMaze;
const
   maze1 : array[0..7]  of integer =
      ( 200,  40,  50,  40,  50, 160, 100, 160 );
   maze2 : array[0..7]  of integer =
      ( 100,  80, 100, 120, 200, 120, 200, 240 );
   maze3 : array[0..3]  of integer =
      (   0, 200, 100, 200 );
   maze4 : array[0..7]  of integer =
      ( 150, 160, 150, 240,  50, 240,  50, 280 );
   maze5 : array[0..3]  of integer =
      ( 150,  80, 300,  80 );
   maze6 : array[0..3]  of integer =
      ( 250,  80, 250, 160 );
   maze7 : array[0..3]  of integer =
      ( 100, 280, 100, 320 );
   maze8 : array[0..7]  of integer =
      ( 150, 280, 250, 280, 250, 240, 300, 240 );
```

```pascal
      maze9 : array[0..5] of integer =
         ( 250,   40, 350,   40, 350,   80 );
      maze10: array[0..11] of integer =
         ( 200, 200, 300, 200, 300, 120,
           400, 120, 400,  80, 400, 160 );
      maze11: array[0..5] of integer =
         ( 300, 280, 350, 280, 350, 160 );
      maze12: array[0..3] of integer =
         ( 400,   0, 400,  40 );
      maze13: array[0..7] of integer =
         ( 450, 120, 450,  40, 550,  40, 550,  80 );
      maze14: array[0..7] of integer =

         ( 500,  80, 500, 160, 400, 160, 400, 240 );
      maze15: array[0..3] of integer =
         ( 400, 280, 400, 320 );
      maze16: array[0..9] of integer =
         ( 550, 120, 550, 200, 450,
           200, 450, 280, 550, 280 );
      maze17: array[0..3] of integer =
         ( 500, 240, 600, 240 );
var
   i, j : integer;
     vp : ViewPortType;
   PtSz : integer;
begin
   SetColor( MaxColors - 1 );    { Set draw color to white }
   SetViewPort( 0, 0, 639, 349, True );
   SetTextStyle( DefaultFont, HorizDir, 1 );
   OutTextXY( 20, 330,
              'Use Arrow Keys to move ''George'' or ' +
              '<Q>uit to exit program');

   SetViewPort( 0, 0, 600, 320, True );
   SetLineStyle( SolidLn, 0, NormWidth );
   GetViewSettings( vp );
   Rectangle( 0, 0, vp.x2 - vp.x1, vp.y2 - vp.y1 );

   PtSz := SizeOf( PointType );
   OutTextXY( 10, 20, 'START' );
   DrawPoly( SizeOf( maze1 ) div PtSz, maze1 );
   DrawPoly( SizeOf( maze2 ) div PtSz, maze2 );
   DrawPoly( SizeOf( maze3 ) div PtSz, maze3 );
   DrawPoly( SizeOf( maze4 ) div PtSz, maze4 );
   DrawPoly( SizeOf( maze5 ) div PtSz, maze5 );
   DrawPoly( SizeOf( maze6 ) div PtSz, maze6 );
   DrawPoly( SizeOf( maze7 ) div PtSz, maze7 );
   DrawPoly( SizeOf( maze8 ) div PtSz,  maze8 );
   DrawPoly( SizeOf( maze9 ) div PtSz,  maze9 );
```

```pascal
      DrawPoly( SizeOf( maze10 ) div PtSz, maze10 );
      DrawPoly( SizeOf( maze11 ) div PtSz, maze11 );
      DrawPoly( SizeOf( maze12 ) div PtSz, maze12 );
      DrawPoly( SizeOf( maze13 ) div PtSz, maze13 );
      DrawPoly( SizeOf( maze14 ) div PtSz, maze14 );
      DrawPoly( SizeOf( maze15 ) div PtSz, maze15 );
      DrawPoly( SizeOf( maze16 ) div PtSz, maze16 );
      DrawPoly( SizeOf( maze17 ) div PtSz, maze17 );
      OutTextXY( 550, 300, 'FINISH' );
end;
procedure FlashImage( x, y : integer );
var
   i, j, k : integer;
begin
   for i := 1 to 3 do
      for j := 0 to 3 do
         for k := 0 to 1 do
         begin
            PutImage( x, y, Flash[j]^, XOrPut );
            sound( random(100) + 100 );
         end;
   nosound;
end;
procedure PositionImage( Step : integer );
var
   x, y : integer;
begin
   x := XPos; y := YPos;
   case Move of
      Right, Left : inc( x, 8 );
      Up,    Down : inc( y, 5 );
   end;
   PutImage( x, y, Man[ Move, Step ]^, XOrPut );
end;
function TestMove : boolean;
var
   i : integer;   Result : boolean;
begin
   Result := True;
   case Move of
      Right: for i := XPos+47 to XPos+96 do
                if GetPixel( i, YPos+5 ) <> 0
                   then Result := False;
      Left: for i := XPos downto XPos-50 do
                if GetPixel( i, YPos+5 ) <> 0
                   then Result := False;
      Up: for i := YPos downto YPos-40 do
```

```pascal
                        if GetPixel( XPos+5, i ) <> 0
                           then Result := False;
            Down: for i := YPos+37 to YPos+76 do
                        if GetPixel( XPos+5, i ) <> 0
                           then Result := False;
      end; { case }
      TestMove := Result;
   end;
procedure TakeStep( x, y, Step : integer );
   begin
      PositionImage( Step );
      delay( TimeOut );
      PositionImage( Step );
      inc( XPos, x );
      inc( YPos, y );
      if Step <> NStep then LastMove := Step;
   end;
procedure MoveImage( NextStep : integer );
   var
      i, XFake, YFake, XStep, YStep, XFlash, YFlash :
integer;
   begin
      PositionImage( NStep );
      Move := NextStep;
      PositionImage( NStep );
      case Move of
         Right: begin  XFake  :=  5;   YFake  :=  0;
                       XStep  :=  5;   YStep  :=  0;
                       XFlash :=  5;   YFlash :=  0;   end;
         Left:  begin  XFake  := -5;   YFake  :=  0;
                       XStep  := -5;   YStep  :=  0;
                       XFlash :=  2;   YFlash :=  0;   end;
         Up:    begin  XFake  :=  0;   YFake  := -5;
                       XStep  :=  0;   YStep  := -4;
                       XFlash :=  0;   YFlash :=  2;   end;
         Down:  begin  XFake  :=  0;   YFake  :=  5;
                       XStep  :=  0;   YStep  :=  4;
                       XFlash :=  0;   YFlash :=  0;   end;
      end; { case }
      if not TestMove then
      begin
         PositionImage( NStep );
         inc( XPos, XFake );
         inc( YPos, YFake );
         PositionImage( LStep );
         FlashImage( XPos+XFlash, YPos+YFlash );
         PositionImage( LStep );
```

```
            dec( XPos, XFake );
            dec( YPos, YFake );
            PositionImage( NStep );
         end else
         begin
            PositionImage( NStep );
            inc( XPos, XStep );
            inc( YPos, YStep );
            if LastMove <> 0 then
            begin
               for i := 1 to 2 do
               begin
                  TakeStep( XStep, YStep, LStep );
                  TakeStep( XStep, YStep, NStep );
                  TakeStep( XStep, YStep, RStep );
                  TakeStep( XStep, YStep, NStep );
               end;
               TakeStep( XStep, YStep, LStep );
               PositionImage( NStep );
               delay( TimeOut );
            end else
            begin
               for i := 1 to 2 do
               begin
                  TakeStep( XStep, YStep, RStep );
                  TakeStep( XStep, YStep, NStep );
                  TakeStep( XStep, YStep, LStep );
                  TakeStep( XStep, YStep, NStep );
               end;
               TakeStep( XStep, YStep, RStep );
               PositionImage( NStep );
               delay( TimeOut );
            end;
         end;
   end;
procedure StartGame;
   var
      Ch   : char;
      Quit : boolean;
   begin
      Quit := False;
      Move := Right;
      LastMove := Right;
      PositionImage( NStep );
      while not Quit do
      begin
         Ch := ReadKey;
         case upcase( Ch ) of
```

```pascal
                    #$00 : begin
                             Ch := ReadKey;
                             case Ch of
                                'M' : MoveImage( Right );
                                'K' : MoveImage( Left );
                                'H' : MoveImage( Up );
                                'P' : MoveImage( Down );
                             end;                                  {case}
                           end;
                    'Q' : Quit := True;                      { exit! }
            end; { case }
        end;
   end;
procedure ClearImages;
   var
      i, j : integer;
   begin
      for i := 0 to 2 do dispose( Flash[i] );
      for i := 0 to 3 do
         for j := 0 to 2 do dispose( Man[i,j] );
   end;

begin
   XPos := 3;  YPos := 3;   { initial position for maze  }
   ErrorCode := 0;          { reports any graphics errors }
   Initialize;                        { set graphics mode }
   OutTextXY(10,10,' One Moment Please ');
   SetActivePage( 1 );
   CreateImages;                      { create and save images }
   SetActivePage( 0 );
   ClearViewPort;
   CreateMaze;                        { build the maze    }
   StartGame;                         { now run the demo  }
   ClearImages;                       { free memory used  }
   CloseGraph;                        { restore text mode }
end.
```

ANIMATE2.PAS

```pascal
program Animate2;

uses GRAPH, CRT;

const
   BRIEF = 100;             { change value to slow images }
   ASTEP = 5;                       { degrees for movement }
var
```

```pascal
    GraphDriver,               { graphics device driver    }
    GraphMode,                 { graphics mode value       }
    MaxColors,                 { maximum colors available  }
    ErrorCode,                 { reports any graphics errors }
    rcolor,   lcolor,          { right and left leg colors }
    urangle,  ulangle,      { upper right & left leg angles }
    lxknee,   lyknee, rxknee, ryknee,
                               { coordinates for knees     }
    lrangle,  llangle,      { lower right & left leg angles }
    lxfoot,   lyfoot, rxfoot, ryfoot,
                               { coordinates for feet      }
    ujoint,   ljoint,          { length of leg joints      }
    xpos,     ypos,            { body coordinates (center) }
    xoffset,  Count, i : integer;
                               { number of images written  }
procedure Initialize;
   begin
      GraphDriver := DETECT;
      InitGraph( GraphDriver, GraphMode, '\TP\BGI' );
      ErrorCode := GraphResult;
      if ErrorCode <> grOk then
      begin
         writeln(' Graphics System Error: ',
                 GraphErrorMsg( ErrorCode ) );
         halt( 1 );
      end;
      MaxColors := GetMaxColor + 1;
   end;
function Rad( degrees: integer ): real;
   begin
      Rad := PI * degrees / 180;
   end;
function RSin( degrees: integer ): real;
   begin
      RSin := sin( Rad( degrees ) );
   end;
function RCos( degrees: integer ): real;
   begin
      RCos := cos( Rad( degrees ) );
   end;
function N2S( Val, Digit : integer ): string;
   var
      Buffer : string;
   begin
      str( Val:Digit, Buffer );
```

```pascal
            N2S := Buffer;
        end;
procedure Pause;
    var
        Ch : char;
    begin
        while KeyPressed do Ch := ReadKey;
        Ch := ReadKey;
    end;
procedure CreateField;
    const
        Base = 152;
    begin
        Line( 0, Base, 639, Base );
        Rectangle( 100, Base-10, 120, Base );
        Rectangle( 150, Base-15, 175, Base );
        Rectangle( 255, Base-20, 300, Base );
        Rectangle( 375, Base-10, 420, Base );
    end;
procedure PlotKnot;
    var
        i, j, k : integer;
    begin
        k := GetColor;
        for i := -1 to 1 do
            for j := -1 to 1 do
                PutPixel( GetX+i, GetY+j, k );
    end;
procedure BodyImage( color : integer );
    var
        i, j, left, right, top, bottom, x, y : integer;
    begin
        SetColor( color );
        if color <> 0 then SetColor( lcolor );
        MoveTo( lxfoot, lyfoot );
        PlotKnot;
        LineTo( lxknee, lyknee );
        PlotKnot;
        LineTo( xpos, ypos );
        PlotKnot;
        if color <> 0 then SetColor( rcolor );
        LineTo( rxknee, ryknee );
        PlotKnot;
        LineTo( rxfoot, ryfoot );
        PlotKnot;
        if color <> 0 then SetColor( MaxColors-1 );
```

```
        bottom := ypos+10;
        top    := ypos-5;
        left   := xpos-11;
        right  := xpos+11;
        Line( xpos,  ypos,  left,   top     );
        Line( xpos,  ypos,  right,  top     );
        Line( xpos,  ypos,  xpos,   bottom  );
        Line( left,  top,   right,  top     );
        Line( left,  top,   xpos,   bottom  );
        Line( right, top,   xpos,   bottom  );
        y := 1;
        OutTextXY( xoffset, y, N2S( Count, 3 ) );
        inc( Count );
    end;

procedure StartWalker;
    begin
        lxknee := lxfoot;
        lyknee := lyfoot - ljoint;
        xpos   := round( RSin( ulangle )
                         * ujoint ) + lxfoot;
        ypos   := round( RCos( ulangle )
                         * ujoint ) + lyfoot - ljoint;
        rxfoot := round( RSin( urangle )
                         * ujoint ) + xpos;
        rxknee := rxfoot;
        ryknee := ryfoot - ljoint;
        BodyImage( MaxColors-1 );
    end;

procedure RaiseWalker;
    var
        xknee, yknee : integer;
    begin

        while( ulangle <= 150 ) do
        begin
           inc( ulangle, ASTEP );
           xknee := xpos -
                    trunc( RSin( ulangle ) * ujoint );
           yknee := ypos -
                    trunc( RCos( ulangle ) * ujoint );
           BodyImage( 0 );
           lxknee := xknee;
           lyknee := yknee;
           lrangle := trunc( 180 / PI *
                      ArcTan( ( lxfoot - lxknee ) /
                              ( lyfoot - lyknee ) ) );
           llangle := lrangle;
           lxknee := trunc( lxfoot -
```

```pascal
                            RSin( llangle ) * ljoint );
            rxknee := trunc( rxfoot +
                            RSin( lrangle ) * ljoint );
            ryknee := trunc( lyfoot -
                            RCos( llangle ) * ljoint );
            lyknee := ryknee;
            ypos := trunc( lyknee +
                            RCos( ulangle ) * ujoint );
            BodyImage( 15 );
        end;
        urangle := ulangle;
        lrangle := 0;
        llangle := 0;
    end;
procedure GroundImage;
    begin
        while GetPixel( lxfoot, lyfoot+3 ) <> 0 do
        begin
            BodyImage( 0 );
            inc( lyknee );   inc( ryknee );
            inc( lyfoot );   inc( ryfoot );
            inc( ypos );
            BodyImage( MaxColors-1 );
        end;
    end;
procedure WalkRight;
    var
        i : integer;
    begin
        for i := 1 to ( 30 div ASTEP ) do
        begin                    { swing right foot up 30 degrees }
            BodyImage( 0 );
            inc( lrangle, ASTEP );
            rxfoot := trunc( rxknee +
                    RSin( lrangle ) * ljoint );
            ryfoot := trunc( ryknee +
                    RCos( lrangle ) * ljoint );
            BodyImage( MaxColors-1 );
            delay( BRIEF );
        end;

        for i := 1 to ( 30 div ASTEP ) do
        begin                    { adjust left leg to advance foot }
            BodyImage( 0 );
            inc( llangle, ASTEP );
            lxknee := lxfoot +
                    trunc( RSin( llangle ) * ljoint );
            lyknee := lyfoot -
```

```
                        trunc( RCos( llangle ) * ljoint );
        xpos    := lxknee +
                        trunc( RSin( ulangle ) * ujoint );
        ypos    := lyknee +
                        trunc( RCos( ulangle ) * ujoint );
        rxknee := xpos +
                        trunc( RSin( urangle ) * ujoint );
        ryknee := ypos -
                        trunc( RCos( urangle ) * ujoint );
        rxfoot := rxknee +
                        trunc( RSin( lrangle ) * ljoint );
        ryfoot := ryknee +
                        trunc( RCos( lrangle ) * ljoint );
        BodyImage( MaxColors-1 );
        delay( BRIEF );
end;

for i := 1 to ( 30 div ASTEP ) do
begin                   { bring right leg back to standing }
        BodyImage( 0 );
        dec( lrangle, ASTEP );
        rxknee := rxfoot -
                        trunc( RSin( lrangle ) * ljoint );
        ryknee := ryfoot -
                        trunc( RCos( lrangle ) * ljoint );
        xpos    := rxknee -
                        trunc( RSin( urangle ) * ujoint );
        ypos    := ryknee +
                        trunc( RCos( urangle ) * ujoint );
        lxknee := xpos -
                        trunc( RSin( ulangle ) * ujoint );
        lyknee := ypos  -
                        trunc( RCos( ulangle ) * ujoint );
        lxfoot := lxknee -
                        trunc( RSin( llangle ) * ljoint );
        lyfoot := lyknee +
                        trunc( RCos( llangle ) * ljoint );
        BodyImage( MaxColors-1 );
        delay( BRIEF );
end;

for i := 1 to ( 30 div ASTEP ) do
begin                   { bring left leg back to standing  }
        BodyImage( 0 );
        dec( llangle, ASTEP );
        lxfoot := lxknee -
                        trunc( RSin( llangle ) * ljoint );
        lyfoot := lyknee +
                        trunc( RCos( llangle ) * ljoint );
```

```pascal
            BodyImage( MaxColors-1 );
            delay( BRIEF );
         end;

         GroundImage;
      end;

begin
   Initialize;                         { set graphics mode      }
   urangle := 30;   ulangle := 30;     { initial values for     }
   lrangle := 0;    llangle := 0;      { charlie (walker)       }
   ujoint  := 30;   ljoint  := 30;
   lxfoot  := 30;   lyfoot  := 150;    ryfoot := 150;
   rcolor  := BLUE; lcolor  := RED;
   OutTextXY( 1, 1, ' Count := ' );
   xoffset := TextWidth(' Count := ');
   CreateField;
   StartWalker;
   RaiseWalker;
   for i := 1 to 20 do WalkRight;
   Pause;
   CloseGraph;                         { restore text mode      }
end.
```

CHAPTER 11

Image Manipulation and Image Files

Two subjects will be covered in this chapter: the basic principles required to store and retrieve an image as a disk file and other methods for manipulating an existing image. I'll begin with background relevant to both topics—the structure of an image.

When Turbo Pascal saves an image of a portion of the screen, the screen image is encoded or compressed to minimize memory usage. For example, assume an image that is 41 by 41 pixels in size. If each pixel value were stored as an 8-bit char value, the image would require 1,681 bytes of memory. But, in a monographic mode, each pixel location contains only two bits of real information: the video bit and the intensity bit. At the other extreme, in EGA/VGA color modes, each pixel contains six bits of information: the RrGgBb color bits (see Chapter 12 for more detail on color video data). Instead of 1,681 bytes, only 1,261 bytes of actual information are required to be saved and, for a monochrome image, only 421 bytes.

Turbo Pascal, however, goes one step further and uses a data compression algorithm to minimize the memory requirements, reducing 1,681 EGA/VGA pixels to a mere 990 bytes of image data (about a 42 percent savings over storing the image as char data). In monographic modes, similar compression results in even greater savings.

The data compression and deciphering is automatic and is handled whenever GetImage and PutImage are called—and there is no need to worry about the mechanisms involved. But there is one item of information in the data image that is useful to know about. The first four bytes of data contain the x- and y-axis size of the image coded as *X_lsb*, *X_msb*, *Y_lsb*, *Y_msb*.

Therefore, for the above example, the first four bytes of the image would read *28h*, *00h*, *28h*, *00h* (28h = 40 decimal) with the **L**east**S**ignificant**B**yte first and the **M**ost**S**ignificant**B**yte second. Notice that the size value is not stored as 41, but as 40—a minimum axis size of 1 being reasonably assumed.

Image Files: Storage and Retrieval

When using graphics images, instead of placing the code description for a series of images in your program, it is often more convenient to create an image—or several images—once and to store these as external image files, recalling them if and when necessary for use in the application program.

For example, in the line-graph demo presented previously, four images were used to represent four different types of stock or four different types of company. In a real application, this line graph might have required dozens or hundreds of image symbols, even though only a few would be needed at any particular time. Instead of including the coding to create each of these in the application program and wasting time to draw each image and memory to store the images, a more efficient approach would be to use a separate image creation utility program, store the images as external files, and read the image files when required by the application. This is simple to accomplish, and the method is illustrated in Chapter 15.

Since the image size is included in the image (and, therefore, in the image file), all you need to know in order to retrieve an image, is the filename.

The FileImg.Pas Demo

The demo program, FileImg.Pas, will show how this is accomplished; first, by creating a image (*Flash*); then by storing it as a diskfile (IMAGE.OUT) and; finally, by retrieving the image as Flash2. FileImg begins by declaring two pointers:

```
Flash1, Flash2 : pointer;
```

It then initializes the graphics system, selecting random colors and fill patterns for the actual demonstration. When done, FileImg waits for a key entry before it releases the memory allocated for the images and exits.

```
begin
   Initialize;                        {  set graphics mode       }
   randomize;                         {  create and save image   }
   SetColor( random(MaxColors)+1 );
   SetFillStyle( random(11)+1, random(MaxColors)+1 );
```

```
FillPoly( sizeof( pflash ) div sizeof( PointType ),
         pflash );
```

The flash image is adapted from an earlier animation program, using one of the image patterns demonstrated.

```
const
   pflash : array[ 1..18 ] of integer =
         ( 100, 40, 110, 60, 100, 70, 120, 65, 140, 80,
           130, 60, 140, 50, 120, 55, 100, 40 );
```

The *Flash* image is created by calling SaveImage, but in this application, SaveImage has been modified slightly to accept a fifth parameter, *Size*. *Size* is passed by address so that the calculated value will be returned for further use. This is not an absolute requirement because the ImageSize function can be called at any time, but it is convenient and the size information will be needed by FileImage.

```
Flash := SaveImage( 100, 40, 140, 80, Size );
```

The FileImage function is passed the image pointer (*Flash*), the size of the image (*Size* returned by SaveImage), and the filename where the image will be stored.

```
FileImage( Flash, 40, 40, 'IMAGE.OUT' );
```

The ReadImage function requires only the filename, returning a pointer to the new image retrieved from the disk. For confirmation, the retrieved image is written to the screen.

```
Flash2 := ReadImage( 'IMAGE.OUT' );
PutImage( 300, 300, Flash2^, CopyPut );
```

The SaveImage procedure operates exactly as before, except for the added parameter, *Size*.

```
function SaveImage( left, top, right, bottom: integer;
                    var Size: word ): pointer;
   var
      image : pointer;
   begin
      Size := ImageSize( left, top, right, bottom );
      GetMem( image, Size );
      GetImage( left, top, right, bottom, image^ );
      PutImage( left, top, image^, XOrPut );
      SaveImage := image;
   end;
```

The FileImage procedure is the key to storing an image on disk. It accepts four parameters: *Image*, a pointer to the image to be written; *Xsize* and *Ysize*, the sizes of the image; and the filename.

```
procedure FileImage( Image: pointer;
                     Xsize, Ysize: byte;
                     Filename: string );
  var
     f : file of byte;        i, j : integer;
     k : byte;                size : word;
  begin
```

The image passed to the procedure is written to the screen at a fixed location. If desired, an alternate video page can be used at this point to execute these operations "out of sight" or to prevent interference with an existing screen image.

```
    { SetActivePage( 1 );  }   { use alternate video page }
    { SetVisualPage( 1 );  }   { optional : make visible  }
    size := xsize * ysize;
    PutImage( 100, 100, Image^, CopyPut );
```

After the image is written to the screen, a file of byte size is declared and the x and y image sizes are written as the first two bytes.

```
    assign( f, FileName );
    rewrite( f );
    write( f, xsize );
    write( f, ysize );
```

Next, the image bytes are written to the file. This is done without attempting to compress the file image. The image size, compressed or raw, makes little difference in an application of this type since the disk storage system allocates file storage in blocks, not in terms of the actual size required.

```
    for i := 0 to xsize do
      for j := 0 to ysize do
      begin
         k := GetPixel( 100+i, 100+j );
         write( f, k );
      end;
```

If a large number of images are required for an application, multiple images could be combined in a single file—heading the file with an array of bytes indicating the start point and size of each image within the file. In this case, image compression might have some value; otherwise, it's pointless.

```
    close( f );
    PutImage( 100, 100, image^, XOrPut );
```

```
   { SetActivePage( 0 );   }{ restore original video page }
   { SetVisualPage( 0 );   }{ restore visual video page  }
end;
```

Lastly, the file (*f*) is closed and the image is XOr'ed to the screen for erasure.

Using the ReadImage function, retrieving the image from the created file is almost as simple as creating and saving it, but in this application, only one parameter is required—the filename. ReadImage declares three byte variables: *xsize*, *ysize*, and *k*; a file handle, *f*; and *temp*, a local pointer to reference the image.

```
function ReadImage( filename: string ): pointer;
   var
      i, j : integer;        f : file of byte;
      size : word;           xsize, ysize, k : byte;
      temp : pointer;
```

f is opened as a file of byte size and, as the first step, the x and y size parameters are retrieved.

```
   begin
      assign( f, filename );
      reset( f );
      read( f, xsize );
      read( f, ysize );
```

Next, the image bytes are read from the file and written to the screen, recreating the image.

```
      for i := 0 to xsize do
         for j := 0 to ysize do
         begin
            read( f, k );
            PutPixel( 200+i, 200+j, k );
         end;
      close( f );
```

As shown, the screen size of the image is contained in the image data and, therefore, ImageSize will be called locally to determine *size*. This is particularly convenient since your program will not know how much memory is needed for an image retrieved from disk and memory must be allocated before the image can be saved.

```
      size := ImageSize( 0, 0, xsize, ysize );
      temp := SaveImage( 200, 200,
                         200+xsize, 200+ysize, size );
      ReadImage := temp;
   end;
```

It's done. Only a bit more work required than when the image file was written. The image file was opened and read, beginning with the image size data, the memory size was calculated and memory was allocated. Finally, the image pointer was returned to the calling function.

Files With Multiple Images

While it is possible to write several images to a single file, doing so is not recommended (though it may be necessary for some applications).

I am not going to attempt to offer any hard and fast rules for creating multiple-image files; instead, here are considerations and suggestions which should help when programming this type of application.

First, are the images all going to be the same size? Or will there be several different size images in a single file? In either case, the handling can be similar, but, if the images are all exactly the same size, then positioning the file pointer to seek a specific image becomes simpler. If the images differ only slightly in size, then it may be worthwhile to make them all the size of the largest, for convenience. If the images are all different sizes, then retrieval becomes a matter of reading succesive images until the desired item is reached.

Or does it?

How are you going to retrieve the four bytes of information that tell you the screen image size and, therefore, the size of the data to read?

One alternative would be to create a file header—an index to the images within the file—consisting of either the size of each successive image or the offset, in bytes, of the image position within the file. Remember, the data has no way to tell you that it is the beginning of an image and there are no reserved flag bytes with graphics images. Any value could occur in an image.

Second, how are you going to write multiple images to a file? The file append option, used when the file is opened, is the obvious choice. However, when writing the file, should you add a few nulls between items? Or create a specific pattern of bits to insert between entries as a safety?

Actually, if your handling is accurate at all, such safeties shouldn't be necessary. And, if your handling isn't accurate, these won't help much anyway. Your best bet is not to depend on fancy insertions.

Third, if you do need multiple images in a single file, it can be done. It can be done easier in C (specifically Turbo C) than in Pascal (and certainly easier than BASIC).

More Image Manipulation

The second principal topic in this chapter is image manipulation. In Chapter 10, images were rotated 180 degrees or flipped left for right, simple transpositional manipulations in four basic directions.

But a mere four directions is a rather limited choice of orientations. What about a true image rotation? The computer is great at crunching numbers and can calculate coordinate transformations without even raising a sweat, so why not use this capability?

The demo program, ROTATE.PAS, will show two types of rotation: direct image rotation and calculated image rotation.

Direct Image Rotation

In direct image rotation, an existing image is rotated pixel by pixel to create a second image, which is a duplication of the first, but which has a different orientation.

At the same time, each pixel in the specified image area is tested to see if it is non-zero, since there's no point in rotating background pixels.

If the pixel value is not zero—if it does contain visual information—then the pixel's position is read as an x-axis/y-axis offset from a center point. Nominally, an image is rotated egocentrically (self-centered), but provisions can be made to rotate an image eccentrically by specifying the necessary zero point coordinates.

In either case, the pixel's position, as an x-axis/y-axis offset, is converted to an angle and a vector distance (the hypotenuse of a right triangle formed by the x and y distances—see *Vector Calculations*). The pixel angle is then incremented by the rotation angle and the vector distance is reconverted to an x-axis/y-axis offset which becomes the new pixel position. Since overwriting the original image would be self-defeating, each rotated pixel offset is plotted from a new center position to create a new, rotated image.

As ROTATE.PAS will demonstrate, the rotated image is not always as smooth as the original, due to variations in the calculation that result from small changes in angles (both in the original pixel coordinates and the rotated vector angle), and return fractional values which must be reduced to integer coordinates for the actual plot. Basically, the higher the screen resolution, the smoother the rotated image will appear, but these calculated image rotations cannot be smoothed entirely when carried out on a pixel by pixel basis.

Calculated Image Rotation

The second method of image rotation does not apply to all types of images, but for any image generated primarily using the Turbo Pascal Arc and Line functions, the line and arc coordinates can be rotated, and a new image is generated. These coordinate rotations are carried out in the same manner as for direct image rotation.

One obvious exception exists: the Ellipse function cannot be rotated by rotating coordinates since there is no provision for circular elongation, except directly along the x-axis or the y-axis. Also, the Circle function, which is a special case of Ellipse, is not affected by coordinate rotation.

When coordinate rotation is practical, there are advantages. The resulting images are smoother than those produced by direct image rotation and creating the image is generally faster since fewer calculations are required.

Video Aspect Adjustments

As ROTATE.PAS will demonstrate (unless you are using a VGA system), the video aspect ratio also needs to be taken into account when rotating either pixels or image element coordinates. In some cases, as with the text legend in the center of the image, the rotated text is clearest when no aspect correction is applied, but the rest of the image is definitely distorted.

The ROTATE.PAS Demo

The image rotation facilities demonstrated in this program are designed less as plug-in utilities than as a demonstration of how image rotation procedures can be created. Four basic methods are shown: direct (pixel) image rotation and calculated image rotation; both with and without video aspect correction.

This demonstration is written primarily for EGA/VGA systems. The demo will run on CGA, but the bottom portion of the display will be off of the screen.

To begin, the program initializes the graphics system (setting the video aspect ratio), then calls ShowImageRotation and ShowCoordRotation with an angle (in degrees) for rotation. Acceptable values are *0..360*, though values outside of this range will be adjusted to fit.

```
begin
   Initialize;
   ShowLineRotation;
   Pause;
   ClearDevice;
   ShowImageRotation( 180 );
   ShowCoordRotation( 180 );
   Pause;
   CloseGraph;
end.
```

The ShowImageRotation function creates a simple screen image, then demonstrates rotation using the four methods.

```
procedure ShowImageRotation( degrees : integer );
   var
      i, j, cx, cy, Point, radius : integer;
   begin
      radius := 50;
      SetTextJustify( CenterText, TopText );
      OutTextXY( 320, 10, 'Original' );
      cx := 320;
      cy := 100;
      Circle( cx, cy, radius );
      Line( cx - radius,
            cy + round( radius * AspR ),
            cx + radius,
            cy - round( radius * AspR ) );
      Line( cx + radius,
            cy - round( radius * AspR ),
            cx + radius,
            cy - round( ( radius - 20 ) * AspR ) );
      Line( cx + radius,
            cy - round( radius * AspR ),
            cx + radius - 20,
            cy - round( radius * AspR ) );
      OutTextXY( 320, 100, 'Horizontal?' );
```

In the original image, a circle is drawn with an arrow crossing it at an angle of 45 degrees and the question *Horizontal?* is written across the center. This original image has been created in white, but now two colored circles will be written to the right and left to act as reference marks for the subsequent image rotations.

```
      SetColor(RED);
      cx := 160;
      Circle( cx, cy, radius );
      SetColor(GREEN);
      cx := 480;
      Circle( cx, cy, radius );
      SetColor(WHITE);
```

Two captions are added to show the selected rotation angle:

```
      cx := 160; cy := 30;
      OutTextXY( cx, cy, 'Figure rotated ' +
                 N2S( degrees, 3 ) + ' degrees');
      inc( cy, 10 );
      OutTextXY( cx, cy, 'without aspect correction');
      cx := 480; cy := 30;
      OutTextXY( cx, cy, 'Figure rotated ' +
                 N2S( degrees, 3 ) + ' degrees');
      inc( cy, 10 );
      OutTextXY( cx, cy, 'using aspect correction');
```

Now, the original image is rotated using RotatePoint to the left and AdjRotatePoint to the right. If you are using a VGA system (or another with a 1:1 vertical:horizontal pixel ratio), the two images will be essentially the same.

```
      for i := -50 to 50 do
      for j := -50 to 50 do
      begin
         Point := GetPixel( 320+i, 100+j );
         if Point > 0 then
         begin
            cx := i;
            cy := j;
            RotatePoint( cx, cy, degrees );
            PutPixel( 160+cx, 100+cy, Point );
            cx := i;
            cy := j;
            AdjRotatePoint( cx, cy, degrees );
            PutPixel( 480+cx, 100+cy, Point );
         end;
      end;
   end;
```

ShowCoordRotation

On the bottom half of the screen (not visible on CGA systems), two more captions are written for the coordinate rotation demonstrations.

The first coordinate rotation—in red and to the left—is done without using video aspect ratio corrections in the calculations. The *AspR* factor appearing here is the same as was used to correct the original figure, but it does not further affect the values created by the RotateLine function.

As you will notice, the text insertion that was rotated in the first half of this demonstration will not appear in this portion. Turbo Pascal does not offer provisions for fractional rotation of the graphics text fonts. Also, except for 90-degree increments, the graphic text fonts tend to appear rather distorted, even when direct image rotation is used.

```
      radius := 50;
      cx := 160;   cy := 250;
```

The x and y coordinates set the center point for the new image and the original line formulas are repeated using the new reference point.

```
         Circle( cx, cy, radius );
         RotateLine( cx, cy, degrees,
                     cx - radius,
                     cy + round( radius * AspR ),
                     cx + radius,
                     cy - round( radius * AspR ) );
```

```
          RotateLine( cx, cy, degrees,
                      cx + radius,
                      cy - round( radius * AspR ),
                      cx + radius,
                      cy - round( ( radius - 20 ) * AspR ));
          RotateLine( cx, cy, degrees,
                      cx + radius,
                      cy - round( radius * AspR ),
                      cx + radius-20,
                      cy - round( radius * AspR ) );
```

The second coordinate rotation—in green and to the right—does use video aspect ratios in the coordinate calculation.

```
     SetColor(GREEN);
     cx := 480;   cy := 250;
     Circle( cx, cy, radius );
     AdjRotateLine( cx, cy, degrees,
                    cx - radius,
                    cy + round( radius * AspR ),
                    cx + radius,
                    cy - round( radius * AspR ) );
     AdjRotateLine( cx, cy, degrees,
                    cx + radius,
                    cy - round( radius * AspR ),
                    cx + radius,
                    cy - round((radius-20) * AspR ));
     AdjRotateLine( cx, cy, degrees,
                    cx + radius,
                    cy - round( radius * AspR ),
                    cx + radius - 20,
                    cy - round( radius * AspR ) );
  end;
```

RotateLine

In the RotateLine procedure, the *cx* and *cy* parameters are the center point, *degrees* is the angle for rotation, and *x1*, *y1*, *x2*, and *y2* are the begin and end points for the line to be rotated.

```
procedure RotateLine( cx, cy, degrees,
                      x1, y1, x2, y2 : integer );
   begin
```

The begin and end coordinate pairs are converted to offsets relative to the center point coordinates.

```
        dec( x1, cx );     dec( y1, cy );
        dec( x2, cx );     dec( y2, cy );
```

The offset pairs are rotated using RotatePoint.

```
RotatePoint( x1, y1, degrees );
RotatePoint( x2, y2, degrees );
```

A new line is drawn using the Line function and passing parameters as the centerpoint coordinates, plus the x-axis and y-axis offsets returned by the RotatePoint function.

```
   Line( cx+x1, cy+y1, cx+x2, cy+y2 );
end;
```

AdjRotateLine

The AdjRotateLine procedure works the same way as RotateLine except for calling AdjRotatePoint instead of RotatePoint.

```
procedure AdjRotateLine( cx, cy, degrees,
                         x1, y1, x2, y2 : integer );
  begin
     dec( x1, cx );   dec( y1, cy );
     dec( x2, cx );   dec( y2, cy );
     AdjRotatePoint( x1, y1, degrees );
     AdjRotatePoint( x2, y2, degrees );
     Line( cx+x1, cy+y1, cx+x2, cy+y2 );
  end;
```

AdjRotatePoint

The AdjRotatePoint function is an intermediate procedure calling the Rotate-Point function after adjusting the *YOff* (y-axis offset) value using the aspect ratio. In this case, the offset is being normalized to the same value it would have if plotted against the x-axis instead of being plotted on the y-axis (or, as if the x and y pixel sizes were the same).

```
procedure AdjRotatePoint( var XOff, YOff : integer;
                          degrees : integer );
  var
     X0, Y0 : integer;
  begin
     X0 := XOff;
     Y0 := round( YOff / AspR );
     RotatePoint( X0, Y0, degrees );
```

After RotatePoint returns the rotated value, the y-axis value (*Y0*) is corrected for the screen aspect ratio.

```
     XOff := X0;
     YOff := round( Y0 * AspR );
  end;
```

Both values (the coordinate pair) are returned to the calling function after rotation.

RotatePoint

The RotatePoint function carries out the actual calculations, accepting x-axis and y-axis offset values (which may be positive or negative distances) and the rotation angle in degrees.

```
procedure RotatePoint( var X, Y : integer;
                       degrees : integer );
   var
      X0, Y0, HypLen, AngR, AngO : real;
      SnX, SnY : integer;
   begin
      Y0 := Y;
      X0 := X;
      SnX := 1;
      SnY := 1;
      if X < 0 then
      begin
         SnX := -1;
         SnY := -1;
      end;
```

The offset parameters are accepted as local variables of type *real*. At the same time, preliminary values are calculated for the magnitude (+/–) of the final calculated values.

Since Turbo Pascal lacks C's hypot function, an equivalent function conveniently returns a vector distance calculated from the two offset values.

```
      HypLen := Hypot( X0, Y0 );
```

And the vector angle is calculated, using the offset coordinates, as a value in radians.

```
      if abs( X0 ) > 0
         then AngO := ArcTan( -1 * Y0 / X0 )
         else if Y0 < 0 then AngO :=      PI / 2
                        else AngO := 3 * PI / 2;
```

If the absolute value of *X0* is greater than 0, atan2 returns the angle in radians. Alternatively, if *X0* is zero, then the y-axis offset is the determining factor and the angle can be either *PI/2* or *3*PI/2*, depending on whether the y-axis offset is positive or negative.

The value in *degrees* is also converted to a local parameter value in radians and the original angle (*AngO*) is added.

```
      AngR := Ang0 + ( degrees / 180 ) * PI;
      if AngR >= 2*PI then AngR := AngR - 2 * Pi;
```

If the result is greater than *2*PI*, *AngR* is returned to the normal range (*0..2*PI*).

The next step is to check which quadrant *AngR* falls in and assign the necessary vector polarity. This is because the vector coordinates will be calculated as absolute values and the *SnX* and *SnY* flags will be used to determine the actual sign (+/-) of the results. This is done as a correction for the fact that the calculated coordinate values will not match the coordinate values needed for screen positions.

```
      if ( AngR > 0 ) AND ( AngR <= PI )
         then SnY := SnY * -1;
      if ( AngR > PI/2 ) AND ( AngR <= 3*PI/2 )
         then SnX := SnX * -1;
```

Now the vector distance (*HypLen*) and the rotated vector angle (*AngR*) are returned to the new coordinate values (*X0* and *Y0*). Depending on which half of the quadrants (see Figure 11-1) *AngR* falls in, either *X0* is calculated using the cosine or *Y0* is calculated using the sine of the angle with the other coordinate calculated as the remaining side of a right triangle.

```
      if ( AngR >= PI/4 ) AND ( AngR <= 3*PI/4 ) OR
         ( AngR >= 5*PI/4 ) AND ( AngR <= 7*PI/4 ) then
      begin
         X0 := HypLen * cos( AngR );
         Y0 := sqrt( sqr( HypLen ) - sqr( X0 ) );
      end else
      begin
         Y0 := HypLen * sin( AngR );
         X0 := sqrt( sqr( HypLen ) - sqr( Y0 ) );
      end;
```

Finally, the absolute values of *X0* and *Y0* are converted to integer values, multiplied by their sign, and returned as *X* and *Y* coordinates.

```
      X := round( abs( X0 ) ) * SnX;
      Y := round( abs( Y0 ) ) * SnY;
   end;
```

Vector Calculations

I've shown you how to rotate a point, but haven't explained in any detail the why or how of it. If your high school or college trig is a bit rusty, you may be wondering about the previous calculations.

Let me first remind you of a few facts that you already know, but which you need to keep firmly in the forefront of your mind in order to understand what's happening here.

With computer graphics, all screen positions are described as x,y coordinates beginning with a 0,0 coordinate in the upper-left corner of the screen. The upper-left screen position is normally referenced as 1,1 in Turbo Pascal or in Turbo C, but, to the computer, this is still the 0,0 reference point (and before DOS receives the C or Pascal coordinates they are changed to match this zero-origin system).

In screen coordinates, x-axis values increase from left to right and y-axis values increase from top to bottom. All of this should be familiar to computer programmers.

In the Cartesian coordinate system (rectangular parallel coordinates), however, the x-axis values also increase from left to right (with negative values left of the 0,0 coordinate), but the y-axis values increase from bottom to top with the negative values on the y-axis lying below the 0,0 coordinate. Since the Cartesian coordinate system is well established (predating computers) it has priority and all trigometric conversions from x,y coordinate values assume Cartesian values initially. Likewise, all conversions from polar coordinates (vector angle and magnitude) yield results compatible with the Cartesian system, not the screen coordinate system. Therefore, some minor—but important—adaptations will be necessary.

But first, in order to rotate an image, a center point for rotation is required and this point becomes a new 0,0 reference point, though it has no relationship to the screen origin 0,0 point. This center point reference is quite arbitrary, is for local (program) reference only, and can be anywhere on the screen (or even off the screen, if you desire).

Each rotated point, however, is now referenced in terms of an X and Y offset from this 0,0 coordinate. If the center point is located at screen coordinates 100,145 and the point to be rotated is at screen coordinates 50,175, then the rotation coordinates will be −50,30. (By convention, the x-axis coordinate is always given first, and the first coordinate is always the x-axis.)

In Chapter 10, left-right and mirror image transformations were made simply by changing the sign of the offset (relative to a new center coordinate). True rotation, however, cannot be accomplished this easily and requires something other than the x,y coordinate system.

To rotate a point, the point's x,y coordinates must first be converted to a polar vector. A vector consists of two values: an angle and a length. For our purposes, the angle will always be in the range $0..2*PI$ $(0..360°)$ and the length (magnitude) will always be a positive value. Negative vector angles and angles greater than $2*PI$ are possible and valid as are negative vector magnitudes, but since these can always be normalized without loss of information, only normalized vectors are used in these calculations (besides, it's simpler).

Since engineers were among the principal earlier users of computers, and engineers—bless their tinker-toy hearts—prefer radian angles to degree/minute/second angles, computer trig functions commonly use angles expressed in radians instead of degrees. While both systems begin with a zero angle, 180 degrees equals PI radians and 360 degrees equals 2*PI radians, while other angles are commonly expressed either as decimal radians or as radian fractions (see Figure 11-1).

Figure 11-1: Sine/Cosine Angle Values

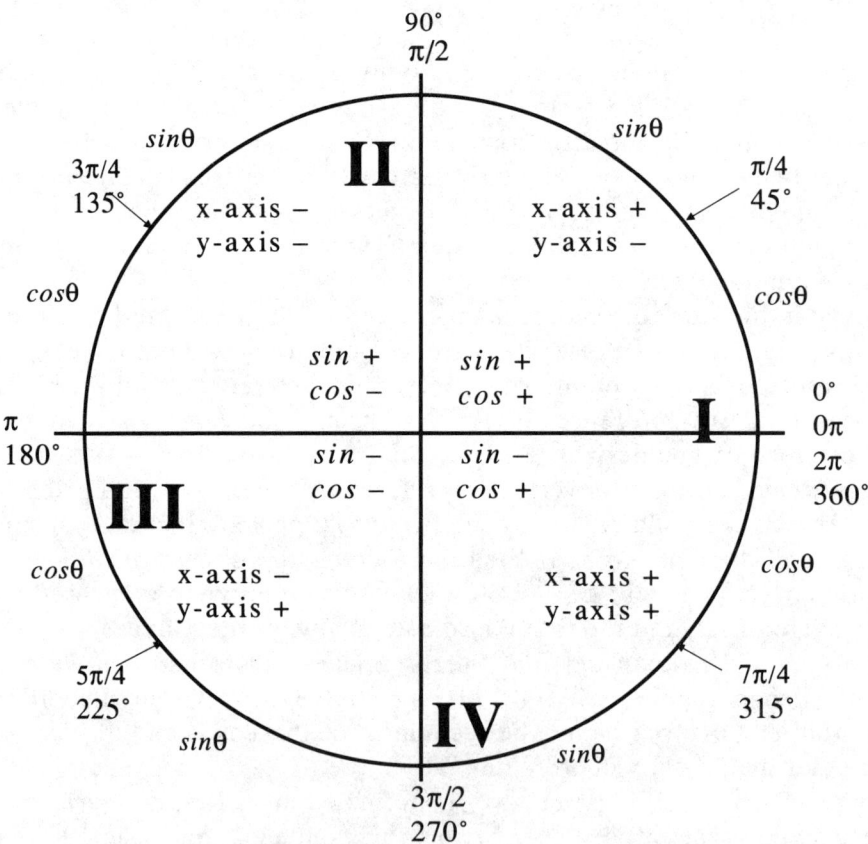

Angle values are shown both in radians and degrees. The signs for the sine and cosines of angles in each quadrant are shown for normal polar coordinates, while the x-axis and y-axis signs are shown for the screen coordinate system.

Now, back to calculating a polar (vector) coordinate from the screen position coordinates. To get the vector magnitude (*HypLen*), the Hypot function returns the square root of the sum of the squares of the two arguments (following the Pythagorean Theorem):

```
HypLen = Hypot( X0, Y0 );
```

And the ArcTan function conveniently transforms the x,y coordinates into a vector angle, with one exception: an x-offset value of 0.

```
AngO := ArcTan( -1 * Y0 / X0 )
```

Before covering the exception, however, there is another point to discuss.

Notice the *–1* in the above formula? The value for *Y0* is precisely opposite in sign to what the ArcTan function expects because the normal math functions treat positive values as 1st Quadrant points. This means that a positive value for *Y0* is expected to be above the 0,0 coordinate, as if the screen 0,0 point were at the bottom-left corner of the screen.

Since this is a screen coordinate system, however, a positive vertical value is down and negative is up; therefore, *Y0* is multiplied by –1 to change its sign before the angle is calculated (and this discrepancy between normal and screen coordinates will appear again in these calculations).

The ArcTan function returns values in the range *–PI..PI* and is accurate when the *x* parameter approaches 0, but not helpful when the *x* parameter equals zero (and the angles could be *PI/2* or *–PI/2*). If the value of *X0* is zero, then the *Y0* parameter is used to determine the angle:

```
    else if Y0 < 0 then AngO :=     PI / 2
                   else AngO := 3 * PI / 2;
```

The x,y coordinates have been converted to a vector angle and magnitude (size, length, distance) which can be rotated. Rotation becomes a simple matter of adding the rotation angle to the vector angle (or subtracting the rotation angle, but here rotation has been limited to the counter-clockwise direction). That's it. The vector has been rotated.

This has been the easy part—the vector must be restored to x,y coordinates before it can be used, which is the whole point of doing this.

Again, please refer to Figure 11-1. The original and rotation angles have already been summed together as *AngR*. If the value of *AngR* lies in the range *PI/2..3*PI/2* then the vector is in the 2nd or 3rd quadrants and sign of X is inverted. (*SnX* and *SnY* were initialized as +1 and then adjusted for the original angle's quadrant.)

```
if ( AngR > PI/2 ) AND ( AngR <= 3*PI/2 )
    then SnX := SnX * -1;
```

Likewise, if the value of *AngR* lies in the range *0..PI*, the vector angle is in the 1st or 2nd quadrants and the sign of Y is inverted for the screen coordinate system, which is the only one that counts here.

```
if ( AngR > 0 ) AND ( AngR <= PI )
   then SnY := SnY * -1;
```

Normally, the sign of the sine of the angle would determine the sign of X, while the sign of the cosine of the angle would determine the sign of Y—except that in the screen coordinate system, this would be correct for X and invalid for Y and the x,y results are going to be calculated in a slightly different manner.

If the angle lies in the range *PI/4..3*PI/4* or in the range *5*PI/4..7*PI/4*, then the x-axis value (*X0*) will be calculated using the cosine of the angle and the y-axis value will be calculated as the square root of the difference of the squares of the remaining sides (again, using the Pythagorean Theorem).

```
if ( AngR >= PI/4 ) AND ( AngR <= 3*PI/4 ) OR
   ( AngR >= 5*PI/4 ) AND ( AngR <= 7*PI/4 ) then
begin
   X0 := HypLen * cos( AngR );
   Y0 := sqrt( sqr( HypLen ) - sqr( X0 ) );
end else
```

Otherwise, the same calculations are carried out, but using the sin of the angle to find the y-axis value and using Pythagoras' rule for the x-axis.

```
begin
   Y0 := HypLen * sin( AngR );
   X0 := sqrt( sqr( HypLen ) - sqr( Y0 ) );
end;
```

The reason for this is accuracy. By using sin and cos only within the angle ranges where each yields the greatest accuracy (using sin where the y-axis value is greater than the x-axis value and cos where the x-axis value is greater), and calculating the remaining value using the Pythagorean Theorem, the resulting position coordinates are as accurate as possible and the image rotation is smoother. This is also why the local variables, *X0* and *Y0*, are *real* rather than *integer* values.

Notice also the italicized *sin*θ and *cos*θ in Figure 11-1 showing the ranges where each function yields the greater accuracy.

Now, since either the x or y value was calculated using the square root function, one of these is a positive value. (Since the square root of a number could be either positive or negative, sqrt always returns a positive value.) If only the sin and cos functions had been used, then the y-axis value could simply be inverted (multiplied by −1) to correct it for the screen coordinate system. Instead, the absolute values of both *X0* and *Y0* are multiplied by the sign values determined earlier, then returned as screen coordinate integers.

```
X = round( abs( X0 ) ) * SnX;
Y = round( abs( Y0 ) ) * SnY;
```

If this is confusing, please refer to the text and to Figure 11-1, remembering that the coordinate values used are screen coordinates, that the y-axis values are negative toward the top of the screen, and that the angle increases in the counterclockwise direction. It really isn't a matter of difficulty as much as of careful calculations and making allowance for the differences between the Cartesian coordinate system and the screen coordinate system.

Other Image Rotation Options

When the direct image rotation was demonstrated, each pixel was tested and the background pixels were ignored. Further selective rotation could be applied, however, and different color values could be rotated separately, by different angles or in different directions.

Since in EGA/VGA modes the same color hues can be assigned to different palette entries and rotation can be made on the basis of the palette entry rather than the actual hue, it becomes practical to rotate one part of an image while leaving another portion—apparently the same color—unaffected.

Including Text Rotations

Earlier, when discussing graphics text options, I pointed out the fact that only two text orientations were supported. Using direct image rotation even upside-down text becomes possible and, with care, some other text angles are practical though not as convenient as the directly supported text presentations.

Summary

These are tools for your usage, develop and employ them as you see fit. The possibilities, if not endless, are certainly vast and a bit of imagination should suggest a variety of interesting options.

FILEIMG.PAS

```
{=====================================}
{     Saving an image as a data file  }
{=====================================}

uses GRAPH, CRT;
const
```

```pascal
      pflash : array[ 1..18 ] of integer =
            ( 100, 40, 110, 60, 100, 70, 120, 65, 140, 80,
              130, 60, 140, 50, 120, 55, 100, 40 );
var
   GraphDriver,
   GraphMode,
   MaxColors,
   ErrorCode : integer;
   Size, xasp, yasp : word;
   AspectRatio : real;
   Flash, Flash2 : pointer;
function N2S( Val, Digit: integer ): string;
   var
      Buffer : string[10];
   begin
      str( Val:Digit, Buffer );
      N2S := Buffer;
   end;
procedure Pause;
   var
      Ch : char;
   begin
      while KeyPressed do Ch := ReadKey;
      Ch := ReadKey;
   end;
procedure Initialize;
   begin
      GraphDriver := DETECT;
      InitGraph( GraphDriver, GraphMode, '\TP\BGI' );
      ErrorCode := GraphResult;
      if ErrorCode <> grOk then
      begin
         writeln(' Graphics System Error: ',
                   GraphErrorMsg( ErrorCode ) );
         halt( 1 );
      end;
      MaxColors := GetMaxColor;
      GetAspectRatio( xasp, yasp );
      AspectRatio := xasp / yasp;
   end;
function SaveImage( left, top, right, bottom: integer;
                    var size: word ): pointer;
   var
      image : pointer;
   begin
      size := ImageSize( left, top, right, bottom );
```

Chapter 11: Image Manipulation and Image Files

```
            GetMem( image, size );
            GetImage( left, top, right, bottom, image^ );
            PutImage( left, top, image^, XOrPut );
            SaveImage := image;
         end;
   procedure FileImage( image: pointer; xsize, ysize: byte;
   filename: string );
      var
         f : file of byte;        i, j : integer;
         k : byte;                size : word;
      begin
         size := xsize * ysize;
      {  SetActivePage( 1 );   }
      {  SetVisualPage( 1 );   }
         PutImage( 100, 100, image^, CopyPut );
         assign( f, FileName );
         rewrite( f );
         write( f, xsize );
         write( f, ysize );
         for i := 0 to xsize do
            for j := 0 to ysize do
            begin
               k := GetPixel( 100+i, 100+j );
               write( f, k );
            end;
         close( f );
         PutImage( 100, 100, image^, XOrPut );
      {  SetActivePage( 0 );   }
      {  SetVisualPage( 0 );   }
      end;
   function ReadImage( filename: string ): pointer;
      var
         i, j : integer;         f : file of byte;
         size : word;            xsize, ysize, k : byte;
         temp : pointer;
      begin
      {  SetActivePage( 1 );   }
      {  SetVisualPage( 1 );   }
         assign( f, filename );
         reset( f );
         read( f, xsize );
         read( f, ysize );
         size := xsize * ysize;
         for i := 0 to xsize do
            for j := 0 to ysize do
            begin
               read( f, k );
```

```pascal
                PutPixel( 200+i, 200+j, k );
            end;
        close( f );
        size := ImageSize( 0, 0, xsize, ysize );
        temp := SaveImage( 200, 200,
                          200+xsize, 200+ysize, size );
    {   SetActivePage( 0 );   }
    {   SetVisualPage( 0 );   }
        ReadImage := temp;
    end;
begin
    Initialize;
    randomize;
    SetColor( random(MaxColors)+1 );
    SetFillStyle( random(11)+1, random(MaxColors)+1 );
    FillPoly( sizeof( pflash ) div sizeof( PointType ),
              pflash );
    Flash := SaveImage( 100, 40, 140, 80, Size );
    FileImage( Flash, 40, 40, 'IMAGE.OUT' );
    Flash2 := ReadImage( 'IMAGE.OUT' );
    PutImage( 300, 300, Flash2^, CopyPut );
    Pause;
    dispose( Flash );
    dispose( Flash2 );
    CloseGraph;
end.
```

ROTATE.PAS

```pascal
    {=================================================}
    { Rotating an image using Turbo Pascal Graphics }
    {=================================================}
uses GRAPH, CRT;

var
    GraphDriver,
    GraphMode,
    MaxColors,
    ErrorCode : integer;
    AspR : real;
    xasp, yasp : word;
function N2S( Val, Digit : integer ): string;
    var
        Buffer : string;
    begin
        str( Val:Digit, Buffer );
        N2S := Buffer;
    end;
```

```pascal
function R2S( Val: real; Digit, Decimal : integer ):
string;
   var
      Buffer : string;
   begin
      str( Val:Digit:Decimal, Buffer );
      R2S := Buffer;
   end;
procedure Initialize;
   begin
      GraphDriver := DETECT;
      InitGraph( GraphDriver, GraphMode, '\TP\BGI' );
      ErrorCode := GraphResult;
      if ErrorCode <> grOk then
      begin
         writeln(' Graphics System Error: ',
                 GraphErrorMsg( ErrorCode ) );
         halt( 1 );
      end;
      MaxColors := GetMaxColor + 1;
      GetAspectRatio( xasp, yasp );
      AspR := xasp / yasp;
   end;
procedure Pause;
   var
      Ch : char;
   begin
      SetColor(WHITE);
      SetTextJustify( CenterText, BottomText );
      OutTextXY( GetMaxX div 2, GetMaxY,
                 'press any key ...' );
      while KeyPressed do Ch := ReadKey;
      Ch := ReadKey;
   end;
procedure ClearLabel( cx, cy : integer; Txt : string );
   begin
      SetViewPort( cx-200, cy-4, cx+200, cy+6, True );
      ClearViewPort;
      SetViewPort( 0, 0, GetMaxX, GetMaxY, True );
      OutTextXY( cx, cy, Txt );
   end;
function Hypot( X, Y : real ): real;
   begin
      Hypot := sqrt( sqr( X ) + sqr( Y ) );
   end;
procedure RotatePoint( var X, Y : integer;
```

```pascal
                        degrees : integer );
   var
      X0, Y0, HypLen, AngR, AngO : real;
      SnX, SnY : integer;
begin
   Y0 := Y;
   X0 := X;
   SnX := 1;
   SnY := 1;
   if X < 0 then
   begin
      SnX := -1;
      SnY := -1;
   end;
   HypLen := Hypot( X0, Y0 );
   if abs( X0 ) > 0
      then AngO := ArcTan( -1 * Y0 / X0 )
      else if Y0 < 0 then AngO :=     PI / 2
                     else AngO := 3 * PI / 2;
   AngR := AngO + ( degrees / 180 ) * PI;
   if AngR >= 2*PI then AngR := AngR - 2 * Pi;
   if ( AngR > 0 ) AND
      ( AngR <= PI )
      then SnY := SnY * -1;
   if ( AngR > PI/2 ) AND
      ( AngR <= 3*PI/2 )
      then SnX := SnX * -1;
   if ( AngR >= PI/4 ) AND ( AngR <= 3*PI/4 ) OR
      ( AngR >= 5*PI/4 ) AND ( AngR <= 7*PI/4 ) then
   begin
      X0 := HypLen * cos( AngR );
      Y0 := sqrt( sqr( HypLen ) - sqr( X0 ) );
   end else
   begin
      Y0 := HypLen * sin( AngR );
      X0 := sqrt( sqr( HypLen ) - sqr( Y0 ) );
   end;
   X := round( abs( X0 ) ) * SnX;
   Y := round( abs( Y0 ) ) * SnY;
end;
procedure AdjRotatePoint( var XOff, YOff : integer;
degrees : integer );
   var
      X0, Y0 : integer;
   begin
      X0 := XOff;
      Y0 := round( YOff / AspR );
      RotatePoint( X0, Y0, degrees );
```

```
            XOff := X0;
            YOff := round( Y0 * AspR );
        end;
    procedure RotateLine( cx, cy, degrees,
                          x1, y1, x2, y2 : integer );
        begin
            dec( x1, cx );    dec( y1, cy );
            dec( x2, cx );    dec( y2, cy );
            RotatePoint( x1, y1, degrees );
            RotatePoint( x2, y2, degrees );
            Line( cx+x1, cy+y1, cx+x2, cy+y2 );
        end;
    procedure AdjRotateLine( cx, cy, degrees,
                             x1, y1, x2, y2 : integer );
        begin
            dec( x1, cx );    dec( y1, cy );
            dec( x2, cx );    dec( y2, cy );
            AdjRotatePoint( x1, y1, degrees );
            AdjRotatePoint( x2, y2, degrees );
            Line( cx+x1, cy+y1, cx+x2, cy+y2 );
        end;
    procedure ShowImageRotation( degrees : integer );
        var
            i, j, cx, cy, Point, radius : integer;
        begin
            radius := 50;
            SetTextJustify( CenterText, TopText );
            OutTextXY( 320, 10, 'Original' );
            cx := 320;
            cy := 100;
            Circle( cx, cy, radius );
            Line( cx - radius,
                  cy + round( radius * AspR ),
                  cx + radius,
                  cy - round( radius * AspR ) );
            Line( cx + radius,
                  cy - round( radius * AspR ),
                  cx + radius,
                  cy - round( ( radius - 20 ) * AspR ) );
            Line( cx + radius,
                  cy - round( radius * AspR ),
                  cx + radius - 20,
                  cy - round( radius * AspR ) );
            OutTextXY( 320, 100, 'Horizontal?' );
            SetColor(RED);
            cx := 160;
            Circle( cx, cy, radius );
```

```pascal
            SetColor(GREEN);
            cx := 480;
            Circle( cx, cy, radius );
            SetColor(WHITE);
            cx := 160; cy := 30;
            OutTextXY( cx, cy, 'Figure rotated ' +
                       N2S( degrees, 3 ) + ' degrees');
            inc( cy, 10 );
            OutTextXY( cx, cy, 'without aspect correction');
            cx := 480; cy := 30;
            OutTextXY( cx, cy, 'Figure rotated ' +
                       N2S( degrees, 3 ) + ' degrees');
            inc( cy, 10 );
            OutTextXY( cx, cy, 'using aspect correction');
            for i := -50 to 50 do
            for j := -50 to 50 do
            begin
                Point := GetPixel( 320+i, 100+j );
                if Point > 0 then
                begin
                    cx := i;
                    cy := j;
                    RotatePoint( cx, cy, degrees );
                    PutPixel( 160+cx, 100+cy, Point );
                    cx := i;
                    cy := j;
                    AdjRotatePoint( cx, cy, degrees );
                    PutPixel( 480+cx, 100+cy, Point );
                end;
            end;
        end;
    procedure ShowCoordRotation( degrees : integer );
        var
            i, j, cx, cy, Point, radius : integer;
        begin
            radius := 50;
            cx := 160; cy := 180;
            OutTextXY( cx, cy, 'Coordinates rotated ' +
                       N2S( degrees, 3 ) + ' degrees');
            inc( cy, 10 );
            OutTextXY( cx, cy, 'without aspect correction');
            cx := 480; cy := 180;
            OutTextXY( cx, cy, 'Coordinates rotated ' +
                       N2S( degrees, 3 ) + ' degrees');
            inc( cy, 10 );
            OutTextXY( cx, cy, 'using aspect correction');
            SetColor(RED);
            cx := 160;   cy := 250;
```

```
            Circle( cx, cy, radius );
            RotateLine( cx, cy, degrees,
                        cx - radius,
                        cy + round( radius * AspR ),
                        cx + radius,
                        cy - round( radius * AspR ) );
            RotateLine( cx, cy, degrees,
                        cx + radius,
                        cy - round( radius * AspR ),
                        cx + radius,
                        cy - round( ( radius - 20 ) * AspR ));
            RotateLine( cx, cy, degrees,
                        cx + radius,
                        cy - round( radius * AspR ),
                        cx + radius-20,
                        cy - round( radius * AspR ) );
            SetColor(GREEN);
            cx := 480;  cy := 250;
            Circle( cx, cy, radius );
            AdjRotateLine( cx, cy, degrees,
                           cx - radius,
                           cy + round( radius * AspR ),
                           cx + radius,
                           cy - round( radius * AspR ) );
            AdjRotateLine( cx, cy, degrees,
                           cx + radius,
                           cy - round( radius * AspR ),
                           cx + radius,
                           cy - round((radius-20) * AspR ));
            AdjRotateLine( cx, cy, degrees,
                           cx + radius,
                           cy - round( radius * AspR ),
                           cx + radius - 20,
                           cy - round( radius * AspR ) );
     end;
procedure ShowLineRotation;
    var
        X0, Y0, X1, Y1, i, j : integer;
    begin
        X0 := 60;
        Y0 := 60;
        OutTextXY( 10, 10,
                   ' Line rotated in 10 degree steps ');
        Line( 150, 100, 150+X0, 100+Y0 );
        j := 1;
        for i := 1 to 35 do
        begin
            inc( j );
```

```
            if j >= MaxColors then j := 1;
            if MaxColors > 4 then SetColor( j );
            X1 := X0;
            Y1 := round( Y0 / AspR );
            RotatePoint( X1, Y1, i * 10 );
            Line( 150, 100, 150 + X1,
                  round( 100 + Y1 * AspR ) );
            delay( 100 );
         end;
    end;
begin
    Initialize;
    ShowLineRotation;
    Pause;
    ClearDevice;
    ShowImageRotation( 180 );
    ShowCoordRotation( 180 );
    Pause;
    CloseGraph;
end.
```

CHAPTER 12

Colors and Color Selection

This chapter is concerned primarily with colors and color selections in EGA/VGA modes and, secondarily, with CGA and Monochrome systems.

This restriction is not intended as a put down of CGA or Monochrome video modes, but is simply a recognition of the fact that CGA systems have limited color capabilities and Monochrome systems have effectively none.

Video Signal Cues

On Monochrome systems, graphic video output is limited to two bits of information per pixel: a video on/off and an intensity bit (see Table 12-1).

Table 12-1: System Video Attributes

BIT #	MONOCHROME	COLOR RGBI	COLOR EGA
0	n/a	Blue	Primary Blue
1	n/a	Green	Primary Green
2	n/a	Red	Primary Red
3	Video	n/a	Secondary Blue
4	Intensity	Intensity	Secondary Green
5	n/a	n/a	Secondary Red

On CGA systems, the **RGBI** (**R**ed, **G**reen, **B**lue, and **I**ntensity) color system is used with four bits of information per graphics pixel, but combinations are limited to four, predefined palettes of three colors plus background color (as shown in Table 12-3). The background color in each palette is BLACK by default, but can be selected from the entire range of 16 colors shown in Table 12-2.

Table 12-2: CGA Color Values

COLOR DEC	VALUES HEX	4-BIT BINARY	COLOR COMPONENTS	CONSTANT/COLOR NAME
0	0	0000	. . . .	Black
1	1	0001	. . . B	Blue
2	2	0010	. . G .	Green
3	3	0011	. . G B	Cyan
4	4	0100	. R . .	Red
5	5	0101	. R . B	Magenta
6	6	0110	. R G .	Brown
7	7	0111	. R G B	LightGray
8	8	1000	I . . .	DarkGray
9	9	1001	I . . B	LightBlue
10	A	1010	I . G .	LightGreen
11	B	1011	I . G B	LightCyan
12	C	1100	I R . .	LightRed
13	D	1101	I R . B	LightMagenta
14	E	1110	I R G .	Yellow
15	F	1111	I R G B	White

On EGA/VGA systems, the **RrGgBb** color system uses six bits of information per pixel for a total of 64 colors/hues. The default colors for this palette are shown in Table 12-4.

CGA Colors

For CGA systems, 16 possible colors are supported, as shown in Table 12-2. In text modes, any of these colors can be selected as foreground color, though only the first eight colors are valid as background colors. Using Turbo C graphics, the AT&T driver (modes ATT400C0..ATT400C3) and the MCGA driver (modes MCGAC0..MCGAC3) operate in the same fashion as CGA modes, CGAC0..CGAC3. Similarly, color operation in the CGAHI mode is duplicated by the MCGAMED, MCGAHI, ATT400MED, and ATT400HI modes.

As shown in Table 12-2, each color is defined by four register bits controlling the red, green, and blue hues and an intensity control. Each hue (color gun) has two settings: low and high intensity. When the Intensity bit is TRUE

(ON), all color guns are set high. If Intensity is FALSE, all color guns respond as low.

Table 12-3: CGA Color Palette

PALETTE COLOR	HEX	4-BIT BINARY	COLOR COMPONENTS	CONSTANT/COLOR NAME
PALETTE NUMBER 0 (CGAC0)				+
0	0	0000	. . . .	Black
1	A	1010	I . G .	LightGreen
2	B	1100	I R . .	LightRed
3	C	1110	I R G .	Yellow
PALETTE NUMBER 1 (CGAC1)				+
0	0	0000	. . . .	Black
1	B	1011	I . G B	LightCyan
2	D	1101	I R . B	LightMagenta
3	F	1111	I R G B	White
PALETTE NUMBER 2 (CGAC2)				
0	0	0000	. . . .	Black
1	2	0010	. . G .	Green
2	4	0100	. R . .	Red
3	6	0110	. R G .	Brown
PALETTE NUMBER 3 (CGAC3)				
0	0	0000	. . . .	Black
1	3	0011	. . G B	Cyan
2	5	0101	. R . B	Magenta
3	7	0111	.R G B	LightGray

Blue is generated by turning on the blue gun at low intensity; LightBlue also turns on the blue gun, but because of the Intensity flag, is turned on high and produces a brighter color. In the same fashion, turning on both the green and blue guns produces Cyan; adding the Intensity signal produces LightCyan.

As a minor oddity, notice that enabling the Intensity signal alone (with the red, green, and blue guns off), still produces a response from all three of the color guns, though their output is very low, and the result is DarkGray. You might consider this a bug that has been turned into a feature.

In graphics modes, the CGA system supports multiple colors only in the four low resolution, 320x200 pixel modes (C0, C1, C2, and C3). Each of these modes selects one of the predefined 4-color palettes shown in Table 12-3.

By default, the background color in each palette is Black, but may be changed to any of the 16 CGA colors (see Table 12-2) using the SetBkColor function. The SetPalette and SetAllPalette functions—used in EGA/VGA modes to change palette colors—are not applicable in CGA modes. There is, however, one exception: the function SetPalette(PaletteIndex, color) can be used with a *PaletteIndex* of zero (background), as an alternative to the SetBkColor function.

The CGA colors Blue (value 1), DarkGray (value 8), and LightBlue (value 9) do not appear in any of the defined palettes. These can, of course, be used as background colors.

Table 12-4: EGA/VGA Default Palette

PALETTE REGISTER	DEFAULT HEX	COLOR VALUE 6-BIT BINARY	COLOR COMPONENTS	CONSTANTS/ COLOR NAME
0	0	000 000	. . . . . .	EGABlack
1	1	000 001	. . . . . B	EGABlue
2	2	000 010	. . . . G .	EGAGreen
3	3	000 011	. . . . G B	EGACyan
4	4	000 100	. . . R . .	EGARed
5	5	000 101	. . . R . B	EGAMagenta
6	14	010 100	. g . R . .	EGABrown
7	7	000 111	. . . R G B	EGALightGray
8	38	111 000	r g b . . .	EGADarkGray
9	39	111 001	r g b . . B	EGALightBlue
A	3A	111 010	r g b . G .	EGALightGreen
B	3B	111 011	r g b . G B	EGALightCyan
C	3C	111 100	r g b R . .	EGALightRed
D	3D	111 101	r g b R . B	EGALightMagenta
E	3E	111 110	r g b R G .	EGAYellow
F	3F	111 111	r g b R G B	EGAWhite

CGA High Resolution

In any of the high resolution modes (CGAHi, MCGAMed, or ATT400Med at 640x200 pixels; MCGAHi at 640x480 pixels or ATT400Hi at 640x400 pixels), two colors are supported: a black background and a color foreground. The foreground color is selected from the 16 CGA colors using the SetBkColor function. *No, this is not an error.* Due to a quirk in the CGA hardware, the SetBkColor function is used to select the CGAHi foreground color. The background color remains black. All pixels with a value of 1 are displayed in the foreground color, pixels with a value of 0 remain black.

The IBM8514 and VGA Video Adapters

At the other extreme, the highest color resolution is provided by the IBM-8514 video card and the IBM8514 mode or by the VGA video card using the VGA256.BGI driver (see Appendix E), both of which are supported by the SetRGBPalette function.

The SetRGBPalette function allows custom color definition for a palette of 256 colors. To maintain compatibility with other video adapters, however, the first 16 palette entries are predefined by the .BGI drivers to correspond to the default EGA/VGA color palette entries.

All 256 palette entries (numbered 0..255) can be defined individually by three integer color arguments: red, green, and blue. While the arguments passed to the SetRGBPalette function are integer values, only the six most-significant bits of the lower (LSB) byte are actually used to set the palette color value (values from 0 to 252 in steps of four, i.e., arguments of 252, 253, 254, and 255 are treated identically since the six most-significant bits are the same and only the two least-significant bits differ).

EGA/VGA Color

EGA/VGA video modes offer a palette of 16 colors selected from a spectrum of 64 possible hues. In actual fact, VGA systems are capable of wider color ranges, having 256 color registers and 256 possible hues. When using Turbo Pascal procedures, they are effectively limited to the EGA color range, though they still support the higher resolutions. For information on developing special handling for VGA color systems, see Appendix E.

For the present, the topic is restricted to color handling within the capabilities of Turbo Pascal and restricted to the EGA color range of 64 hues.

The EGA/VGA modes also begin with a default palette of 16 hues. Unlike the CGA color system using 4-bit colors, each EGA/VGA color is defined by a 6-bit value. This is commonly called an **RrGgBb** color system.

The **RrGgBb** color system provides two flags (and two signals) for each of the three color guns: a primary **R**ed and secondary **r**ed, a primary **B**lue and secondary **b**lue, and a primary **G**reen and secondary **g**reen. (By custom, the primary color is capitalized and the secondary is in lowercase.)

It may help to think of the **RrGgBb** system as analogous to the **RBGI** system, except that the secondary colors act as individual intensity flags for each of the primary color guns.

Just as DarkGray was created in CGA by turning on the Intensity flag but leaving off all of the color flags, EGADarkGray turns on the **rgb** (intensity) flags while leaving the **RGB** (primary) color guns turned off. On the other hand, where the CGA system created Brown by mixing the Red and Green guns, EGABrown is created by mixing the Red color gun with the green intensity flag—mixing Red with a very low Green produces a deep Brown.

Aside from the EGABrown, the default palette colors for EGA/VGA are the same as the CGA colors except that three intensity signals (**rgb**) are used in place of a single intensity flag—gang-controlling all three color guns.

A Wider Range of Hues

One of the advantages of EGA/VGA, in addition to being able to use 16 colors in high resolution modes, is being able to select your palette from 64 separate hues.

To be frank, some of these 64 colors are not particularly appealing and the precise tone of a particular hue is subject to the color balance adjustments on the monitor used, but beauty is, as always, in the eye and monitor of the beholder. For an example of the range of color, Table 12-5 shows 11 varieties of yellow, ranging from a color value of 06, which matches the CGA Brown to a color value of 62, which corresponds to EGAYellow.

Table 12-5: EGA Yellows

COLOR VALUES			
DEC	HEX	6-BIT BINARY	SECONDARY AND PRIMARY COMPONENTS
06	06h	000 110	. . . R G .
14	0Eh	001 110	. . b R G .
18	12h	010 010	. g . . G .
22	16h	010 110	. g . R G .
26	1Ah	011 010	. g b . G .
30	1Eh	011 110	. g b R G .
38	26h	100 110	r . . R G .
46	2Eh	101 110	r . b R G .
54	36h	110 110	r g . R G .
55	37h	110 111	r g . R G B
62	3Eh	111 110	r g b R G .

Looking at the color components shown in Table 12-5, you will notice all of the yellows include Green and, with two exceptions, blend Red. In one case, color value 18, is actually high intensity Green, but depending on the surrounding colors and background, this may be recognized as either Yellow, Green, or Chartreuse. The precise recognition and label applied to any color is largely a matter of subjective perception.

Manipulating Color and Hue

In the EGA/VGA color system, specific color values can be created by manipulating the combinations of primary and secondary flags for each color gun. Each of the three color guns has four settings: completely off, low intensity (color off, intensity on), normal (color on, intensity off), and high (color on, intensity on)—for a total of 43 or 64 colors.

If you need to manipulate colors directly, these bit-values can be set directly to build a specific color value, then you can assign the created value to the EGA/VGA palette.

For example, suppose that you need three pure greens. Bit 1 controls the Green color gun (bit 0 at the right is blue) and bit 4 is the Green intensity flag, so the three pure greens would be 16 (010 000 or **.g. . . .**), 2 (000 010 or **. . . .G.**), and 18 (010 010 or **.g. .G.**), in order of intensity.

The first green (color value 16) is a dark green, appearing as khaki against some backgrounds. The second (color value 2) is a pure green and corresponds to EGAGreen, while the third green (color value 18) is a bright or chartreuse green and, depending on surroundings, appears almost yellow (and, if you noticed, is also included in the yellows in Table 12-5).

But there is another green that does not appear among these possibilities. This fourth green is EGALightGreen, color value 58 (111 010 or **rgb .G.**). In this case, the **rgb** produces DarkGray (which, since we're working with light emission and not color absorption/reflection, is also soft white). The dark gray is added to the Green color gun for a lighter green without becoming chartreuse.

To show some of these relationships and to provide a convenient method of examining the variety of possible colors, two demo programs, COLCUBE.C and COLORS.C, are provided.

Please note that both of these demo programs will operate only on EGA/VGA capable systems. No provision has been made to adapt them for CGA systems; they are for high resolution color systems only.

The Color Relations Cube

The COLCUBE.C program uses the default color palette to create a doubled cube showing the relationships between primary and secondary colors.

The physical spectrum, as seen in the rainbow or displayed by a prism, begins with Red and proceeds to Orange, Yellow, Green, Blue, and ends with Violet. To create our computer color spectrum, we have only the Red, Green, and Blue colors to work with. These three primary colors are, however, the three that the eye best perceives and by combining these as light, the eye perceives colors that are not actually present.

In the case of a T.V. signal, these same three colors are used to generate everything from subtle ranges of flesh tones to the intense flashing headlines favored by automobile dealers on late-night movie ads. The T.V., using analog signals, is able to offer finer gradations and combinations of primary colors than the computer which, in EGA/VGA mode, is limited to four values.

Notice that the figure created by COLCUBE.C (see Figure 12-1) has four main axes: red, green, blue, and white (or intensity). The human retina has three types of color receptors believed to correspond to the three primary colors. However, color perception is not limited to recognition of these three values, but also to the relative intensity of each and the balance between these.

Figure 12-1: Color Cube

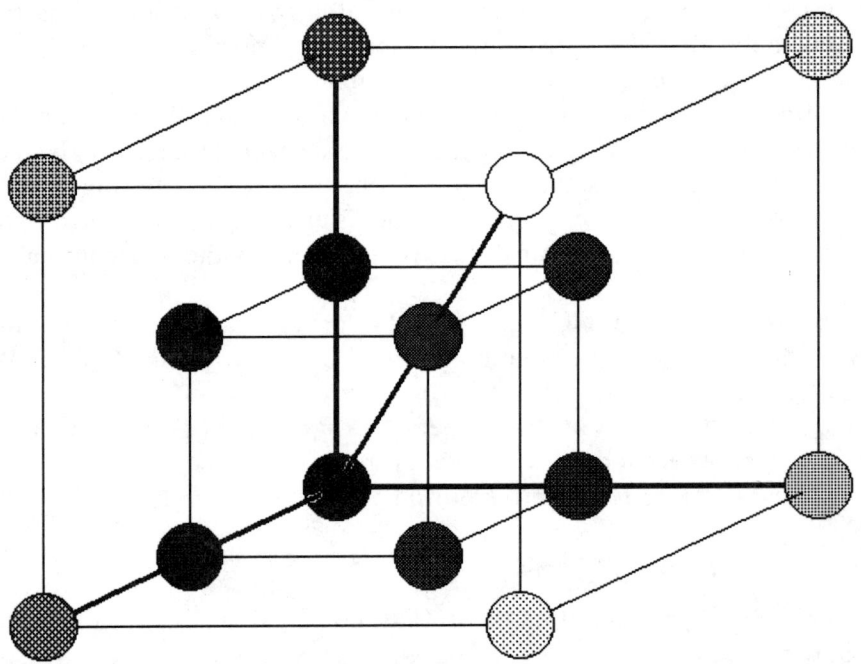

A balanced combination of all three colors is perceived as gray or white, depending on overall intensity (see Chapter 17).

As mentioned, how colors are perceived is affected by other colors surrounding them and COLCUBE shows this effect by swapping the EGABlack and EGAWhite colors between palette color 0 (background) and palette color 15.

The COLORS.PAS Demo

The COLORS.PAS demo (see Figure 12-2) is simple overall, beginning with three global variables: *radius*, which sets the size for the display Circles; *StepForward*, which is used as a Boolean flag to determine whether the colors are incremented or decremented; and *palette*, which is the color palette structure. The structure type *PaletteType* is defined in the GRAPH unit.

Figure 12-2: Colors Demo

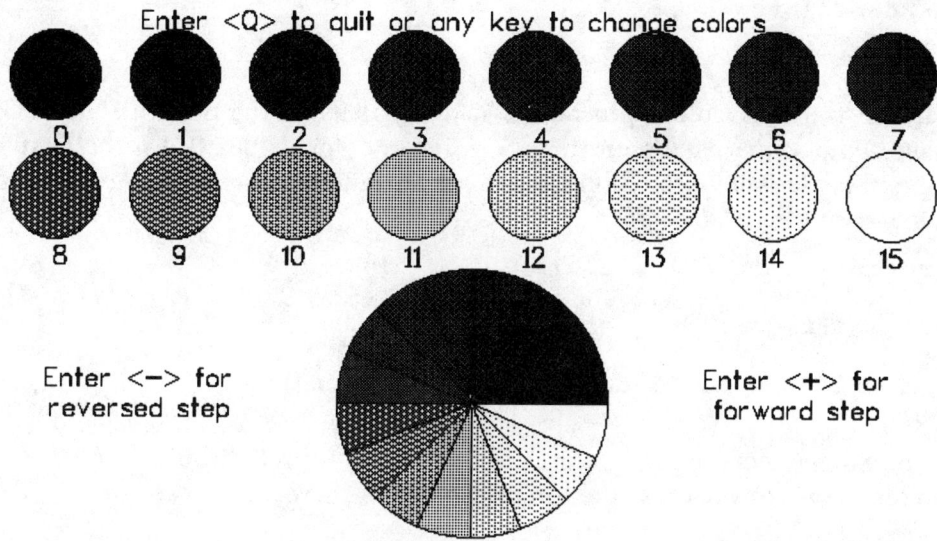

The program starts the graphics system using the same Initialize procedure as virtually all of the other programs in this book.

The SetTextJustify and SetTextStyle procedures pick a font and text justification for the screen display, then write the appropriate messages to the screen.

```
begin
   Initialize;
   radius := 30;
   StepForward := True;
   SetTextJustify( CenterText, CenterText );
   SetTextStyle( SansSerifFont, HorizDir, 1 );
   OutTextXY( 320, 10,
      'Enter <Q> to quit or any key to change colors' );
   OutTextXY( 100, 250, 'Enter <-> for' );
   OutTextXY( 100, 270, 'reversed step' );
   OutTextXY( 540, 250, 'Enter <+> for' );
   OutTextXY( 540, 270, 'forward step' );
```

Next, a special palette is created by the InitializeColors procedure. ShowColors writes 16 colored Circles in two rows, ColorWheel creates a pie chart with the same 16 colors and, with the screen set up and drawn, StepColors is ready to show you through the 64 EGA/VGA color values.

```
    InitializeColors;
    ShowColors;
    ColorWheel;
    StepColors;
    CloseGraph;
end.
```

In the InitializeColors procedure, instead of using the default EGA/VGA palette colors, the palette entries are reset to color values 0..15, the first 16 colors. The SetPalette function assigns the unsigned integer values to the index elements in the *palette* structure.

```
procedure InitializeColors;
var
    i : integer;
begin
    for i := 0 to 15 do SetPalette( i, i );
end;
```

The ShowColors procedure uses a single loop from 0 through 7 to draw 16 Circles in two rows across the top portion of the screen.

```
procedure ShowColors;
var
    i : integer;
begin
    GetPalette( palette );
    for i := 0 to 7 do
    begin
```

The first row of Circles use the first eight palette colors: (*palette.color[0]..palette.color[7]*). At the moment, these are also the first eight possible color values, but it is the palette entry value that is assigned to the screen pixels, not the color value contained by each palette entry.

```
        SetFillStyle( SolidFill, i );
        Circle( 80*i+40, 50, radius );
        FloodFill( 80*i+40, 50, GetColor );
```

The LabelColors function labels each colored Circle with the color value, not the palette item number.

```
        LabelColors( i );
```

The second row of Circles takes the second set of palette item assignments (*palette.color[8]..palette.color[15]*).

```
         SetFillStyle( SolidFill, i+8 );
         Circle( 80*i+40, 130, radius );
         FloodFill( 80*i+40, 130, GetColor );
         LabelColors( i+8 );
      end;
end;
```

The LabelColors procedure is called with one argument specifying the palette entry number, then reads the value in *palette.colors[i]*, and writes this value on the screen next to the colored Circle. While the rest of the screen will not be rewritten as colors change, the labels for the specific color values are rewritten each time a palette entry is changed.

```
procedure LabelColors( i : integer );
var
   Buffer : string;
begin
   str( palette.colors[i]:2, buffer );
   if i > 7 then PrnNum( 80*i-600, 138+radius, buffer )
            else PrnNum( 80*i+40,   58+radius, buffer );
end;
```

The ColorWheel function draws a second display in the form a of pie graph that has 16 slices filled with the 16 palette colors.

```
procedure ColorWheel;
var
   i : integer;
begin
   for i := 0 to 15 do
   begin
      SetFillStyle( SolidFill, 15-i );
      PieSlice( 320, 270, trunc( i*22.5 ),
                trunc( (i+1)*22.5 ), radius*3 );
   end;
end;
```

The last element in this demo is the StepColors procedure.

```
procedure StepColors;
var
   i, ThisColor : integer;
   Ch : char;
   Done : boolean;
```

The *Done* variable is initialized as False, setting up a loop condition that will continue until *Done* becomes True. Until then, StepColors waits for a keyboard entry.

An entry of "Q" or "q" increments *Done* to allow an exit; an entry of "−" or "+" selects a direction for the colors to change.

```pascal
begin
   Done := False;
   while not Done do
   begin
      Ch := upcase( ReadKey );
      Done := Ch = 'Q';
      if Ch = '-' then StepForward := False;
      if Ch = '+' then StepForward := True;
      if not Done then
      begin
```

Any keyboard entry that has not set the exit condition allows a second loop to increment or decrement the current palette color values. The loop steps through the 16 palette entries with *ThisColor* taking the value of each palette entry (*palette.colors[i]*) in turn, then *ThisColor* is incremented or decremented as appropriate with a final test to ensure that the resulting color value remains within the range 0..63.

```pascal
         for i := 0 to 15 do
         begin
            ThisColor := palette.colors[i];
            if StepForward then inc( ThisColor )
                           else dec( ThisColor );
            if ThisColor < 0 then ThisColor := 63;
            if ThisColor > 63 then ThisColor := 0;
```

Finally, SetPalette sets *palette.colors[i]* to the new color value, GetPalette updates the *palette* record, LabelColors updates the screen label, and a delay of 30 milliseconds is executed before the loop continues.

```pascal
            SetPalette( i, ThisColor );
            GetPalette( palette );
            LabelColors( i );
            delay(30);
         end;
      end;
   end;
end;
```

When you run this demo, notice the screen colors change *immediately* when a new value is passed to SetPalette. If you would like to see a more pronounced demonstration of this effect, increase the value in *delay(30);* and add another delay before updating the color label on screen.

Remember, the only action required to change a screen color is to assign a new value to the appropriate palette entry. This action will update the entire screen on the next sweep refresh cycle, regardless of window or viewport settings or which video page is currently active.

This speed of change also allows other effects. For example, you could define several palettes as an array of type palette; for example, *AltPalette : array[0..9] of PaletteType* declares an array of 10 alternate palettes numbered 0..9 which can be used to save any array of colors.

```
for i := 0 to 16 do
   palette.colors[i] = AltPalette[ NewPalette ].colors[i];
```

The loop can assign any of these as *NewPalette* to the active *palette* definition.

Summary

Without going into tedious detail on the theories of color perception or the current fashions in colors and the technical aspects of how the color monitors and video cards function, you've seen the essentials of how the several different video modes use color and what color instructions are accepted in different modes.

In conclusion, here are a pair of colorful (pun intended) demo programs. Take them apart and play with them for a while. Try a few experiments and see what happens. Also, have a shot at building color values as previously described, these results can also be interesting.

And, try using the shift operators (shl and shr) directly on the color values (not on the palette entry numbers). The effects are unusual.

Take a bit of time, relax, play with the color assignments and see what happens. You may find something fascinating or useful, or both.

ColorCub.PAS

```
              { Color Chart for EGA Mode/Palettes }
uses GRAPH, CRT;
const
   dx   : array[0..2] of integer = ( 235, 380,  525 );
   dzx  : array[0..2] of integer = (   0, -90, -180 );
   yFac : array[0..2] of integer = (  46,  27,    8 );
   zyFac: array[0..2] of integer = (   0,   6,   12 );
var
   dy, dzy : array[0..2] of integer;
   GraphDriver, GraphMode, ErrorCode,
   MaxColors, Radius, VAdj, i : integer;
   Colors : boolean;
```

```pascal
procedure Initialize;
begin
   GraphDriver := DETECT;
   InitGraph( GraphDriver, GraphMode, '\TP\BGI' );
   ErrorCode := GraphResult;
   if ErrorCode <> grOk then
   begin
      writeln(' Graphics System Error: ',
              GraphErrorMsg( ErrorCode ) );
      halt( 1 );
   end;
end;
procedure SetCircle( X1, Y1, Z1, Color : integer );
begin
   SetFillStyle( SolidFill, Color );
   SetLineStyle( SolidLn, 0, 1 );
   SetColor( EGAWhite );
   Circle( dx[X1]+dzx[Z1], dy[Y1]+dzy[Z1], Radius );
   SetColor( EGABlack );
   Circle( dx[X1]+dzx[Z1],
           dy[Y1]+dzy[Z1], Radius div 2 );
   FloodFill( dx[X1]+dzx[Z1]+1,
              dy[Y1]+dzy[Z1]+1, EGAWhite );
   SetColor( EGALightGray );
end;
procedure CLine( X1, Y1, Z1, X2, Y2, Z2, Wt : integer );
begin
   SetLineStyle( SolidLn, 0, Wt );
   Line( dx[X1]+dzx[Z1], dy[Y1]+dzy[Z1],
         dx[X2]+dzx[Z2], dy[Y2]+dzy[Z2] );
end;
procedure ColorCube;
begin
   SetColor( EGARed );
   CLine( 0, 0, 0, 1, 0, 0, 3 );
   CLine( 1, 0, 0, 2, 0, 0, 3 );
   CLine( 1, 0, 0, 1, 1, 0, 1 );
   CLine( 1, 0, 0, 1, 0, 1, 1 );
   SetCircle( 1, 0, 0, EGARed );
   SetColor( EGABlue );
   CLine( 0, 0, 0, 0, 1, 0, 3 );
   CLine( 0, 1, 0, 0, 2, 0, 3 );
   CLine( 0, 1, 0, 1, 1, 0, 1 );
   CLine( 0, 1, 0, 0, 1, 1, 1 );
   SetCircle( 0, 1, 0, EGABlue );
   SetColor( EGAGreen );
   CLine( 0, 0, 0, 0, 0, 1, 3 );
```

```
   CLine( 0, 0, 1, 0, 0, 2, 3 );
   CLine( 0, 0, 1, 1, 0, 1, 1 );
   CLine( 0, 0, 1, 0, 1, 1, 1 );
   SetCircle( 0, 0, 1, EGAGreen );
   SetColor( EGALightGray );
   CLine( 0, 0, 0, 1, 1, 1, 3 );
   CLine( 1, 1, 1, 2, 2, 2, 3 );
   SetCircle( 0, 0, 0, EGABlack );
   CLine( 0, 1, 1, 1, 1, 1, 1 );
   SetCircle( 0, 1, 1, EGACyan );
   CLine( 1, 1, 0, 1, 1, 1, 1 );
   SetCircle( 1, 1, 0, EGAMagenta );
   CLine( 1, 0, 1, 1, 1, 1, 1 );
   SetCircle( 1, 0, 1, EGABrown );
   SetCircle( 1, 1, 1, EGALightGray );
   SetColor( EGALightRed );
   CLine( 2, 0, 0, 2, 2, 0, 1 );
   CLine( 2, 0, 0, 2, 0, 2, 1 );
   SetCircle( 2, 0, 0, EGALightRed );
   SetColor( EGALightBlue );
   CLine( 0, 2, 0, 0, 2, 2, 1 );
   CLine( 0, 2, 0, 2, 2, 0, 1 );
   SetCircle( 0, 2, 0, EGALightBlue );
   SetColor( EGALightGreen );
   CLine( 0, 0, 2, 2, 0, 2, 1 );
   CLine( 0, 0, 2, 0, 2, 2, 1 );
   SetCircle( 0, 0, 2, EGALightGreen );
   CLine( 2, 2, 0, 2, 2, 2, 1 );
   SetCircle( 2, 2, 0, EGALightMagenta );
   CLine( 0, 2, 2, 2, 2, 2, 1 );
   SetCircle( 0, 2, 2, EGALightCyan );
   CLine( 2, 0, 2, 2, 2, 2, 1 );
   SetCircle( 2, 0, 2, EGAYellow );
   SetCircle( 2, 2, 2, EGAWhite );
end;

procedure ColorSwitch;
var
   Done : boolean;
   Ch : char;
begin
   Done := False;
   while not Done do
   begin
      Ch := Upcase( ReadKey );
      if Ch = 'Q' then Done := True else
      if Colors then
      begin
         SetPalette( 0, EGABlack );
```

```pascal
            SetPalette( 15, EGAWhite );
            Colors := False;
         end else
         begin
            SetPalette( 0, EGAWhite );
            SetPalette( 15, EGABlack );
            Colors := True;
         end;
      end;
   end;
end;

begin
   Initialize;
   Colors := False;
   Radius := 20;
   VAdj := GetMaxY div 60;
   for i := 0 to 2 do
   begin
       dy[i] :=  yFac[i] * VAdj;
       dzy[i] := zyFac[i] * VAdj;
   end;
   OutTextXY( 10, 10,
      'Enter <Q> to quit or any key to change colors' );
   ColorCube;
   ColorSwitch;
   PrintPause( GraphDriver, FALSE );
   CloseGraph;                              { restore text mode }
end.
```

Colors.PAS

```pascal
            { Color Chart for EGA Mode/Palettes }
uses GRAPH, CRT;

var
   GraphDriver, GraphMode,
   MaxColors, ErrorCode, radius : integer;
   palette : PaletteType;
   StepForward : boolean;

procedure Initialize;
begin
   GraphDriver := DETECT;
   InitGraph( GraphDriver, GraphMode, '\TP\BGI' );
   ErrorCode := GraphResult;
   if ErrorCode <> grOk then
   begin
      writeln(' Graphics System Error: ',
```

```
                    GraphErrorMsg( ErrorCode ) );
         halt( 1 );
      end;
   end;
procedure PrnNum( x, y : integer; Buffer : string );
begin
   SetViewPort( x-20, y-4, x+20, y+9, True );
   ClearViewPort;
   SetViewPort( 0, 0, GetMaxX, GetMaxY, True );
   OutTextXY( x, y, buffer );
end;
procedure LabelColors( i : integer );
var
   Buffer : string;
begin
   str( palette.colors[i]:2, buffer );
   if i > 7 then PrnNum( 80*i-600, 138+radius, buffer )
            else PrnNum( 80*i+40,   58+radius, buffer );
end;
procedure ShowColors;
var
   i : integer;
begin
   GetPalette( palette );
   for i := 0 to 7 do
   begin
      SetFillStyle( SolidFill, i );
      Circle( 80*i+40, 50, radius );
      FloodFill( 80*i+40, 50, GetColor );
      LabelColors( i );
      SetFillStyle( SolidFill, i+8 );
      Circle( 80*i+40, 130, radius );
      FloodFill( 80*i+40, 130, GetColor );
      LabelColors( i+8 );
   end;
end;
procedure ColorWheel;
var
   i : integer;
begin
   for i := 0 to 15 do
   begin
      SetFillStyle( SolidFill, 15-i );
      PieSlice( 320, 270, trunc( i*22.5 ),
                trunc( (i+1)*22.5 ), radius*3 );
   end;
end;
```

```pascal
procedure StepColors;
var
   i, ThisColor : integer;
   Ch : char;
   Done : boolean;
begin
   Done := False;
   while not Done do
   begin
      Ch := upcase( ReadKey );
      Done := Ch = 'Q';
      if Ch = '-' then StepForward := False;
      if Ch = '+' then StepForward := True;
      if not Done then
      begin
         for i := 0 to 15 do
         begin
            ThisColor := palette.colors[i];
            if StepForward then inc( ThisColor )
                           else dec( ThisColor );
            if ThisColor < 0 then ThisColor := 63;
            if ThisColor > 63 then ThisColor := 0;
            SetPalette( i, ThisColor );
            GetPalette( palette );
            LabelColors( i );
            delay(30);
         end;
      end;
   end;
end;
procedure InitializeColors;
var
   i : integer;
begin
   for i := 0 to 15 do SetPalette( i, i );
end;
begin
   Initialize;
   radius := 30;
   StepForward := True;
   SetTextJustify( CenterText, CenterText );
   SetTextStyle( SansSerifFont, HorizDir, 1 );
   OutTextXY( 320, 10,
      'Enter <Q> to quit or any key to change colors' );
   OutTextXY( 100, 250, 'Enter <-> for' );
   OutTextXY( 100, 270, 'reversed step' );
   OutTextXY( 540, 250, 'Enter <+> for' );
```

```
    OutTextXY( 540, 270, 'forward step' );
    InitializeColors;
    ShowColors;
    ColorWheel;
    StepColors;
    CloseGraph;
end.
```

CHAPTER 13

Using A Mouse With Graphics Displays

When an input device is required with a graphics display (except text graphics), the obvious choice is to use the mouse as the primary selection mechanism and the cursor keys as the secondary device.

The mouse can be used in two different fashions. First, by reading the mouse output codes as an analog of the cursor keys and second, by directly incorporating a mouse driver in your program and interpreting mouse events.

Reading Mouse Events as Cursor Keys

This method uses the default mouse interface (the MOUSE.COM or MOUSE.SYS driver) supplied with the physical mouse hardware and requires little special provision by the programmer. When the mouse is moved left, the system receives the two codes (scan and char codes) *00h*, *48h*, just as if the left arrow key had been pressed. This assumes that the scan and char key codes are being read directly from the input device or port. Similarly, the left mouse button returns the same code (*0Dh*) as pressing the Enter key on the keyboard.

However, with a Logitech mouse (and many others), these key response codes can be reassigned or even interpreted as macro instructions (see your mouse manual for details) and it can be difficult to ensure that the appropriate responses will always be returned by the mouse software.

A Direct Mouse Interface

For most graphics applications, indirectly interpreting the mouse input (treating the mouse as a keyboard analog) is unreliable for several reasons: the mouse movement and key responses may not be assigned correctly, the returned information is less complete than can be read directly from the mouse, little or no control can be exercised over the mouse parameters, and the program loop time may produce a delay in responding to the mouse movement.

For these reasons, most graphics applications seek to exercise a direct interface with the mouse device, allowing the program to set mouse parameters and to read mouse events and position directly. The following mouse interface procedures allow you (via your program) to:

- restrict mouse movement to a specific screen area
- read the mouse screen position directly
- change the mouse response rates and adjust vertical and horizontal mouse-to-screen movement ratios
- read mouse keys as both make and break events and test individual key-down status
- select graphics mouse cursors or create new graphics mouse cursor patterns
- selectively hide or display the mouse cursor

Many of these capabilities will be demonstrated in the MousePtr program at the end of this chapter.

Mouse Driver Types

For VGA graphics, Logitech mouse driver 4.0 or later (or the equivalent from Microsoft or your mouse vendor) should be used. On earlier versions, the graphics mouse cursor may not appear in VGA modes using vertical resolutions greater than 350 pixels.

If you are using VGA or higher resolution and do not have a suitable mouse driver, you have two choices: use a lower resolution or get an updated mouse driver (or both).

To force an application to use a lower resolution mode, instead of calling InitGraph with the predefined DETECT value, enter the video driver ID and a specific mode for operation, such as: *GraphDriver := VGA;* (9) and *GraphMode := VGAMed;* (2) to select a 640 by 350, 16 color video mode.

The Mouse Unit

To provide mouse interface functions, for both text and graphics applications, the program MOUSE.PAS will compile the MOUSE.TPU unit, supplying four object mouse types: TextMouse, GraphicMouse, TextLightPen, and GraphicLightPen.

The TextMouse object is obviously for text applications, while the GraphicMouse object is used for graphics applications. The remaining two mouse objects, TextLightPen, and GraphicLightPen, provide light-pen emulation equivalents for text and graphic modes. However, only the graphics interface applications will be demonstrated here—the corresponding text interface applications are relatively simple and differ only in minor elements and require little explanation.

The Mouse unit and the GraphicsMouse object will be used extensively by the programs in Chapters 14 and 15 to demonstrate the graphics control objects and icon objects. Also, in this chapter, the MousePtr program will be used to both demonstrate the graphics mouse object and to provide a utility program to create a graphics mouse cursor.

However, if you are not familiar with object-oriented programming, further information can be found in *Object-Oriented Programming in Turbo Pascal 5.5*, available from Addison-Wesley Publishing Company.

The MOUSE and MOUSEPTR programs are also available on disk, as source codes, together with the other utilities and demo programs appearing in this book.

Mouse Types

To begin, there are currently two basic types of mouse in use: the Microsoft (two button) mouse and the Logitech (three button) mouse. Most mice will conform to one of these two standards.

The basic Microsoft mouse supports 16 mouse functions (functions 0..15) and has two buttons, each producing a make and a break response capable of being read as pressed or released. The Logitech mouse supports all features of the Microsoft mouse, but adds two additional mouse functions (functions 16 and 19) and a third (middle) button.

The procedures in the Mouse unit include both the Microsoft and Logitech mouse functions and the MOUSEPTR program will operate with either type of mouse though the third button (functions 16 and 19) will not be supported by the Microsoft mouse.

These mouse procedures presume the presence of two items: a hardware mouse and a mouse device driver, both of which are supplied by the mouse manufacturer or vendor. The hardware mouse may be either a serial or bus mouse and the mouse device driver may be either MOUSE.COM or MOUSE.SYS (normally both device drivers are supplied with each mouse).

The Object Mouse Unit

For an object unit, all procedures, functions, and constants available to calling applications are defined in the INTERFACE section of the unit code, beginning with three type definitions:

```
type
   Position = record
                BtnStatus,
                opCount,
                xPos, yPos  : integer;
              end;
```

The *Position* data type is used to interrogate the mouse. It returns *BtnStatus*, which reports the status of each button; *opCount*, which reports how many times a specified button has been pressed or released; and *xPos* and *yPos*, which report the mouse position at the time of the last button event.

```
   EventRec = record
                Event,
                BtnStatus,
                XPos, YPos : word;
              end;
```

The EventRec record returns four unsigned word values. *Event* is the mouse event register mask that selects which mouse events should be reported, *BtnStatus* reports the status of the mouse buttons, and *XPos* and *YPos* report the location where the last event occurred.

```
   GCursor  =  record
                 ScreenMask,
                 CursorMask : array [0..15] of word;
                 hotX, hotY : integer;
               end;
```

The final variable type, *GCursor*, is used to set the graphic mouse cursor. It consists of two arrays of words defining the screen and cursor masks and two integer values for the cursor hot spot. A series of constants are also defined and, because these are defined in the INTERFACE section, may be used directly by the application programs.

```
const
   ButtonL  = 0;
   ButtonR  = 1;
   ButtonM  = 2;
```

The *ButtonL*, *ButtonR*, and *ButtonM* constants identify the left, right, and middle mouse buttons.

```
Software  = 0;
Hardware  = 1;
```

The *Software* and *Hardware* constants identify the type of text cursor.

```
OFF       = 0;
ON        = 1;
```

The Mouse Cursor

Each graphics cursor is defined as a screen mask and a cursor mask. The graphics mouse cursor is written to the screen in such a fashion that the existing screen information is not destroyed. It is done, first by ANDing the screen mask image with the existing screen contents, then XORing the cursor mask image with the result. The bit effects of writing the screen and cursor masks are shown in Table 13-1.

Table 13-1: Screen and Cursor Mask Effects

SCREEN MASK BIT	CURSOR MASK BIT	DISPLAY BIT
0	0	0
0	1	1
1	0	Unaffected
1	1	Inverted

The default graphics cursor is the left-angled arrow pattern shown in Figure 13-1. Here the screen mask is used to selectively block the background image around the cursor image, creating a border to make the cursor visible even when the background image color is the same.

The graphics cursor definition contains more than just the cursor image. It also contains two coordinates specifying the cursor's *hot spot* or target pixel. The cursor hot spot values may be in the range −16..16 though, normally, only coordinates in the range 0..15 would be chosen because negative coordinates lie outside (above and to the left) the cursor image.

In Figures 13-1 through 13-5, the graphics cursor hot spots are shown by small crossed arrows. In all of the images defined here, the hot spot lies within the cursor image.

Five graphics mouse cursors are also predefined and may be used by GraphicMouse or GraphicLightPen objects, see Figures 13-1 through 13-5.

The Arrow Cursor

The Arrow cursor is not only the default graphics cursor (created by the mouse software itself), but is also supplied as a defined image so it can be loaded by the application after another cursor image has been used.

```
    arrow : GCursor =
      ( ScreenMask : ( $1FFF, $0FFF, $07FF, $03FF,
                       $01FF, $00FF, $007F, $003F,
                       $001F, $003F, $01FF, $01FF,
                       $E0FF, $F0FF, $F8FF, $F8FF );
        CursorMask : ( $0000, $4000, $6000, $7000,
                       $7800, $7C00, $7E00, $7F00,
                       $7F80, $7C00, $4C00, $0600,
                       $0600, $0300, $0300, $0000 );
        hotX : $0001;  hotY : $0001 );
```

The Reset method can be used to restore the default arrow cursor after another graphics cursor has been selected, but in some circumstances, you may prefer to have an alternate arrow cursor that can be loaded without having to call the Reset method.

Figure 13-1: Mouse Default Graphics Cursor

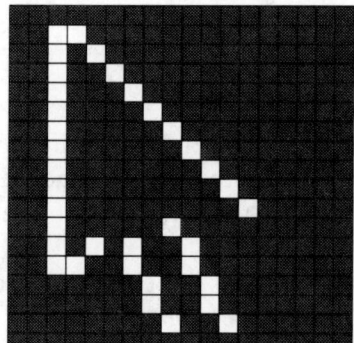

Left, the default graphics cursor is shown against a matching background. Against a contrasting background, only the cursor mask image would appear.
Below (left and right), the screen mask and cursor mask are shown separately.

Screen Mask

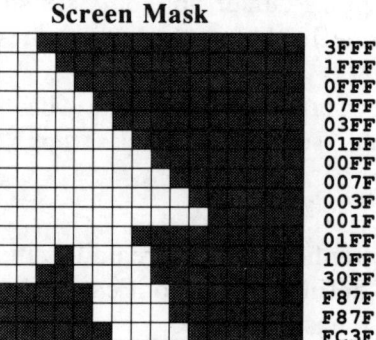

```
3FFF
1FFF
0FFF
07FF
03FF
01FF
00FF
007F
003F
001F
01FF
10FF
30FF
F87F
F87F
FC3F
```

Cursor Mask

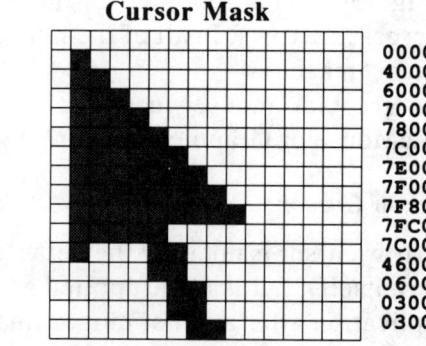

```
0000
4000
6000
7000
7800
7C00
7E00
7F00
7F80
7FC0
7C00
4600
0600
0300
0300
```

Figure 13-2: Check Cursor

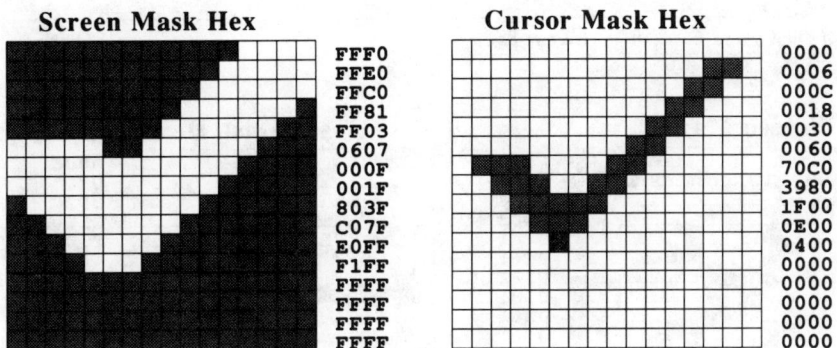

The Check Cursor

The Check cursor is useful for item selection, lists, or radio buttons (see Chapter 14).

```
check : GCursor =
    ( ScreenMask : ( $FFF0, $FFE0, $FFC0, $FF81,
                     $FF03, $0607, $000F, $001F,
                     $803F, $C07F, $E0FF, $F1FF,
                     $FFFF, $FFFF, $FFFF, $FFFF );
      CursorMask : ( $0000, $0006, $000C, $0018,
                     $0030, $0060, $70C0, $3980,
                     $1F00, $0E00, $0400, $0000,
                     $0000, $0000, $0000, $0000 );
      hotX : $0005;  hotY : $0010 );
```

The Cross Cursor

For the Cross cursor (cross-hairs) graphics cursor, notice that both an interior and exterior border are created, allowing the cursor to be visible against any background. Notice also that existing screen pixels at the center of the cursor, the target spot, are never overwritten by either the screen or cursor masks.

```
cross : GCursor =
    ( ScreenMask : ( $F01F, $E00F, $C007, $8003,
                     $0441, $0C61, $0381, $0381,
                     $0381, $0C61, $0441, $8003,
                     $C007, $E00F, $F01F, $FFFF );
      CursorMask : ( $0000, $07C0, $0920, $1110,
                     $2108, $4004, $4004, $783C,
                     $4004, $4004, $2108, $1110,
```

```
                        $0920, $07C0, $0000, $0000 );
     hotX : $0007;    hotY : $0007 );
```

Figure 13-3: Cross Graphics Cursor

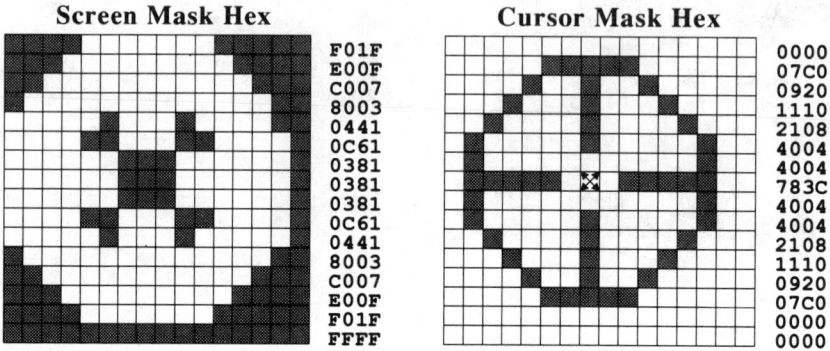

The Glove Cursor

The Glove cursor is popularly used to indicate visually that the mouse is on a button control or that a frame corner or other graphics control object has been selected. See the icon demo in Chapter 15 for an example of how the Glove cursor can be used.

```
glove : GCursor =
    ( ScreenMask : ( $F3FF, $E1FF, $E1FF, $E1FF,
                     $E1FF, $E049, $E000, $8000,
                     $0000, $0000, $07FC, $07F8,
                     $9FF9, $8FF1, $C003, $E007 );
      CursorMask : ( $0C00, $1200, $1200, $1200,
                     $1200, $13B6, $1249, $7249,
                     $9249, $9001, $9001, $8001,
                     $4002, $4002, $2004, $1FF8 );
      hotX : $0004;   hotY : $0000 );
```

The Ibeam Cursor

The Ibeam cursor is popular in graphics text applications such as Ventura Publisher or Presentation Manager when text information is presented using graphics-generated characters and when the cursor must be aligned with the graphics text images. Notice that the screen mask produces a complete outline that surrounds the cursor image so the cursor is visible against any background.

Figure 13-4: Glove Graphics Cursor

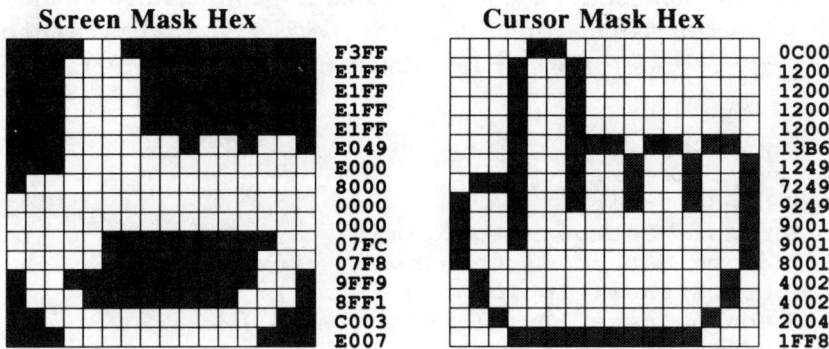

Figure 13-5: IBeam Graphics Cursor

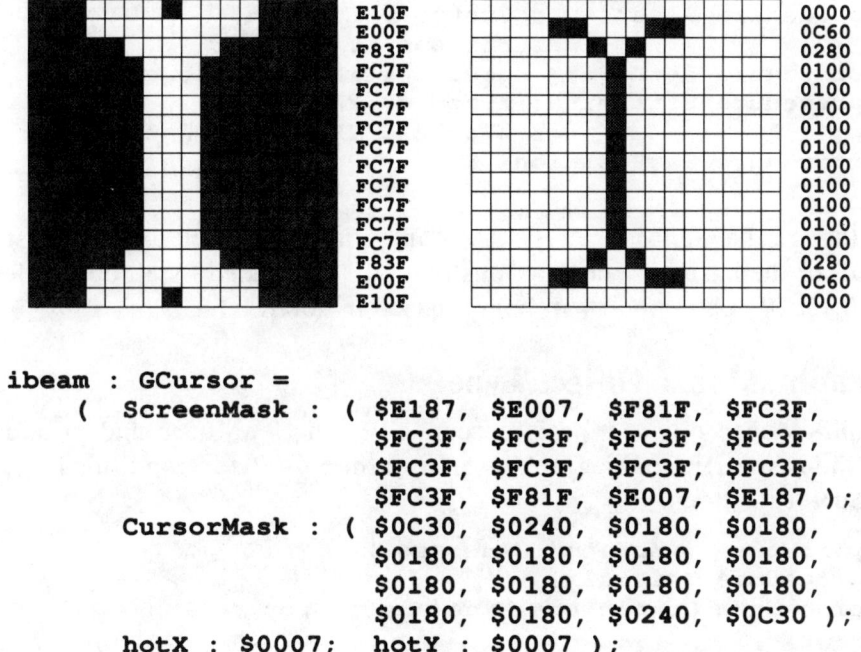

```
ibeam : GCursor =
    ( ScreenMask : ( $E187, $E007, $F81F, $FC3F,
                     $FC3F, $FC3F, $FC3F, $FC3F,
                     $FC3F, $FC3F, $FC3F, $FC3F,
                     $FC3F, $F81F, $E007, $E187 );
      CursorMask : ( $0C30, $0240, $0180, $0180,
                     $0180, $0180, $0180, $0180,
                     $0180, $0180, $0180, $0180,
                     $0180, $0180, $0240, $0C30 );
      hotX : $0007;   hotY : $0007 );
```

The GenMouse Object Type

The GenMouse object type is the ancestor object type for all other mouse objects, but is not intended for use by itself. Instead, applications should only declare object variables of one of the descendent object types, such as GraphicMouse for graphics applications or TextMouse for text-based programs.

```
type
   GenMouse = object
      x, y : integer;
      visible : Boolean;
      function  TestMouse: boolean;
      procedure SetAccel( threshold : integer );
      procedure Show( Option : Boolean );
      procedure InstallTask( Mask : word );
      procedure ClearEvent;
      procedure GetPosition( var BtnStatus,
                             XPos, YPos : integer );
      procedure QueryBtnDn( button : integer;
                            var mouse : Position );
      procedure QueryBtnUp( button : integer;
                            var mouse : Position );
      procedure ReadMove( var XMove, YMove : integer );
      procedure Reset( var Status : Boolean;
                       var BtnCount : integer );
      procedure SetRatio( horPix, verPix : integer );
      procedure SetLimits( XPosMin, YPosMin,
                           XPosMax, YPosMax : integer );
      procedure SetPosition( XPos, YPos : integer );
   end;
```

Even though the GenMouse type is not intended to be used directly, it still defines all of the basic object functions that will be needed by all descendent mouse objects. Each method will be discussed in detail later.

The GraphicMouse Object Type

The GraphicMouse object type is descended from GenMouse and provides three methods specific to the graphics mouse: the Initialize, ConditionalHide, and SetCursor methods.

```
GraphicMouse = object( GenMouse )
   procedure Initialize;
   procedure ConditionalHide( left, top,
                              right, bottom : integer );
   procedure SetCursor( cursor : GCursor );
end;
```

The Initialize method is provided to establish default conditions for the graphics mouse. Notice however that TextMouse defines its own Initialize method—which is not the same as GraphicMouse.Initialize!

The ConditionalHide and SetCursor methods, as well as the Initialize method, will be discussed in more detail presently.

Other Mouse Object Types

The TextMouse and TextLightPen object types are not discussed here in detail, but are included in the Mouse unit for use in text applications.

The GraphicLightPen object type is a descendent of GraphicMouse with the addition of a method providing lightpen mouse emulation—not a popular requirement but sometimes useful.

```
TextMouse = object( GenMouse )
   procedure Initialize;
   procedure SetCursor( ctype, C1, C2 : word );
end;
GraphicLightPen = object( GraphicMouse )
   procedure LightPen( Option : Boolean );
end;
TextLightPen = object( TextMouse )
   procedure LightPen( Option : Boolean );
end;
```

The Implementation Section

The Implementation section of a unit contains the details of procedures and functions (or, in this case, methods). However, the specific elements within the Implementation section, are not directly accessible to applications using the unit, but *are* accessible via the methods defined in the Interface section.

For example, the three units, Crt, Graph and Dos, which are used within the Implementation section are not available to the application using the unit (unless the application contains its own, separate "uses" statement), nor is the *Regs* variable visible outside the unit.

```
IMPLEMENTATION

uses Crt, Graph, Dos;
var
   Regs : registers;
```

In the same fashion, the Lower and Upper functions are local to the unit and can only be used by the methods within the unit. They will not be accessible to the application calling the unit nor to descendents of any of the objects defined within the unit, except through the methods defined in the Interface section.

```
function Lower( n1, n2 : integer ) : integer;
   begin
      if n1 < n2 then Lower := n1
                 else Lower := n2;
   end;
function Upper( n1, n2 : integer ) : integer;
   begin
      if n1 > n2 then Upper := n1
                 else Upper := n2;
   end;
```

Likewise the following MouseHandler definition can only be used by methods defined within the unit; it is not otherwise accessible.

```
procedure MouseHandler( Flags, CS, IP, AX, BX, CX, DX,
                        SI, DI, DS, ES, BP : word );
   INTERRUPT;
   begin
      mEvent.Event     := AX;
      mEvent.BtnStatus := BX;
      mEvent.xPos      := CX;
      mEvent.yPos      := DX;
      { exit processing for far return to driver }
      inline( $8B/$E5/                { MOV SP, BP }
              $5D/                    { POP BP }
              $07/                    { POP ES }
              $1F/                    { POP DS }
              $5F/                    { POP DI }
              $5E/                    { POP SI }
              $5A/                    { POP DX }
              $59/                    { POP CX }
              $5B/                    { POP BX }
              $58/                    { POP AX }
              $CB );                  { RETF }
   end;
```

GenMouse Implementation

The methods that were declared for the GenMouse object (and its descendents) in the Interface section are defined in the Implementation section, beginning with the TestMouse method.

The TestMouse Method

The TestMouse method is provided to test for the presence—in the system—of a mouse and mouse driver and operates by testing the system memory for a key value indicating that a mouse is installed and viable.

```
function GenMouse.TestMouse : Boolean;
   const
      iret = 207;
   var
      dOff, dSeg : integer;
   begin
      dOff := MemW[0000:0204];
      dSeg := MemW[0000:0206];
      if( ( dSeg = 0 ) or ( dOff = 0 ) )
         then TestMouse := FALSE
         else TestMouse := Mem[dSeg:dOff] <> iret;
   end;
```

The Reset Method

The Reset method calls mouse interrupt 33h, function 00h to reset the mouse to the default conditions.

```
procedure GenMouse.Reset( var Status : Boolean; var
BtnCount : integer );
   begin
      regs.AX := $00;
      intr($33,regs);
      Status   := regs.AX <> 0;
      BtnCount := regs.BX;
   end;
```

The Reset method returns the Boolean flag *Status* indicating the mouse is present. If no mouse is found, a 0 (zero) value is returned; if a mouse is present, a -1 is returned. *BtnCount* reports the number of buttons present on the mouse (2 or 3). This function is always called to initialize the mouse or to reset the graphics mouse cursor to the default cursor image (the left-slanted arrow image).

The Show Method

The Show method is used both to hide and to show the mouse cursor. The mouse driver provides two separate interrupt functions, show (01h) and hide (02h) to control the visibility of the mouse cursor. Because multiple calls to the show function will require multiple calls to the hide function (and vice versa), this can easily cause confusion.

Instead, the Show method uses two Boolean conditional flags, *Option* and *Visible*, so that only one call is ever required to hide or reveal the mouse cursor. The Show method is called with *Option* parameter, specifying TRUE to make the mouse cursor visible or FALSE to hide the mouse cursor.

```
procedure GenMouse.Show( Option : Boolean );
   begin
      if Option and not Visible then
      begin
         regs.AX := $01;
         Visible := TRUE;
         intr($33,regs);
      end else
      if Visible and not Option then
      begin
         regs.AX := $02;
         Visible := FALSE;
         intr($33,regs);
      end;
   end;
```

In this fashion, the single instruction *Show(False)* will always hide the mouse cursor and the instruction *Show(True)* will always make the mouse cursor visible.

An initial value for the *Visible* flag is set by the GraphicMouse.Initialize or TextMouse.Initialize methods.

The GetPosition Method

The GetPosition method returns three values reporting on the mouse position and mouse buttons status by calling interrupt 33h, function 03h.

```
procedure GenMouse.GetPosition( var BtnStatus,
                                XPos, YPos : integer );
   begin
      regs.AX := $03;
      intr($33,regs);
      BtnStatus := regs.BX;
      XPos      := regs.CX;
      YPos      := regs.DX;
   end;
```

The GetPosition reports the current mouse position—regardless of button events—either in screen pixels (for graphics modes) or in character cell pixel coordinates (for text modes).

In graphics modes, the position reported is always the pixel coordinates of the mouse cursor's hot spot, using normal screen coordinates from the 0,0 origin at the upper left of the screen. This position is reported independently of viewport (window) settings and is always an absolute screen position.

In text modes, the position is again reported in pixel coordinates, but the pixel coordinates reported are those of the character cell where the mouse text cursor is located. Thus, if a screen character cell is 8 pixels by 8 pixels and the reported position is 16,32, then the text cursor is in the third column and the fifth row. A position of 0,0 is the first column and first row character position.

Again, the reported position is independent of any windows that may be in effect and is always in absolute screen coordinates.

Hint: you might like to create separate GetPosition methods for the text and graphics mouse objects with provisions allowing the text version to report in column/row coordinates.

The BtnStatus value returns the present conditions of each of the mouse buttons, but only the three least-significant-bits are relevant. Bit 0 corresponds to the left button, bit 1 to the right button, and bit 2 to the middle button (for three-button mice). If any button is down, the corresponding bit value is set. If the button is up, the bit value is zero.

The SetPosition Method

The SetPosition method calls interrupt 33h, function 04h to set the mouse cursor to a specified screen position.

```
procedure GenMouse.SetPosition( XPos, YPos : integer );
   begin
      regs.AX := $04;
      regs.CX := XPos;
      regs.DX := YPos;
      intr($33,regs);
   end;
```

The x- and y-axis values must be within the valid ranges for the current video mode.

In text modes (see GetPosition) the x- and y-axis values are still specified as pixel values but will be rounded automatically to the nearest character boundaries.

The QueryBtnDn Method

The QueryBtnDn method is called with an argument specifying one of the mouse buttons and returns a record structure (*mouse : Position*). This reports if the queried button has been pressed (but is not necessarily down now), how many times the button has been pressed (since the last call querying its status) and the mouse cursor coordinates the last time the queried button was pressed.

```pascal
procedure GenMouse.QueryBtnDn( button : integer;
                               var mouse : Position );
   begin
      regs.AX := $05;
      regs.BX := button;
      intr($33,regs);
      mouse.BtnStatus := regs.AX;
      mouse.opCount   := regs.BX;
      mouse.xPos      := regs.CX;
      mouse.yPos      := regs.DX;
   end;
```

The *BtnStatus* value reports the present status of all of the buttons, while *opCount* reports only on the queried button and indicates how many times, if any, the button has been pressed since last queried. The *xPos* and *yPos* values return the position of the mouse on the last button down event (if any). The button count and position information are reset by this call.

The QueryBtnUp Method

The QueryBtnUp method is essentially the same as QueryBtnDn, except the reported button event is the release of the specified button rather than the button down event.

```pascal
procedure GenMouse.QueryBtnUp( button : integer;
                               var mouse : Position );
   begin
      regs.AX := $06;
      regs.BX := button;
      intr($33,regs);
      mouse.BtnStatus := regs.AX;
      mouse.opCount   := regs.BX;
      mouse.xPos      := regs.CX;
      mouse.yPos      := regs.DX;
   end;
```

The SetLimits Method

The SetLimits method is the mouse equivalent of the Windows or ViewPort functions, establishing minimum and maximum horizontal and vertical ranges for the mouse cursor and restricting cursor movements to the defined area.

```pascal
procedure GenMouse.SetLimits( XPosMin, YPosMin,
                              XPosMax, YPosMax: integer);
   begin
      regs.AX := $07;                     { set horizontal limits }
```

```
      regs.CX := Lower(XPosMin,XPosMax);
      regs.DX := Upper(XPosMin,XPosMax);
      intr($33,regs);
      regs.AX := $08;                    { set vertical limits }
      regs.CX := Lower(YPosMin,YPosMax);
      regs.DX := Upper(YPosMin,YPosMax);
      intr($33,regs);
   end;
```

Both horizontal and vertical limits are set by a single method even though two mouse interrupt calls are required: interrupt 33h, functions 07h and 08h.

If the mouse cursor is outside the area specified when the limits are set, the mouse cursor position is corrected until it lies within the validated screen area. Also, if the minimum value specified is larger than the maximum value, the two values are exchanged automatically.

If you are using EGA or VGA video (or other, high-resolution video), the default x and y mouse screen limits *may not* match the actual screen size in pixels. Always call the SetLimits method to set the actual required screen margins.

The ReadMove Method

The ReadMove method reports absolute mouse movement as vertical and horizontal step counts (the distance the mouse has moved in *mickeys* or $1/200$-inch increments) since the last call to this function.

```
procedure GenMouse.ReadMove( var XMove, YMove: integer );
   begin
      regs.AX := $0B;
      intr($33,regs);
      XMove := regs.CX;
      YMove := regs.DX;
   end;
```

Some mice report only 100 mickeys/inch, others 200 mickeys/inch and some—such as the newest "HiRes" mice—go as high as 320 mickeys/inch. The vertical and horizontal step count is reported as a signed integer in the range −32768..32767. Positive values specify motions from left to right or from top to bottom (with the mouse cord pointing "up" or away from the user).

Since the total mouse distance that can be reported is slightly less than 14 feet (in any direction from a starting point of 0,0), this is adequate for virtually any application short of a computer odometer.

Because the SetAccel method is enabled by default and, with fast mouse movement, can report 600 mickeys per inch or higher, the ReadMove method is not accurate for measuring distances, unless the speed threshold is reset to a very large value such as 7FFFh.

With this proviso, however, ReadMove could be used with the mouse for measurements ... within limits.

The SetRatio Method

The SetRatio method sets the amount of mouse motion (*mickeys*) required to move the screen cursor eight pixels horizontally or vertically.

```
procedure GenMouse.SetRatio( horPix, verPix : integer );
   begin
      regs.AX := $0F;
      regs.CX := horPix;
      regs.DX := verPix;
      intr($33,regs);
   end;
```

The default values are eight mickeys per eight pixels horizontal and sixteen mickeys per pixel vertical. For a 200 mickey/inch mouse, these settings will require 3.2 inches horizontal and 2.0 inches vertical movement to cover a 640x200 pixel screen (assuming there is no acceleration).

The SetAccel Method

The SetAccel method calls interrupt 33h, function 13h to set a threshold speed (in mickeys/second) over which the mouse driver will add in an acceleration factor. Using this feature, when the mouse is moved quickly, the mouse cursor is moved farther for the same physical distance (for a given hand movement) than if it is moved slowly.

```
procedure GenMouse.SetAccel( threshold : integer );
   begin
      regs.AX := $13;
      regs.DX := threshold;
      intr($33,regs);
   end;
```

The acceleration factor used by mouse drivers varies. Some use a fixed acceleration of two; others (including Logitech) use a variable acceleration factor determined by the speed of the mouse movement.

To cancel the acceleration factor, simply call SetAccel with an unreasonably large argument, such as 7FFFh, to establish a threshold that will not be reached; unless, of course, your hand is faster than a speeding bullet. (Though, in actual fact, a speed setting of 7FFFh is only about 9.3 MPH or 450 RPM on the mouse ball, assuming a standard of 200 mickeys/inch.)

To restore acceleration, call SetAccel with a speed threshold of 0.

The Event Handler Methods

The event handler procedure itself is not provided as a method for any of the mouse object types, though a MouseHandler procedure has been defined together with the InstallTask and ClearEvent methods. These are not demonstrated because they can often be temperamental.

The InstallTask method passes an event mask and the address of the user-defined subroutine, which is called by the mouse driver when any of the events defined by the mask occur.

```
procedure GenMouse.InstallTask;
  begin
      regs.AX := $0B;
      regs.CX := Mask;
      regs.DX := ofs(MouseHandler);
      regs.ES := seg(MouseHandler);
      intr($33,regs);
  end;
```

Mask values passed to this event handler routine are shown in Figure 13-6.

The *Logitech Programmer's Reference Manual* includes a caution recommending that as little time as possible be spent in the event handler. Use it with caution.

The ClearEvent method resets the mEvent.Event to a null value.

Figure 13-6: The Flag Register Bits

The mask value 007Fh (EVENTMASK) excludes everything except bits 0..6 (unshaded) of the 16-bit register. These seven flag bits are defined as shown.

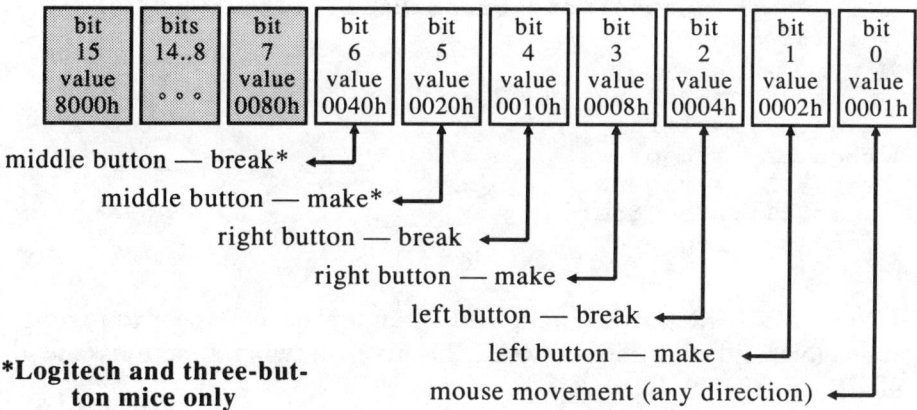

```pascal
procedure GenMouse.ClearEvent;
   begin
      mEvent.Event := 0;
   end;
```

The GraphicMouse Methods

Three additional methods are provided which are specific to the graphics mouse object (and its descendent, GraphicLightPen). These methods are not available to the TextMouse object.

The SetCursor Method

The SetCursor method allows selection of different graphics cursors, including the five predefined graphics cursors in the Mouse unit.

```pascal
procedure GraphicMouse.SetCursor( cursor : GCursor );
   begin
      regs.AX := $09;
      regs.BX := cursor.hotX;
      regs.CX := cursor.hotY;
      regs.DX := Ofs( cursor.ScreenMask );
      regs.ES := Seg( cursor.ScreenMask );
      intr($33,regs);
   end;
```

The ConditionalHide Method

The ConditionalHide method is implemented by the Logitech mouse (and compatibles) only and is not valid for the Microsoft mouse. This allows the user to define an area of the screen where the mouse cursor will be automatically hidden.

```pascal
procedure GraphicMouse.ConditionalHide( left, top, right,
bottom : integer );
   begin
      regs.AX := $0A;
      regs.CX := left;
      regs.DX := top;
      regs.SI := right;
      regs.DI := bottom;
      intr($33,regs);
   end;
```

The ConditionalHide method is useful when updating a specific region of the screen, to avoid conflicts between the pixel drawing functions and the mouse cursor image.

The ConditionalHide setting is automatically reset by a call to interrupt 33h, function 01h (show), but is not recommended for several reasons. With EGA/VGA systems, for example, this function may not operate correctly.

Instead, I recommend calling the *Show(FALSE)* method before executing any screen update operations and then calling *Show(TRUE)* when finished— as will be demonstrated presently in the MousePtr program.

The GraphicMouse Initialize Method

The GraphicMouse Initialize method sets default conditions for the graphics mouse, including setting the mouse limits to the full screen size, establishing an initial value for the *Visible* flag, placing the mouse cursor at the center of the screen, and making the cursor visible.

```
procedure GraphicMouse.Initialize;
   begin
      Visible := FALSE;
      SetLimits( 0, 0, GetMaxX, GetMaxY );
      SetCursor( arrow );
      SetPosition( GetMaxX div 2, GetMaxY div 2 );
      Show( TRUE );
   end;
```

Other Object Mouse Methods

Several additional mouse methods are defined in the mouse unit, for text mouse and lightpen objects, which will not be demonstrated in this book. These do, however, deserve at least a brief mention.

The TextMouse Initialize Method

The Initialize method used by the TextMouse object is similar to the GraphicsMouse Initialize. It sets the cursor *Visible* flag, establishes the mouse screen (window) limits, selects the default underline text cursor type, positions the cursor and makes it visible.

```
procedure TextMouse.Initialize;
   begin
      Visible := FALSE;
      SetLimits( lo(WindMin)*8, hi(WindMin)*8,
                 lo(WindMax)*8, hi(WindMax)*8 );
      SetCursor( Hardware, 6, 7 );
      SetPosition( 0,0 );
      Show( TRUE );
   end;
```

The TextMouse SetCursor Method

Setting the mouse cursor in text modes is a bit different than the graphics mode cursor.

```
procedure TextMouse.SetCursor( cType, c1, c2 : word );
   begin
      regs.AX := $0A;
      regs.BX := cType;
      regs.CX := c1;
      regs.DX := c2;
      intr($33,regs);
   end;
```

The *cType* argument selects either the *Hardware* or *Software* cursor type while the *c1* and *c2* arguments set the cursor for the appropriate type.

The Software Text Cursor

The software text cursor is a character or character attribute that replaces and/or changes the screen character cell where the mouse cursor is positioned. The software cursor is defined by two 16-bit values: the screen mask and the cursor mask.

The screen mask is ANDed with the existing screen character and attribute, then the cursor mask is XORed with the resulting value. For further details, experimentation is suggested.

Table 13-2: Software Text Cursor Marks

BIT	DESCRIPTION
15	Blinking (1) Or Non-blinking (0) Character
14..12	Background Color
11	Foreground Intensity, High (1) Or Low (0)
10..8	Foreground Color
7..0	Character Code

The Hardware Cursor

The hardware cursor is the conventional text cursor written to the screen by the video controller and is defined by the scan lines of the character cell as shown in Table 13-3.

Table 13-3: Cursor Size Settings

VIDEO TYPE (MODE)	MONOCHROME (07h)	TEXT (00-03h)
Default Start/Stop	9h/0Ah	06h/07h
Block Start/Stop	00h/0Ah	00h/0Bh

The LightPen Methods

The two lightpen methods allow lightpen mouse emulation in either text or graphics modes and are called with Boolean arguments to turn emulation on or off.

```
procedure TextLightPen.LightPen( Option : Boolean );
   begin
      if Option then regs.AX := $0D
                else regs.AX := $0E;
      intr($33,regs);
   end;
procedure GraphicLightPen.LightPen( Option : Boolean );
   begin
      if Option then regs.AX := $0D
                else regs.AX := $0E;
      intr($33,regs);
   end;
```

The MousePtr Utility

The MousePtr utility is provided both as a demonstration for the Mouse unit and the GraphicMouse object and as a convenient utility for creating custom graphic mouse cursors for use in your own applications.

The MousePtr screen is nominally sized for EGA resolutions (350 pixels vertical) but does not apply any type of adjustment for the screen aspect ratio. Thus, on VGA systems, the grids are nominally square, but on EGA, the grids are rectangular (as are the pixels comprising the mouse cursors). For CGA video, spacing modifications will be required.

The MousePtr utility begins by drawing two 16x16 grids—the left grid for the screen mask and the right for the cursor mask—and then adds a series of option buttons across the bottom of the screen. Since this is strictly a mouse relevant operation, no provisions are made for operating any of the button selectors except by using the mouse.

Button Operations

Most of the option buttons are self-explanatory or, if they aren't, will explain themselves through experimentation. However, a few brief comments may be useful.

Both the Screen and Cursor grids are the enlarged equivalents of a mouse cursor pixel image and individual pixels may be turned on or off by clicking the left mouse button within the grid square.

The Clear and Invert buttons operate precisely as their labels suggest, each operating on its respective grid. The Copy to Screen button copies the cursor mask bit for bit to the screen mask. The Make from Cursor button creates a screen mask from the cursor mask image, leaving a one-pixel border around the cursor image.

The HotSpot button allows selection of a target pixel, which will be the mouse cursor's hot spot. When selected, the button changes color and the next pixel selected—in either the screen or cursor masks—will become the new hot spot and will be indicated by a color shift. The default hot spot is the 0,0 pixel or the upper-left corner.

Even though a mouse cursor may have a valid hot spot that lies outside of the 16 by 16 pixel image (x/y values are valid in the range −16..16), no provisions are made here to select positions outside of the active grid. If variant coordinates are required, the .CUR file created by the Save Pointer option can be edited directly.

The Use Pointer button (bottom row) makes a new, active mouse cursor from the current cursor and screen masks and the current hot spot settings. The Arrow Pointer button restores the default, slanted-arrow mouse cursor.

Selecting the Load Pointer button, see Figure 13-7, writes a new prompt at the top center of the screen, requesting a filename to load a cursor image. All cursor files are assumed to have the extension .CUR. Notice also that the active mouse cursor has been switched to the IBeam cursor and remains located at the current character position.

The Save Pointer button uses a prompt similar to the Load Pointer option, requesting a filename (a maximum of eight characters), and again assuming the .CUR extension.

Both save and load operations use ASCII text files that contain a cursor description in a format compatible with Turbo Pascal program codes. The .CUR files can be imported directly into a program, see Figure 13-8 for a sample output file.

Finally, the remaining Quit button requires no comment. I should, however, caution you that no protection has been supplied to prevent an accidental exit. After all, you're the programmer and you're supposed to be smarter than the average user, right?

Summary

The object mouse unit, MOUSE.TPU, will be required by several of the later programs in this book, but is also an extremely useful unit for graphics and text programming applications in general.

Figure 13-7: The MousePtr Display

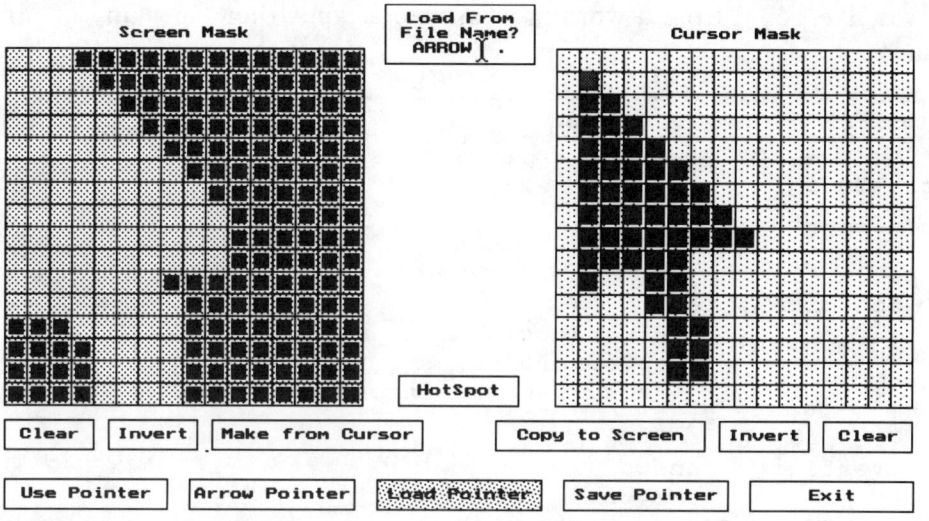

Figure 13-8: MousePtr's Output File: IBEAM.CUR

```
const
   IBEAM : GCursor =
   (  ScreenMask : ( $E10F, $E00F, $E00F, $F83F,
                     $FC7F, $FC7F, $FC7F, $FC7F,
                     $FC7F, $FC7F, $FC7F, $FC7F,
                     $F83F, $E00F, $E00F, $E10F );
      CursorMask : ( $0000, $0C60, $0280, $0100,
                     $0100, $0100, $0100, $0100,
                     $0100, $0100, $0100, $0100,
                     $0100, $0280, $0C60, $0000 );
      hotX : $0007;   hotY : $0007 );
```

The second program, MOUSEPTR.PAS, not only demonstrates the use of the GraphicMouse object, but also provides a convenient utility to create custom graphics mouse cursor images.

In Chapter 14, notice how much more convenient Button object controls would have been if used in place of the control button rectangles demonstrated in the MOUSEPTR program. Avoiding use of the control objects unit to create the current demo program—since the control object subject had not yet been discussed—not only made the program code much longer than an object version, but also took much more time to write.

Having quickly become accustomed to the convenience of object programming, it also felt like a major step backwards to not use an existing object unit, it was like going from a word processor to a typewriter (speaking of nightmares).

Mouse.PAS

```pascal
unit MOUSE;

INTERFACE

type
   Position = record
                 BtnStatus,
                 opCount,
                 xPos, yPos   : integer;
              end;

   EventRec = record
                 Event,
                 BtnStatus,
                 XPos, YPos : word;
              end;

   GCursor =  record
                 ScreenMask,
                 CursorMask : array [0..15] of word;
                 hotX, hotY : integer;
              end;

var
   mEvent : EventRec;

const
   ButtonL  = 0;
   ButtonR  = 1;
   ButtonM  = 2;
   Software = 0;
   Hardware = 1;
   OFF      = 0;
   ON       = 1;

            {=======================================}
            { five graphics cursors are predefined }
            { for use with GraphicMouse            }
            {=======================================}

   arrow : GCursor =              { default graphics cursor }
       ( ScreenMask : ( $1FFF, $0FFF, $07FF, $03FF,
                        $01FF, $00FF, $007F, $003F,
```

Chapter 13: Using a Mouse with Graphics Display 251

```
                            $001F,  $003F,  $01FF,  $01FF,
                            $E0FF,  $F0FF,  $F8FF,  $F8FF );
            CursorMask : (  $0000,  $4000,  $6000,  $7000,
                            $7800,  $7C00,  $7E00,  $7F00,
                            $7F80,  $7C00,  $4C00,  $0600,
                            $0600,  $0300,  $0300,  $0000 );
            hotX : $0001;   hotY : $0001 );
    check : GCursor =                { check mark graphics cursor }
        (   ScreenMask : (  $FFF0,  $FFE0,  $FFC0,  $FF81,
                            $FF03,  $0607,  $000F,  $001F,
                            $803F,  $C07F,  $E0FF,  $F1FF,
                            $FFFF,  $FFFF,  $FFFF,  $FFFF );
            CursorMask : (  $0000,  $0006,  $000C,  $0018,
                            $0030,  $0060,  $70C0,  $3980,
                            $1F00,  $0E00,  $0400,  $0000,
                            $0000,  $0000,  $0000,  $0000 );
            hotX : $0005;   hotY : $0010 );
    cross : GCursor =                { circle with cross hairs }
        (   ScreenMask : (  $F01F,  $E00F,  $C007,  $8003,
                            $0441,  $0C61,  $0381,  $0381,
                            $0381,  $0C61,  $0441,  $8003,
                            $C007,  $E00F,  $F01F,  $FFFF );
            CursorMask : (  $0000,  $07C0,  $0920,  $1110,
                            $2108,  $4004,  $4004,  $783C,
                            $4004,  $4004,  $2108,  $1110,
                            $0920,  $07C0,  $0000,  $0000 );
            hotX : $0007;   hotY : $0007 );
    glove : GCursor =                { glove or hand image cursor }
        (   ScreenMask : (  $F3FF,  $E1FF,  $E1FF,  $E1FF,
                            $E1FF,  $E049,  $E000,  $8000,
                            $0000,  $0000,  $07FC,  $07F8,
                            $9FF9,  $8FF1,  $C003,  $E007 );
            CursorMask : (  $0C00,  $1200,  $1200,  $1200,
                            $1200,  $13B6,  $1249,  $7249,
                            $9249,  $9001,  $9001,  $8001,
                            $4002,  $4002,  $2004,  $1FF8 );
            hotX : $0004;   hotY : $0000 );
    ibeam : GCursor =                           { I-beam cursor }
        (   ScreenMask : (  $E10F,  $E00F,  $F83F,  $FC7F,
                            $FC7F,  $FC7F,  $FC7F,  $FC7F,
                            $FC7F,  $FC7F,  $FC7F,  $FC7F,
                            $FC7F,  $F83F,  $E00F,  $E10F );
            CursorMask : (  $0000,  $0C60,  $0280,  $0100,
                            $0100,  $0100,  $0100,  $0100,
                            $0100,  $0100,  $0100,  $0100,
                            $0100,  $0280,  $0C60,  $0000 );
```

```pascal
                hotX : $0007;  hotY : $0007 );
type
   GenMouse = object
      x, y : integer;
      visible : Boolean;
      function  TestMouse: boolean;
      procedure SetAccel( threshold : integer );
      procedure Show( Option : Boolean );
      procedure InstallTask( Mask : word );
      procedure ClearEvent;
      procedure GetPosition( var BtnStatus,
                             XPos, YPos : integer );
      procedure QueryBtnDn( button : integer;
                            var mouse : Position );
      procedure QueryBtnUp( button : integer;
                            var mouse : Position );
      procedure ReadMove( var XMove, YMove : integer );
      procedure Reset( var Status : Boolean;
                       var BtnCount : integer );
      procedure SetRatio( horPix, verPix : integer );
      procedure SetLimits( XPosMin, YPosMin,
                           XPosMax, YPosMax : integer );
      procedure SetPosition( XPos, YPos : integer );
   end;

   GraphicMouse = object( GenMouse )
      procedure Initialize;
      procedure ConditionalHide( left, top,
                                 right, bottom : integer );
      procedure SetCursor( cursor : GCursor );
   end;

   TextMouse = object( GenMouse )
      procedure Initialize;
      procedure SetCursor( ctype, C1, C2 : word );
   end;

   GraphicLightPen = object( GraphicMouse )
      procedure LightPen( Option : Boolean );
   end;

   TextLightPen = object( TextMouse )
      procedure LightPen( Option : Boolean );
   end;

IMPLEMENTATION
uses Crt, Graph, Dos;
var
   Regs : registers;
```

```
      function Lower( n1, n2 : integer ) : integer;
         begin                                       { local function }
            if n1 < n2 then Lower := n1
                       else Lower := n2;
         end;
      function Upper( n1, n2 : integer ) : integer;
         begin                                       { local function }
            if n1 > n2 then Upper := n1
                       else Upper := n2;
         end;
   procedure MouseHandler( Flags, CS, IP, AX, BX, CX, DX,
                           SI, DI, DS, ES, BP : word );
      INTERRUPT;
      begin
         mEvent.Event     := AX;
         mEvent.BtnStatus := BX;
         mEvent.xPos      := CX;
         mEvent.yPos      := DX;
         { exit processing for far return to driver }
         inline( $8B/$E5/                   { MOV SP, BP }
                 $5D/                       { POP BP }
                 $07/                       { POP ES }
                 $1F/                       { POP DS }
                 $5F/                       { POP DI }
                 $5E/                       { POP SI }
                 $5A/                       { POP DX }
                 $59/                       { POP CX }
                 $5B/                       { POP BX }
                 $58/                       { POP AX }
                 $CB );                     { RETF   }
      end;

            {===========================================}
            { implementation methods for GeneralMouse }
            {===========================================}
   function GenMouse.TestMouse : Boolean;
      const
         iret = 207;
      var
         dOff, dSeg : integer;
      begin
         dOff := MemW[0000:0204];
         dSeg := MemW[0000:0206];
         if( ( dSeg = 0 ) or ( dOff = 0 ) )
            then TestMouse := FALSE
            else TestMouse := Mem[dSeg:dOff] <> iret;
```

```pascal
      end;
procedure GenMouse.Reset( var Status : Boolean; var
BtnCount : integer );
   begin
      regs.AX := $00;          { reset to default conditions }
      intr($33,regs);
      Status   := regs.AX <> 0;              { mouse present }
      BtnCount := regs.BX;                    { button count }
   end;
procedure GenMouse.SetAccel( threshold : integer );
   begin
      regs.AX := $13;
      regs.DX := threshold;
      intr($33,regs);
   end;
procedure GenMouse.Show( Option : Boolean );
   begin
      if Option and not Visible then
      begin
         regs.AX := $01;               { show mouse cursor }
         Visible := TRUE;
         intr($33,regs);
      end else
      if Visible and not Option then
      begin
         regs.AX := $02;               { hide mouse cursor }
         Visible := FALSE;
         intr($33,regs);
      end;
   end;
procedure GenMouse.GetPosition( var BtnStatus,
                                XPos, YPos : integer );
   begin                                      { function 03h }
      regs.AX := $03;
      intr($33,regs);
      BtnStatus := regs.BX;
      XPos      := regs.CX;
      YPos      := regs.DX;
   end;
procedure GenMouse.SetPosition( XPos, YPos : integer );
   begin
      regs.AX := $04;
      regs.CX := XPos;
      regs.DX := YPos;
      intr($33,regs);
```

```
        end;
procedure GenMouse.SetRatio( horPix, verPix : integer );
   begin
      regs.AX := $0F;
      regs.CX := horPix;                  { horizontal ratio }
      regs.DX := verPix;                  { vertical ratio   }
      intr($33,regs);
   end;
procedure GenMouse.QueryBtnDn( button : integer;
                               var mouse : Position );
   begin
      regs.AX := $05;                              { function 05h }
      regs.BX := button;
      intr($33,regs);
      mouse.BtnStatus := regs.AX;
      mouse.opCount := regs.BX;
      mouse.xPos    := regs.CX;
      mouse.yPos    := regs.DX;
   end;
procedure GenMouse.QueryBtnUp( button : integer;
                               var mouse : Position );
   begin
      regs.AX := $06;
      regs.BX := button;
      intr($33,regs);
      mouse.BtnStatus := regs.AX;
      mouse.opCount := regs.BX;
      mouse.xPos    := regs.CX;
      mouse.yPos    := regs.DX;
   end;
procedure GenMouse.SetLimits( XPosMin, YPosMin,
                              XPosMax, YPosMax: integer);
   begin
      regs.AX := $07;                     { horizontal limits }
      regs.CX := Lower(XPosMin,XPosMax);
      regs.DX := Upper(XPosMin,XPosMax);
      intr($33,regs);
      regs.AX := $08;                     { vertical limits }
      regs.CX := Lower(YPosMin,YPosMax);
      regs.DX := Upper(YPosMin,YPosMax);
      intr($33,regs);
   end;
procedure GenMouse.ReadMove( var XMove,
                             YMove : integer );
   begin
```

```pascal
        regs.AX := $0B;
        intr($33,regs);
        XMove := regs.CX;
        YMove := regs.DX;
    end;
procedure GenMouse.InstallTask;
    begin
        regs.AX := $0B;
        regs.CX := Mask;
        regs.DX := ofs(MouseHandler);
        regs.ES := seg(MouseHandler);
        intr($33,regs);
    end;
procedure GenMouse.ClearEvent;
    begin
        mEvent.Event := 0;
    end;
            {=========================================}
            { implementation method for GraphicsMouse }
            {=========================================}
procedure GraphicMouse.SetCursor( cursor : GCursor );
    begin
        regs.AX := $09;
        regs.BX := cursor.hotX;
        regs.CX := cursor.hotY;
        regs.DX := Ofs( cursor.ScreenMask );
        regs.ES := Seg( cursor.ScreenMask );
        intr($33,regs);
    end;
procedure GraphicMouse.ConditionalHide( left, top, right,
bottom : integer );
    begin
        regs.AX := $0A;                         { function 0Ah }
        regs.CX := left;
        regs.DX := top;
        regs.SI := right;
        regs.DI := bottom;
        intr($33,regs);
    end;
procedure GraphicMouse.Initialize;
    begin
        Visible := FALSE;
        SetLimits( 0, 0, GetMaxX, GetMaxY );
        SetCursor( arrow );
        SetPosition( GetMaxX div 2, GetMaxY div 2 );
```

```pascal
            Show( TRUE );
         end;

            {=====================================}
            { implementation method for TextMouse }
            {=====================================}
procedure TextMouse.Initialize;
   begin
      Visible := FALSE;
      SetLimits( lo(WindMin)*8, hi(WindMin)*8,
                 lo(WindMax)*8, hi(WindMax)*8 );
      SetCursor( Hardware, 6, 7 );
      SetPosition( 0,0 );
      Show( TRUE );
   end;
procedure TextMouse.SetCursor( cType, c1, c2 : word );
   begin
      regs.AX := $0A;                         { function 10h }
      regs.BX := cType;       { 0 = software, 1 = hardware }
      regs.CX := c1;       { screen mask or scan start line }
      regs.DX := c2;       { cursor mask or scan stop line }
      intr($33,regs);
   end;
            {========================================}
            { implementation method for TextLightPen }
            {========================================}
procedure TextLightPen.LightPen( Option : Boolean );
   begin
      if Option then regs.AX := $0D        { turn pen on  }
                else regs.AX := $0E;       { turn pen off }
      intr($33,regs);
   end;
            {============================================}
            { implementation method for GraphicsLightPen }
            {============================================}
procedure GraphicLightPen.LightPen( Option : Boolean );
   begin
      if Option then regs.AX := $0D        { turn pen on  }
                else regs.AX := $0E;       { turn pen off }
      intr($33,regs);
   end;
end.
```

MousePtr.PAS

```pascal
program MousePointer;
uses Crt, Graph, Mouse;
type
   Str20 = string[20];
var
   GMouse     : GraphicMouse;
   TMouse     : TextMouse;
   mButton    : Position;
   NewCursor  : GCursor;
   GDriver, GMode, GError, i, j, Buttons,
      XIndex, YIndex, HotSpotX, HotSpotY : integer;
   Exit, HotSpotSelect, MStatus : Boolean;
   outline : array[1..5] of pointtype;
   Screen, Cursor : array[0..15,0..15] of Boolean;
   Ch : char;
procedure BoxItem( x, y, w, h : integer; text : str20 );
   begin
      SetTextJustify( CenterText, CenterText );
      Rectangle( x, y, x+w, y+h );
      OutTextXY( x+(w div 2), y+(h div 2), text );
   end;
procedure FillSquare( x1, y1, x2, y2,
                      FillStyle, Color : integer );
   var
      outline : array[1..5] of PointType;
   begin
      outline[1].x := x1;   outline[1].y := y1;
      outline[2].x := x2;   outline[2].y := y1;
      outline[3].x := x2;   outline[3].y := y2;
      outline[4].x := x1;   outline[4].y := y2;
      outline[5] := outline[1];
      SetFillStyle( FillStyle, Color );
      FillPoly( sizeof(outline) div sizeof( PointType ),
               outline );
   end;
procedure EraseSquare( x1, y1, x2, y2 : integer );
   var
      i, j : integer;
   begin
      FillSquare( x1, y1, x2, y2, SolidFill, BLACK );
   end;
procedure Beep;
   begin
      Sound( 220 ); delay( 100 ); NoSound;
                  delay( 50 );
```

```pascal
            Sound( 440 ); delay( 100 ); NoSound;
        end;
function StrToHex( WorkStr: string ): word;
    var
        TempVal : word;
    begin
        TempVal := $0000;
        for i := 1 to length(WorkStr) do
        begin
            TempVal := TempVal shl 4;
            case WorkStr[i] of
                '1'..'9': inc( TempVal,
                                ord( WorkStr[i] ) - $30 );
                'A'..'F': inc( TempVal,
                                ord( WorkStr[i] ) - $37 );
            end; {case}
        end;
        StrToHex := TempVal;
    end;
function HexToStr( NumVal : word ): string;
    const
        HexStr = '0123456789ABCDEF';
    var
        Temp : string[4];
        CVal : byte;
          i : integer;
    begin
        Temp := '';
        for i := 1 to 4 do
        begin
            CVal := ( NumVal and $000F ) + 1;
            NumVal := NumVal shr 4;
            Temp := copy( HexStr, CVal, 1 ) + Temp;
        end;
        HexToStr := Temp;
    end;
procedure MakeCursor;
    var
        i, j : integer;
        TBit : word;
    begin
        with NewCursor do
        begin
            hotX := HotSpotX;
            hotY := HotSpotY;
            for i := 0 to 15 do
            begin
```

```pascal
                    ScreenMask[i] := $0000;
                    CursorMask[i] := $0000;
                end;
                for i := 0 to 15 do
                begin
                    TBit := $0001;
                    for j := 0 to 15 do
                    begin
                        CursorMask[i] := CursorMask[i] shl 1;
                        if Cursor[j,i] then inc( CursorMask[i] );
                        ScreenMask[i] := ScreenMask[i] shl 1;
                        if Screen[j,i] then inc( ScreenMask[i] );
                    end;
                end;
            end;
        end;
    procedure UseNewCursor;
        begin
            MakeCursor;
            GMouse.Show( FALSE );
            GMouse.SetCursor( NewCursor );
            GMouse.Show( TRUE );
        end;
    procedure PaintScreen( X, Y : integer );
        var
            Color : integer;
        begin
            if ( X = HotSpotX ) and ( Y = HotSpotY )
                then Color := LIGHTRED
                else Color := WHITE;
            GMouse.Show( FALSE );
            if Screen[X,Y] then
                FillSquare( (X+1)*15+3, (Y+2)*15+3,
                            (X+2)*15-3, (Y+3)*15-3,
                            SolidFill, Color )
            else
                FillSquare( (X+1)*15, (Y+2)*15,
                            (X+2)*15, (Y+3)*15,
                            CloseDotFill, WHITE );
            GMouse.Show( TRUE );
            SetColor( WHITE );
        end;
    procedure PaintCursor( X, Y : integer );
        var
            Color : integer;
        begin
            if ( X = HotSpotX ) and ( Y = HotSpotY )
```

```
            then Color := LIGHTRED
            else Color := WHITE;
    GMouse.Show( FALSE );
    if Cursor[X,Y] then
        FillSquare( (X+1)*15+369, (Y+2)*15,
                    (X+2)*15+366, (Y+3)*15-3,
                    SolidFill, Color )
    else
        FillSquare( (X+1)*15+369, (Y+2)*15,
                    (X+2)*15+369, (Y+3)*15,
                    WideDotFill, Color );
    GMouse.Show( TRUE );
    SetColor( WHITE );
    end;
procedure HotSpotComplete;
    var
        X, Y : integer;
    begin
        X := HotSpotX;
        Y := HotSpotY;
        PaintCursor( X, Y );
        PaintScreen( X, Y );
        GMouse.Show( FALSE );
        HotSpotSelect := FALSE;
        SetColor( WHITE );
        SetTextJustify( CenterText, CenterText );
        BoxItem(   279, 250, 80, 20, 'HotSpot' );
        GMouse.Show( TRUE );
    end;
procedure SetHotSpot;
    var
        X, Y : integer;
    begin
        X := HotSpotX;
        Y := HotSpotY;
        HotSpotX := -1;
        HotSpotY := -1;
        PaintCursor( X, Y );
        PaintScreen( X, Y );
        GMouse.Show( FALSE );
        HotSpotSelect := TRUE;
        SetColor( RED );
        SetTextJustify( CenterText, CenterText );
        BoxItem(   279, 250, 80, 20, 'HotSpot' );
        SetColor( WHITE );
        GMouse.Show( TRUE );
    end;
```

```pascal
procedure ScreenLayout;
   var
      j : integer;
   begin
      j := GetMaxX;
      SetTextJustify( CenterText, CenterText );
      OutTextXY( 135, 20, 'Screen Mask' );
      OutTextXY( 504, 20, 'Cursor Mask' );
      HotSpotComplete;
         { screen mask items }
      BoxItem(  15, 280,  60, 20, 'Clear' );
      BoxItem(  85, 280,  60, 20, 'Invert' );
      BoxItem( 155, 280, 140, 20, 'Make from Cursor' );
         { cursor mask items }
      BoxItem( 564, 280,  60, 20, 'Clear' );
      BoxItem( 494, 280,  60, 20, 'Invert' );
      BoxItem( 344, 280, 140, 20, 'Copy to Screen' );
         { control options }
      BoxItem(  15, 320, 110, 20, 'Use Pointer' );
      BoxItem( 140, 320, 110, 20, 'Arrow Pointer' );
      BoxItem( 265, 320, 110, 20, 'Load Pointer' );
      BoxItem( 390, 320, 110, 20, 'Save Pointer' );
      BoxItem( 515, 320, 110, 20, 'Exit' );
   end;
procedure ClearScreen;
   var
      i, j : integer;
   begin
      for i := 0 to 15 do
         for j := 0 to 15 do
            if Screen[i,j] then
            begin
               Screen[i,j] := FALSE;
               PaintScreen( i, j );
            end;
   end;
procedure ClearCursor;
   var
      i, j : integer;
   begin
      for i := 0 to 15 do
         for j := 0 to 15 do
            if Cursor[i,j] then
            begin
               Cursor[i,j] := FALSE;
               PaintCursor( i, j );
            end;
```

```
      end;
procedure InvertScreen;
   var
      i, j : integer;
   begin
      for i := 0 to 15 do
         for j := 0 to 15 do
            begin
               Screen[i,j] := not Screen[i,j];
               PaintScreen( i, j );
            end;
   end;
procedure InvertCursor;
   var
      i, j : integer;
   begin
      for i := 0 to 15 do
         for j := 0 to 15 do
            begin
               Cursor[i,j] := not Cursor[i,j];
               PaintCursor( i, j );
            end;
   end;
procedure ScreenSet( mButton : Position );
   var
      x, y : integer;
   begin
      x := mButton.xPos div 15 - 1;
      y := mButton.yPos div 15 - 2;
      if HotSpotSelect then
      begin
         HotSpotX := x;
         HotSpotY := y;
         HotSpotComplete;
      end else
      begin
         Screen[x,y] := not Screen[x,y];
         PaintScreen( x, y );
      end;
   end;
procedure CursorSet( mButton : Position );
   var
      x, y : integer;
   begin
      x := ( mButton.xPos - 384 ) div 15;
      y := mButton.yPos div 15 - 2;
```

```pascal
            if HotSpotSelect then
            begin
                HotSpotX := x;
                HotSpotY := y;
                HotSpotComplete;
            end else Cursor[x,y] := not Cursor[x,y];
            PaintCursor( x, y );
        end;
procedure CursorToScreen;
    var
        i, j : integer;
    begin
        for i := 0 to 15 do
            for j := 0 to 15 do
                begin
                    Screen[i,j] := Cursor[i,j];
                    PaintScreen( i, j );
                end;
    end;
procedure ScreenFromCursor;
    var
        i, j, x, y : integer;
        Test : boolean;
    begin
        for i := 0 to 15 do
            for j := 0 to 15 do
                begin
                    Test := TRUE;
                    for x := -1 to 1 do
                        for y := -1 to 1 do
                            if( i+x in [0..15] ) and
                               ( j+y in [0..15] ) and
                              Cursor[i+x,j+y] then
                                  Test := FALSE;
                    Screen[i,j] := Test;
                    PaintScreen( i, j );
                end;
    end;
procedure SavePointer;
    var
        i, j, k : integer;
        Ch : char;
        CF : text;
        Done : Boolean;
        FileName : string[12];
    begin
        i := 0;
```

```
Done := FALSE;
FileName := '........';
SetViewPort( 269, 0, 369, 42, TRUE );
SetTextJustify( CenterText, CenterText );
GMouse.SetCursor( ibeam );
repeat
   inc(i);
   GMouse.Show( FALSE );
   ClearViewPort;
   SetColor( LightRed );
   Rectangle( 0, 0, 100, 40 );
   OutTextXY( 50, 10, 'Save As');
   OutTextXY( 50, 20, 'File Name?' );
   OutTextXY( 50, 30, FileName);
   GMouse.Show( TRUE );
   GMouse.SetPosition( 285+i*8,30 );
   repeat until KeyPressed;
   Ch := ReadKey;
   case Ch of
        #$0D : Done := TRUE;
        #$08 : if( i > 1 ) then dec( i,2 );
      '0'..'9',
             ' ',
      'A'..'Z',
      'a'..'z': if( i > 8 ) then
                   begin
                       Beep;
                       dec(i,1);
                   end else FileName[i] := UpCase(Ch);
   end; {case}
until Done;
GMouse.SetCursor( arrow );
GMouse.Show( FALSE );
ClearViewPort;
GMouse.Show( TRUE );
for i := 8 downto 1 do
   if ( FileName[i] = '.' ) or
      ( FileName[i] = ' ' )
      then FileName[0] := chr(i-1);
FileName := FileName+'.CUR';
SetViewPort( 0, 0, GetMaxX, GetMaxY, TRUE );
MakeCursor;
if FileName <> '' then
begin
   Assign( CF, FileName );
   Rewrite( CF );
   writeln( CF, 'const');
   write( CF, '    ' +
          copy( FileName, 1, length(FileName)-4 ) );
```

```pascal
            writeln( CF, ' : GCursor =');
            with NewCursor do
            begin
               writeln( CF, '    (   ScreenMask : ( $',
                     HexToStr(ScreenMask[0]), ', $',
                     HexToStr(ScreenMask[1]), ', $',
                     HexToStr(ScreenMask[2]), ', $',
                     HexToStr(ScreenMask[3]), ',' );
               for i := 1 to 3 do
               begin
                  write( CF, '                            $',
                     HexToStr(ScreenMask[i*4  ]), ', $',
                     HexToStr(ScreenMask[i*4+1]), ', $',
                     HexToStr(ScreenMask[i*4+2]), ', $',
                     HexToStr(ScreenMask[i*4+3]) );
                  if i < 3 then writeln( CF, ',' )
                           else writeln( CF, ' ); ' );
               end;
               writeln( CF, '        CursorMask : ( $',
                     HexToStr(CursorMask[0]), ', $',
                     HexToStr(CursorMask[1]), ', $',
                     HexToStr(CursorMask[2]), ', $',
                     HexToStr(CursorMask[3]), ',' );
               for i := 1 to 3 do
               begin
                  write( CF, '                            $',
                     HexToStr(CursorMask[i*4  ]), ', $',
                     HexToStr(CursorMask[i*4+1]), ', $',
                     HexToStr(CursorMask[i*4+2]), ', $',
                     HexToStr(CursorMask[i*4+3]) );
                  if i < 3 then writeln( CF, ',' )
                           else writeln( CF, ' ); ' );
               end;
               writeln( CF, '        hotX : $',
                        HexToStr(hotX),
                          '; hotY : $',
                        HexToStr(hotY), ' );' );
            end;
            writeln( CF );
            Close( CF );
         end else Beep;
      end;
procedure LoadPointer;
   var
      i, j, k : integer;
      Ch : char;
      CF : text;
      Done : Boolean;
```

```
      FileName : string[12];
      WorkText : string;
      TempVal  : word;
begin
   i := 0;
   Done := FALSE;
   FileName := '........';
   SetViewPort( 269, 0, 369, 42, TRUE )
   SetTextJustify( CenterText, CenterT\
   GMouse.SetCursor( ibeam );
   repeat
      inc(i);
      GMouse.Show( FALSE );
      ClearViewPort;
      SetColor( LightRed );
      Rectangle( 0, 0, 100, 40 );
      OutTextXY( 50, 10, 'Load From');
      OutTextXY( 50, 20, 'File Name?' );
      OutTextXY( 50, 30, FileName);
      GMouse.Show( TRUE );
      GMouse.SetPosition( 285+i*8,30 );
      repeat until KeyPressed;
      Ch := ReadKey;
      case Ch of
           #$0D : Done := TRUE;
           #$08 : if( i > 1 ) then dec( i,2 );
           '0'..'9',
               ' ',
           'A'..'Z',
           'a'..'z': if( i > 8 ) then
                     begin
                        Beep;
                        dec(i,1);
                     end else FileName[i] := UpCase(Ch);
      end; {case}
   until Done;
   GMouse.SetCursor( arrow );
   SetColor( White );
   GMouse.Show( FALSE );
   ClearViewPort;
   SetViewPort( 0, 0, GetMaxX, GetMaxY, TRUE );
   GMouse.Show( TRUE );
   for i := 8 downto 1 do
      if( FileName[i] = '.' ) or
         ( FileName[i] = ' ' )
         then FileName[0] := chr(i-1);
   if FileName <> '' then
   begin
      FileName := FileName+'.CUR';
```

```
Assign( CF, FileName );
{$I-} Reset( CF ); {$I+}
if( IOresult = 0 ) then
begin
   ClearScreen;
   ClearCursor;
   i := 0;
   repeat
      readln( CF, WorkText );
      if Pos('$',WorkText) > 0 then
         for j := 1 to 4 do
         begin
            while WorkText[1] <> '$' do
               delete(WorkText,1,1);
            delete(WorkText,1,1);
            TempVal :=
               StrToHex(copy(WorkText,1,4));
            case i of
               0..15: for k := 0 to 15 do
                  begin
                     if(TempVal AND $8000)<>0
                     then begin
                        Screen[k,i] := TRUE;
                        PaintScreen(k,i);
                     end;
                     TempVal := TempVal shl 1;
                  end;
               16..31: for k := 0 to 15 do
                  begin
                     if(TempVal AND $8000)<>0
                     then
                        Cursor[k,i-16] := TRUE;
                        PaintCursor(k,i-16);
                     TempVal := TempVal shl 1;
                  end;
               32: HotSpotX := TempVal;
               33: begin
                  HotSpotY := TempVal;
                  PaintCursor( HotSpotX, HotSpotY );
                  PaintScreen( HotSpotX, HotSpotY );
                  j := 4;          { break out of loop }
               end;
            end; {case}
            inc( i );
         end;
   until i > 33;
   Close( CF );
end else Beep;
```

```pascal
            end else Beep;
        end;
begin
    GDriver := Detect;
    InitGraph( GDriver, GMode, '\TP\BGI' );
    SetGraphMode( 1 );
    GError := GraphResult;
    if GError <> grOk then
    begin
        writeln('Graphics error: ',GraphErrorMsg(GError));
        writeln('Program aborted...');
        halt(1);
    end;
    ClearDevice;
    Exit := FALSE;
    ScreenLayout;
    for i := 0 to 15 do
        for j := 0 to 15 do
        begin
            Screen[i,j] := TRUE;
            Cursor[i,j] := TRUE;
        end;
    ClearCursor;
    ClearScreen;
    GMouse.Reset( mStatus, Buttons );
    if mStatus then
    begin
        SetWriteMode( CopyPut );
        GMouse.Initialize;
        with GMouse do
        repeat
            QueryBtnDn( ButtonL, mButton );
            if mButton.opCount > 0 then
            begin
                case mButton.yPos of
                    30..270 :            { screen or cursor grids }
                        case mButton.xPos of
                            15..255 : ScreenSet( mButton );
                            279..359 : if mButton.yPos >= 250
                                          then SetHotSpot;
                            384..624 : CursorSet( mButton );
                        end; { case mButton.xPos }
                    280..300 :       { screen or cursor commands }
                        case mButton.xPos of
                            15..75:  ClearScreen;
                            85..145: InvertScreen;
                            155..295: ScreenFromCursor;
                            364..484: CursorToScreen;
```

```
                        494..554: InvertCursor;
                        564..624: ClearCursor;
                      end; { case mButton.XPos }
                320..340 :          { general command options }
                  case mButton.xPos of
                       15..125: UseNewCursor;
                      140..250: SetCursor( arrow );
                      265..375: LoadPointer;
                      390..500: SavePointer;
                      515..625: Exit := TRUE;
                   end; { case mButton.xPos }
              end; { case mButton.yPos }
           end;
        until Exit;
     end;
     TMouse.Reset( mStatus, Buttons );
     TMouse.SetCursor( hardware, 11, 12 );
     Beep;
end.
```

CHAPTER 14

Buttons, Scrollbars, and Control Objects

The point of graphics programming and a graphics mouse is to provide your applications with graphics controls.

In Chapter 13, as a first step in this direction, the GraphicMouse object was demonstrated by the MousePtr utility in which a number of screen controls were mouse-operated. Each of these control buttons, however, required specific code to create the button image, to write a label to each button box, and to test the mouse coordinates each time a button was pressed to decide which control had been selected.

Any changes in the layout of the screen could only be accomplished by changing every program element that applied to each control element changed.

In brief, both creating the program and revising the program entailed laborious attention to detail as well as presenting considerable opportunity for errors. Of course, when any opportunity for error exists, the guiding principles of the universe become actively engaged to ensure that such an error will occur.

But there are also ways to reduce the probabilities of error without giving up graphics controls. And, since the amount of work required to create these controls can also be reduced—or eliminated—by creating graphic control objects instead of individual graphic controls, suddenly graphics controls become more convenient than conventional application controls.

Graphic Control Objects

The object-oriented programming extensions provided by Turbo Pascal 5.5 offer a variety of conveniences for the programmer. One area where the conveniences are most impressive (if only in the visual sense) is in creating graphic control objects.

For graphics applications, a control object has to fill five major criteria and should be able to:

- create and maintain its own screen display
- change size and position if required
- change appearance as appropriate to its function (buttons, for example, change visual state to indicate a mouse hit or selection state)
- respond to a mouse event directly or indirectly (the minimum requirement is that an object must be able to test the mouse event coordinates against its own position and size and report a hit when it occurs)
- the graphic control object must be able to erase itself from the screen and, if required, remove itself from memory

Other tasks and capabilities will also be assigned to graphic control objects, but these five are the absolute minimum which will be demanded of any graphics control. But these are also the tasks which, in conventional programming, are the hardest to accomplish and require the major portion of the programmer's time in developing an application and in revising and debugging the program.

With a graphic control object, however, only one instance of a specific object type requires the programmer's attention—the first one created.

Once the first instance of an object has been created and debugged, any number of clones of the object can be created, without each instance requiring repetitive debugging and problem solving.

Furthermore, creating a new object type descended from a working object requires less time and work than writing a new feature using conventional programming. This is because much of the task is inherited from the ancestor object and does not require laborious repetition. Nor is there the probability of additional errors.

If any additional inducement is required, once an graphic control object unit has been created, the graphic controls can be used as if they were extensions to Turbo Pascal.

Creating Graphic Control Objects

The graphic control unit (GCONTROL.TPU) will provide four object types, though only three are actually control objects: Button, RadioButton, and

ScrollBar. The fourth object type, VueMeter, is a graphics analog of an older tuning or metering device popular in electronics applications before the days of digital displays.

Before discussing the graphics control objects, however, the GControl unit uses three other units: Crt, Graph, and Mouse. The first two are standard units supplied by Turbo Pascal and the third unit, Mouse.TPU, supplies the various mouse object types (see Chapter 13).

Also, an ancestor object type, Point, provides the primal ancestor for the other object types.

The Point Object Type

The Point object is provided as a generic ancestor for all graphic objects, supplying the basic position and color variables, a reference variable for restoring viewport settings and a variety of methods which will be needed by most descendent object types. (The Point object type is neither illustrated nor demonstrated.)

```
Point = object
    x, y, Color : integer;
    VRef : ViewPortType;
```

Since the Point object type and its methods are declared in the Interface section of the unit, objects of type Point can be created by applications using the unit, even though this is not the intended use of the Point type.

The real reason for the Point type appearing as a separate type and in the Interface section is so the Point variables and methods can be used, not only by the current object types, but also by other descendent object types that may be created by calling on the GCONTROL.TPU unit without having the source code for the unit.

If you are not familiar with how descendent object types are created, a more complete explanation is provided in *Object-Oriented Programming in Turbo Pascal 5.5*, available from Addison-Wesley Publishing Company.

Point.Init

The Point object type is supplied with a variety of basic methods, beginning with the Init constructor, which is used to initialize a Point object instance. Each descendent object type will have its own, different initialization procedure providing the required handling.

```
constructor Point.Init;
   begin
      GetViewSettings( VRef );
   end;
```

In this case, the Init method does nothing by itself except save the viewport settings that are in effect when the object is created.

Point.Create

The Create method, for the Point object, is called with three parameters; the first two specify screen location and the third sets the color.

```
procedure Point.Create( PtX, PtY, C : integer );
   begin
      SetLoc( PtX, PtY );
      Color := C;
      Draw;
   end;
```

Point.Move

The Move method accepts only two coordinate parameters and moves an existing object from its present location. It begins by calling the Erase method, changing the position coordinates by calling SetLoc and then calling the Draw method to recreate the object at its new location.

```
procedure Point.Move( PtX, PtY : integer );
   begin
      Erase;
      SetLoc( PtX, PtY );
      Draw;
   end;
```

Point.Draw

The Draw method requires no parameters and draws the object on the screen using the object instance's position and color parameters. Normally the Draw method would only be called by other object methods. It might be called directly by an application if; for example, some other process had overwritten the object image and it was necessary to restore the screen image.

```
procedure Point.Draw; virtual;
   begin
      PutPixel( x, y, Color );
   end;
```

Point.RestoreViewPort

Many graphic objects use Turbo Pascal's SetViewPort procedure to establish local viewport settings during various screen operations. Before establishing their own viewport settings, the object types created here save the viewport parameters that existed when the object was first created and, when their tasks are completed, call the RestoreViewPort method to reset the original viewport parameters stored in *VRef*.

```
procedure Point.RestoreViewPort;
   begin
      with VRef do
         SetViewPort( X1, Y1, X2, Y2, Clip );
   end;
```

Point.SetColor

The SetColor method provides a means of changing the color of an instance of Point by reassigning the Color parameter and then calling the Draw method.

```
procedure Point.SetColor( C : integer );
   begin
      Color := C;
      Draw;
   end;
```

Point.SetLoc

The SetLoc method simply changes the location coordinates of an object and will be inherited, as a virtual method, by all descendent object types. SetLoc is a virtual method because it calls on other object methods, but, to operate correctly for descendent objects, must call on the descendent and not ancestor methods.

```
procedure Point.SetLoc( PtX, PtY : integer ); virtual;
   begin
      x := PtX + VRef.X1;
      y := PtY + VRef.Y1;
   end;
```

As defined, the SetLoc method does nothing except to set the location coordinates as an offset relative to the viewport origin. It is called by the Create and Move methods.

Point.Erase

The Erase method uses a local integer to save the current instance's Color value. It then changes the color to background color before calling the Draw method to erase the screen image; finally, it resets the Color variable to the saved value.

```
procedure Point.Erase; virtual;
   var
      Temp : integer;
   begin
```

```
      Temp  := Color;
      Color := GetBkColor;
      Draw;
      Color := Temp;
   end;
```

Three function methods: GetColor, GetX, and GetY, return object instance values to the calling application.

```
function  Point.GetColor : integer;
   begin
      GetColor := Color;
   end;
function  Point.GetX : integer;
   begin
      GetX := x - VRef.X1;
   end;
function  Point.GetY : integer;
   begin
      GetY := y - VRef.Y1;
   end;
```

In the case of the latter two functions, the object instance values are corrected so that the viewport settings return the same values which were the original parameters—or their equivalents if the object's position has changed since it was created. In effect, the coordinate system under which an object is created remains in effect for all method calls to the object. This is a provision that makes the object independent of any viewport changes and greatly simplifies the object's operations.

As mentioned, the Point object type is not really intended for direct use by an application, particularly since each object consists of one screen pixel, but requires several bytes for its definition. As a means of manipulating single pixels, this is simply not efficient, but it is an effective ancestor type for more complicated objects.

Mouse Access

Because the graphic objects, in order to function autonomously, must be able to access the mouse object directly, two variables—*GMouse* and *TMouse*—are declared as global variables in the Interface section of the unit.

```
var
   GMouse : GraphicMouse;
   TMouse : TextMouse;
```

Because these appear in the Interface section, they are immediately available to the application using the unit and do not have to be redefined within the application program.

TMouse is supplied, of course, so that the mouse can be reset to text mode operation before the program exits (see CTRLTEST.PAS for an example).

The Button Object Type

The Button object type is the basic graphic control object; it provides the screen analog of a physical button. An instance of button may have any of three button styles which are defined as

```
ButtonType = ( Rounded, Square, ThreeD );
```

and are shown in Figure 14-1.

Figure 14-1: Three Button Object Styles

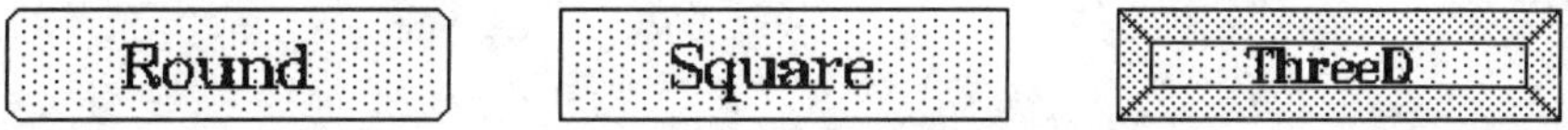

The Button object is a direct descendent of the Point object type; therefore, it inherits the position, color, and viewport setting variables along with Point's methods. Button also adds several new variables:

```
Exist, State, Rotate : boolean;
DblClkTime, FontSize,
TypeFace, SizeX, SizeY : integer;
ThisButton : ButtonType;
BtnTxt : STR40;
```

ThisButton describes the button's style, *SizeX* and *SizeY* are obvious, and the *BtnTxt* variable is the label string displayed on the button.

The Boolean *State* determines whether the button is selected and offers visual feedback in the form of a color inversion. The *Exist* and *Rotate* flags are primarily internal and will be discussed later. Likewise, *FontSize* is usually set by the object itself while *TypeFace* is the screen font style used to label the button.

The variable *DblClkTime* is a sampling delay for a mouse double-click selection.

Button Methods

The Button object type defines an even two dozen methods in addition to the methods inherited from the Point object type.

Now, if this sounds like a great deal of fuss for a simple button object, remember that because methods are defined does not mean you are forced to use all of them. Also remember that Turbo Pascal's *smart linking* only includes procedures (in the compiled .EXE) which are actually used. Simply because methods are provided in the object unit does not mean that these will be included as fact in the .EXE program.

In this case particularly, this plethora of methods are defined to provide complete access to all of Button's characteristics and capabilities. They're there, but you don't have to use them!

Button.Init

The first method, as always, is the Init method, which is also a *constructor* method—essential for dynamic object instances—and it sets the button style, location, size, color, and text label.

```
constructor Button.Init( WhatType : ButtonType;
                PtX, PtY, Width, Height, C : integer;
                Text : STR40 );
   begin
      GetViewSettings( VRef );
      SetButtonType( WhatType );
      SetTypeSize( 10 );
      SetTypeFace( TriplexFont );
      SetViewPort( 0, 0, GetMaxX, GetMaxY, ClipOn );
      SetTextJustify( CenterText, CenterText );
      SetLoc( PtX, PtY );
```

The Init method begins by calling several other Button methods to assign the various parameters. At the same time, some conditions are set by default, such as the text justification settings and the default *DblClkTime*.

```
      DblClkTime := 50;
```

Width and *Height* have minimum values.

```
      if Width < 20 then SizeX := 20
                    else SizeX := Width;
      if Height < 20 then SizeY := 20
                     else SizeY := Height;
      if SizeY > SizeX then Rotate := TRUE
                       else Rotate := FALSE;
```

The *Rotate* flag is determined by relationship between the horizontal and vertical button sizes. If the button is taller than it is wide, then *Rotate* is set so that the button label will be written vertically, rather than horizontally.

Lastly, the button *Color* is set, *State* is initialized as False, the button's existence is confirmed, the text label is set, and the button itself is written to the screen by calling the Draw method.

```
      Color   := C;
      State   := FALSE;
      Exist   := TRUE;
      BtnTxt  := Text;
      Draw;
   end;
```

Button.Done

The next Button method is the Done method, which is a *destructor* method.

```
destructor Button.Done;
   begin
      Erase;
   end;
```

With static instances of Button, the Done method is redundant because the Erase method can be called directly to delete an object's screen image. However, when dynamic objects are used, a destructor method is vital to permit disposal of memory when the object is no longer needed.

In having the Done method call the Erase method, both tasks are accomplished by one application instruction—this is good programming practice.

Button.SetOutline

The SetOutline method is declared in the Interface section, making it available to applications though it is not intended for use by applications at all. By declaring SetOutline as a method rather than a local procedure, it is available to descendent object types, thus avoiding the need for you to reinvent this procedure.

```
procedure Button.SetOutline( var RectArr: RectOutline;
                             x1, y1, x2, y2 : integer );
   begin
      RectArr[1].x := x1;    RectArr[1].y := y1;
      RectArr[2].x := x1;    RectArr[2].y := y2;
      RectArr[3].x := x2;    RectArr[3].y := y2;
      RectArr[4].x := x2;    RectArr[4].y := y1;
      RectArr[5]   := RectArr[1];
   end;
```

Obviously, the SetOutline method has only one task to accomplish: assigning four coordinates (two corner pairs) to a rectangular array of points and returning the array to the calling procedure for further use.

Button.Draw

One of the procedures using the SetOutline procedure is the Draw method which creates the object's screen image. Since the Button object can have three different styles as well as varying sizes and label orientations, the Draw method is moderately complex and tracks several preexisting conditions, such as color and viewport settings, so that these can be restored to their previous settings when the image is completed.

```
procedure Button.Draw; virtual;
   const
      radius = 6;
      offset = 3;
   var
      RectArr : RectOutline;
      AlignX, AlignY, TempSize, TextLen,
      i, BtnWd, BtnHt, TextDir, OldColor : integer;
   begin
      OldColor := Graph.GetColor;
```

Before anything is drawn, the GraphicMouse object is called to turn off the mouse cursor, regardless of where the cursor may be on the screen, so that it does not interfere with the new screen image.

```
      GMouse.Show( FALSE );
```

Next, a new viewport is created to limit drawing operations to the image area required for the button, then it sets the text justification and drawing color.

```
      SetViewPort( x, y, x+SizeX, y+SizeY, ClipOn );
      SetTextJustify( CenterText, CenterText );
      Graph.SetColor( color );
```

Notice that the Graph unit's SetColor procedure is explicitly referenced here. If this were not done (if the command simply *called* SetColor), then it would be Button.SetColor that was called, which, in turn, calls Button.Draw, which would again call Button.SetColor—and the result would be an annoying closed loop.

Such conflicts are not entirely hopeless and you might like to try an experiment at this point in the program by removing the explicit reference in favor of a general reference. (The recursive nature of the problem will produce a stack overflow condition in, depending on your CPU clock speed and stack size, one to five minutes.)

This is one of the more subtle traps of object-oriented programming because it is very common for multiple object types to have the same method names, particularly when they are related by descendence. It is also common for object method names to duplicate existing procedure names, particularly when the method function parallels an existing function.

But explicitly referencing a graph unit function, for example, avoids this conflict and object methods may be explicitly referenced. And, in the Draw method especially, the Graph unit will be explicitly referenced. For the Square button style, drawing the button image is quite simple and requires calling the Graph.Rectangle feature only.

```
case ThisButton of
Square:
   begin
      Graph.Rectangle( 0, 0, SizeX, SizeY );
      BtnWd := SizeX - 10;
      BtnHt := SizeY - 10;
   end;
```

For the ThreeD button style, the drawing operations are slightly more complicated, and require an outer rectangle, shading, an inner rectangle, and four lines to complete the 3-D image.

```
ThreeD:
   begin
      Graph.Rectangle( 0, 0, SizeX, SizeY );
      SetOutline( RectArr,1,1,SizeX-1,SizeY-1 );
      SetFillStyle( CloseDotFill, color );
      SetLineStyle( UserBitLn, 0, NormWidth );
      FillPoly( sizeof(RectArr) div
                sizeof(PointType), RectArr );
      SetLineStyle( SolidLn, 0, NormWidth );
      Graph.Rectangle( 2*radius, 2*radius,
                       SizeX-2*radius,
                       SizeY-2*radius );
      Line( 0, 0, 2*radius, 2*radius );
      Line( 0, SizeY, 2*radius, SizeY-2*radius );
      Line( SizeX, 0, SizeX-2*radius, 2*radius );
      Line( SizeX, SizeY,
            SizeX-2*radius, SizeY-2*radius );
      BtnWd := SizeX-4*radius;
      BtnHt := SizeY-4*radius;
   end;
else
```

The default case, Rounded, is the most complex of all because the button outline is built up from four partial arcs for the corners and then four lines to complete the sides.

```pascal
    begin
      ThisButton := Rounded;
      with Graph do
      begin
        Arc( SizeX-radius, radius,
             0, 90, radius );
        Arc( radius, radius,
             90, 180, radius );
        Arc( radius, SizeY-radius,
             180, 270, radius );
        Arc( SizeX-radius, SizeY-radius,
             270, 360, radius );
        Line( radius, 0, SizeX-radius, 0 );
        Line( radius, SizeY,
                SizeX-radius, SizeY );
        Line( 0, radius, 0, SizeY-radius );
        Line( SizeX, radius,
                SizeX, SizeY-radius );
      end;
      BtnWd := SizeX-2*radius;
      BtnHt := SizeY-2*radius;
    end;
end; { case }
```

Next, a separate case statement is used to fill RectArr with the coordinates for the center of each button style.

```pascal
case ThisButton of
  Square,
  Rounded: SetOutline( RectArr, offset, offset,
                       SizeX-offset, SizeY-offset );
  ThreeD:  SetOutline( RectArr, 2*radius+1,
                       2*radius+1,
                       SizeX-2*radius-1,
                       SizeY-2*radius );
end; { case }
```

Then the actual fill is executed according to the button *State*, using the FillPoly procedure from the Graph unit with a blank line style to outline the filled area.

```pascal
if State then SetFillStyle( SolidFill, color )
         else SetFillStyle( WideDotFill, color );
SetLineStyle( UserBitLn, 0, NormWidth );
FillPoly( sizeof(RectArr) div sizeof(PointType),
```

```
            RectArr );
   SetLineStyle( SolidLn, 0, NormWidth );
```

After the button image is completed, the button's label still needs to be drawn, but before drawing the text string, the text direction (*TextDir*) has to be determined.

```
       TextDir := HorizDir;
       if Rotate then
       begin
          TextDir := VertDir;
          TextLen := BtnWd;
          BtnWd := BtnHt;
          BtnHt := TextLen;
       end;
```

The text font size must be selected to fit the button size, or at least to approximate the best fit possible.

```
       SetTextStyle( TypeFace, TextDir, FontSize );
       for i := FontSize downto 1 do
          if( TextWidth(BtnTxt) > BtnWd ) then
             SetTextStyle( TypeFace, TextDir, i ) else
             if( TextHeight(BtnTxt) > BtnHt ) then
                SetTextStyle( TypeFace, TextDir, i );
       TextLen := ord( BtnTxt[0] );
```

First the font size is stepped down until the character height fits within the button space—in effect, using the largest font which will fit both horizontally and vertically within the button.

But, even at the smallest font size, the length of the label may still exceed the available space so a second test is executed to truncate the string length — if necessary—to ensure a fit.

```
       while( TextWidth(copy(BtnTxt,1,TextLen))>BtnWd ) do
          dec( TextLen );
       AlignX := SizeX div 2 - 3;
       AlignY := SizeY div 2 - 3;
       if BtnTxt[TextLen] = ' ' then dec( TextLen );
       if State then Graph.SetColor( GetBkColor );
```

And, finally, if the button *State* is set, then the label needs to be drawn in the background color instead of the button color.

```
       OutTextXY( AlignX,AlignY,copy(BtnTxt,1,TextLen) );
       if State then Graph.SetColor( color );
       SetViewPort( 0, 0, GetMaxX, GetMaxY, ClipOn );
       GMouse.Show( TRUE );
       Graph.SetColor( OldColor );
    end;
```

The remainder of the process is simply housekeeping, restoring the original viewport settings, making the mouse cursor visible again, and restoring the original drawing color.

Button.Erase

The Erase method doesn't bother with the Draw method, but simply resets the viewport before using the ClearViewPort command to erase the screen image—but please note, the mouse cursor is still turned off before the screen is cleared and turned on afterwards.

```
procedure Button.Erase; virtual;
  begin
     if Exist then
     begin
        GMouse.Show( FALSE );
        SetViewPort( x, y, x+SizeX, y+SizeY, ClipOn );
        ClearViewPort;
        SetViewPort( 0, 0, GetMaxX, GetMaxY, ClipOn );
        GMouse.Show( TRUE );
     end;
  end;
```

Button.ButtonHit

The ButtonHit method is central to all graphic control objects and returns a Boolean result to the calling application, confirming button selection by a mouse hit.

```
function Button.ButtonHit: boolean; virtual;
  var
     Result : boolean;
     BtnStatus, XPos, YPos : integer;
  begin
     Result := FALSE;
     GMouse.GetPosition( BtnStatus, XPos, YPos );
```

A couple of different approaches were possible in creating the ButtonHit method. One option might have been to pass mouse coordinates to the Button-Hit method, but this was rejected as unnecessarily awkward.

Instead, when the ButtonHit is asked for a check, ButtonHit itself calls the GraphicMouse object to request mouse button status and coordinates. Because several button objects or other control objects may be requesting this same information, the GetPosition method is called rather than the QueryBtnDn method which reports a prior mouse button event but resets this event information each time it is called. Instead, the GetPosition method requests current button information and retrieves both the present, immediate status of all buttons and the current mouse position.

If, and only if, the left button is down, the mouse coordinates are tested against button's position and size coordinates.

```
if( BtnStatus AND $01 ) = $01 then
    Result := ( XPos >= x )
          AND ( XPos <= x+SizeX )
          AND ( YPos >= y )
          AND ( YPos <= y+SizeY );
```

Using four Boolean tests for the position may seem awkward compared to testing the x and y positions against a set as *[x..x+SizeX]*, but in Turbo Pascal there are two problems preventing this. First, these element descriptions are not valid set descriptors and, second, set elements are limited to the range 0..255—which would cover only a portion of the screen.

Using four Boolean tests, even combined using the AND operator, may appear verbose, but is actually an efficient method.

If the local flag, *Result*, is true, then ButtonHit, rather than relying on the calling application, calls the Invert method before returning the hit report to the calling program.

```
    if Result then Invert;
    ButtonHit := Result;
end;
```

Button.DoubleClick

A second selection method, DoubleClick, is also provided, reporting only if the Button instance has been selected by two quick mouse clicks instead of a single button hit event.

```
function Button.DoubleClick: boolean; virtual;
   var
      Result : boolean;
      BtnEvent : Position;
   begin
      Result := FALSE;
      if ButtonHit then
```

The DoubleClick method begins by calling the ButtonHit method to ask if the current button instance has been hit at all. If so, then the mouse object's QueryBtnDn method is called immediately to clear the mouse registers of the current button event.

```
       begin
          GMouse.QueryBtnDn( ButtonL, BtnEvent );
```

Next, a brief delay is executed (by default, 50 milliseconds) and the mouse is queried again for a second button event.

```
delay( DblClkTime );
GMouse.QueryBtnDn( ButtonL, BtnEvent );
```

If the left mouse button has been hit a second time within the delay period, there's no point in testing the location of the hit again, we can simply assume that this was a double-click event and report it as such.

```
            Result := BtnEvent.opCount  0;
         end;
         if not Result AND GetState then
            SetState( FALSE );
         DoubleClick := Result;
      end;
```

One bit of housekeeping is included here; if a first button hit occurred, then the button has been inverted. If this was not a double-click, the button needs to be turned off again.

This is a point where you may wish to revise the object handling. If, for example, you want to be able to both select and deselect a button using a double-click, then the handling should be altered to reflect this, perhaps by using the Invert instead of the SetState method.

The *DblClkTime* delay can also be altered, if necessary, via the SetDblClick, IncDblClick, and DecDblClick methods. These methods, together with the remaining methods provided for the Button object, are self-explanatory and will not be discussed in detail here.

The RadioButton Object Type

The RadioButton object type is a circular button and is often used in groups where only one button from a set may be selected at any time. However, provisions for canceling set RadioButtons when a new button is selected are not included in the object type itself, they must be handled by the application.

A selection of RadioButton objects appear in Figure 14-2.

The RadioButton object type, as a descendent of the Button object type, inherits a variety of variables, though not all of these or all of the inherited methods will be used by the RadioButton type.

Instead, the RadioButton adds two new integer variables, *Outline*, which will be the outline color for this button type, and *Radius*, which is the size of the button.

Figure 14-2: Graphics Control Objects

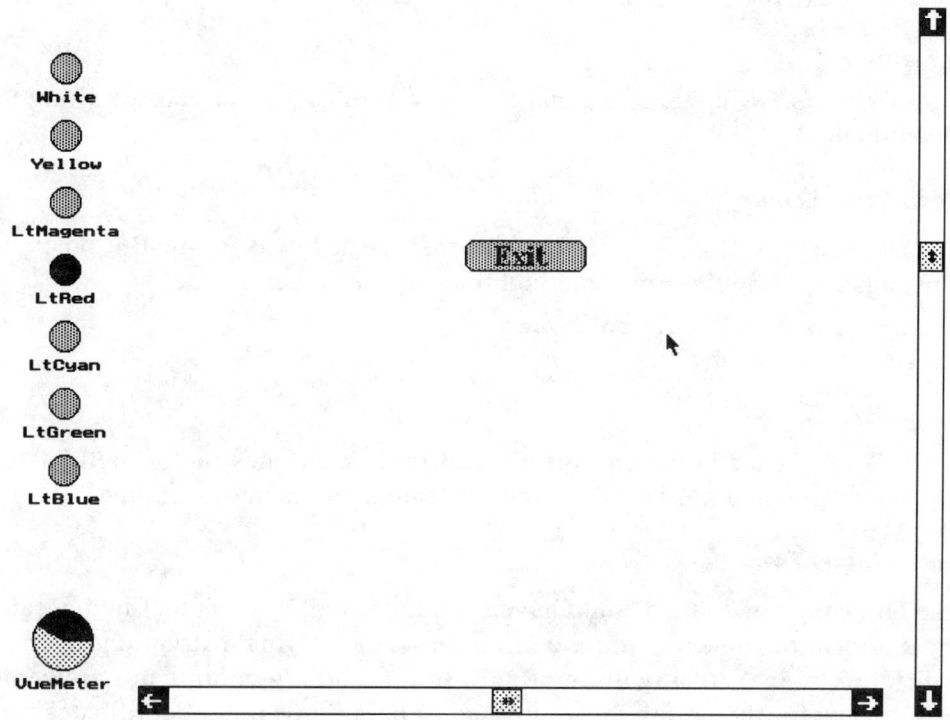

RadioButton.Init

The RadioButton Init method is called with location parameters, button color, radius and a text string that is nominally limited to ten characters in length.

```
constructor RadioButton.Init( PtX, PtY, C, R : integer;
                              Text : STR10 );
   begin
      GetViewSettings( VRef );
      SetTextJustify( CenterText, CenterText );
      SetLoc( PtX, PtY );
      Radius   := R;
```

After preserving the viewport settings and initiating the position and radius variables, Init assigns the outline color by ORing the color parameter with 08h so that the color always has the intensity bit set. If you are using a variant color palette, this provision may need to be altered.

```
         Outline := C OR $08;
         Color   := C;
```

```
      State   := FALSE;
      Exist   := TRUE;
      BtnTxt  := Text;
      Draw;
   end;
```

And the *Color*, *State*, *Exist*, and *BtnTxt* variables are set before calling the Draw method.

RadioButton.Done

The Done method is defined in the same fashion as it was for the Button object type, again calling the Erase method to clear the screen image.

```
destructor RadioButton.Done;
  begin
      Erase;
  end;
```

Unlike most methods, an object's constructor and destructor methods are not inheritable and must be declared separately for each object type.

RadioButton.Draw

The Draw method, which could have been inherited, is also redefined because the RadioButton object requires a different set of drawing instructions to create a different shape. Also, with the RadioButton, the x/y coordinates are center coordinates for the button image instead of being the corner coordinates for a rectangular button.

```
procedure RadioButton.Draw; virtual;
   var
       XAsp, YAsp : word;
      OldColor, i : integer;
   begin
      OldColor := Graph.GetColor;
      RestoreViewPort;
      GetAspectRatio( XAsp, YAsp );
      Graph.SetColor( Outline );
      GMouse.Show( FALSE );
```

Again, the current color and viewport settings are preserved and the mouse pointer is hidden before the object's image is drawn. Then the appropriate fill style is selected, together with the proper color to show the RadioButton instance's *State*.

```
            if State then SetFillStyle( SolidFill, Color ) else
                    SetFillStyle( InterleaveFill, Color );
            FillEllipse( x, y, Radius,
                      Radius * longint( XAsp ) div YAsp );
```

When the FillEllipse function is called to draw the button image—with corrections for the screen aspect ratio—the button outline is drawn using the *Outline* color and filled with pattern and button color.

Instances of the RadioButton object type are generally too small to contain a text label so the *BtnTxt* label is written, centered below the button image before the mouse pointer and the original drawing colors are restored.

```
      SetTextStyle( DefaultFont, HorizDir, 1 );
      OutTextXY( X, Y + Radius + 10, BtnTxt );
      GMouse.Show( TRUE );
      Graph.SetColor( OldColor );
   end;
```

RadioButton.Erase

For the Button object type, the Erase method used the viewport settings and ClearViewPort to erase the button image. This could be used for the RadioButton as well but is not the most practical means because the button label may be omitted in order to space buttons closely or may be included with wider spacing. Therefore, to erase a RadioButton, the Erase method operates in a different fashion, changing both *Color* and *Outline* to the background drawing color and then calling the Draw method to cancel the screen image.

```
procedure RadioButton.Erase; virtual;
   var
      OldColor : integer;
   begin
      OldColor := Color;
      Color := GetBkColor;
      Outline := Color;
      Draw;
      Color := OldColor;
      Outline := OldColor OR $08;
   end;
```

After Draw is finished, the original color values are restored so the RadioButton can be recreated at a new location if necessary.

RadioButton.ButtonHit

The ButtonHit method for the RadioButton object type is also different.

```
function RadioButton.ButtonHit: Boolean; virtual;
   var
      Result : boolean;
      BtnStatus, XPos, YPos, OffX, OffY : integer;
   begin
      Result := FALSE;
```

```
      GMouse.GetPosition( BtnStatus, XPos, YPos );
      if( BtnStatus AND $01 ) = $01 then
      begin
         OffX := abs( XPos - x );
         OffY := abs( YPos - y );
```

In this case, the mouse coordinates are converted to an offset from the RadioButton's center position, an offset that is calculated in absolute distances instead of signed distances.

Comparing the offset distance as a hypotenuse length against the button radius has a tendency, when the values are large (because the mouse is not close to the button), to create a floating-point error. Therefore, two offset tests are made to decide, first, if the mouse event is close to the button tested.

```
      if ( OffX < 2 * Radius ) AND
         ( OffY < 2 * Radius ) then
```

If the mouse event is in the immediate vicinity of the button, then a test is made to decide if the button was actually hit.

```
         Result := trunc( sqrt( sqr( OffX ) +
                               sqr( OffY ) ) ) < radius;
      end;
```

If a hit did occur, then the button's state is set to TRUE and the results are reported to the calling application.

```
      if Result then SetState( TRUE );
      ButtonHit := Result;
   end;
```

With RadioButton controls, buttons cannot be deselected with a mouse hit; instead, any other selected button is turned off (using the inherited SetState method) when a new button is turned on ... just like the station selector on your car radio.

The last two RadioButton methods, SetRadius and GetRadius, should be self-explanatory.

The ScrollBar Object Type

The third control object type provided by the GControl unit is the ScrollBar object. It is probably the most familiar graphics control device since it is used, in one form or another, by virtually every graphics application that requires a display extending beyond the physical limits of a single screen.

In this example, the scrollbars have square end pads and a square thumbpad which can be mouse manipulated to control the position parameters of the calling application. In other implementations, the thumbpad might be variable in width to show, not only a position within a range, but also to show what portion of the total range was shown by the current display. This latter embellishment, however, is left as an exercise for the readers who are invited to create their own scrollbars with whatever revisions and features appeal to their applications. Two scrollbars, horizontal and vertical, appear in Figure 14-2. For the present, two new types are declared for use with scrollbars: HitType and Direction.

```
HitType = ( NONE, RIGHT, UP, HBAR, VBAR, LEFT, DOWN );
Direction = ( Vertical, Horizontal );
```

The ScrollBar object type is declared as a descendent of Button, inheriting all the object variables and methods declared by its ancestors, Point and Button, but declaring several new variables.

```
ScrollBar = object( Button )
   ScrollMove : Direction;
   BarWidth, BarLen,
   LineColor, SPos, Step : integer;
   ThumbPad : pointer;
```

The *ScrollMove* variable determines the orientation, vertical or horizontal, of each ScrollBar instance. The *BarWidth* variable is the thickness of the scrollbar and *BarLen* is the overall length of the scrollbar. The *LineColor* variable is the drawing color for the object image, *SPos* is the position, within the scrollbar, of the thumbpad, and *Step* is an incremental value for the thumbpad movement. The final object variable, *ThumbPad*, is a pointer variable because the scrollbar's thumbpad will be a memory image that is more convenient to move readily than an image drawn directly.

ScrollBar.Init

This Init method is similar to previous examples and creates a ScrollBar instance with a specified location (*PtX* and *PtY*, length (*Size*), outline, and image colors *C1* and *C2*, and *Orientation*).

```
constructor ScrollBar.Init( PtX, PtY,
                    Size, C1, C2 : integer;
                    Orientation : Direction );
   var
      RectArr   : RectOutline;
   begin
```

In this case, *BarWidth* has been set arbitrarily as 20 pixels and with a minimum length (*Size*) of 100 pixels.

```
BarWidth := 20;
GetViewSettings( VRef );
if Size < 100 then Size := 100;
```

The initial thumbpad position is at either the left or the top of the scrollbar (depending on the orientation) and is offset from the physical end by *BarWidth* to leave room for the endpad.

```
SPos := BarWidth + 1;
BarLen := Size;
ScrollMove := Orientation;
Step := BarLen div 100;
```

The object variable, *BarLen*, accepts the specified *Size* parameter and *Step* is set to 1 percent of *BarLen*. The length of the scrollbar, however, is not fixed at this point because it will be adjusted to fit within the viewport if necessary.

```
case ScrollMove of
   Vertical:
   begin
      while BarLen + 2 * BarWidth >
            VRef.Y2 - VRef.Y1 do
         dec( BarLen );
      SizeX := BarWidth;
      SizeY := BarLen + 2 * BarWidth;
      while PtX + BarWidth > VRef.X2 - VRef.X1 do
         dec( PtX );
   end;
   Horizontal:
   begin
      while BarLen + 2 * BarWidth >
            VRef.X2 - VRef.X1 do
         dec( BarLen );
      SizeX := BarLen + 2 * BarWidth;
      SizeY := BarWidth;
      while PtY + BarWidth > VRef.Y2 - VRef.Y1 do
         dec( PtY );
   end;
end; {case}
```

BarWidth is adjusted according to the horizontal or vertical orientation and the inherited *SizeX* and *SizeY* variables are set to provide space for the final scrollbar size, plus the endpads.

Notice, however, that the *Step* size is not adjusted further even if *BarWidth* has changed—a factor you might change if your application has different requirements. Be sure that you have a minimum *Step* of one pixel or it may be very hard to move.

```
SetLoc( PtX, PtY );
LineColor := C1;
Color := C2;
Graph.SetColor( LineColor );
```

```
SetFillStyle( CloseDotFill, Color );
SetTextStyle( DefaultFont, HorizDir, 1 );
SetTextJustify( CenterText, CenterText );
```

The Init method also draws the thumbpad image which will be saved as a memory image.

```
case ScrollMove of
Vertical:
   begin
      SetOutline( RectArr, 2, SPos,
                  BarWidth-2, SPos+BarWidth-1 );
      FillPoly( sizeof(RectArr) div
                sizeof(PointType), RectArr );
      Graph.SetColor( White );
      OutTextXY( BarWidth div 2, SPos +
                 BarWidth div 2, #$12 );
```

For a vertical scrollbar, the double-ended vertical arrow (ASCII 12h) is added to the drawn thumbpad image before the image is saved.

```
      GetMem( ThumbPad,
              ImageSize( 2, SPos, BarWidth - 2,
                         SPos + BarWidth - 1 ) );
      GetImage( 2, SPos, BarWidth-2,
                SPos + BarWidth - 1, ThumbPad^ );
      PutImage( 2, SPos, ThumbPad^, XOrPut );
   end;
```

The horizontal scrollbar is effectively the same, except for *SetOutline* arguments and the positioning of the ASCII character 1Dh before saving the thumbpad image.

```
   Horizontal: ...
      end;
   end; { case }
   Exist := TRUE;
   Draw;
end;
```

Init ends by calling the Draw method.

ScrollBar.Done

In this instance, the Done method is a bit different from previous examples because, after calling the Erase method to remove the screen image, the *ThumbPad* image also needs to be removed from memory.

```
destructor ScrollBar.Done;
   begin
      Erase;
```

```
        Dispose( ThumbPad );
    end;
```

ScrollBar.Draw

This Draw method begins by drawing the scrollbar outline as a solid bar.

```
procedure ScrollBar.Draw; virtual
    var
        RectArr  : RectOutline;
        OldColor : word;
    begin
        OldColor := Graph.GetColor;
        Graph.SetColor( LineColor );
        SetViewPort( x, y, x+SizeX, y+SizeY, ClipOn );
        SetOutline( RectArr, 1, 1, SizeX-1, SizeY-1 );
        SetFillStyle( SolidFill, color );
        SetLineStyle( SolidLn, 0, NormWidth );
        FillPoly( sizeof(RectArr) div sizeof(PointType),
                  RectArr );
```

Next, the end pads are created by drawing two arrow characters, one at each end, using the ASCII characters 18h and 19h for a vertical scrollbar, or 1Bh and 1Ah for a horizontal scrollbar.

```
        Graph.SetColor( GetBkColor );
        SetTextStyle( DefaultFont, HorizDir, 2 );
        case ScrollMove of
            Vertical   : begin
                            OutTextXY( 10, 12, #$18 );
                            OutTextXY( 10, SizeY-10, #$19 );
                         end;
            Horizontal : begin
                            OutTextXY( 10, 12, #$1B );
                            OutTextXY( SizeX-10, 12, #$1A );
                         end;
        end;
```

At this point, the scrollbar consists of a solid bar with an arrow at each end. The next task is to clear the center of the bar.

```
        Graph.SetColor( LineColor );
        SetFillStyle( SolidFill, Graph.GetBkColor );
        case ScrollMove of
            Vertical: SetOutline( RectArr, 1, BarWidth+1,
                                  SizeX-1, SizeY-BarWidth-1 );
            Horizontal: SetOutline( RectArr, BarWidth+1, 1,
                                    SizeX-BarWidth-1, SizeY-1 );
        end; {case}
        FillPoly( sizeof(RectArr) div sizeof(PointType),
                  RectArr );
```

Chapter 14: Buttons, Scrollbars and Control Objects 295

With this done, the original color and viewport settings are restored before the SetThumbPad method is called to add the ThumbPad image.

```
    Graph.SetColor( OldColor );
    RestoreViewPort;
    SetThumbPad;
end;
```

ScrollBar.SetThumbPad

The SetThumbPad method is called to place the ThumbPad image and to erase it before moving. Since the *XOPut* option is used with PutImage, both operations are the same as long as the image location is correct.

```
procedure ScrollBar.SetThumbPad;
  begin
     SetViewPort( x, y, x+SizeX-1, y+SizeY-1, True );
     case ScrollMove of
         Vertical: PutImage( 2,SPos,ThumbPad^,XOrPut );
       Horizontal: PutImage( SPos,2,ThumbPad^,XOrPut );
     end; {case}
     RestoreViewPort;
  end;
```

ScrollBar.ScrollHit

Instead of a Boolean ButtonHit method—because a simple hit report is not sufficient—ScrollBar has a ScrollHit method which returns a *HitType* reporting whether the mouse hit occurred at one of the endpads (and at which), at the thumbpad, or somewhere along the scrollbar.

```
function ScrollBar.ScrollHit: HitType;
  var
     Result : HitType;
     BtnStatus, XPos, YPos : integer;
  begin
     Result := NONE;
```

Like the previous control objects, the ScrollHit method queries the mouse directly for the mouse button status and mouse cursor position, using a series of Boolean tests to determine first if, and then where, the mouse hit occurred.

```
       GMouse.GetPosition( BtnStatus, XPos, YPos );
       if BtnStatus AND $01 = $01 then
       case ScrollMove of
          Vertical:
             if( XPos >= x ) AND
                ( XPos <= x+BarWidth ) AND
                ( YPos >= y ) then
```

```
                    if YPos <= y+BarWidth
                        then Result := UP              else
                    if YPos <= y+BarLen+BarWidth
                        then Result := VBAR            else
                    if YPos <= y+BarLen+BarWidth*2
                        then Result := DOWN;
        Horizontal:
            if( YPos >= y ) AND
               ( YPos <= y+BarWidth ) AND
               ( XPos >= x ) then
                    if XPos <= x+BarWidth
                        then Result := LEFT            else
                    if XPos <= x+BarLen+BarWidth
                        then Result := HBAR            else
                    if XPos <= x+BarLen+BarWidth*2
                        then Result := RIGHT;
    end; {case}
```

If you require a scrollbar that reports only thumbpad and endpad hits, the following format can be used for a vertical scrollbar:

```
if( YPos >= y ) AND ( YPos <= y+BarWidth ) then
    if( XPos >= x ) AND ( XPos <= x+BarWidth )
        then Result := LEFT else
    if( XPos >= x+SPos ) AND
       ( XPos <= x+SPos+BarWidth )
        then Result := HBAR else
    if( XPos >= x+BarLen+BarWidth ) AND
       ( XPos <= x+BarLen+BarWidth*2 )
        then Result := RIGHT;
```

The equivalent will be required for a horizontal scrollbar.

Using either ScrollHit format, after the hit test is completed and, if a hit has occurred, the mouse cursor is turned off before calling the SetThumbPad method to erase the *ThumbPad* image at the current position.

```
if Result <> NONE then
begin
    GMouse.Show( FALSE );
    SetThumbPad;
end;
```

Next, *SPos* is updated according to the hit position (*Result*).

```
case Result of
    LEFT,  UP: dec( SPos, Step );
          HBAR: SPos := XPos - x - 10;
          VBAR: SPos := YPos - y - 10;
    RIGHT, DOWN: inc( SPos, Step );
end; {case}
```

The updated position (*SPos*) is tested to be sure that the applicable limits have not been exceeded before SetThumbPad is called a second time to restore the thumbpad image. The mouse cursor is turned on again.

```
      if Result <> NONE then
   begin
      if SPos < BarWidth then SPos := BarWidth;
      if SPos > BarLen   then SPos := BarLen;
      SetThumbPad;
      GMouse.Show( TRUE );
   end;
```

Finally, *Result* is reported to the calling application.

```
      ScrollHit := Result;
   end;
```

This is another example, like Button and RadioButton, where the control object acts extensively on its own before reporting results back to the calling application. This is also one of the strengths of graphic control objects—their ability to act autonomously—limited, of course, to the extent of the programmer's provisions.

The ScrollHit method's capabilities, of course, do not extend to controlling the calling application which has to execute its own response to changes in the scrollbar's thumbpad position.

ScrollBar.GetPosition

A ScrollBar hit event is probably not, by itself, enough information for the calling application to decide what response to take. Therefore, the GetPosition method returns the scrollbar's thumbpad location.

```
function ScrollBar.GetPosition: integer;
  begin
      GetPosition := SPos;
  end;
```

But the thumbpad position may not mean much to the application, even though the application can also call the inherited GetSize method for a comparison value.

ScrollBar.GetPercent

There is a simpler method of retrieving a relative position report from a scrollbar object: the GetPercent method which returns an integer percentage according to the position of the thumbpad along the scrollbar.

```
function ScrollBar.GetPercent: integer;
  var
```

```
      Percent : integer;
begin
   case ScrollMove of
      Horizontal: Percent := round( (SPos-BarWidth) /
                                    (BarLen-BarWidth)*100 );
        Vertical: Percent := round( (SPos-BarWidth) /
                                    (BarLen-BarWidth)*100 );
   end;
   GetPercent := Percent;
end;
```

This is information the calling application can use for whatever purposes it needs—as will be shown presently in the CTRLTEST demo.

The VueMeter Object Type

The VueMeter is not a graphics control object per se, but it is a simple metering device modeled after a popular electronic device from the ages predating solid state instruments and digital readouts. It displays a pie-sector, analog meter with a range of 0 to 360 degrees. An example of a VueMeter object appears in Figure 14-2.

The VueMeter object type is a descendent of the RadioButton type and declares a single integer object variable, *Closure*, which is the degree of closure of the meter.

VueMeter.Init

The Init method is called with position coordinates *PtX* and *PtY*, color (*C*), radius (*R*), and a caption string, *Text*. *Closure* for the VueMeter is always initialized as one degree.

```
constructor VueMeter.Init( PtX, PtY, C, R : integer;
                           Text : STR10 );
begin
   GetViewSettings( VRef );
   SetTextJustify( CenterText, CenterText );
   SetLoc( PtX, PtY );
   Radius   := R;
   Color    := C;
   Closure  := 1;
   Exist    := TRUE;
   BtnTxt   := Text;
   Draw;
end;
```

VueMeter.Done

The Done method is required to do very little except call the Erase method to remove the screen image.

```
destructor VueMeter.Done;
   begin
      Erase;
   end;
```

VueMeter.Draw

The Draw method for the VueMeter uses the Graph unit's Sector procedure to draw and fill two pie segments, one from 0 to *Closure* degrees and, if *Closure* is less than 360, the second from *Closure* to 360 degrees, completing the circle. The VueMeter's caption (*BtnTxt*) is written below the meter in the same fashion used with the RadioButton.

```
procedure VueMeter.Draw; virtual;
   var
      i : integer;   XAsp, YAsp : word;
   begin
      RestoreViewPort;
      GetAspectRatio( XAsp, YAsp );
      if Closure < 0   then Closure := 0;
      if Closure > 360 then Closure := 360;
      GMouse.Show( FALSE );
      Graph.SetColor( Color );
      SetFillStyle( SolidFill, Color );
      Sector( x, y, 0, Closure, Radius,
              Radius * longint( XAsp ) div YAsp );
      SetTextStyle( DefaultFont, HorizDir, 1 );
      SetTextJustify( CenterText, CenterText );
      OutTextXY( X, Y + Radius + 10, BtnTxt );
      Graph.SetColor( White );
      SetFillStyle( CloseDotFill, Color );
      if Closure < 360 then
         Sector( x, y, Closure, 360, Radius,
                 Radius * longint( XAsp ) div YAsp );
      GMouse.Show( TRUE );
   end;
```

VueMeter.Erase

Like the RadioButton, the Erase method operates using the background color to redraw the VueMeter and caption but does so using a single Sector operation.

```
procedure VueMeter.Erase; virtual;
   var
```

```
      XAsp, YAsp : word;
begin
   GetAspectRatio( XAsp, YAsp );
   GMouse.Show( FALSE );
   Graph.SetColor( GetBkColor );
   SetFillStyle( SolidFill, GetBkColor );
   Sector( x, y, 0, 360, Radius,
           Radius * longint( XAsp ) div YAsp );
   SetTextStyle( DefaultFont, HorizDir, 1 );
   SetTextJustify( CenterText, CenterText );
   OutTextXY( X, Y + Radius + 10, BtnTxt );
   Graph.SetColor( White );
   GMouse.Show( TRUE );
end;
```

VueMeter.Select, .Close, .Open

The Select, Close, and Open methods each accept an integer argument (*Degrees*) to set, increment, or decrement the *Closure* variable before calling the Draw method. No range checks are executed by any of these methods since a single range check is included in the Draw method.

```
procedure VueMeter.Select( Degree: integer );
   begin
      Closure := Degree;
      Draw;
   end;
procedure VueMeter.Close( Degree: integer );
   begin
      inc( Closure, Degree );
      Draw;
   end;
procedure VueMeter.Open( Degree: integer );
   begin
      dec( Closure, Degree );
      Draw;
   end;
```

Other Meter Objects

A variety of other meter objects are also possible, ranging from the "catseye" tuning meters which appeared in a variety of applications in early radio and electronics equipment, to the conventional "moving needle" meters which have been used in VOM equipment, auto dashboards and other applications for a century or more.

These sound like antiques, and perhaps they are. The scrollbar objects, however, are simply visual analogs of slidebar potentiometers and the button objects are analogs of physical button switches.

One reason for using any of these objects is because visual analogs of non-digital instruments are frequently still easier to understand, even if less precise, than digital displays. I won't recommend using them for every application, but occasionally, these may be preferable to more conventional digital displays.

In the CtrlTest demo following, the analog VueMeter will be demonstrated in one very simple application. Take a look at it and think about it.

The CtrlTest Demonstration

The CtrlTest demo program is a simple example employing two ScrollBar objects for position, eight RadioButtons for colors, one VueMeter totaling the percentage positions of the two ScrollBars, and a single Button object which is positioned by the scrollbars, changes color in response to the radio buttons and terminates the demo when double-clicked by the mouse pointer (see Figure 14-2).

The CtrlTest demo uses four units: the Crt and Graph units, which are standard Turbo Pascal units; the Mouse unit, which appeared in Chapter 13; and the GControl unit created in this chapter. Once these units are provided, the CtrlTest demo itself is extremely simple, consisting of several object variable declarations and the main procedure, with no subprocedures. The variable declarations, however, deserve a few comments:

```
var
   mButton : Position;
   Status  : Boolean;
```

The *mButton* and *Status* variables provide mouse access, but please note that no mouse object is declared by the program because the GControl unit has already provided the mouse object declaration in its Interface section.

The GControl unit cannot declare the specific object instances which the program will use; only the object types. Thus, in CtrlTest's var declarations, the actual object instances that will be used are defined as follows:

```
ExitButton : Button;
CatsEye : VueMeter;
PHScroll, PVScroll : ^ScrollBar;
RButton : array[RMin..RMax] of ^RadioButton;
```

Notice that *ExitButton* and *CatsEye* are declared as static objects and *PHScroll*, *PVScroll*, and *RButton* are pointers to dynamic object instances.

In this example the declarations of static versus dynamic object instances are principally a matter of personal preference. All of the objects might have been declared as static instances or might have been dynamic. The only real criterion for such choices is that dynamic instances are always used when the program needs to release object instances—when they're no longer needed—to free memory for other tasks or when very large arrays of objects are needed. Otherwise, it is merely a matter of preference and convenience.

The demo program begins by calling the graphic mouse Reset method to enable the mouse for graphics operation and then tests the returned *Status* flag to be sure that the mouse is present before proceeding.

```
GMouse.Reset( Status, BtnCount );
if Status then
begin
   ClearDevice;
   GMouse.Initialize;
```

If the mouse is present and capable, then the viewport is cleared and the mouse is initialized for graphics operation. Both the objects require initialization, but notice that static and dynamic instances are initialized in slightly different fashions. The *RButton* instances are dynamic and, therefore, require the New procedure to allocate memory for each instance.

```
for i := RMin to RMax do
   New( RButton[i],
      Init( 50, 360-45*i, i+8, 10, ColorStr[i] ) );
```

In earlier versions of Turbo Pascal, the New procedure accepted only one parameter: a pointer variable for the address of the allocated dynamic variable. Beginning with Turbo Pascal 5.5, the New procedure's syntax has been extended so that the constructor invocation is accepted as a second parameter.

The older syntax is still acceptable

```
for i := RMin to RMax do
begin
   RButton[i] := New( RadioButton );
   RButton[i].Init( 50, 360-45*i, i+8, 10,
ColorStr[i] );
end;
```

but is also less convenient!

If you have noticed that, in the first example, New was called as a procedure and, in the second example, as a function, give yourself a pat on the back. This is neither discrepancy nor error because, with the extended syntax, New can now be called either way, but like a C function, the returned function value can be ignored because the value was also returned in the variable (first) parameter. If desired, the first syntax can also be written as:

```
for i := RMin to RMax do
    Ptr[i] := New( RButton[i],
        Init( 50, 360-45*i, i+8, 10, ColorStr[i] ) );
```

in which case, the pointer address would be returned both to RButton^ and to Ptr^—a double value, so to speak.

For the static instance, *CatsEye*, no memory allocation is required and only the Init method is called.

```
CatsEye.Init( 50, GetMaxY-50,
              LightRed, 20, 'VueMeter' );
```

Before creating the scrollbars and the *ExitButton*, a graphics window is established and the viewport settings are saved using the *VRef* variable.

```
SetViewPort( 100, 0, GetMaxX, GetMaxY, ClipOn );
GetViewSettings( VRef );
```

The two scrollbars and *ExitButton* are created within the viewport. Remember, each of these control object instances includes a record of the viewport settings when it was created and will reset the default viewport to these parameters. Also, the VueMeter and RadioButton instances lie outside the viewport created for the scrollbars and *ExitButton*.

```
New( PHScroll,
     Init( 0, GetMaxY, VRef.X2-VRef.X1-80,
           Green, LightGreen, Horizontal ) );
New( PVScroll,
     Init( GetMaxX, 0, GetMaxY,
           Green, LightGreen, Vertical ) );
```

Both of the scrollbar objects instances are dynamic and use the New procedure to allocate memory, but *ExitButton* is static and only requires initialization.

```
with ExitButton do
    Init( Rounded,
          PHScroll^.GetPosition-20,
          PVScroll^.GetPosition,
          80, 20, LightRed, 'Exit' );
RButton[4]^.SetState( TRUE );
```

As one last task before starting the real work, the RadioButton for the initial color selection (LightRed) is turned on.

The main program loops, waiting for *ExitButton* to report a DoubleClick event. While waiting, it executes another *repeat..until* loop that continues until a left mouse button release event occurs.

```
while not ExitButton.DoubleClick do
repeat
```

Because the combination of a *while not..do* and *repeat..until* loop may sound like overkill, I'll begin by explaining a bit. The *while not ExitButton* loop is the main loop, terminating only when a double-click event is registered. The *repeat..until* button released loop provides a continuous response when the mouse button is held down to drag a scrollbar thumbpad or to produce a repeat response from one of the endpads.

If this is still not clear, experiment with the demo program and all will become so.

In the mean time, the first event(s) tested are the scrollbars. Both scrollbars are queried via the ScrollHit method and, if either reports a hit of any kind, then the *ExitButton*'s Move method is called with the two scrollbars' GetPosition methods as parameters.

```
if( PHScroll^.ScrollHit <> NONE ) or
  ( PVScroll^.ScrollHit <> NONE ) then
begin
    ExitButton.Move( PHScroll^.GetPosition-20,
                     PVScroll^.GetPosition );
```

In other words, the several objects are told to talk to each other and work things out among themselves. After all, as long as they can talk the same language, why should I bother acting as an interpreter?

The same thing is done with the VueMeter except that the scrollbars' GetPercent responses are converted to degrees (just a minor bit of translation).

```
CatsEye.Select(
    round((PHScroll^.GetPercent/100*180) +
          (PVScroll^.GetPercent/100*180)));
end;
```

The next task—still within the *repeat..until* loop—is a *for* loop that steps through the RadioButton array, asking each if it recognizes a mouse hit.

```
for i := RMin to RMax do
    if RButton[i]^.ButtonHit then
    begin
```

If one of the RadioButtons has been hit, then a second loop turns off all of the buttons before turning the hit button back on again. In this case, even though the RadioButton responded automatically to the hit by turning itself on, the second loop turned it off and; therefore, an external call is required to reenable the button to show its state.

```
          for j := RMin to RMax do
              RButton[j]^.SetState( FALSE );
          RButton[i]^.SetState( TRUE );
          ExitButton.SetColor(RButton[i]^.GetColor);
          CatsEye.SetColor( RButton[i]^.GetColor );
      end;
```

Finally, *ExitButton* and *CatsEye* are notified of the new color, after which each will erase and redraw itself. Also, the mouse is asked for a button release event to decide if the *repeat..until* loop can be closed.

```
      GMouse.QueryBtnUp( ButtonL, mButton );
  until mButton.opCount > 0;
```

Remember, the *while not...do* loop is still in effect until *ExitButton* receives a double-click and it will continue with the inner loop testing all other button events until this happens.

Once the exit instruction has been received, then the static buttons' Erase methods are called to remove the screen images. The *delay* instructions are provided for illustration only.

```
      ExitButton.Erase;                    delay( 500 );
      CatsEye.Erase;                       delay( 500 );
```

In the previous two instructions, the object instances were static, but the dynamic object instances require a different handling. For these, the Dispose procedure is used with the object's Done method as a second parameter.

```
      for i := RMin to RMax do begin
         Dispose( RButton[i], Done );   delay( 500 );
      end;
      Dispose( PHScroll, Done );          delay( 500 );
      Dispose( PVScroll, Done );          delay( 500 );
```

Like the New procedure, the Dispose procedure has also been extended by Turbo Pascal 5.5 and can be used for conventional memory uses and, by specifying an object destructor method as the second parameter, to dispose of object using a single call. The alternative, following the older format, of requiring two instructions, is:

```
      PVScroll^.Done;
      Dispose( PVScroll );
```

Obviously, the extended syntax is more convenient. Don't forget, a separate call to the Erase method to remove the screen image is not necessary because the Done method includes a screen erase call for the object image.

```
      end;
      CloseGraph;
      TMouse.Initialize;
end.
```

Of course, the program ends by closing the graphics mode and by resetting the system mouse to text mode by initializing the text mouse object. Depending on the mouse software and system in use, this may not be necessary, but it is certainly common courtesy to do so!

Summary

The graphics control objects created in the GControl unit demonstrate the basic requirements of interactive objects. These can be used as is in other applications or as the basis for your own custom control objects.

The Mouse and GControl units will be used again, in the following chapter to create icon images that are also mouse-interactive, though in a different fashion.

GCONTROL.PAS / GCONTROL.TPU

```
unit GControl;

INTERFACE

uses Crt, Graph, Mouse;

type
   STR40 = string[40];
   STR10 = string[10];
   RectOutline = array[1..5] of PointType;

   Point = object
      x, y, Color : integer;
      VRef : ViewPortType;
      constructor Init;
      procedure Create( PtX, PtY, C : integer );
      procedure Move( PtX, PtY : integer );
      procedure Draw; virtual;
      procedure RestoreViewPort;
      procedure SetColor( c : integer );
      procedure SetLoc( PtX, PtY : integer ); virtual;
      procedure Erase; virtual;
      function  GetColor : integer;
      function  GetX : integer;
      function  GetY : integer;
   end;

   ButtonType = ( Rounded, Square, ThreeD );
   Button = object( Point )
```

```
              {========inherited=========}
              {  x, y, Color : integer;   }
              {  VRef : ViewPortType;     }
              {===========================}

    Exist, State, Rotate : boolean;
    DblClkTime,
    FontSize, TypeFace, SizeX, SizeY : integer;
    ThisButton : ButtonType;
    BtnTxt : STR40;
    constructor Init( WhatType : ButtonType;
               PtX, PtY, Width, Height, C : integer;
               Text : STR40 );
    destructor  Done;
    procedure DecDblClick;
    procedure Draw; virtual;
    procedure Erase; virtual;
    procedure IncDblClick;
    procedure Invert;
    procedure Move( PtX, PtY : integer ); virtual;
    procedure SetButtonType( WhatType : ButtonType );
    procedure SetColor( C : integer );
    procedure SetDblClick( Time: integer );
    procedure SetLabel( Text : STR40 );
    procedure SetOutline( var RectArr: RectOutline;
                      x1, y1, x2, y2 : integer );
    procedure SetState( BState : boolean );
    procedure SetTypeFace( TxtFont : integer );
    procedure SetTypeSize( TxtSize : integer );
    function   ButtonHit: boolean; virtual;
    function   DoubleClick: boolean; virtual;
    function   GetDblClick: integer;
    function   GetHeight : integer;
    function   GetState : boolean;
    function   GetTextSize : integer;
    function   GetType : ButtonType;
    function   GetWidth : integer;
end;

RadioButton = object( Button )
```

```
          {===========inherited==============}
          {   x, y, Color, FontSize,          }
          {   TypeFace, SizeX, SizeY : integer; }
          {   Exist, State, Rotate : boolean;  }
          {   ThisButton : ButtonType;         }
          {   VRef : ViewPortType;             }
          {   BtnTxt : STR40;                  }
          {====================================}
     Outline, Radius : integer;
     constructor Init( PtX, PtY, C, R : integer;
                       Text : STR10 );
     destructor Done;
     procedure Draw;   virtual;
     procedure Erase;  virtual;
     procedure SetRadius( R : integer );
     function  GetRadius : integer;
     function  ButtonHit : boolean; virtual;
  end;

  VueMeter = object( RadioButton )
          {===========inherited==============}
          {   x, y, Color, FontSize, TypeFace, }
          {   SizeX, SizeY, Radius : integer;  }
          {   Exist, State, Rotate : boolean;  }
          {   ThisButton : ButtonType;         }
          {   VRef : ViewPortType;             }
          {   BtnTxt : STR40;                  }
          {====================================}
     Closure : integer;
     constructor Init( PtX, PtY, C, R : integer;
                       Text : STR10 );
     destructor Done;
     procedure  Draw;   virtual;
     procedure  Erase;  virtual;
     procedure  Select( Degree: integer );
     procedure  Close( Degree: integer );
     procedure  Open( Degree: integer );
  end;

  HitType = ( NONE, RIGHT, UP, HBAR, VBAR, LEFT, DOWN );
  Direction = ( Vertical, Horizontal );
  ScrollBar = object( Button )
```

```
        {============inherited================}
        {   x, y, Color, FontSize,              }
        {   TypeFace, SizeX, SizeY : integer;   }
        {   Exist, State, Rotate : boolean;     }
        {   ThisButton : ButtonType;            }
        {   VRef : ViewPortType;                }
        {   BtnTxt : STR40;                     }
        {=======================================}
      ScrollMove : Direction;
      BarWidth, BarLen,
      LineColor, SPos, Step : integer;
      ThumbPad : pointer;
      constructor Init( PtX, PtY, Size, C1, C2 : integer;
                        Orientation : Direction );
      destructor Done;
      procedure SetLoc( PtX, PtY : integer ); virtual;
      procedure Draw; virtual;
      procedure SetThumbPad;
      function  GetPosition: integer;
      function  GetDirection: Direction;
      function  GetPercent: integer;
      function  ScrollHit: HitType;
   end;

var
   GMouse : GraphicMouse;
   TMouse : TextMouse;

IMPLEMENTATION
         {=======================================}
         { implementation for object type Point }
         {=======================================}

constructor Point.Init;
   begin
      GetViewSettings( VRef );
   end;

procedure Point.SetLoc;                    { PtX, PtY : integer }
   begin
      x := PtX + VRef.X1;
      y := PtY + VRef.Y1;
   end;

procedure Point.Draw;
   begin
      PutPixel( x, y, Color );
   end;
```

```pascal
procedure Point.Create;                         { PtX, PtY, C : integer }
   begin
      SetLoc( PtX, PtY );
      Color := C;
      Draw;
   end;
procedure Point.Erase;
   var
      Temp : integer;
   begin
      Temp := Color;
      Color := GetBkColor;
      Draw;
      Color := Temp;
   end;
procedure Point.Move;                           { PtX, PtY : integer }
   begin
      Erase;
      SetLoc( PtX, PtY );
      Draw;
   end;
procedure Point.RestoreViewPort;
   begin
      with VRef do
         SetViewPort( X1, Y1, X2, Y2, Clip );
   end;
procedure Point.SetColor;                       { C : integer }
   begin
      Color := C;
      Draw;
   end;
function  Point.GetColor;
   begin
      GetColor := Color;
   end;
function  Point.GetX;
   begin
      GetX := x - VRef.X1;
   end;
function  Point.GetY;
   begin
      GetY := y - VRef.Y1;
   end;
```

```
{========================================}
{ implementation for object type Button }
{========================================}
constructor Button.Init;              { WhatType : ButtonType }
    begin                  { PtX, PtY, Width, Height, C : integer }
        GetViewSettings( VRef );     {            Text : STR40     }
        SetButtonType( WhatType );
        SetTypeSize( 10 );
        SetTypeFace( TriplexFont );
        SetViewPort( 0, 0, GetMaxX, GetMaxY, ClipOn );
        SetTextJustify( CenterText, CenterText );
        SetLoc( PtX, PtY );
        DblClkTime := 50;
        if Width < 20 then SizeX := 20
                      else SizeX := Width;
        if Height < 20 then SizeY := 20
                       else SizeY := Height;
        if SizeY > SizeX then Rotate := TRUE
                         else Rotate := FALSE;
        Color  := C;
        State  := FALSE;
        Exist  := TRUE;
        BtnTxt := Text;
        Draw;
    end;
procedure Button.DecDblClick;
    begin
        if DblClkTime > 25 then
            dec( DblClkTime, 5 );
    end;
procedure Button.IncDblClick;
    begin
        if DblClkTime < 100 then
            inc( DblClkTime, 5 );
    end;
procedure Button.SetDblClick;
    begin
        DblClkTime := Time;
        if DblClkTime < 25 then DblClkTime := 25;
        if DblClkTime > 100 then DblClkTime := 100;
    end;
function Button.GetDblClick: integer;
    begin
        GetDblClick := DblClkTime;
    end;
```

```pascal
destructor Button.Done;
   begin
      Erase;
   end;

{==========================================================}
{ local procedure for Button functions AND descendents    }
{==========================================================}
procedure Button.SetOutline;         { var RectArr: RectOutline }
   begin                             { x1, y1, x2, y2 : integer }
      RectArr[1].x := x1;    RectArr[1].y := y1;
      RectArr[2].x := x1;    RectArr[2].y := y2;
      RectArr[3].x := x2;    RectArr[3].y := y2;
      RectArr[4].x := x2;    RectArr[4].y := y1;
      RectArr[5] := RectArr[1];
   end;
procedure Button.Draw;
   const
      radius = 6;                                    { radius }
      offset = 3;                         { offset for fill }
   var
      RectArr : RectOutline;
      AlignX, AlignY, TempSize, TextLen,
      i, BtnWd, BtnHt, TextDir, OldColor : integer;
   begin
      OldColor := Graph.GetColor;
      GMouse.Show( FALSE );
      SetViewPort( x, y, x+SizeX, y+SizeY, ClipOn );
      SetTextJustify( CenterText, CenterText );
      Graph.SetColor( color );
      case ThisButton of
      Square:
         begin
            Graph.Rectangle( 0, 0, SizeX, SizeY );
            BtnWd := SizeX - 10;
            BtnHt := SizeY - 10;
         end;
      ThreeD:                                    { 3-D Outline }
         begin
            Graph.Rectangle( 0, 0, SizeX, SizeY );
            SetOutline( RectArr,1,1,SizeX-1,SizeY-1 );
            SetFillStyle( CloseDotFill, color );
            SetLineStyle( UserBitLn, 0, NormWidth );
            FillPoly( sizeof(RectArr) div
                        sizeof(PointType), RectArr );
            SetLineStyle( SolidLn, 0, NormWidth );
            Graph.Rectangle( 2*radius, 2*radius,
```

```
                        SizeX-2*radius,
                        SizeY-2*radius );
         Line( 0, 0, 2*radius, 2*radius );
         Line( 0, SizeY, 2*radius, SizeY-2*radius );
         Line( SizeX, 0, SizeX-2*radius, 2*radius );
         Line( SizeX, SizeY,
               SizeX-2*radius, SizeY-2*radius );
         BtnWd := SizeX-4*radius;
         BtnHt := SizeY-4*radius;
      end;
  else                                         { default case }
     begin
        ThisButton := Rounded;
                  { draw corners }
        Graph.Arc( SizeX-radius, radius,
                   0, 90, radius );
        Graph.Arc( radius, radius,
                   90, 180, radius );
        Graph.Arc( radius, SizeY-radius,
                   180, 270, radius );
        Graph.Arc( SizeX-radius, SizeY-radius,
                   270, 360, radius );
                   { draw sides }
        Graph.Line( radius, 0, SizeX-radius, 0 );
        Graph.Line( radius, SizeY,
                    SizeX-radius, SizeY );
        Graph.Line( 0, radius, 0, SizeY-radius );
        Graph.Line( SizeX, radius,
                    SizeX, SizeY-radius );
        BtnWd := SizeX-2*radius;
        BtnHt := SizeY-2*radius;
     end;
end; { case }

case ThisButton of                             { fill button }
   Square,
   Rounded: SetOutline( RectArr, offset, offset,
                        SizeX-offset, SizeY-offset );
   ThreeD:  SetOutline( RectArr, 2*radius+1,
                        2*radius+1,
                        SizeX-2*radius-1,
                        SizeY-2*radius );
end; { case }

                  { show State }
if State then SetFillStyle( SolidFill, color )
         else SetFillStyle( WideDotFill, color );
SetLineStyle( UserBitLn, 0, NormWidth );
FillPoly( sizeof(RectArr) div sizeof(PointType),
```

```pascal
                        RectArr );
        SetLineStyle( SolidLn, 0, NormWidth );
                { adjust fonts AND string to fit }
        TextDir := HorizDir;        { horizontal text display }
        if Rotate then
        begin                       { vertical text display }
            TextDir := VertDir;
            TextLen := BtnWd;       { swap width AND height }
            BtnWd := BtnHt;
            BtnHt := TextLen;
        end;
        SetTextStyle( TypeFace, TextDir, FontSize );
        for i := FontSize downto 1 do
            if( TextWidth(BtnTxt) > BtnWd ) then
                SetTextStyle( TypeFace, TextDir, i ) else
              if( TextHeight(BtnTxt) > BtnHt ) then
                SetTextStyle( TypeFace, TextDir, i );
        TextLen := ord( BtnTxt[0] );
        while( TextWidth(copy(BtnTxt,1,TextLen))>BtnWd ) do
            dec( TextLen );
        AlignX := SizeX div 2 - 3;
        AlignY := SizeY div 2 - 3;
        if BtnTxt[TextLen] = ' ' then dec( TextLen );
        if State then Graph.SetColor( GetBkColor );
                        { add label }
        OutTextXY( AlignX,AlignY,copy(BtnTxt,1,TextLen) );
        if State then Graph.SetColor( color );
        SetViewPort( 0, 0, GetMaxX, GetMaxY, ClipOn );
        GMouse.Show( TRUE );
        Graph.SetColor( OldColor );
    end;
procedure Button.Erase;
    begin
        if Exist then
        begin
            GMouse.Show( FALSE );
            SetViewPort( x, y, x+SizeX, y+SizeY, ClipOn );
            ClearViewPort;
            SetViewPort( 0, 0, GetMaxX, GetMaxY, ClipOn );
            GMouse.Show( TRUE );
        end;
    end;
procedure Button.Move;                  { PtX, PtY : integer }
    begin
        Erase;
        SetLoc( PtX, PtY );
```

```
      Draw;
   end;
procedure Button.SetLabel;                   {  Text : STR40  }
   begin
      BtnTxt := Text;
      Draw;
   end;
procedure Button.SetColor;                   {  C : integer  }
   begin
      Color := C;
      Draw;
   end;
procedure Button.SetState;                   { BState : boolean }
   begin
      if( State <> BState ) then Invert;
   end;
procedure Button.SetTypeSize;                { TxtSize : integer }
   begin
      FontSize := TxtSize;
   end;
procedure Button.SetTypeFace;                { TxtFont : integer }
   begin
      TypeFace := TxtFont;
   end;
procedure Button.SetButtonType;    { WhatType : ButtonType }
   begin
      ThisButton := WhatType;
   end;
procedure Button.Invert;
   begin
      State := not State;
      Draw;
   end;
function Button.GetWidth;
   begin
      GetWidth := SizeX;
   end;
function Button.GetHeight;
   begin
      GetHeight := SizeY;
   end;
function Button.GetState;
   begin
```

```pascal
            GetState := State;
      end;
function Button.GetTextSize;
   begin
         GetTextSize := FontSize;
   end;
function Button.GetType;
   begin
         GetType := ThisButton;
   end;
function Button.ButtonHit: Boolean;
   var
         Result : boolean;
         BtnStatus, XPos, YPos : integer;
   begin
         Result := FALSE;
         GMouse.GetPosition( BtnStatus, XPos, YPos );
         if( BtnStatus AND $01 ) = $01 then
             Result := ( XPos >= x ) AND
                       ( XPos <= x+SizeX ) AND
                       ( YPos >= y ) AND ( YPos <= y+SizeY );
         if Result then Invert;
         ButtonHit := Result;
   end;
function Button.DoubleClick: Boolean;
   var
         Result : boolean;
         BtnEvent : Position;
   begin
         Result := FALSE;
         if ButtonHit then                          { first hit  }
         begin
             GMouse.QueryBtnDn( ButtonL, BtnEvent );
             delay( DblClkTime );                   { wait a bit }
             GMouse.QueryBtnDn( ButtonL, BtnEvent );
             Result := BtnEvent.opCount  0;         { second hit }
         end;
         if not Result AND GetState then
             SetState( FALSE );
         DoubleClick := Result;
   end;
```

```pascal
{=============================================}
{ implementation for object type RadioButton  }
{=============================================}
constructor RadioButton.Init;     { PtX, PtY, C, R : integer }
   begin                          {             Text : STR10 }
      GetViewSettings( VRef );
      SetTextJustify( CenterText, CenterText );
      SetLoc( PtX, PtY );
      Radius  := R;
      Outline := C OR $08;
      Color   := C;
      State   := FALSE;
      Exist   := TRUE;
      BtnTxt  := Text;
      Draw;
   end;
destructor RadioButton.Done;
   begin
      Erase;
   end;
procedure RadioButton.Draw;
   var
       XAsp, YAsp : word;
       OldColor, i : integer;
   begin
      OldColor := Graph.GetColor;
      RestoreViewPort;
      GetAspectRatio( XAsp, YAsp );
      Graph.SetColor( Outline );
      GMouse.Show( FALSE );
      if State then SetFillStyle( SolidFill, Color ) else
              SetFillStyle( InterleaveFill, Color );
      FillEllipse( x, y, Radius,
                   Radius * longint( XAsp ) div YAsp );
      SetTextStyle( DefaultFont, HorizDir, 1 );
      OutTextXY( X, Y + Radius + 10, BtnTxt );
      GMouse.Show( TRUE );
      Graph.SetColor( OldColor );
   end;
procedure RadioButton.Erase;
   var
      OldColor : integer;
   begin
      OldColor := Color;
      Color := GetBkColor;
      Outline := Color;
```

```pascal
         Draw;
         Color := OldColor;
         Outline := OldColor OR $08;
      end;
procedure RadioButton.SetRadius;
   begin
      Radius := R;
   end;
function RadioButton.GetRadius;
   begin
      GetRadius := Radius;
   end;
function RadioButton.ButtonHit: Boolean;
   var
      Result : boolean;
      BtnStatus, XPos, YPos, OffX, OffY : integer;
   begin
      Result := FALSE;
      GMouse.GetPosition( BtnStatus, XPos, YPos );
      if( BtnStatus AND $01 ) = $01 then
      begin
         OffX := abs( XPos - x );
         OffY := abs( YPos - y );

     {=============================================}
     { provision to prevent floating-point error }
     {=============================================}

         if ( OffX < 2 * Radius ) AND
            ( OffY < 2 * Radius ) then
            Result := trunc( sqrt( sqr( OffX ) +
                              sqr( OffY ) ) ) < radius;
      end;
      if Result then SetState( TRUE );
      ButtonHit := Result;
   end;

          {=============================================}
          { implementation for object type VueMeter }
          {=============================================}
constructor VueMeter.Init;          { PtX, PtY, C, R : integer }
   begin                            {          Text : STR10    }
      GetViewSettings( VRef );
      SetTextJustify( CenterText, CenterText );
      SetLoc( PtX, PtY );
      Radius   := R;
      Color    := C;
```

```pascal
        Closure := 1;
        Exist   := TRUE;
        BtnTxt  := Text;
        Draw;
    end;
destructor VueMeter.Done;
    begin
        Erase;
    end;
procedure VueMeter.Draw;
    var
        i : integer;    XAsp, YAsp : word;
    begin
        RestoreViewPort;
        GetAspectRatio( XAsp, YAsp );
        if Closure < 0   then Closure := 0;
        if Closure > 360 then Closure := 360;
        GMouse.Show( FALSE );
        Graph.SetColor( Color );
        SetFillStyle( SolidFill, Color );
        Sector( x, y, 0, Closure, Radius,
                Radius * longint( XAsp ) div YAsp );
        SetTextStyle( DefaultFont, HorizDir, 1 );
        SetTextJustify( CenterText, CenterText );
        OutTextXY( X, Y + Radius + 10, BtnTxt );
        Graph.SetColor( White );
        SetFillStyle( CloseDotFill, Color );
        if Closure < 360 then
            Sector( x, y, Closure, 360, Radius,
                    Radius * longint( XAsp ) div YAsp );
        GMouse.Show( TRUE );
    end;
procedure VueMeter.Erase;
    var
        XAsp, YAsp : word;
    begin
        GetAspectRatio( XAsp, YAsp );
        GMouse.Show( FALSE );
        Graph.SetColor( GetBkColor );
        SetFillStyle( SolidFill, GetBkColor );
        Sector( x, y, 0, 360, Radius,
                Radius * longint( XAsp ) div YAsp );
        SetTextStyle( DefaultFont, HorizDir, 1 );
        SetTextJustify( CenterText, CenterText );
        OutTextXY( X, Y + Radius + 10, BtnTxt );
        Graph.SetColor( White );
```

```pascal
            GMouse.Show( TRUE );
    end;
procedure VueMeter.Select( Degree: integer );
    begin
        Closure := Degree;
        Draw;
    end;
procedure VueMeter.Close( Degree: integer );
    begin
        inc( Closure, Degree );
        Draw;
    end;
procedure VueMeter.Open( Degree: integer );
    begin
        dec( Closure, Degree );
        Draw;
    end;

            {==========================================}
            { implementation for object type ScrollBar }
            {==========================================}
constructor ScrollBar.Init;
                        { PtX, PtY, Size, C1, C2 : integer }
    var                 { Orientation : Direction          }
        RectArr  : RectOutline;
    begin
        BarWidth := 20;
        GetViewSettings( VRef );
        if Size < 100 then Size := 100;
        SPos := BarWidth+1;
        BarLen := Size;
        ScrollMove := Orientation;
        Step := BarLen div 100;
        case ScrollMove of
           Vertical:
           begin
              while BarLen + 2 * BarWidth >
                    VRef.Y2 - VRef.Y1 do
                 dec( BarLen );
              SizeX := BarWidth;
              SizeY := BarLen + 2 * BarWidth;
              while PtX + BarWidth > VRef.X2 - VRef.X1 do
                 dec( PtX );
           end;
           Horizontal:
           begin
```

```
            while BarLen + 2 * BarWidth >
                VRef.X2 - VRef.X1 do
                dec( BarLen );
            SizeX := BarLen + 2 * BarWidth;
            SizeY := BarWidth;
            while PtY + BarWidth > VRef.Y2 - VRef.Y1 do
                dec( PtY );
        end;
end; {case}
SetLoc( PtX, PtY );
LineColor := C1;
Color := C2;
            {=== draw scrollbar thumbpad ===}
Graph.SetColor( LineColor );
SetFillStyle( CloseDotFill, Color );
SetTextStyle( DefaultFont, HorizDir, 1 );
SetTextJustify( CenterText, CenterText );
case ScrollMove of
Vertical:
    begin
        SetOutline( RectArr, 2, SPos,
                    BarWidth-2, SPos+BarWidth-1 );
        FillPoly( sizeof(RectArr) div
                    sizeof(PointType), RectArr );
        Graph.SetColor( White );
        OutTextXY( BarWidth div 2, SPos +
                    BarWidth div 2, #$12 );
        GetMem( ThumbPad,
                ImageSize( 2, SPos, BarWidth - 2,
                            SPos + BarWidth - 1 ) );
        GetImage( 2, SPos, BarWidth-2,
                    SPos + BarWidth - 1, ThumbPad^ );
        PutImage( 2, SPos, ThumbPad^, XOrPut );
    end;
Horizontal:
    begin
        SetOutline( RectArr, SPos, 2,
                    SPos+BarWidth-1, BarWidth-2 );
        FillPoly( sizeof(RectArr) div
                    sizeof(PointType), RectArr );
        Graph.SetColor( White );
        OutTextXY( SPos + BarWidth div 2,
                    BarWidth div 2 + 1, #$1D );
        GetMem( ThumbPad,
                ImageSize( SPos, 2,
                            SPos + BarWidth - 1,
                            BarWidth - 2 ) );
        GetImage( SPos, 2, SPos + BarWidth - 1,
```

```pascal
                              BarWidth - 2, ThumbPad^ );
                  PutImage( SPos, 2, ThumbPad^, XOrPut );
              end;
      end; { case }
      Exist := TRUE;
      Draw;
   end;
procedure ScrollBar.SetLoc;
   begin
      X := VRef.X1 + PtX;
      Y := VRef.Y1 + PtY;
   end;
procedure ScrollBar.SetThumbPad;
   begin
      SetViewPort( x, y, x+SizeX-1, y+SizeY-1, True );
      case ScrollMove of
          Vertical: PutImage( 2,SPos,ThumbPad^,XOrPut );
          Horizontal: PutImage( SPos,2,ThumbPad^,XOrPut );
      end; {case}
      RestoreViewPort;
   end;
procedure ScrollBar.Draw;
   var
      RectArr  : RectOutline;
      OldColor : word;
   begin
      OldColor := Graph.GetColor;
      Graph.SetColor( LineColor );
      SetViewPort( x, y, x+SizeX, y+SizeY, ClipOn );
                {=== scrollbar outline ===}
      SetOutline( RectArr, 1, 1, SizeX-1, SizeY-1 );
      SetFillStyle( SolidFill, color );
      SetLineStyle( SolidLn, 0, NormWidth );
      FillPoly( sizeof(RectArr) div sizeof(PointType),
                RectArr );
                   {=== scrollbar arrows ===}
      Graph.SetColor( GetBkColor );
      SetTextStyle( DefaultFont, HorizDir, 2 );
      case ScrollMove of
         Vertical    : begin
                          OutTextXY( 10, 12, #$18 );
                          OutTextXY( 10, SizeY-10, #$19 );
                       end;
         Horizontal  : begin
                          OutTextXY( 10, 12, #$1B );
                          OutTextXY( SizeX-10, 12, #$1A );
```

```
                                 end;
            end;
{=========================================================}
{   SetLineStyle( SolidLn, 0, ThickWidth );               }
{   case ScrollMove of                                    }
{       Vertical: begin                                   }
{                     Line( 10,  4,    4, 12 );           }
{                     Line( 10,  4,   16, 12 );           }
{                     Line( 10,  4,   10, 16 );           }
{                     Line( 10, SizeY-4,    4, SizeY-12 ); }
{                     Line( 10, SizeY-4,   16, SizeY-12 ); }
{                     Line( 10, SizeY-4,   10, SizeY-16 ); }
{                 end;                                    }
{       Horizontal: begin                                 }
{                     Line(  4, 10,   12,  4 );           }
{                     Line(  4, 10,   12, 16 );           }
{                     Line(  4, 10,   16, 10 );           }
{                     Line( SizeX-4, 10, SizeX-12,  4 ); }
{                     Line( SizeX-4, 10, SizeX-12, 16 ); }
{                     Line( SizeX-4, 10, SizeX-16, 10 ); }
{                 end;                                    }
{   end;                                                  }
{   SetLineStyle( SolidLn, 0, NormWidth );                }
{=========================================================}
              {=== clear scrollbar center ===}
      Graph.SetColor( LineColor );
      SetFillStyle( SolidFill, Graph.GetBkColor );
      case ScrollMove of
          Vertical: SetOutline( RectArr, 1, BarWidth+1,
                                SizeX-1, SizeY-BarWidth-1 );
         Horizontal: SetOutline( RectArr, BarWidth+1, 1,
                                SizeX-BarWidth-1, SizeY-1 );
      end; {case}
      FillPoly( sizeof(RectArr) div sizeof(PointType),
                RectArr );
           {=== restore default color settings ===}
      Graph.SetColor( OldColor );
      RestoreViewPort;
      SetThumbPad;
   end;
destructor ScrollBar.Done;
   begin
      Erase;
      Dispose( ThumbPad );
   end;
function ScrollBar.GetPosition;
   begin
```

```pascal
            GetPosition := SPos;
    end;
function ScrollBar.GetPercent;
    var
        Percent : integer;
    begin
        case ScrollMove of
            Horizontal: Percent := round( (SPos-BarWidth) /
                                          (BarLen-BarWidth)*100 );
              Vertical: Percent := round( (SPos-BarWidth) /
                                          (BarLen-BarWidth)*100 );
        end;
        GetPercent := Percent;
    end;
function ScrollBar.GetDirection;
    begin
        GetDirection := ScrollMove;
    end;
function ScrollBar.ScrollHit;
    var
        Result : HitType;
        BtnStatus, XPos, YPos : integer;
    begin
        Result := NONE;
        GMouse.GetPosition( BtnStatus, XPos, YPos );
        if BtnStatus AND $01 = $01 then
        case ScrollMove of
            Vertical:
                if( XPos >= x ) AND
                  ( XPos <= x+BarWidth ) AND
                  ( YPos >= y ) then
                   if YPos <= y+BarWidth
                       then Result := UP            else
                   if YPos <= y+BarLen+BarWidth
                       then Result := VBAR          else
                   if YPos <= y+BarLen+BarWidth*2
                       then Result := DOWN;
            Horizontal:
                if( YPos >= y ) AND
                  ( YPos <= y+BarWidth ) AND
                  ( XPos >= x ) then
                   if XPos <= x+BarWidth
                       then Result := LEFT          else
                   if XPos <= x+BarLen+BarWidth
                       then Result := HBAR          else
                   if XPos <= x+BarLen+BarWidth*2
```

```pascal
                          then Result := RIGHT;
        end; {case}


{==========================================================}
{    alternate form for thumbpad and endpad hits only      }
{==========================================================}
{                                                          }
{    if( YPos >= y ) AND ( YPos <= y+BarWidth ) then        }
{       if( XPos >= x ) AND ( XPos <= x+BarWidth )          }
{          then Result := LEFT else                         }
{       if( XPos >= x+SPos ) AND                            }
{          ( XPos <= x+SPos+BarWidth )                      }
{          then Result := HBAR else                         }
{       if( XPos >= x+BarLen+BarWidth ) AND                 }
{          ( XPos <= x+BarLen+BarWidth*2 )                  }
{          then Result := RIGHT;                            }
{==========================================================}

        if Result <> NONE then
        begin
           GMouse.Show( FALSE );
           SetThumbPad;
        end;
        case Result of
           LEFT,    UP: dec( SPos, Step );
                  HBAR: SPos := XPos - x - 10;
                  VBAR: SPos := YPos - y - 10;
           RIGHT, DOWN: inc( SPos, Step );
        end; {case}
        if Result <> NONE then
        begin
           if SPos < BarWidth then SPos := BarWidth;
           if SPos > BarLen   then SPos := BarLen;
           SetThumbPad;
           GMouse.Show( TRUE );
        end;
        ScrollHit := Result;
     end;

        (* =========== end of methods ============= *)

end.
```

CTRLTEST.PAS

```pascal
program Control_Object_Test;
uses Crt, Graph, Mouse, GControl;
const
   RMin = 1;
```

```pascal
            RMax = 7;
            ColorStr : array[1..7] of string[10] =
                       ( 'LtBlue', 'LtGreen', 'LtCyan', 'LtRed',
                         'LtMagenta', 'Yellow', 'White' );
   var
      mButton : Position;                        { mouse position   }
      VRef : ViewPortType;                       { viewport coords  }
      Status : Boolean;                          { mouse status     }
      GDriver, GMode, GError, i, j, BtnCount : integer;
                  { === object list === }
      ExitButton : Button;                       { static  object   }
      CatsEye : VueMeter;                        { static  object   }
      PHScroll, PVScroll : ^ScrollBar;           { dynamic objects  }
      RButton : array[RMin..RMax] of ^RadioButton;
                                                 { dynamic objects  }
   begin
      GDriver := Detect;
      InitGraph( GDriver, GMode, '\TP\BGI' );
      GError := GraphResult;
      if GError <> grOk then
      begin
         writeln( 'Graphics error: ',
                  GraphErrorMsg(GError) );
         writeln( 'Program aborted...' );
         halt(1);
      end;
      GMouse.Reset( Status, BtnCount );
      if Status then
      begin
         ClearDevice;
         GMouse.Initialize;
             {======================================}
             {    set up graphic control objects    }
             {======================================}
         for i := RMin to RMax do
            New( RButton[i],
                Init( 50, 360-45*i, i+8, 10, ColorStr[i] ) );
         CatsEye.Init( 50, GetMaxY-50,
                       LightRed, 20, 'VueMeter' );
         SetViewPort( 100, 0, GetMaxX, GetMaxY, ClipOn );
         GetViewSettings( VRef );
         New( PHScroll,
              Init( 0, GetMaxY, VRef.X2-VRef.X1-80,
                    Green, LightGreen, Horizontal ) );
         New( PVScroll,
              Init( GetMaxX, 0, GetMaxY,
                    Green, LightGreen, Vertical ) );
```

```
   with ExitButton do
   begin
      Init( Rounded,
            PHScroll^.GetPosition-20,
            PVScroll^.GetPosition,
            80, 20, LightRed, 'Exit' );
      RButton[4]^.SetState( TRUE );
   end;
               {===========================}
               {    start demo program     }
               {===========================}
   while not ExitButton.DoubleClick do
   repeat
      if( PHScroll^.ScrollHit <> NONE ) or
        ( PVScroll^.ScrollHit <> NONE ) then
      begin
         ExitButton.Move( PHScroll^.GetPosition-20,
                          PVScroll^.GetPosition );
         CatsEye.Select(
            round((PHScroll^.GetPercent/100*180) +
                  (PVScroll^.GetPercent/100*180)));
      end;
      for i := RMin to RMax do
         if RButton[i]^.ButtonHit then
         begin
            for j := RMin to RMax do
               RButton[j]^.SetState( FALSE );
            RButton[i]^.SetState( TRUE );
            ExitButton.SetColor(RButton[i]^.GetColor);
            CatsEye.SetColor( RButton[i]^.GetColor );
         end;
      GMouse.QueryBtnUp( ButtonL, mButton );
   until mButton.opCount > 0;
               {===========================}
               {    clean up objects       }
               {===========================}
ExitButton.Erase;                     delay( 500 );
CatsEye.Erase;                        delay( 500 );
for i := RMin to RMax do begin
   Dispose( RButton[i], Done );       delay( 500 );
end;
Dispose( PHScroll, Done );            delay( 500 );
Dispose( PVScroll, Done );            delay( 500 );
```

```
                        {========================}
                        {    and exit to text    }
                        {========================}
   end;
   CloseGraph;                 { restore text mode and ...        }
   TMouse.Initialize;          { reset mouse for text operation   }
end.
```

CHAPTER 15

Creating Icons

With the increasing popularity of graphics applications many programs (and programmers) have abandoned text menus and labeled buttons in favor of icon-based applications like those pioneered by Apple computers, Microsoft Windows and more recently, Presentation Manager.

In many cases, such as the Apple Macintosh where text labels appear almost as if they were minor afterthoughts, graphic icons have been taken to extremes, which many consider more hindrance than help. In other cases, such as Presentation Manager, icons appear principally in an informative or a convenience capacity, rather than as the primary interactive element.

Regardless of your likes or dislikes, icons are a natural element of graphic programming and can be used in whatever fashions your preferences and applications dictate. Of course, if you find icons intensely distasteful or irritating, then you are under no obligation to use them. After all, what goes around comes around; I have no interest in imposing strictures on your programming.

Take or leave icons as you wish, but remember, they are a valid element of graphics programming and will appear more often in the future.

Creating Icon Images

Icons can serve as screen symbols and as buttons to summon or control applications or subprocedures. Since control buttons have been shown in other demonstrations, this chapter will be concerned with the images used for icons and a simple demo where the mouse maneuvers the icon around the screen.

For the business line graph (Chapter 9), the symbols used were created in various fashions—by defining bit maps, by drawing images, etc.—but, for general applications, a more versatile and consistent method of creating icons and bit images is required; hence, the IconEdit utility.

The IconEdit Utility

The IconEdit utility provides a simple bit-map editor that can create icon images up to 32 pixels square in monochrome or color, can save and retrieve images from disk and can invert images or change color to monochrome.

Most graphics systems using icons have used monochrome icons even though some, such as the Macintosh, allow colors to be assigned to icons. Multicolored icons, however, are relatively uncommon even though color monitors are increasingly common. In the case of the icon editor, multicolored icons are supported or monochrome icons may be created with a color specified. The monochrome icons, of course, require less memory—both as disk files and in RAM.

The size limitations (32x32) are arbitrary and can easily be increased if desired. In most cases, a 32-bit square image is more than sufficient, while smaller sizes are sometimes preferred, as for the line graph demo appearing in Chapter 9.

Smaller image sizes are readily available through vertical and horizontal size options. In general, when creating an icon, you should start with the default (large) image size and reduce the grid size after the image is completed. Also, the IconEdit utility requires the Mouse and GControl units created in previous chapters. If you do not have these compiled already, both units should be completed before attempting to create the IconEdit program or before running the IconDemo program. All of these, together with the other programs and units created in this book, are available on a program disk available from Addison-Wesley Publishing (please see the coupon at the back of the book).

The IconEdit utility, itself, is not particularly complex and provides a drawing grid with various option and color buttons. The mouse draws on the grid using the selected color when the left button is down or using the background color when the right button is down. Other than this, the drawing program is self-explanatory.

A few comments on how icons are saved as files are in order.

Figure 15-1: The IconEdit Display

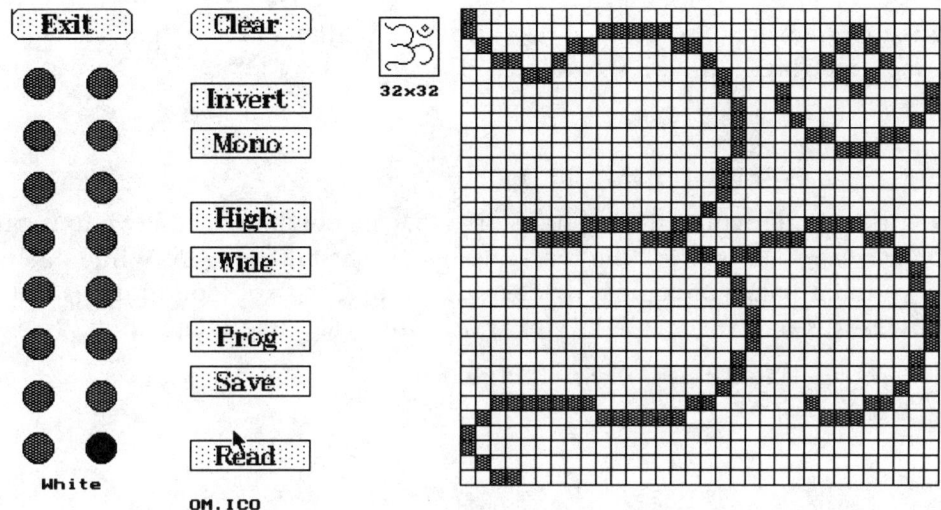

The Icon Image Files

The WriteImageProg procedure is used to save a created icon bit image as a disk file but the file save procedure begins with a pair of tests to determine if the icon image can be saved in a monochrome format or if a multicolored format is required. Before testing for either condition, the first two bytes written to the output file are the horizontal and vertical sizes of the icon image. After this, the first test is to retrieve the state of the MonoBtn button. If this is set (TRUE) then the image will be saved as monochrome.

```
          CFlag := not MonoBtn.GetState;
```

If *CFlag* is not set by the first test, a second test is executed by checking the entire *image* array to decide if more than one color is present. This is done by setting the *C1* variable to the first non-background color entry encountered and then comparing all subsequent non-background entries against this color value. If a second color entry is encountered, then multicolor is assumed and *CFlag* is set as TRUE.

```
            if CFlag then
          begin
             CFlag := not CFlag;
             for i := 0 to HSize do
                for j := 0 to HSize do
                   if image[i,j] <> 0 then
                      if C1 = 0 then C1 := image[i,j] else
```

```
            if C1 <> image[i,j] then
               CFlag := TRUE;
   end;
```

If the icon image is color, then the third byte written to the output file is the multicolored flag, *C2*, with the value $FF.

```
   if CFlag then
   begin
      write( fil, C2 );
```

Next, for a multicolored icon, pairs of pixels are combined with two four-bit color values (0..15 or 00h..0Fh) creating one, eight-bit file byte. While this is only minimal image encoding, a 16-color, 32 by 32 pixel icon requires only 515 bytes to store, versus slightly over one kilobyte without encoding.

```
      for i := 0 to HSize do
      begin
         C2 := 0;
         k := 0;
         for j := 0 to VSize do
         begin
            inc( k );
            C2 := C2 shl 4;
            inc( C2, image[i,j] );
            if k = 2 then
            begin
               k := 0;
               write( fil, C2 );
            end;
         end;
         if k <> 0 then
         begin
            C2 := C2 shl 4;
            write( fil, C2 );
         end;
      end;
   end else
```

For a monochrome icon, the third file byte is the active palette color (00h..0Fh). This color is the currently selected working color, *not* the color used to create the icon image. By selecting different drawing colors before saving an icon image to file, the icon can be saved in a different color than it was drawn and, depending on whether you find this useful or a nuisance, you may consider it a feature or a bug.

```
   begin
      write( fil, ActiveColor );
```

For a monochrome icon, after writing a single byte to establish the color used, the image itself is stored as an array of Boolean bits with eight True/False bits per file byte.

```
for i := 0 to HSize do
   for j := 0 to 3 do
      if j*8 <= VSize then
      begin
         C2 := 0;
         for k := 0 to 7 do
         begin
            C2 := C2 shl 1;
            if j*8+k <= VSize then
               if image[ i, j*8+k ] <> 0 then
                  inc( C2 );
         end;
         write( fil, C2 );
      end;
end;
```

Note that each row of pixels in the icon image begins a new file byte even if the vertical size of the image is not a multiple of eight bits. While this is not the absolute optimum for data compression, it does simplify encoding and decoding and a 32 by 32 icon requires only 67 bytes versus 515 bytes for a multicolored icon.

Of course, depending on system parameters, file size minimums may result in 256 to 1,024 bytes being allocated to store a 67-byte icon image. You may wish to consider combining several icon data sets into a single file. This, however, is left as an exercise for the reader.

The Icon Object

The icon object type is defined in the demo program IconDemo.PAS, but could be included in the GCONTROL unit or even redefined as a descendent of the Button object type. Unlike previous object types, however, the icon object type is not created as a separate unit and supplies only minimal object methods. It may be elaborated as desired.

Figure 15-2 shows the IconDemo program which loads four icon images from disk files and supplies a single exit button. For demonstration purposes, you will have to create your own icon images and alter the loaded filenames to match.

The icons can be dragged around the screen using the mouse or can be selected by a double-click, in which case the program will respond by writing a brief response to the screen and sounding a two-tone note. In actual practice, of course, double-clicking on an icon should produce a more definitive result.

The Icon object is similar to the Button object demonstrated previously. It is generally self-explanatory.

Figure 15-2: IconDemo Showing Four Icons, a Mouse Pointer, and a Button

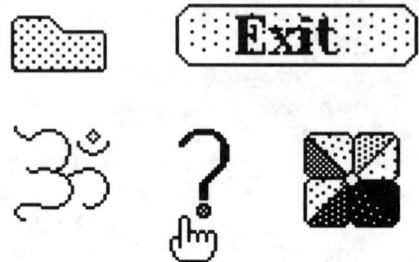

IconEdit.Pas

```pascal
program Icon_Image_Editor;
uses Crt, Graph, Mouse, GControl;
const
   GridColor = Blue;
var
   mButton : Position;                       { mouse position   }
   VRef : ViewPortType;                      { viewport coords  }
   Status : Boolean;                         { mouse status     }
   OrgPalette : PaletteType;
   ActiveColor, HSize, VSize : byte;
   PixColor, BtnStatus, XPos, YPos,
   GDriver, GMode, GError, i, j, BtnCount : integer;
   Image : array[0..31,0..31] of byte;
               { === object list === }
   ExtBtn, ClrBtn, MonoBtn, HighBtn, WideBtn,
   InvBtn, ProgBtn, SaveBtn, ReadBtn: Button;
                                             { static  objects }
   RButton : array[0..15] of ^RadioButton;
                                             { dynamic objects }
procedure FillSquare( x1, y1, x2, y2,
                      FillStyle, Color : integer );
   var
      OrgColor : integer;
      outline : array[1..5] of PointType;
   begin
```

```pascal
        OrgColor := Graph.GetColor;
        Graph.SetColor( GridColor );
        outline[1].x := x1;   outline[1].y := y1;
        outline[2].x := x2;   outline[2].y := y1;
        outline[3].x := x2;   outline[3].y := y2;
        outline[4].x := x1;   outline[4].y := y2;
        outline[5] := outline[1];
        SetFillStyle( FillStyle, Color );
        FillPoly( sizeof(outline) div sizeof( PointType ),
                  outline );
        Graph.SetColor( OrgColor );
    end;
procedure EraseSquare( x1, y1, x2, y2 : integer );
    var
        i, j : integer;
    begin
        FillSquare( x1, y1, x2, y2, SolidFill, BLACK );
    end;
procedure Beep;
    begin
        Sound( 220 );  delay( 100 );  NoSound;
                       delay(  50 );
        Sound( 440 );  delay( 100 );  NoSound;
    end;
function StrToHex( WorkStr: string ): word;
    var
        TempVal : word;
    begin
        TempVal := $0000;
        for i := 1 to length(WorkStr) do
        begin
            TempVal := TempVal shl 4;
            case WorkStr[i] of
                '1'..'9': inc( TempVal,
                                ord( WorkStr[i] )-$30 );
                'A'..'F': inc( TempVal,
                                ord( WorkStr[i] )-$37 );
            end; {case}
        end;
        StrToHex := TempVal;
    end;
function HexToStr( NumVal : word ): string;
    const
        CharStr : string[16] = '0123456789ABCDEF';
    var
        Temp : string[4];
```

```pascal
            i : integer;
   begin
      Temp := ',';
      for i := 1 to 2 do
      begin
         Temp := copy( CharStr,
                       (NumVal AND $000F)+1, 1 ) + Temp;
         NumVal := NumVal shr 4;
      end;
      HexToStr := ' $'+Temp;
   end;
procedure PaintGrid;
   var
      Temp1, Temp2 : string;
   begin
      GMouse.Show( FALSE );
      SetViewPort( 246, 06, 286, 86, TRUE );
      ClearViewPort;
      Rectangle( 0, 0, HSize+8, VSize+8 );
      str( HSize+1, Temp1 );
      str( VSize+1, Temp2 );
      SetTextJustify( CenterText, CenterText );
      SetTextStyle( DefaultFont, HorizDir, 1 );
      OutTextXY( 20, 50, Temp1 + 'x' + Temp2 );
      SetViewPort( 300, 0, GetMaxX, GetMaxY, TRUE );
      ClearViewPort;
      SetViewPort( 0, 0, GetMaxX, GetMaxY, TRUE );

      for i := 0 to HSize do
         for j := 0 to VSize do
         begin
            FillSquare( i*10+300, j*10,
                        i*10+310, j*10+10,
                        InterleaveFill, Image[i,j] );
            PutPixel( 250 + i, 10 + j, Image[i,j] );
         end;
      GMouse.Show( TRUE );
   end;
procedure NoteColor;
   const
      ColorNames : array[0..15] of string[10] =
      ( 'Black', 'Blue', 'Green', 'Cyan', 'Red',
        'Magenta', 'Brown', 'LightGray', 'DarkGray',
        'LightBlue', 'LightGreen', 'LightCyan',
        'LightRed', 'LtMagenta', 'Yellow', 'White' );
   begin
      SetViewPort( 0, 310, 80, 330, TRUE );
```

```
            Graph.SetColor( ActiveColor );
            SetTextStyle( DefaultFont, HorizDir, 1 );
            SetTextJustify( CenterText, CenterText );
            ClearViewPort;
            OutTextXY( 40, 10, ColorNames[ActiveColor] );
            SetViewPort( 0, 0, GetMaxX, GetMaxY, TRUE );
        end;
    procedure ClearImage;
        var
            i, j : integer;
        begin
            for i := 0 to HSize do
                for j := 0 to VSize do
                    Image[i,j] := 0;
            PaintGrid;
            ClrBtn.SetState( FALSE );
            if InvBtn.GetState then
                InvBtn.SetState( FALSE );
        end;
    procedure InvertImage;
        var
            i, j : integer;
        begin
            for i := 0 to HSize do
                for j := 0 to VSize do
                    Image[i,j] := Image[i,j] XOR $0F;
            PaintGrid;
        end;
    procedure Monochrome;
        var
            i, j : integer;
        begin
            if InvBtn.GetState then
            begin
                for i := 0 to HSize do
                    for j := 0 to VSize do
                        Image[i,j] := Image[i,j] AND $0F;
                PaintGrid;
            end;
            if MonoBtn.GetState then
            begin
                GetPalette( OrgPalette );
                for i := 1 to 15 do
                    SetPalette( i,
                                OrgPalette.Colors[ActiveColor] );
            end else
                SetAllPalette( OrgPalette );
```

```pascal
            delay( 100 );
        end;
function GetSize: integer;
    var
        TempStr : string;
        R,Value : integer;
            Ch  : char;
    begin
        TempStr := '';
        SetTextJustify( LeftText, TopText );
        SetTextStyle( DefaultFont, HorizDir, 1 );
        SetViewPort( 120, 330, GetMaxX, 340, TRUE );
        repeat
            ClearViewPort;
            OutTextXY( 1, 1, 'Size (10..32): '+TempStr );
            Ch := ReadKey;
            case upcase(Ch) of
                '0'..'9' : TempStr := TempStr+ upcase(Ch);
                    #$7F,
                    #$08 : if ord( TempStr[0] ) > 0 then
                               TempStr[0] :=
                                   chr( ord( TempStr[0] ) -1 );
            end; {case}
        until Ch = #$0D;
        ClearViewPort;
        if ord( TempStr[0] ) = 0
            then Value := 0
            else val( TempStr, Value, R );
        SetViewPort( 0, 0, GetMaxX, GetMaxY, TRUE );
        GetSize := Value;
    end;
procedure SetWidth;
    var
        Result : integer;
    begin
        Result := GetSize;
        if( Result < 10 ) OR ( Result > 32 ) then Beep else
        begin
            HSize := Result-1;
            PaintGrid;
        end;
        WideBtn.SetState( FALSE );
    end;
procedure SetHeight;
    var
        Result : integer;
    begin
```

```pascal
            Result := GetSize;
            if( Result < 10 ) OR ( Result > 32 ) then Beep else
            begin
                VSize := Result-1;
                PaintGrid;
            end;
            HighBtn.SetState( FALSE );
        end;
    function ReadName( Note: string ): string;
        var
            TempStr : string;
            Ch : char;
        begin
            TempStr := '';
            SetColor( White );
            SetTextJustify( LeftText, TopText );
            SetTextStyle( DefaultFont, HorizDir, 1 );
            SetViewPort( 120, 330, GetMaxX, 340, TRUE );
            repeat
                ClearViewPort;
                OutTextXY( 1, 1, Note + TempStr );
                Ch := ReadKey;
                case upcase(Ch) of
                    'A'..'Z',
                    '0'..'9',
                    '\',  ':',
                    '.',  '_' : TempStr := TempStr+ upcase(Ch);
                        #$7F,
                        #$08 : if ord( TempStr[0] ) > 0 then
                                    TempStr[0] :=
                                        chr( ord( TempStr[0] )-1 );
                end; {case}
            until Ch = #$0D;
            ClearViewPort;
            SetViewPort( 0, 0, GetMaxX, GetMaxY, TRUE );
            ReadName := TempStr;
        end;
    procedure ReportError( ErrNum : integer );
        var
            Temp : string;
        begin
            str( ErrNum, Temp );
            SetTextJustify( LeftText, TopText );
            SetTextStyle( DefaultFont, HorizDir, 1 );
            SetViewPort( 120, 330, GetMaxX, 350, TRUE );
            ClearViewPort;
            SetColor( LightRed );
```

```pascal
         OutTextXY( 1, 1, 'File error '+ Temp +
             ' occurred: press Enter to continue' );
         SetColor( White );
         readln;
         ClearViewPort;
         SetViewPort( 0, 0, GetMaxX, GetMaxY, TRUE );
      end;
procedure SaveImage;
   var
      C1, C2 : byte;
      i, j, k : integer;
      fil : file of byte;
      FileName : string;
      CFlag : boolean;
   begin
      C1 := 0;
      C2 := $FF;
      CFlag := FALSE;
      FileName := ReadName( 'Write image: ' );
      if FileName = '' then
      begin
         Beep;
         SaveBtn.SetState( FALSE );
         Exit;
      end;
      OutTextXY( 120, 330, FileName );
      Assign( fil, FileName );
      {$I-} Rewrite( fil ); {$I+}
      i := IOresult;
      if i <> 0 then ReportError( i ) else
      begin
         write( fil, HSize, VSize );
         CFlag := not MonoBtn.GetState;
         if CFlag then
         begin
            CFlag := not CFlag;
            for i := 0 to HSize do
               for j := 0 to HSize do
                  if image[i,j] <> 0 then
                     if C1 = 0 then C1 := image[i,j] else
                        if C1 <> image[i,j] then
                           CFlag := TRUE;
         end;
         if CFlag then
         begin                              { multicolored image }
            write( fil, C2 );               { multicolored flag  }
            for i := 0 to HSize do
            begin
```

```
                    C2 := 0;
                    k := 0;
                    for j := 0 to VSize do
                    begin
                       inc( k );
                       C2 := C2 shl 4;
                       inc( C2, image[i,j] );
                       if k = 2 then
                       begin
                          k := 0;
                          write( fil, C2 );
                       end;
                    end;
                    if k <> 0 then
                    begin
                       C2 := C2 shl 4;
                       write( fil, C2 );
                    end;
                 end;
              end else
              begin                              { monochrome image }
                 write( fil, ActiveColor );      { palette color }
                 for i := 0 to HSize do
                    for j := 0 to 3 do
                       if j*8 <= VSize then
                       begin
                          C2 := 0;
                          for k := 0 to 7 do
                          begin
                             C2 := C2 shl 1;
                             if j*8+k <= VSize then
                                if image[ i, j*8+k ] <> 0 then
                                   inc( C2 );
                          end;
                          write( fil, C2 );
                       end;
              end;
              Close( fil );
           end;
           SaveBtn.SetState( FALSE );
        end;
procedure ReadImage;
    var
        C1, C2 : byte;
        i, j, k : integer;
        fil : file of byte;
        FileName : string;
        CFlag : boolean;
```

```pascal
begin
   CFlag := FALSE;
   FileName := ReadName( 'Read Image: ' );
   if FileName = '' then
   begin
      Beep;
      ReadBtn.SetState( FALSE );
      Exit;
   end;
   OutTextXY( 120, 330, FileName );
   Assign( fil, FileName );
   {$I-} Reset( fil ); {$I+}
   i := IOresult;
   if i <> 0 then
      ReportError( i ) else
   begin
      read( fil, HSize, VSize, C1 );
      if C1 = $FF then CFlag := TRUE;
      if CFlag then
      begin                              { multicolored image }
         for i := 0 to HSize do
            for j := 0 to VSize div 2 do
            begin
               read( fil, C2 );
               image[i, j*2 ] := C2 shr 4;
               if VSize >= j*2+1 then
                  image[i, j*2+1 ] := C2 AND $0F;
            end;
      end else
      begin                              { monochrome image }
         for i := 0 to HSize do
            for j := 0 to 3 do
               if j*8 <= VSize then
               begin
                  read( fil, C2 );
                  for k := 0 to 7 do
                  begin
                     if j*8+k <= VSize then
                        if C2 AND $80 <> 0
                           then image[i,j*8+k] := C1
                           else image[i,j*8+k] := 0;
                     C2 := C2 shl 1;
                  end;
               end;
      end;
      Close( fil );
   end;
   PaintGrid;
```

```pascal
            ReadBtn.SetState( FALSE );
        end;
procedure WriteImageProg;
    const
        TextLen = 68;
    var
        FileName, ImageName, FileStr, IndentStr : string;
        C1, C2 : byte;
        i, j, k : integer;
        fil : text;
        CFlag : boolean;
        Ch : char;
    begin
        C1 := 0;
        C2 := $FF;
        CFlag := FALSE;
        FileName := ReadName( 'Write image program: ' );
        ImageName := ReadName( 'Image name? ' );
        if( FileName = '' ) or ( ImageName = '' ) then
        begin
            Beep;
            ProgBtn.SetState( FALSE );
            Exit;
        end;
        OutTextXY( 120, 330, FileName +
                   ' (' + ImageName + ')' );
        Assign( fil, FileName );
        {$I-} Rewrite( fil ); {$I+}
        i := IOresult;
        if i <> 0 then ReportError( i ) else
        begin
            IndentStr := '                ';
            CFlag := not MonoBtn.GetState;
            if CFlag then
            begin
                CFlag := not CFlag;
                for i := 0 to HSize do
                    for j := 0 to HSize do
                        if image[i,j] <> 0 then
                            if C1 = 0 then C1 := image[i,j] else
                                if C1 <> image[i,j] then
                                    CFlag := TRUE;
            end;
            if CFlag
                then str( 3 + ( HSize+1 ) *
                             ( VSize div 2 + 1 ), FileStr )
                else str( 3 + ( HSize+1 ) *
                             ( VSize div 8 + 1 ), FileStr );
```

```pascal
        (*========================================================*)
        (* const                                                  *)
        (* Image : array[ 1.. count ] of byte =                   *)
        (* { ( HSize, VSize, CFlag or Color, bt, bt, bt, ... ); } *)
        (*     ( HSize, VSize, CFlag, ??, ??, ??, ??, etc );      *)
        (*========================================================*)
                writeln( fil, '    const' );
                writeln( fil, '       ' + ImageName +
                              ' : array[ 1..'
                           + FileStr + ' ] of byte = ' );
                writeln( fil, '       {  ( HSize, VSize, CFlag' +
                  ' or ColorVal, bt, bt, bt, bt, bt, ... ); }' );
                FileStr := '          (' + HexToStr( HSize )
                                         + HexToStr( VSize );

                if CFlag then
                begin                            { multi-color image }
                   FileStr := FileStr + HexToStr( C2 );
                   for i := 0 to HSize do
                   begin
                      C2 := 0;
                      k := 0;
                      for j := 0 to VSize do
                      begin
                         inc( k );
                         C2 := C2 shl 4;
                         inc( C2, image[i,j] );
                         if k = 2 then
                         begin
                            k := 0;
                            FileStr := FileStr + HexToStr( C2 );
                            if ord( FileStr[0] ) > TextLen then
                            begin
                                writeln( fil, FileStr );
                                FileStr := IndentStr;
                            end;
                         end;
                      end;
                   end;
                   if k <> 0 then
                   begin
                      C2 := C2 shl 4;
                      FileStr := FileStr + HexToStr( C2 );
                      if ord( FileStr[0] ) > TextLen then
                      begin
                          writeln( fil, FileStr );
                          FileStr := IndentStr;
                      end;
```

```
                    end;
                end;
            end else
            begin                           { monochrome image }
                FileStr := FileStr + HexToStr( ActiveColor );
                                            { palette color    }
                for i := 0 to HSize do
                    for j := 0 to 3 do
                        if j*8 <= VSize then
                        begin
                            C2 := 0;
                            for k := 0 to 7 do
                            begin
                                C2 := C2 shl 1;
                                if j*8+k <= VSize then
                                    if image[ i, j*8+k ] <> 0 then
                                        inc( C2 );
                            end;
                            FileStr := FileStr + HexToStr( C2 );
                            if ord( FileStr[0] ) > TextLen then
                            begin
                                writeln( fil, FileStr );
                                FileStr := IndentStr;
                            end;
                        end;
            end;
            if FileStr[0] > IndentStr[0] then
                FileStr[0] := chr( ord( FileStr[0] ) - 1 );
            FileStr := FileStr + ' );';
            writeln( fil, FileStr );
            Close( fil );
        end;
        ProgBtn.SetState( FALSE );
    end;

begin
    GDriver := Detect;
    InitGraph( GDriver, GMode, '\TP\BGI' );
    GError := GraphResult;
    if GError <> grOk then
    begin
        writeln( 'Graphics error: ',
                 GraphErrorMsg(GError) );
        writeln( 'Program aborted...' );
        halt(1);
    end;
    GMouse.Reset( Status, BtnCount );
    if Status then
    begin
```

```pascal
      HSize := 31;
      VSize := 31;
      ClearDevice;
      GMouse.Initialize;
         {=====================================}
         {     set up graphic control objects       }
         {=====================================}
      for i := 0 to 7 do
         New( RButton[i], Init(18,50+35*i,i,10,'' ) );
      for i := 8 to 15 do
         New( RButton[i], Init(60,50+35*(i-8),i,10,'') );
      ExtBtn.Init( Rounded,    0,   0, 80, 20,
                   LightRed,    'Exit'   );
      ClrBtn.Init( Rounded, 120,   0, 80, 20,
                   LightRed,    'Clear'  );
      InvBtn.Init(  Square, 120,  50, 80, 20,
                   LightGreen, 'Invert' );
      MonoBtn.Init( Square, 120,  80, 80, 20,
                   LightGreen, 'Mono'   );
      HighBtn.Init( Square, 120, 130, 80, 20,
                   Yellow,      'High'   );
      WideBtn.Init( Square, 120, 160, 80, 20,
                   Yellow,      'Wide'   );
      ProgBtn.Init( Square, 120, 210, 80, 20,
                   LightCyan,   'Prog'   );
      SaveBtn.Init( Square, 120, 240, 80, 20,
                   LightCyan,   'Save'   );
      ReadBtn.Init( Square, 120, 290, 80, 20,
                   White,       'Read'   );
      ActiveColor := WHITE;
      NoteColor;
      RButton[ActiveColor]^.SetState( TRUE );
      for i := 0 to 31 do
         for j := 0 to 31 do
            Image[i,j] := 0;
      PaintGrid;
               {===========================}
               {     start demo program       }
               {===========================}
      while not ExtBtn.ButtonHit do
      repeat
         GMouse.GetPosition( BtnStatus, XPos, YPos );
         if( XPos < 120 ) AND
            ( BtnStatus AND $01 = $01 ) then
```

```
         begin
            for i := 0 to 15 do
               if RButton[i]^.ButtonHit then
               begin
                  GMouse.Show( FALSE );
                  for j := 0 to 15 do
                  RButton[j]^.SetState( FALSE );
                  RButton[i]^.SetState( TRUE );
                  ActiveColor := i;
                  NoteColor;
                  GMouse.Show( TRUE );
               end;
         end else
         if( XPos < 300 ) AND
            ( BtnStatus AND $01 = $01 ) then
         begin
            if ClrBtn.ButtonHit   then ClearImage;

            if InvBtn.ButtonHit   then InvertImage;
            if MonoBtn.ButtonHit  then Monochrome;

            if HighBtn.ButtonHit  then SetHeight;
            if WideBtn.ButtonHit  then SetWidth;

            if ProgBtn.ButtonHit  then WriteImageProg,
            if SaveBtn.ButtonHit  then SaveImage;

            if ReadBtn.ButtonHit  then ReadImage;
         end else
         begin
            if BtnStatus AND $02 = $02
               then PixColor := GetBkColor
               else PixColor := ActiveColor;
            if BtnStatus AND $03 <> 0 then
               for i := 0 to HSize do
                  for j := 0 to VSize do
                     if ( XPos >= i*10+300 ) AND
                        ( XPos <  i*10+310 ) AND
                        ( YPos >= j*10 ) AND
                        ( YPos <  j*10+10 ) then
                     if Image[i,j] <> PixColor then
                     begin
                        GMouse.Show( FALSE );
                        Image[i,j] := PixColor;
                        FillSquare( i*10+300, j*10,
                                    i*10+310, j*10+10,
                                    InterleaveFill,
                                    Image[i,j] );
                        PutPixel( 250+i, 10+j,
                                  Image[i,j] );
```

```pascal
                            GMouse.Show( TRUE );
                         end;
               end;
               GMouse.QueryBtnUp( ButtonL, mButton );
            until mButton.opCount > 0;
                      {========================}
                      {     clean up objects    }
                      {========================}
            for i := 0 to 15 do
               Dispose( RButton[i], Done );
            ExtBtn.Erase;
                      {========================}
                      {    and exit to text     }
                      {========================}
      end;
      CloseGraph;                 { restore text mode and ...          }
      TMouse.Initialize;          { reset mouse for text operation }
end.
```

IconDemo.Pas

```pascal
program Icon_Demo_Program;

uses Crt, Graph, Mouse, GControl;

type
   Image = object
             ImgPtr : pointer;
             DblClkTime,
             X, Y, XOfs, YOfs : integer;
             HSize, VSize : byte;
             State : boolean;
             constructor Init( FileName : string );
             destructor  Done;
             procedure Show( Status : boolean );
             procedure MoveTo( XPos, YPos : integer );
             procedure Drag;
             function MouseSelect(
                 var MouseX, MouseY: integer ): boolean;
          end;

constructor Image.Init( FileName: string );
   var
      C1, C2 : byte;
      i, j, k : integer;
      fil : file of byte;
   begin
      Assign( fil, FileName );
```

```pascal
            {$I-} Reset( fil ); {$I+}
            i := IOresult;
            if i = 0 then
            begin
               SetActivePage(1);
               read( fil, HSize, VSize, C1 );
               if C1 = $FF then
               begin                            { multicolored image }
                  for i := 0 to HSize do
                     for j := 0 to VSize div 2 do
                     begin
                        read( fil, C2 );
                        PutPixel( i, j*2, C2 shr 4 );
                        if( j*2+1 <= VSize ) then
                           PutPixel( i, j*2+1, C2 AND $0F );
                     end;
               end else
               begin                            { monochrome image }
                  for i := 0 to HSize do
                     for j := 0 to 3 do
                        if j*8 <= VSize then
                        begin
                           read( fil, C2 );
                           for k := 0 to 7 do
                           begin
                              if j*8+k <= VSize then
                                 if C2 AND $80 <> 0
                                    then PutPixel( i, j*8+k, C1 )
                                    else PutPixel( i, j*8+k, 0 );
                              C2 := C2 shl 1;
                           end;
                        end;
               end;
               Close( fil );
            end;
            GetMem( ImgPtr, ImageSize( 0, 0, HSize, VSize ) );
            GetImage( 0, 0, HSize, VSize, ImgPtr^ );
            PutImage( 0, 0, ImgPtr^, XOrPut );
            State := FALSE;
            SetActivePage(0);
            DblClkTime := 150;
         end;

procedure Image.Show;
   begin
      if Status <> State then
      begin
         GMouse.Show( FALSE );
         PutImage( X, Y, ImgPtr^, XOrPut );
```

```pascal
            inc( State );
            GMouse.Show( TRUE );
         end;
   end;
procedure Image.MoveTo;
   begin
      if State then PutImage( X, Y, ImgPtr^, XOrPut );
      X := XPos;
      Y := YPos;
      PutImage( X, Y, ImgPtr^, XOrPut );
      State := TRUE;
   end;
function Image.MouseSelect;
   var
      Result : boolean;
      BtnEvent : Position;
      BtnStatus : integer;
   begin
      Result := FALSE;
      if ( MouseX >= X ) AND ( MouseX <= X+HSize ) AND
         ( MouseY >= Y ) AND ( MouseY <= Y+VSize ) then
      begin
         GMouse.QueryBtnDn( ButtonL, BtnEvent );
         XOfs := MouseX - X;
         YOfs := MouseY - Y;
         Drag;
         delay( DblClkTime );                    { wait a bit }
         GMouse.QueryBtnDn( ButtonL, BtnEvent );
         Result := BtnEvent.opCount <> 0;   { second hit }
         MouseX := -1;            { mouse position is reset }
         MouseY := -1;            { so next test will fail  }
      end;
      MouseSelect := Result;
   end;
procedure Image.Drag;
   var
      BtnEvent : Position;
      BtnStatus, XPos, YPos, XOld, YOld : integer;
   begin
      XOld := -1;
      YOld := -1;
      GMouse.QueryBtnUp( ButtonL, BtnEvent );
      GMouse.SetCursor( GLOVE );
      Show( FALSE );                     { hide the object }
      repeat
         GMouse.GetPosition( BtnStatus, XPos, YPos );
         if( BtnStatus AND $01 ) = $01 then
```

```pascal
            if( XPos <> XOld ) OR ( YPos <> YOld ) then
            begin
                GMouse.Show( FALSE );
                PutImage( XPos-XOfs, YPos-YOfs,
                          ImgPtr^, XOrPut );
                PutImage( XOld-XOfs, YOld-YOfs,
                          ImgPtr^, XOrPut );
                GMouse.Show( TRUE );
                XOld := XPos;
                YOld := YPos;
            end;
            GMouse.QueryBtnUp( ButtonL, BtnEvent );
         until BtnEvent.opCount <> 0;
         X := XPos - XOfs;     { update the object coordinates }
         Y := YPos - YOfs;       { to the final position          }
         GMouse.SetCursor( ARROW );
      end;

destructor Image.Done;
   begin
      if State then PutImage( X, Y, ImgPtr^, XOrPut );
      Dispose( ImgPtr );
   end;

var
   VRef : ViewPortType;                        { viewport coords }
   Status : Boolean;                           { mouse status    }
   BtnStatus, XPos, YPos,
   GDriver, GMode, GError, i, j, BtnCount : integer;
   BtnEvent : Position;
   ExitButton : Button;
   PixImage : array[1..4] of Image;
   ResponseStr : string;

begin
   GDriver := Detect;
   InitGraph( GDriver, GMode, '\TP\BGI' );
   GError := GraphResult;
   if GError <> grOk then
   begin
      writeln( 'Graphics error: ',
               GraphErrorMsg(GError) );
      writeln( 'Program aborted...' );
      halt(1);
   end;
   GMouse.Reset( Status, BtnCount );
   if Status then
   begin
      ClearDevice;
      GMouse.Initialize;
```

```pascal
         PixImage[1].Init( 'FILEFLDR.ICO' );
         PixImage[2].Init( 'OM.ICO' );
         PixImage[3].Init( 'QUESTION.ICO' );
         PixImage[4].Init( 'RAINBOW3.ICO' );
         for i := 1 to 4 do
            PixImage[i].MoveTo( 40 * i + 60, 100 );
         with ExitButton do
            Init( Rounded, GetMaxX-80, 1, 80, 20,
                  LightRed, 'Exit' );

         {==========================}
         {    start demo program    }
         {==========================}
         while not ExitButton.ButtonHit do
         begin
            GMouse.QueryBtnDn( ButtonL, BtnEvent );
            if BtnEvent.opCount <> 0 then
               for i := 1 to 4 do
                  with PixImage[i] do
                     if MouseSelect( BtnEvent.xPos,
                                     BtnEvent.yPos ) then
                     begin
                        case i of
                           1: ResponseStr := 'Icon One';
                           2: ResponseStr := 'Icon Two';
                           3: ResponseStr := 'Icon Three';
                           4: ResponseStr := 'Icon Four';
                        end; {case}
                        SetTextJustify( LeftText, TopText );
                        OutTextXY( 10, i*20, ResponseStr );
                        sound( 200 ); delay( 100 );
                        sound( 440 ); delay( 100 ); nosound;
                     end;
         end;
         for i := 1 to 4 do              {=============================}
            PixImage[i].Done;            { clean up dynamic objects    }
      end;                               {                             }
      CloseGraph;                        { restore text mode and ...   }
      TMouse.Initialize;                 { reset mouse for text ops    }
end.                                     {=============================}
```

CHAPTER 16

Turtle Graphics

The original concept of Turtle Graphics was proposed by S. Papert and co-workers at MIT as a convenient method of creating graphics without having to understand Cartesian coordinates. This basic vision was a turtle capable of walking along a straight line for a specified distance at a specific angle and drawing a line in its track; rather like the line left by a turtle's tail after coming ashore on a sandy beach.

The basic concept proved very popular. Relatively young children could use the turtle to program images and experienced programmers found turtle graphics an excellent tool capable of creating interesting images using simple algorithms, algorithms much simpler than would be required for similar results using Cartesian coordinate systems.

The turtle implemented here is designed to adapt to various screen and video capabilities, handling colors where hardware supported and adjusting movement to match video screen aspect ratios.

The GRAPH3 unit, which is still included with Turbo Pascal, provides the original turtle functions that were part of Turbo Pascal version 3.0, but are no longer a documented feature in later versions. The present TURTLE.TPU unit, however, does not require the GRAPH3 unit and is implemented as an object-oriented turtle and is compatible with all graphics video resolutions. Warning, the TURTLE unit may not be compatible with all functions in the GRAPH3 unit.

The TURTLE unit provides 28 methods for complete turtle capabilities. Not all of these are intended for direct use, some are written only to be called by other functions, but the complete source code for all of the functions is included. Of course, you are invited to modify or revise these functions for your own "mutant" turtle applications.

Just as with other graphics functions, the turtle graphics operate within a window, but the window is independent of your graphics viewport. Separate turtle-windows and graphics viewports can be in use at the same time without conflicts.

The turtle routines operate on *turtle* or *world* coordinates. The home position at turtle coordinates 0,0 is in the center of the active turtle window with positive turtle coordinates to the right (x-axis) and upwards (y-axis), negative coordinates to the left (x-axis) and down (y-axis). The *turtle angles* follow mapping conventions and begin with 0 degree as up or NORTH, 90 degree to the right or EAST, 180 degree as down or SOUTH and 270 degree as left or WEST.

Both 0 degree and 360 degree are valid angles but all angles or rotations greater than 360 degree or less than 0 degree are translated into the range 0..360 degrees. The four ordinal directions NORTH, EAST, SOUTH, and WEST are constants defined in Turtle.Inc.

I hope you have noticed the turtle coordinates and angles do not correspond with the angles and coordinates used in the Turbo Pascal graphics system or the familiar screen coordinate system. By normal computer conventions (as dictated by the screen address requirements), y-axis values increase from top to bottom, while the turtle y-axis values decrease over the same range. At the same time, the Turbo C graphics system considers the zero angle to lie horizontally to the right (EAST) with angles increasing counterclockwise, while the turtle angles place zero at the top (NORTH) with the angles increasing in a clockwise direction.

These rotations and directions are not arbitrary (well, not entirely). The turtle angles and directions follow long established cultural conventions which are almost instinctive: that the compass (or clock) rotates clockwise, that graphs increase going up, that the king is at the top of the mountain. Alternatively, the rotations and directions that have become familiar to the programmer were forged under different constraints, equally valid but different.

Since the basic concept behind the turtle graphics was to design them to be accessible and acceptable to individuals who are not "computer sophisticated," the turtle angles and directions/values were written to follow the common and familiar conventions. For the same reasons, this set of turtle commands continues to follow the earlier standards, the possible dangers of confusing an occasional programmer notwithstanding.

The Turtle Graphic Commands

The turtle graphics unit does presume that Turbo Pascal has initialized the graphics system and selected a graphics driver and mode. This done, turtle graphics are initialized by their own function: Init.

Turtle.Init

Syntax: `Turtle.Init;`

While turtle graphics do not require any special device drivers or modes, aside from those provided by the normal graphics initialization, the Init method does take care of several important tasks, beginning by calling the Create function to draw a turtle cursor and save an image of the cursor. The Init function also calculates the current screen aspect ratio (*TAsp*), sets up an initial turtle window, and sets several default conditions. These include: pen color as maximum valid color, the turtle cursor is set to visible, screen wrap is off, the turtle pen is down in drawing position, and the initial heading is NORTH (0).

Correction for screen aspect ratio is automatically applied to all y-axis movement.

Turtle.TWindow

Syntax: `Turtle.TWindow( xCenter, yCenter, Width, Height : integer );`

The Turtle.TWindow function defines an area of the screen as the active turtle graphics window. Unlike the graphics window function (SetViewPort), TWindow's first two arguments are the x- and y-axis center coordinates; the last two arguments provide the total width and height for the window.

The window is always centered on the home coordinates (position 0,0 in turtle coordinates, but xCenter, yCenter in absolute screen coordinates) and is established initially to include the entire screen less the three-pixels margin. This default margin is provided to ensure that the PutImage function, which handles the turtle cursor, is not called with coordinates that fall outside the valid full screen limits—an error that would prevent the cursor from appearing correctly.

The Clear method erases the turtle window; the Hide, Show, NoWrap, Wrap, and Delay methods control the turtle display parameters.

Turtle.Clear

Syntax: `Turtle.Clear;`

The Clear method borrows Turbo Pascal's graphics viewport functions to erase the turtle screen, restoring the original graphics viewport settings afterwards.

Turtle.Hide and Turtle.Show

Syntax: **Turtle.Hide;**
Syntax: **Turtle.Show;**

The Hide and Show methods disable and enable the turtle cursor display by controlling the *Visible* flag. Initially, in this program, the turtle is visible—other turtle graphics programs prefer to start the turtle hidden.

Turtle.Wrap and Turtle.NoWrap

Syntax: **Wrap;**
Syntax: **NoWrap;**

The Wrap and NoWrap methods control the turtle response when the turtle window limits are reached. If Wrap is in effect when the turtle reaches the window limits, it will reenter the window at the opposite border.

If NoWrap is in effect, the turtle is allowed to move beyond the turtle window limits (or even outside the screen limits entirely), but the turtle drawing will not extend beyond the window borders.

Turtle.Delay

Syntax: **Turtle.Delay(MilliSeconds : integer);**

By default, the turtle moves as fast as possible, but speed is not always desired. The Delay method allows you to specify a delay in milliseconds between turtle steps (between pixel movements).

Also, if the turtle is off-screen; that is, outside of the turtle window, the time delay is disabled. This can save long waits for elaborate nothings which are taking place outside the active turtle window; it does not otherwise effect the display or off-screen reference points used for lines.

Turtle Movements

The turtle movements are controlled by three factors: position, distance, and direction. The position functions provide for absolute moves, the distance functions provide for movements a specified distance along the current heading, and the direction functions set the movement headings.

Turtle.Home

Syntax: **Turtle.Home;**

The Home method moves the turtle cursor to the home coordinates (0,0) at the center of the turtle window without drawing a line in the process. If a turtle_delay time is in effect, the cursor will be moved immediately, but no further movements will occur until a single delay time has elapsed.

Turtle.SetPosition

Syntax: `Turtle.SetPosition( XAxis, YAxis : integer );`

The SetPosition method immediately moves the turtle cursor to the specified turtle coordinates. No line is drawn by this move. If a turtle_delay time is in effect, the cursor will be moved immediately, but no further movements will occur until a single delay time has elapsed.

Turtle.Forwd

Syntax: `Turtle.Forwd( Distance: integer );`

The Forwd method is the heart of the turtle graphics. The turtle cursor is moved the specified distance from the current position along the current heading. Movement is in one-pixel steps and, if the turtle pen is down (*Draw* = TRUE), a line is drawn using the current *PenColor*. If the turtle pen is up, the turtle cursor is moved (if *Visible* = TRUE) without drawing a line. If *Visible* is FALSE, the turtle cursor is moved invisibly. If *Distance* is negative, movement is executed in the direction opposite the current heading.

If a turtle delay time is in effect, movement will halt after each step until the set delay time has elapsed. This movement delay is used regardless of the *Draw* or *Visible* flag settings.

The Forwd method uses the *RCos* and *RSin* functions to calculate the appropriate x-axis and y-axis distances, while the Step method accomplishes the actual movement.

```
procedure GTurtle.Forwd( Distance: integer );
var
    i, dx, dy, xorg, yorg : integer;
    slope : real;
begin
    yorg := XPos;
    xorg := YPos;
    dx := trunc( RSin( Direction ) * Distance );
    dy := trunc( RCos( Direction ) * Distance * TAsp );
```

Some turtle drivers do not adjust for screen aspect, but in this application, the *TAsp* (aspect ratio) variable is used to adjust vertical and horizontal movements to maintain equal line lengths on the screen in each direction. A movement of 50 units on the x-axis causes the turtle to move 50 pixels. The same distance on the y-axis is adjusted by the aspect ratio for the current graphics driver and mode. See also the DrawStr method.

The next step, after calculating the x- and y-offsets resulting from *Direction* and *Distance*, is a series of decisions. The first is to decide which is greater, *dx* or *dy*.

```
if abs( dx ) > abs( dy ) then
begin
```

When plotting a line, always begin with the axis with greater change, then, for each point along this axis, calculate the minor axis position, but begin by calculating the *slope* of the line.

```
Slope =  dy / dx;
```

If *dx* is positive, an increasing loop is used and a y-axis position is calculated and plotted for each x-axis position.

```
if dx > 0 then
   for i = 1 to dx do
      Step( xorg + i, yorg + trunc(i*slope ) );
```

Otherwise, a decreasing loop is used, but the calculations are the same.

```
   else
      for i = -1 downto dx do
         Step( xorg + i, yorg + trunc(i*slope ) );
end else
```

Alternatively, the x-axis positions are calculated along the y-axis.

```
begin
   Slope = dx / dy;
   if dy > 0 then
      for i = 1 to dy do
         Step( xorg + trunc( i*slope ), yorg + i );
   else
      for i = -1 downto dy do
         Step( xorg + trunc( i*slope ), yorg + i );
end;
end;
```

Turtle.Back

Syntax: `Turtle.Back( Distance: integer );`

The Back method moves the turtle according to the same rules as Forwd except that movement is in the direction opposite the current heading. If *Distance* is negative, then movement is Forwd.

Turtle.DrawStr

Syntax: `Turtle.DrawStr( Scale : integer; DStr : string );`

The DrawStr method differs from the Forwd and Back methods in two important respects: first, no correction is applied for the screen aspect ratio and, second, all movements are executed in absolute pixel steps. The reasons for this are that attempting to draw small closed figures using the slope calculations tends to produce a cumulative error when decimal fractions are rounded to integers. Thus, the resulting endpoints do not always match the start points, leaving jagged or open corners on the figures. By using absolute pixel movements for small closed figures, these errors are eliminated and a smooth, finished appearance is created.

The DrawStr method accepts two parameters, a scale multiplier and an array of characters describing the turtle movements which create a figure, turtle character, logo, or other drawing. For this type of drawing, turtle movement is restricted to eight directions, the four cardinal directions and the four diagonals lying between these. (See the Turtle.Write method for details.)

```
procedure GTurtle.DrawStr;
var
    distance, j, k, x, y : integer;
```

A loop steps through the *charstr* array, acting in response to each element in the instruction string:

```
begin
    for j = 1 to ord( DStr[0] ) do
    begin
        Distance = Scale;
        case DStr[j] of
```

The instruction characters *a..h* set the step direction (see Figure 16-1). As long as either *x* or *y* is not zero, turtle movement will be executed after the case selector is finished. Selecting a direction also causes the turtle to take one step in this direction.

```
'a': begin   x =  0;   y = -1;   end;
'b': begin   x =  1;   y = -1;   end;
'c': begin   x =  1;   y =  0;   end;
'd': begin   x =  1;   y =  1;   end;
'e': begin   x =  0;   y =  1;   end;
'f': begin   x = -1;   y =  1;   end;
'g': begin   x = -1;   y =  0;   end;
'h': begin   x = -1;   y = -1;   end;
```

The instruction characters *m* and *p* call the PenUp and PenDown methods after setting both the *x* and *y* step increments to zero so that no turtle movement is executed in response.

```
'm' : begin   x =  0;   y =  0;
              PenDown;  end;
```

```
'p' : begin    x = 0;   y = 0;
               PenUp;   end;
```

Figure 16-1: Plot Compass for Turtle Directions

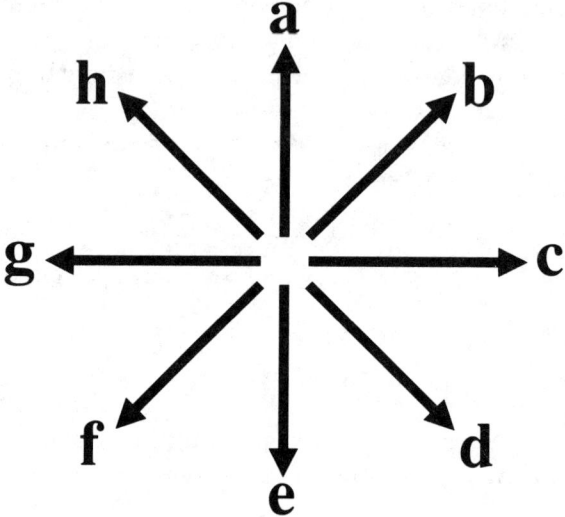

The instruction characters *2..0* continue movement in the active direction, setting the *Distance* according to the scale and the multiplier. Since the instruction which set the direction also resulted in one turtle step (with *Distance* equal to *Scale*), a movement instruction of *1* is ignored entirely, an instruction of *2* is accepted but no action is taken, leaving the value for *Distance := (2 − 1) * Scale*—which is already the value of *Distance*. Instructions *3* through *9* multiply distance by one less than the instruction integer and an instruction of *0* is taken as the equivalent of 10, making *Distance* equal to *Scale* times 9 (10–1).

```
'2'..'9' : Distance :=
              Scale * ( ord( Dstr[j] ) - 49 );
    '0' : Distance := Scale * 9;
    else begin   x := 0;  y := 0;   end;
end; {case}
```

The default case sets null values for the *x* and *y* step values in any case where the instruction character is not recognized, thus preventing error movements. This might be applicable if you wanted to delimit your instruction strings using spaces, commas, dashes, or even several characters to make the instructions easier to read.

Finally, the turtle is stepped along the appropriate heading for the distance set.

```
      for k := 1 to Distance do
          Step( xpos + x, ypos + y );
   end;
end;
```

Turtle.SetHeading

Syntax: `Turtle.SetHeading( Degrees: integer );`

The SetHeading method sets the current heading to an absolute value. The argument *Degrees* can be any integer value or the four cardinal directions (NORTH, EAST, SOUTH, and WEST) defined in the turtle unit can be used.

If a negative value is passed to SetHeadings or if the variable *Degrees* is greater than 360 degrees, then the AdjDirection function corrects the heading value to the range 0..360 degrees.

Turtle.TurnLeft and Turtle.TurnRight

Syntax: `Turtle.TurnLeft( Angle: integer );`
Syntax: `Turtle.TurnRight( Angle: integer );`

The TurnLeft method (counterclockwise) decreases the current heading by *Angle* degrees. TurnRight increases (clockwise) the current heading by *Angle* degrees.

In either function, a negative argument reverses the direction, the current angle is changed, and both *TurnLeft* and *TurnRight* use the AdjDirection function to ensure that the resulting turtle heading remains within the 0..360 degree range.

Turtle Drawing

The turtle graphics unit provides three functions to control the drawing: SetPenColor to select the turtle drawing color, and PenDown and PenUp to lower and raise the pen during movements.

Turtle.SetPenColor

Syntax: `SetPenColor( Color: integer );`

The SetPenColor function selects the turtle drawing color and accepts the color names defined in the Graphics unit. In monochrome modes (CGAHI for example), the drawing color is limited to BLACK or WHITE. In palette selection modes (CGAC0 for example), the drawing colors are limited to the predefined palette selections; otherwise, the drawing color may be any valid color supported.

Turtle.PenUp and Turtle.PenDown

Syntax: `Turtle.PenDown;`
Syntax: `Turtle.PenUp;`

The PenUp and PenDown methods operate exactly as their names imply, setting the *Draw* flag to FALSE or TRUE respectively. If *Draw* is FALSE (set by PenUp), turtle movements do not draw a line. If *Draw* is TRUE (set by PenDown), turtle movements draw a line in the current *PenColor*.

Turtle Information

Functions are also provided to return information about the turtle settings and coordinates.

Turtle.Heading

Syntax: `Angle = Turtle.Heading;`

The Heading method returns an integer value reporting the current turtle heading.

Turtle.WhereT

Syntax: `if Turtle.WhereT ... ;`

The WhereT function returns a Boolean value: TRUE if the current turtle position is within the turtle window limits, FALSE if the turtle is outside the window limits.

Turtle.XCor and Turtle.YCor

Syntax: `xaxis = Turtle.XCor;`
Syntax: `yaxis = Turtle.YCor;`

The XCor and YCor functions return the x-axis and y-axis turtle cursor coordinates.

Turtle Graphics Demo (TUR-DEMO.PAS)

Turtle Graphics are excellent for simple drawing programs or for creating various types of figures and illustrations, while requiring a minimum of programming information. In the Turtle demonstration, two complex figures are generated as examples using simple instructions, then a series of turtle characters and a logo illustration are created using the Write method.

The maze used in the demo in Chapter 10, could also have been drawn using turtle graphics, or a random maze could have been created using turtle graphics and a generation algorithm. In chief, turtle graphics are simply a programming tool, an alternative to the line functions in Turbo Pascal graphics and an entry point for creating complex forms from simple algorithms.

TurtleWrite

The TurtleWrite procedure is not included as a part of the Turtle unit for several reasons, one being that the TurtleWrite procedure has only created instructions with a few, selected characters for demo purposes. Please feel free to extend this utility as desired and even include it in your own Turtle object.

The procedure is called as:

Syntax: TurtleWrite(xaxis, yaxis,
scale, color: integer;
workstr: string);

The TurtleWrite procedure draws characters defined using a simple instruction set that may be employed to create your own fonts, special characters, logos, or other graphic elements.

The character set used in the turtle demo comprises only eight characters and is designed primarily to demonstrate how a font can be created. In general, turtle characters are similar to the "stroked" character fonts provided with Turbo Pascal and Turbo C, though the character images and methods used here are neither as sophisticated, nor as extensive.

The TurtleWrite and DrawChar procedures could be implemented by a variety of methods: the character definitions could be condensed, stored in binary files, or redesigned to include curve calculations (though curves are not provided by the turtle functions) for smoothly rounded characters. The actual method used was chosen primarily for simplicity and for ease of demonstration.

Since curves are not supported, the strokes comprising a character are limited to unit steps in the eight directions shown in Figure 16-1.

Figure 16-2 shows two turtle characters, *e* and *i*, diagrammed as vector strokes with the TurtleWrite instructions.

The beginning and end points for each character are shown as a register mark (a circle enclosing a cross mark). For the character *e*, the complete instruction string reads:

pbama*6b2c4d2e2f2g4edc3bcef2g4h2*pb*2a3mbc2dfg2h*pd7

The italicized instructions are executed pen down, the others pen up.

Figure 16-2: Plot for characters "e" and "i"

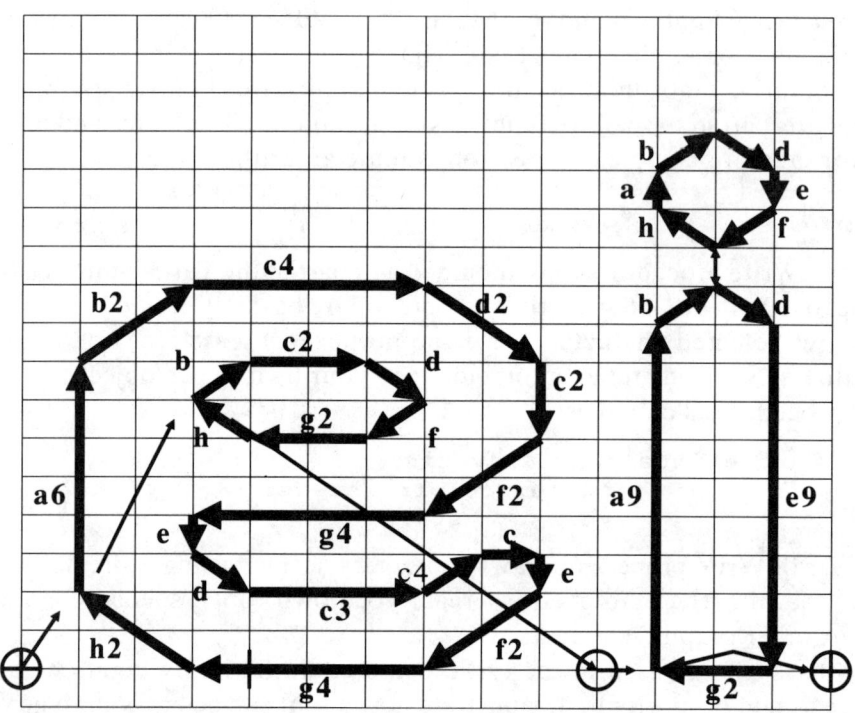

Each stroke begins as a direction and may be followed by a number 2..0 indicating how many steps are to be executed in this direction. If no number follows the direction key, only one step is executed; thus a 1 would be redundent and is not used. A 0 is used for 10 steps and distances greater than 10 steps are coded as multiple instructions. A move right of 16 steps would be coded as *c8c8* rather than *c16*.

In addition to the directions, two other instructions, *p* and *m*, are used. In the instruction string for *e*, the instruction *p* calls PenUp so that the next two move instructions, *ba*, are executed without drawing a line. The instruction *m* calls PenDown and the following instruction groups draw the outside of the character. Next, another PenUp is followed by *b2a3* to position the turtle to draw the eye of the character and the final three instructions, *pd7*, move the turtle without drawing to the terminating position. The turtle ends on the same horizontal as it began, but is one pixel beyond the character, leaving a thin margin on both sides.

The character *i* is coded as: pc*ma9bpamhabdefpemde9g2*pc3. You should be able to follow the coding for these two characters in Figure 16-2, preceding.

The following are the rest of the characters used in the Turtle demonstration together with their code strings (Figures 16-3 through 16-6 show the plots for the remaining turtle characters):

- l is coded as: pb*ma7a7bde7e7fh*pdc2
- r is coded as: pc*ma9bce2b2c2d2eghg2f2e6g2*pc9
- t is coded as: pb2c*ma8g3hbc3a3bde3c3dfg3e7dcdfg2h2*pd2c5

Notice that the character *t* begins at a point inside the left-most extent of the cross bar (as shown by the register mark). This offset provides kerning to allow the character to fit better with other letters, creating a smoother appearance.

Characters may be kerned either left or right and, in many cases, special kerning is assigned to pairs of letters to make them fit together visually. For example, the characters AV are usually kerned to allow the left top of the V to overlap the bottom right of the A. No provision has been made here for pair kerning but it is frequently used in typesetting.

- The *u* is coded as: pba*ma7bde6dc2ba6bde7deghfg4h2*pd2c7

In this case, the character *u* ends immediately at the tail on the right, i of allowing a pixel margin. Like the kerning on the *t,* this provides visual appearance when the character is written as part of a word.

The character *w* is considerably wider than any of the others shov receives only a one-pixel right and left margin. When written toge demo program will show, the characters present a smooth, proportic ance.

As executed in the demo program, the TurtleWrite function is five arguments: the x and y screen position (in turtle coordinates factor, a color argument, and the string to be written.

```
procedure TurtleWrite( x, y, scale, color : inte
                       workstr : string );
const
   LogoStr : string =
            'pcma8a8b2c8c8c8e8e8f2g8g8g8a8a8c8c8c8
            'f2g0g0e5b2c0c0a5f2e3g9g9a3g2e5c7c8c7'
            'f2g0g0e5b2c0c0a5f2e3g9g9a3g2e5c8c8c8pc
var
    i : integer;
```

LogoStr is defined as a constant declaration, but it could also have b passed directly to the DrawStr function from some other source. This handli was chosen only because it was convenient to the demonstration.

The *color* argument allows passing color settings with the string to be displayed. Also, a negative color value can be passed as an argument and will result in a random color selection for each character drawn.

```
begin
  with Tortoise do
  begin
    if color <= MaxColors then SetPenColor( color );
```

Figure 16-3: Plot for Characters l and r

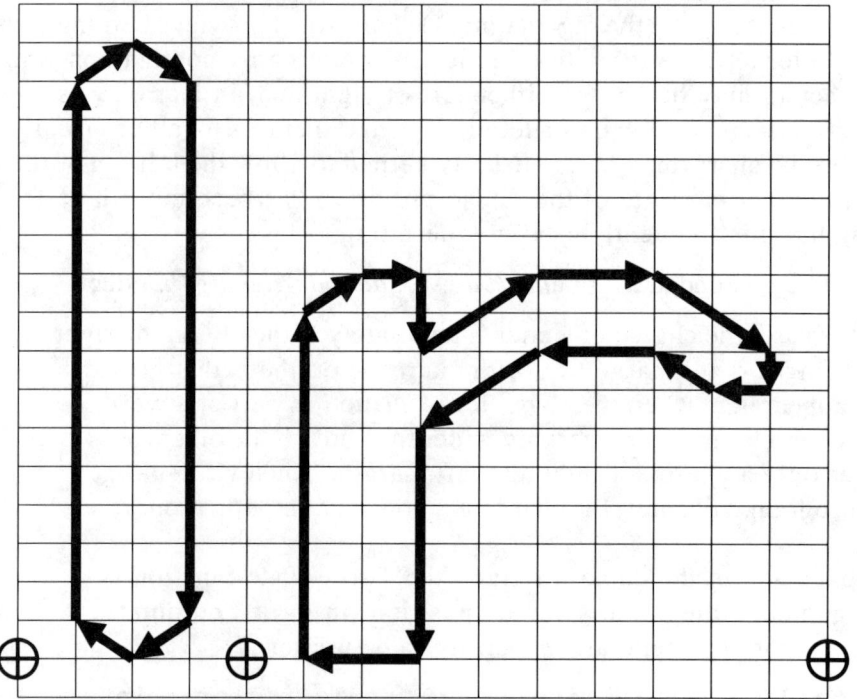

The *scale* factor is a multiplier setting the size of the characters. Negative and zero *scale* factors are not allowed.

```
if scale <= 0 then scale = 1;
```

The initial screen position is set (x, y), then a loop runs through the length of the string to be written:

```
SetPosition( x, y );
for i = 0 to ord( WorkStr[0] ) do
begin
  if color < 0 then
    SetPenColor( random( MaxColors ) + 1 );
```

Figure 16-4: Plot for Character t

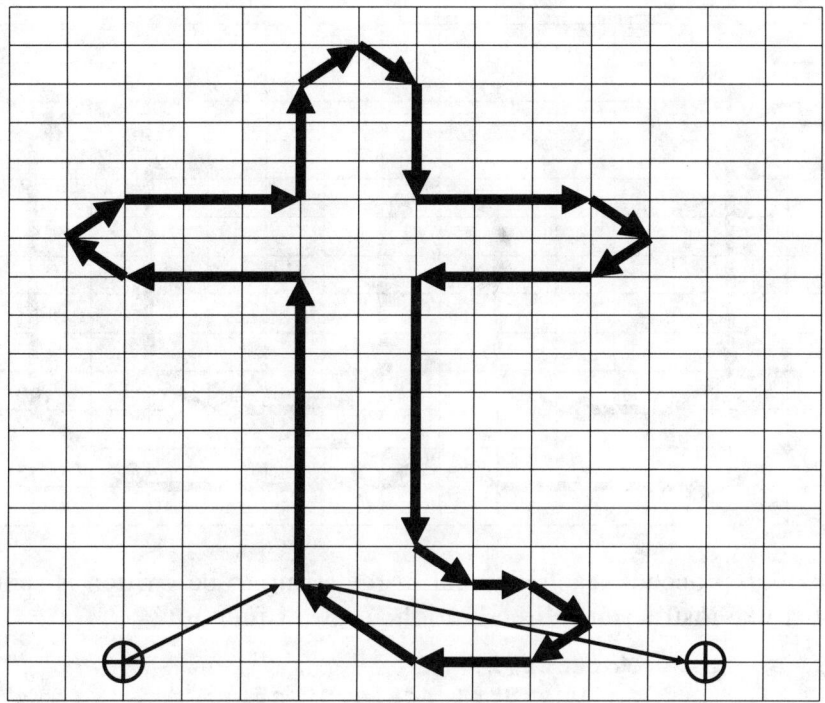

Figure 16-5: Plot for Character u

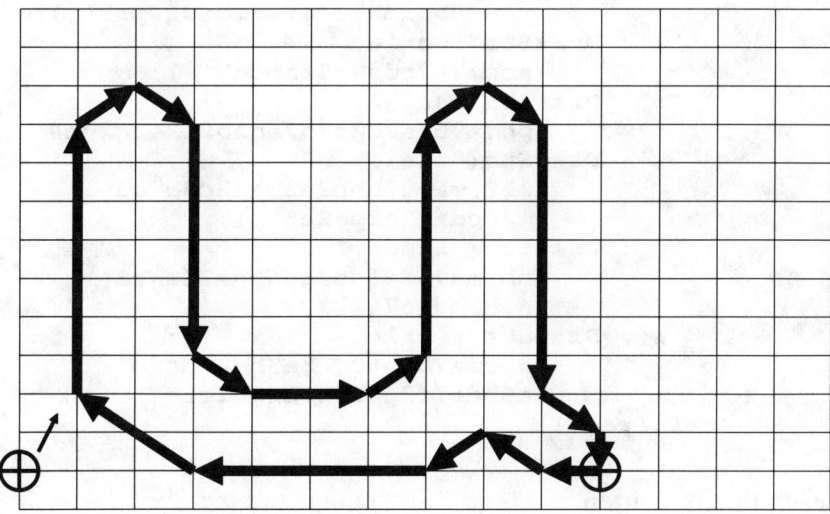

Figure 16-6: Plot for Character w

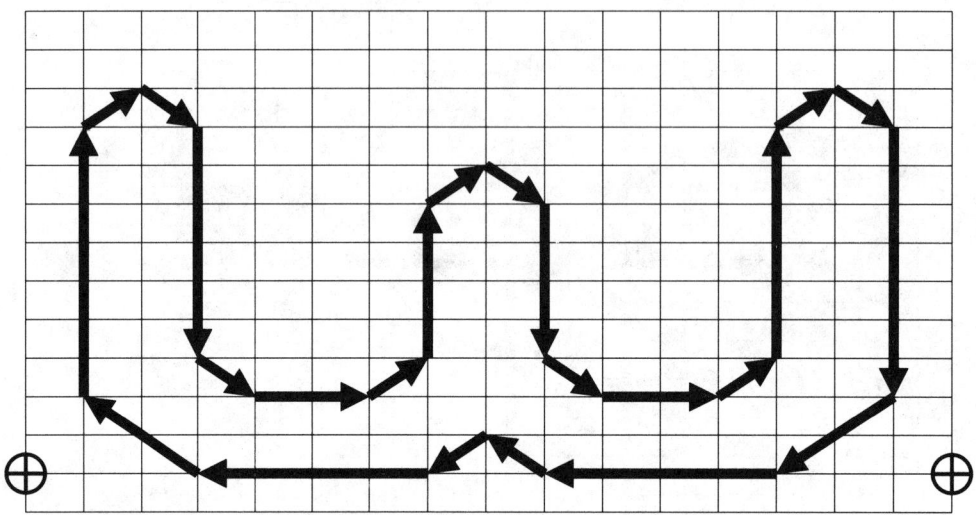

As the loop proceeds, each element of the string to be written is sent as a string of stroke instructions directly to the drawstr function:

```
case WorkStr[i] of
    ' ': DrawStr( scale, 'pc6');
    'e': DrawStr( scale,
            'pbama6b2c4d2e2f2g4edc3bc'
            'ef2g4h2pb2a3mbc2dfg2hpd7' );
    'i': DrawStr( scale,
            'pcma9bpamhabdefpemde9g2pc3' );
    'l': DrawStr( scale,
            'pbma7a7bde7e7fhpdc2' );
    'r': DrawStr( scale,
            'pcma9bce2b2c2d2eghg2f2e6g2pc9' );
    't': DrawStr( scale,
            'pb2cma8g3hbc3a3bde3c3dfg3'
            'e7dcdfg2h2pd2c5' );
    'u': DrawStr( scale,
            'pbama7bde6dc2ba6bde7deghf'
            'g4h2pd2c7' );
    'w': DrawStr( scale,
            'pbama7bde6dc2ba3bde3dc2b'
            'a6bde7f2g4hfg4h2pd2c6c7' );
    end; {case}
end;
```

After each line is written, the logo illustration is added.

```
        DrawStr( scale, LogoStr );
    end;
end;
```

The logo character is a figure known as a double bolix (a bolix is a type of visual paradox).

Unlike most of the letter characters, the logo design could not be drawn in a single continuous line. Two options were possible: one, to use the PenUp function to move to a new location to fill in necessary elements; or, two, to simply trace over existing lines. Since, visually, the two options appear quite similar, the second was chosen and line elements are retraced until the figure is completed.

Display logos can also be created using a variety of drawing programs such as PC Paint, Microsoft Paint, and GEM Draw. They are stored as disk files and subsequently accessed by your program (precise methods vary depending on the utility chosen). A turtle-created logo, however, offers greater flexibility because, as shown in the demo program, it can be scaled to size.

Since individual turtle graphic elements can be defined by instruction strings, as shown with the sample alphabet, picture elements can also be created as turtle graphic instructions using either the TurtleWrite method or via an instruction handler designed to use the Forwd, Back, TurnRight, TurnLeft, and SetHeading functions if you need more flexible line elements. Figure 16-7 shows the plot for my own logo.

Summary

The turtle functions are not designed so much to be used directly as to be called indirectly by other program applications. However, the turtle functions could easily be interfaced to a mouse, joystick, or cursor keys for a drawing utility; combined with various algorithms to trace business data graphs in a moving presentation; or used to create interactive graphic slide shows and show different relations or connections between display elements in interactive stories or programmed instructions.

You might also experiment with revisions to permit separate x- and y-axis scaling. Currently, the TurtleWrite function is best suited to creating balloon or outline typefaces. With minor additions to the DrawStr function, however, the FloodFill function could create solid letters or fill letters using various fill patterns. Another enhancement might be an option to include color changes in the instruction strings.

The turtle functions are simply a tool set, please feel free to enhance, change, and revise them according to your needs and imagination.

Figure 16-7: Plot for author's logo

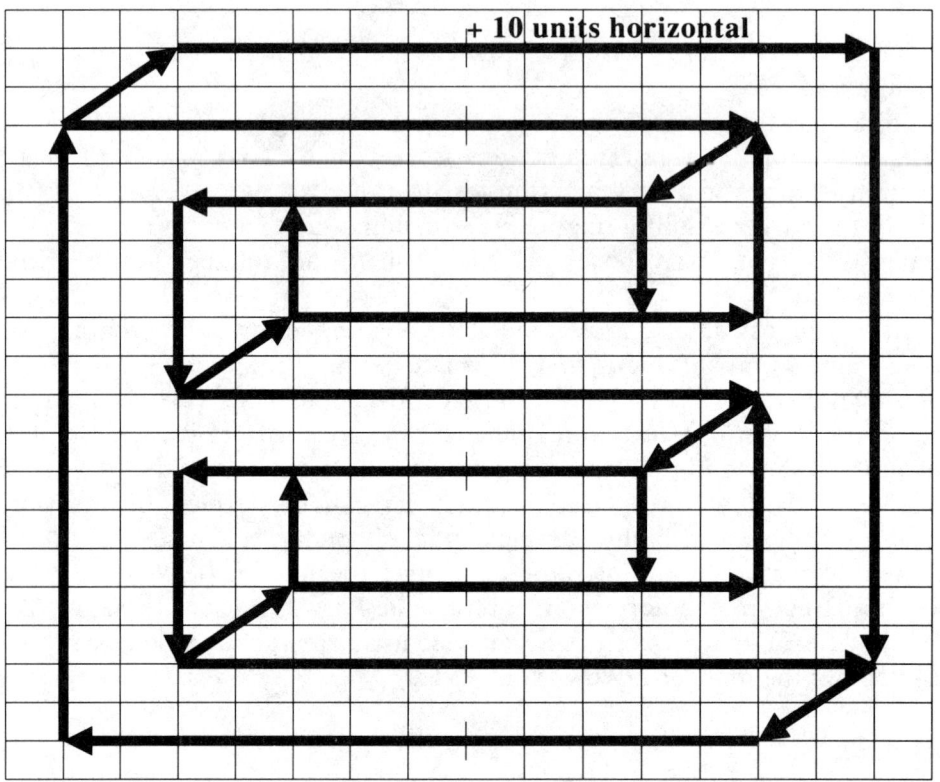

TURTLE.PAS

```
{==================================================}
{    Object Turtle Unit — creates TURTLE.TPU       }
{    Turtle object supports 28 turtle methods      }
{       note: does not require GRAPH3 unit         }
{       works with all graphic resolutions         }
{==================================================}
```

unit TURTLE;

INTERFACE

uses GRAPH, CRT;

const
   NORTH = 0;
   EAST = 90;
   SOUTH = 180;

```
        WEST   = 270;
type
    GTurtle = object
        TAsp : real;
        Visible, WrapOff, Draw : boolean;
        Direction, PenColor, TimeOut,
        XHome, XPos, YHome, YPos,
        Left, Right, Top, Bottom : integer;
                    { turtle limits in abs screen coords }
        TurtlePtr : pointer;
        procedure AdjDirection;
        procedure Back( Distance : integer );
        procedure Clear;
        procedure Create;
        procedure DrawStr( Scale : integer;
                           DStr : string );
        procedure Forwd( Distance : integer );
        procedure Hide;
        procedure Home;
        procedure Init;
        procedure NoWrap;
        procedure PenDown;
        procedure PenUp;
        procedure SetHeading( Degrees: integer );
        procedure SetPenColor( Color: integer );
        procedure SetPosition( XAxis, YAxis: integer );
        procedure Show;
        procedure Step( XStep, YStep: integer );
        procedure TDelay( Time: integer );
        procedure TWindow( XAxis, YAxis,
                          Width, Height: integer );
        procedure TurnLeft( Degrees: integer );
        procedure TurnRight( Degrees: integer );
        procedure Wrap;
        function  Heading: integer;
        function  RCos( Degrees: integer ): real;
        function  RSin( Degrees: integer ): real;
        function  WhereT: boolean;
        function  XCor: integer;
        function  YCor: integer;
    end;

IMPLEMENTATION

            {=====================================}
            {   procedure methods implementation  }
            {=====================================}

procedure GTurtle.AdjDirection;
```

```pascal
      begin
         while( Direction > 360 ) do dec( Direction, 360 );
         while( Direction < 0 )   do inc( Direction, 360 );
      end;
procedure GTurtle.Back;
   begin
      Forwd( Distance * -1 );
   end;
procedure GTurtle.Clear;
   var
      vp : viewporttype;
   begin
      GetViewSettings( vp );
      SetViewPort( Left, Top, Right, Bottom, True );
      ClearViewPort;
      SetViewPort( vp.x1, vp.y1, vp.x2, vp.y2, vp.clip );
      if Visible then
         PutImage( XPos-2, YPos-2, TurtlePtr^, XOrPut );
      Home;
   end;
procedure GTurtle.Create;
   var
      i, j, k : integer;
      temp : pointer;
   begin
      k := GetMaxColor;
      GetMem( temp, ImageSize( 1, 1, 5, 5 ) );
      GetImage( 1, 1, 5, 5, temp^ );
      PutImage( 1, 1, temp^, XOrPut );
      for i := 1 to 5 do
      begin
         PutPixel( i, 3, k );
         PutPixel( 3, i, k );
      end;
      PutPixel( 3, 3, 0 );
      GetMem( TurtlePtr, ImageSize( 1, 1, 5, 5 ) );
      GetImage( 1, 1, 5, 5, TurtlePtr^ );
      PutImage( 1, 1, TurtlePtr^, XOrPut );
      PutImage( 1, 1, temp^, CopyPut );
      dispose( temp );
   end;
procedure GTurtle.DrawStr;
   var
      Distance, j, k, x, y : integer;
   begin
      for j := 1 to ord(DStr[0]) do
```

```
      begin
         Distance := Scale;
         case DStr[j] of
            'a': begin   x := 0;    y := -1;    end;
            'b': begin   x := 1;    y := -1;    end;
            'c': begin   x := 1;    y := 0;     end;
            'd': begin   x := 1;    y := 1;     end;
            'e': begin   x := 0;    y := 1;     end;
            'f': begin   x := -1;   y := 1;     end;
            'g': begin   x := -1;   y := 0;     end;
            'h': begin   x := -1;   y := -1;    end;
            'm': begin   x := 0;    y := 0;
                         PenDown;  end;
            'p': begin   x := 0;    y := 0;
                         PenUp;    end;
         {   '2': Distance := Scale * 1;   }
         {   ...   ...                     }
         {   '9': Distance := Scale * 8;   }
         '2'..'9': Distance :=
                      Scale * ( ord( Dstr[j] ) - 49 );
            '0': Distance := Scale * 9;
            else begin   x := 0;   y := 0;   end;
         end;
         for k := 1 to Distance do
            Step( XPos + x, YPos + y );
      end;
   end;

procedure GTurtle.Forwd;
   var
      i, dx, dy, xorg, yorg : integer;
      slope : real;
   begin
      xorg := XPos;
      yorg := YPos;
      dx := trunc( RSin( Direction ) * Distance );
      dy := trunc( RCos( Direction ) * Distance * TAsp );
      if( abs( dx ) > abs( dy ) ) then
      begin
         slope := dy / dx;
         if( dx > 0 ) then
            for i := 1 to dx do
               Step( xorg + i, yorg + trunc( i*slope ) )
         else
            for i := -1 downto dx do
               Step( xorg + i, yorg + trunc( i*slope ) );
      end else
      begin
         slope := dx / dy;
```

```pascal
            if( dy > 0 ) then
               for i := 1 to dy do
                  Step( xorg + trunc(i*slope ), yorg+i )
            else
               for i := -1 downto dy do
                  Step( xorg + trunc (i*slope), yorg+i );
         end;
      end;
procedure GTurtle.Hide;
   begin
      if Visible then PutImage( XPos-2, YPos-2,
                                  TurtlePtr^, XOrPut );
      Visible := FALSE;
      if TimeOut > 0 then delay( TimeOut );
   end;
procedure GTurtle.Home;
   begin
      if Visible then PutImage( XPos-2, YPos-2,
                                  TurtlePtr^, XOrPut );
      XPos := XHome;
      YPos := YHome;
      if( TimeOut > 0 ) then delay( TimeOut );
      if Visible then PutImage( XPos-2, YPos-2,
                                  TurtlePtr^, XOrPut );
   end;
procedure GTurtle.Init;
   var
      xasp, yasp : word;
   begin
      Create;
      GetAspectRatio( xasp, yasp );
      TAsp := xasp div yasp * -1;
      TWindow( GetMaxX div 2, GetMaxY div 2,
               GetMaxX,       GetMaxY );
      SetPenColor( GetMaxColor );
      TDelay( 0 );
      NoWrap;
      PenDown;
      SetHeading( 0 );
      Show;
   end;
procedure GTurtle.NoWrap;
   begin
      WrapOff := TRUE;
   end;
procedure GTurtle.PenDown;
```

```
      begin
         Draw := TRUE;
      end;
   procedure GTurtle.PenUp;
      begin
         Draw := FALSE;
      end;
   procedure GTurtle.SetHeading;
      begin
         Direction := Degrees;
         AdjDirection;
      end;
   procedure GTurtle.SetPenColor;
      begin
         if( Color < 0 ) then Color := 0;
         if( Color > GetMaxColor ) then
            Color := GetMaxColor;
         PenColor := Color;
         SetColor( PenColor );
      end;
   procedure GTurtle.SetPosition;
      begin
         if Visible then PutImage( XPos-2, YPos-2,
                                    TurtlePtr^, XOrPut );
         XPos := XHome + XAxis;
         YPos := YHome - YAxis;
         if TimeOut > 0 then delay( TimeOut );
         if Visible then PutImage( XPos-2, YPos-2,
                                    TurtlePtr^, XOrPut );
      end;
   procedure GTurtle.Show;
      begin
         if not Visible then PutImage( XPos-2, YPos-2,
                                       TurtlePtr^, XOrPut );
         Visible := TRUE;
         if TimeOut > 0 then delay( TimeOut );
      end;
   procedure GTurtle.Step;
      begin
         if Visible then PutImage( XPos-2, YPos-2,
                                    TurtlePtr^, XOrPut );
         XPos := XStep;
         YPos := YStep;
         if not WrapOff then
         begin
```

```pascal
            if XPos < Left   then inc( XPos, Right)   else
            if XPos > Right  then dec( XPos, Right );
            if YPos < Top    then inc( YPos, Bottom ) else
            if YPos > Bottom then dec( YPos, Bottom );
         end;
         if Draw and WhereT then
            PutPixel( XPos, YPos, PenColor );
         if Visible then PutImage( XPos-2, YPos-2,
                                   TurtlePtr^, XOrPut );
         if ( TimeOut > 0 ) and WhereT then
            delay( TimeOut );
      end;
procedure GTurtle.TDelay( Time: integer );
   begin
      TimeOut := Time;
   end;
procedure GTurtle.TurnLeft;
   begin
      inc( Direction, Degrees );
      AdjDirection;
   end;
procedure GTurtle.TurnRight;
   begin
      dec( Direction, Degrees );
      AdjDirection;
   end;
procedure GTurtle.TWindow;
   var
      xlimit, ylimit : integer;
   begin
      xlimit := GetMaxX - 3;
      ylimit := GetMaxY - 3;
      Left := XAxis - ( Width div 2 );
      while( Left < 3 ) do inc(Left);
      Right := Left + Width;
      while( Right > xlimit ) do dec(Right);
      Top := YAxis - ( Height div 2 );
      while( Top < 3 ) do inc(Top);
      Bottom := Top + Height;
      while( Bottom > ylimit ) do dec(Bottom);
      SetViewPort( Left, Right, Top, Bottom, False );
      ClearViewPort;
      XPos := XAxis;
      YPos := YAxis;
      XHome := XAxis;
      YHome := YAxis;
```

```
        end;
procedure GTurtle.Wrap;
   begin
      WrapOff := FALSE;
   end;

           {=====================================}
           {   function methods implementation   }
           {=====================================}

function GTurtle.Heading: integer;
   begin
      Heading := Direction;
   end;
function GTurtle.RCos;
   begin
      RCos := cos( PI * Degrees / 180 );
   end;
function GTurtle.RSin;
   begin
      RSin := sin( PI * Degrees / 180 );
   end;
function GTurtle.WhereT: boolean;
   begin
      WhereT := ( XPos >= Left ) and ( XPos <= Right )
            and ( YPos >= Top ) and ( YPos <= Bottom );
   end;
function GTurtle.XCor: integer;
   begin
      XCor := XPos - XHome;
   end;
function GTurtle.YCor: integer;
   begin
      YCor := ( YPos - YHome ) * -1;
   end;

                  {===================}
                  {  end of methods   }
                  {===================}

end.
```

Turtle Demo — TUR-DEMO.PAS

```pascal
{================================}
{   Turtle Graphics Demo Program }
{        uses TURTLE.TPU unit    }
{================================}
uses GRAPH, TURTLE, CRT;

var
   GraphDriver, GraphMode,
   MaxColors,   ErrorCode : integer;
   Tortoise : GTurtle;

procedure Initialize;
   begin
      GraphDriver := DETECT;
      InitGraph( GraphDriver, GraphMode, '\TP\BGI' );
      ErrorCode := GraphResult;
      if ErrorCode <> grOk then
      begin
         writeln(' Graphics System Error: ',
                  GraphErrorMsg( ErrorCode ) );
         delay( 1000 );
         halt( 1 );
      end;
      MaxColors := GetMaxColor + 1;
   end;

procedure PrintPause;
   var
      Ch : char;
   begin
      OutTextXY( 10, 10, 'Press any key to continue' );
      while KeyPressed do Ch := ReadKey;
      Ch := ReadKey;
   end;

procedure TurtleHexDemo;
   var
      i, j : integer;
   begin
      with Tortoise do
      begin
         TDelay( 10 );
         SetHeading( SOUTH );
         PenUp;
         Forwd( 100 );
         delay( 500 );
         TDelay( 0 );
```

```
            PenDown;
            SetHeading( 45 );
            for i := 1 to 15 do
            begin
                SetPenColor( i );
                for j := 1 to 6 do
                begin
                    Forwd( 100 + i * 3 );
                    TurnRight( 59 );
                end;
            end;
            Home;
        end;
    end;
procedure TurtleDiamondDemo;
    var
        i, j : integer;
    begin
        with Tortoise do
        begin
            Clear;
            Wrap;
            SetPosition( -100, -100 );
            SetHeading( 45 );
            for i := 1 to 15 do
            begin
                SetPenColor( i );
                for j := 1 to 3 do
                begin   Forwd( 200 );
                        TurnLeft( 90 );   end;
                Forwd( 200 );
            end;
            Home;
        end;
    end;
procedure TurtleWrite( x, y, scale, color : integer;
                      WorkStr : string );
    const
        logostr : string[125] =
                'pcma8a8b2c8c8c8e8e8f2g8g8g8a8a8c8c8c8' +
                'f2g0g0e5b2c0c0a5f2e3g9g9a3g2e5c7c8c7' +
                'f2g0g0e5b2c0c0a5f2e3g9g9a3g2e5c8c8c8pcd';
    var
        i : integer;
    begin
        with Tortoise do
        begin
```

```pascal
            if color <= MaxColors then SetPenColor( color );
            if scale <= 0 then scale := 1;
            SetPosition( x, y );
            for i := 1 to ord( WorkStr[0] ) do
            begin
                if color < 0 then
                    SetPenColor( random( MaxColors ) + 1 );
                case WorkStr[i] of
                    ' ': DrawStr( scale, 'pc6' );
                    'e': DrawStr( scale,
                            'pbama6b2c4d2e2f2g4edc3bcef2g4' +
                            'h2pb2a3mbc2dfg2hpd7' );
                    'i': DrawStr( scale,
                            'pcma9bpamhabdefpemde9g2pc3' );
                    'l': DrawStr( scale,
                            'pbma7a7bde7e7fhpdc2' );
                    'r': DrawStr( scale,
                            'pcma9bce2b2c2d2eghg2f2e6g2pc9' );
                    't': DrawStr( scale,
                           'pb2cma8g3hbc3a3bde3c3dfg3e7dc' +
                           'dfg2h2pd2c5' );
                    'u': DrawStr( scale,
                            'pbama7bde6dc2ba6bde7deghfg4h2pd2c7');
                    'w': DrawStr( scale,
                            'pbama7bde6dc2ba3bde3dc2ba6bde' +
                            '7f2g4hfg4h2pd2c6c7' );
                end; { case }
            end;
            DrawStr( scale, logostr );
        end;
    end;

procedure TurtleWriteDemo;
    begin
        with Tortoise do
        begin
            NoWrap;
            Clear;
            PenUp;
            randomize;
            TDelay( 10 );
            TurtleWrite( -300, -110, 5,
               MaxColors, 'turtle write ' );
            TDelay( 7 );
            TurtleWrite( -300,  -20, 4,
                  random(MaxColors)+1, 'write turtle ' );
            TDelay( 5 );
            TurtleWrite( -300,   55, 3,
                -1, 'turtle write ' );
```

```
            TDelay( 3 );
            TurtleWrite( -300,   110, 2,
                -1, 'write turtle ');
            TDelay( 1 );
            TurtleWrite( -300,   150, 0,
                MaxColors, 'turtle write turtle write ' +
                    'turtle write turtle write turtle' );
            Home;
        end;
    end;
begin
    Initialize;
    Tortoise.Init;
    Tortoise.Show;
    TurtleHexDemo;
    PrintPause;
    TurtleDiamondDemo;
    PrintPause;
    TurtleWriteDemo;
    PrintPause;
    CloseGraph;
end.
```

CHAPTER 17

Graphics Printer Output

Computer graphics are wonderful on screen, but unless you can create these same graphics on paper, they can be quite frustrating. Pasting a computer terminal into a manuscript is close to impossible.

For text modes, the Shift-PrtSc (Shift-PrintScreen) key command is available to send an ASCII screen to the printer and several TSR utilities have been created to execute the same task for a graphics screen. These latter, however, have been notably less than satisfactory. Most work only with specific printers, operate only in specific modes and, when used, may occupy entirely too much resident memory and prevent other applications from running.

In this chapter, two graphics screen print utilities are created providing monochrome outputs using the Epson (dot-matrix) and LaserJet printers (see Chapter 18 for color output using plotters). These graphic output utilities avoid the mentioned problems because they can be tailored for any output device, will adapt to different video modes, and can be incorporated directly into your application program.

Because more people have color monitors on their systems than have color plotters, the LaserJet graphics driver offers, in addition to Portrait and Landscape modes, a Grayscale mode (with two options: normal and inverse gray scales) that translates colors to grays in 16 shades on output.

Please note that all of the graphics output devices shown here are generic drivers. They have been specifically designed to work with most dot-matrix, laserjet, or plotter devices presently marketed or can be easily adapted to work with any devices that require variant handling codes. The standard devices chosen—Epson dot-matrix printers, Hewlett-Packard LaserJet Series II printers, and Hewlett-Packard Plotters—are also de facto industry standards and most devices, regardless of manufacturers' trademarks, use essentially the same control codes and operate in basically the same manner.

One output device type not covered here are the color dot-matrix printers using multicolored ribbons or multicolored inkjets. These devices are not particularly different in theory or operation from the color-pen plotters appearing in Chapter 18 and a specialty driver for this type of device is easily created.

Using the Epson Dot-Matrix Printers

The Epson FX-85 printer is used as the standard device for dot-matrix printers. This ensures compatibility with the MX and RX series and, for the most part, with the LX (inkjet) series, as well as the majority of other manufacturers of dot-matrix printers. Most, if not all, offer graphics modes compatible with the Epson, but you should consult your printer manual for the capabilities of any specific device and adapt the graphics driver as appropriate.

The FX-85 printer offers eight graphics operation modes as shown in Table 17-1. A word of caution: if you are using an Epson printer (or compatible) with the dip switch selection set to "IBM mode" or an IBM dot matrix printer, only graphics modes 0-3 will be available.

Table 17-1: FX-85 Graphics Modes

MODE	DENSITY	DESCRIPTION	SPEED
0	Single	60 dpi	16 in/sec
1	Low Speed Double	120 dpi	8 in/sec
2	High Speed Double	120 dpi	16 in/sec[1]
3	Quadruple	240 dpi	8 in/sec[1]
4	CRT 1	80 dpi	8 in/sec[2]
5	One-to-one	72 dpi	12 in/sec[2]
6	CRT II	90 dpi	3in//sec
7	Dual-Density	144 dpi	3 in/sec[3]

1. Does not print consecutive dots in any one row.
2. Matches screen density of Epson QX-10
3. Plotter modes—provides one-to-one horizontal dot density

While Epson provides mode 4 (CRT I) to match the screen (pixel) density of the QX-10 computer monitor, none of these modes offers an exact match for either CGA or EGA/VGA screen modes. Some, however, provide a better match than others, but this is also dependent on your output orientation.

Portrait Versus Landscape Orientation

Both the laserjet and dot-matrix drivers offer a choice of Landscape or Portrait imaging. The Portrait orientation plots the screen's x-axis across the width of your paper and the y-axis along the length of the paper, producing a half-sheet image. The Landscape orientation matches the long axis of the paper to the screen's x-axis, plotting the screen's y-axis across the width of the paper and producing a single screen image per page. This, in general, is the preferred output orientation.

For each orientation and screen mode, there is a preferred dot-matrix mode to best match the screen image, as shown in Table 17-2.

Table 17-2: Preferred Dot-Matrix Modes for Graphics

DIRECTION	CGA	EGA	VGA
PORTRAIT	3 / 7	1 / 7	1 / 7
LANDSCAPE	0	0	5

Dot-Matrix Mode Criteria

Three criteria apply in printer mode selection for a graphics screen output.

First, the number of dots per inch (dpi) must be high enough to map the screen pixels within the physical page limits. Using a resolution of 60 dpi (mode 0) in Portrait orientation would require a paper width greater than eight inches. For a 13-inch wide printer, 60 dpi would be acceptable for plotting 640 pixels horizontal, but on an eight-inch printer, only 480 pixels would be plotted before the margins were exceeded.

Second, the dots per inch horizontal and the lines per inch vertical must be balanced to achieve an output image close to your screen image. The horizontal dpi can be varied, the vertical cannot (or not easily).

Third, since the image is plotted one to one (one pixel/one dot), the higher the printer density (dots per inch), the smaller the resulting image. For example, mode 3 will plot an entire screen image, in Portrait mode in a width of only 2.7 inches (and in very distorted proportions).

The modes shown are not dictated by fiat. I suggest that you experiment with your own equipment, try the various modes, and see firsthand how each matches output and screen image. In this particular application, a picture is quite literally worth a thousand words.

Remember, though, the higher the number of dots per inch (dpi), the smaller the resulting image horizontally. If you need both the dense bit imaging and a larger image, for a dot matrix, rewrite the graphics driver to output two (or more) printer dots per screen pixel. See also Gray Scaling which uses 16 dots per pixel (at 300 dpi) for color conversion with a laserjet and compare this approach with Epson's mode 3 Quadruple density (240 dpi).

Note also, for CGA modes C0..C3 (low resolution), printer mode 0 works well in Portrait orientation.

Calculating The Dot-Matrix Graphics Character

When the dot-matrix printer is used for normal (alphanumeric) output, an 8-bit character code selects a 9x9 pin pattern from the printer's ROM character sets. In graphics modes, however, only eight of these pins are used and an 8-bit character is sent for every horizontal printhead position with each bit of this character code controlling one of the active pins.

The graphics character is calculated with the top pin controlled by bit 7 of the character, the bottom pin controlled by bit 0. Three examples of graphic character calculations are shown in Figure 17-1.

Figure 17-1: Individual Pin Calculation

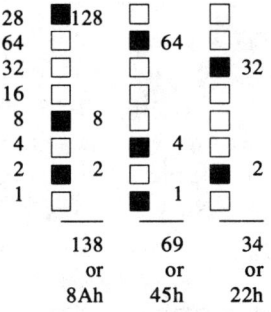

The graphics character code for the dot-matrix print head is calculated as an 8-bit character with bit 7 for the top pin (value 128) and bit 0 for the bottom pin (value 1). The character code sent is the sum of the values for the pins desired to print.

Graphics results are shown here in both decimal and hexadecimal codes.

On the dot-matrix, a series of graphics characters prints eight horizontal rows of dots, then the paper is advanced and the print head returned for the next row. In Portrait mode, each print line accounts for eight screen pixel rows and each character is generated from eight vertical pixels (see Figure 17-2).

In Landscape mode, the print direction and paper advance remain constant, but the screen pixels are scanned as horizontal sets of eight pixels with a print line beginning at the top right of the screen and moving down. Subsequent print lines begin by scanning eight horizontal pixels at the top of the screen but with the horizontal scan position moved eight pixels left while the final print line scans the left-most portion of the screen (see Figure 17-3).

Figure 17-2: Calculating Bit-Image Characters for the Dot-Matrix

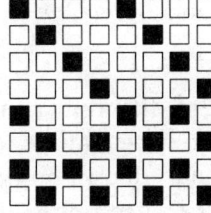

In PORTRAIT mode, the pixels would be read as eight vertical sets (left to right) as 8Ah, 45h, 22h,15h, 8Ah, 45h, 2Ah and 15h and transmitted in this order.

In LANDSCAPE mode, the pixels would be read as eight horizontal sets (top to bottom) as 11h, 22h, 44h, 88h, 51h, AAh, 55h and AAh and tranmitted in this order. Remember, the high order bit is to the right, the low order bit to the left.

Figure 17-3: Mapping Screen to Paper in LANDSCAPE Mode

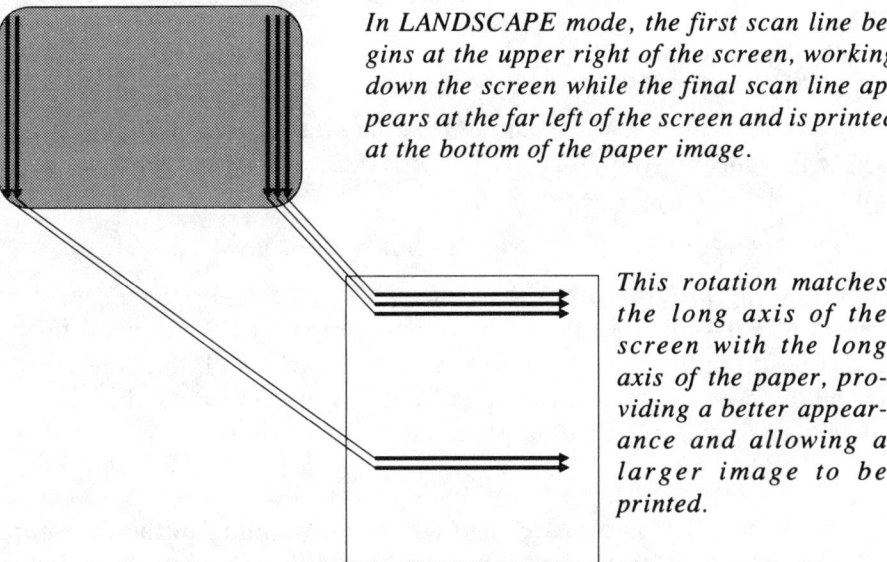

In LANDSCAPE mode, the first scan line begins at the upper right of the screen, working down the screen while the final scan line appears at the far left of the screen and is printed at the bottom of the paper image.

This rotation matches the long axis of the screen with the long axis of the paper, providing a better appearance and allowing a larger image to be printed.

PrintGraph—Dot-Matrix Graphics Driver

To describe the PrintGraph function (dot-matrix driver) as simplicity itself would be demeaning to a very smooth programming function. The PrintGraph function is precisely this: very simple and very smooth.

Before calling PrintGraph, I suggest defining two constants that will be used by the calling function to specify the output orientation desired:

```
const
   PORTRAIT  = 0;
   LANDSCAPE = 1;
```

For convenience, the Escape character is also defined as a constant.

```
ESC = #$1B;
```

Two parameters are required to call PrintGraph, *Mode* and *Direction*.

```
procedure PrintGraph( Mode, Direction : integer );
```

The *Mode* parameter is a provision allowing you to test different printer modes. If and when you've settled on a preferred printer graphics mode, this calling parameter can be eliminated with mode constants supplied in *both* the *PORTRAIT* and *LANDSCAPE* options. Also, if you prefer to use only Landscape or Portrait orientation, the second parameter (*Direction*) can also be eliminated with the *case* provisions rewritten for the preferred option.

In either case, a few local variables are required:

```
var
    i, j, k, m, Msb, Lsb, MaxX, MaxY : integer;
begin
    MaxX := GetMaxX;
    MaxY := GetMaxY;
```

The last two variables, *MaxX* and *MaxY*, may duplicate similar declarations elsewhere in your program, but this will not interfere with their local declaration and these values will be needed.

```
SetViewPort( 0, 0, MaxX, MaxY, False );
```

If your calling program has other settings in effect—or if you want other settings in effect—this can be changed or eliminated. If you need to map a smaller area, it can be done by setting the limits to match the desired screen region, but be sure the data width specifications are set to match.

The printer should be set to graphics mode:

```
write( Lst, ESC,'A',#$07 );
```

In Turbo Pascal, *Lst* is a predefined file corresponding to the first parallel port. If you need a different output port, change this designation accordingly.

The string instruction tells the printer to set line spacing as $n/72$. In this case the *character* 07h specifies $7/72$ (about 82 dpi vertical spacing). Valid settings for *n* are 0..85.

Next, output orientation is selected as Portrait or Landscape:

```
case Direction of
    PORTRAIT: begin
```

The next step is to give the printer a graphics mode command and to specify how wide each line will be (how many dot positions will be plotted). The *Mode* value was specified when PrintGraph was called and, in *PORTRAIT* orientation, this width would be the 640 pixels horizontally on the screen (assuming high resolution modes).

However, since the Epson printer can only accept 8-bit data, the 640 dot specification is reduced to two 8-bit arguments: *Lsb* and *Msb*. Since *MaxX* will have a value of 639 returned by GetMaxX, the argument used to calculate *Lsb* and *Msb* is incremented by one.

```
Lsb := MaxX AND $00FF;
Msb := MaxX SHR 8;
```

A loop begins at the top of the screen. Each loop, however, will plot eight vertical pixels.

```
for j := 0 to MaxY div 8 do
begin
```

The arguments *Mode*, *Lsb*, and *Msb* are passed as char values (unsigned 8-bit integers) with the *ESC** argument indicating that a graphics mode is being selected.

```
write( Lst, ESC, '*', char( Mode ),
       char( Lsb ), char( Msb ) );
```

This graphics mode setting is valid only for one line. After a graphics mode command and line length parameters are sent, the next *x* data bytes (set by the *Lsb* and *Msb* arguments) received are interpreted as graphics pin instructions, regardless of their contents! The graphics mode settings command initializes each and every graphics data line transmitted to the printer.

Now another loop begins, starting at the left screen margin and progressing across the screen to *MaxX*.

```
for i := 0 to MaxX do
begin
```

The character *m* is set to null (0) at the start of each step, then an inner loop steps from *0* through *7* to read eight screen pixels (vertically).

```
m := 0;
for k := 0 to 7 do
begin
```

As the inner loop executes, the character *m* is shifted left one bit. If the current pixel is not *0* (black or background palette entry), then *m* is incremented (the right-most or zero bit is set). As the loop continues and *m* is shifted left, each bit moves up, and a new null bit becomes the low-order bit.

```
m := m SHL 1;
if GetPixel( i, j*8+k ) <> 0
    then inc( m );
end;
```

After the inner loop is finished, the resulting character is output to the printer.

```
        write( Lst, char( m ) );
    end;
```

When the line is finished, the CR/LF codes are explicitly sent to the printer to advance the print head to the beginning of the next line.

```
        write( Lst, #$0D, #$0A );
      end;
    end;
```

Instead of explicitly sending the CR/LF codes, the writeln procedure could be used *in most cases*, but this might fail with some printers (depending on printer options and compiler settings) while specifying the transmission of both characters has the advantage of certainty.

This process continues until the entire screen has been read, eight pixels at a time, and transferred to the printer in the form of a graphics character.

In the Landscape mode, the process is the same except that a different graphics string length is calculated using *MaxY* instead of *MaxX* and the screen image is read, starting at the top right and moving down and left, eight horizontal pixels at a byte (pun intended).

```
    LANDSCAPE: begin
      Lsb := MaxY AND $00FF;
      Msb := MaxY SHR 8;
      j := 0;
      repeat
```

Unlike the Portrait mode, here the screen image is read beginning at the bottom of the screen and working up.

```
            write( Lst, ESC, '*', char( Mode ),
                   char( Lsb ), char( Msb ) );
            for i := MaxY downto 0 do
            begin
               m := 0;
               for k := 0 to 7 do
               begin
                  m := m SHL 1;
                  if GetPixel( j+k, i ) <> 0
                     then inc( m );
               end;
               write( Lst, char( m ) );
            end;
            write( Lst, #$0D, #$0A );
            inc( j, 8 );
         until j >= MaxX-1;
```

```
      end;
   end; { case }
```

Finally, after the entire screen image has been transmitted to the printer, a form feed character is sent to advance the paper.

```
   write( Lst, #$0C );
end;
```

This completes the image transmission process. Simple.

Using The Laserjet Printer Utility

A graphics screen dump to a laserjet printer is no more difficult than printing to a dot-matrix, but there are differences both in the capabilities of the laserjet and in how the laserjet is treated.

First, the laserjet is capable of printing a finer dot-image than a dot-matrix printer—up to 300 dpi—but most laserjets also support four distinct dot resolutions: 75 dpi, 100 dpi, 150 dpi and 300 dpi. At 75 dpi, the image dots are 16 times as large (4x4) as the dots produced at 300 dpi and, naturally, only 1/16 as much information can be mapped to a page. Similarly, the 100 dpi and 150 dpi resolutions create dot sizes that are submultiples of the 300 dpi resolution.

Second, the resolution used does not affect the output speed. The time required to generate a graphics output is determined only by the amount of bit information sent to the printer (transmission time) and not by the resolution setting used by the printer to map the information to the page. The same image generated at 300 dpi and at 75 dpi will require the same output time.

Third, the selected dot resolution does not directly affect the relative x/y-axis spacing. While the x-axis spacing is determined by the dot resolution, the y-axis line spacing is directly under the control of the program. Screen aspect ratios can be matched on output with excellent results and, if desired, deliberate distortions can be introduced.

In sum, since the laserjet labors under fewer *mechanical* constraints than a dot-matrix, the resulting output is capable of much higher resolution and of more faithful reproduction of the original video screen image. Because of this lack of mechanical constraints, the laserjet is controlled in a different manner than a dot-matrix with two principal differences in operation.

First, each row (or column) of screen pixels is mapped one for one to the laserjet output scan. Thus, in Portrait mode, instead of reading successive groups of eight vertical pixels, as was done for the dot matrix, the screen image is read by rows, with each successive eight pixels transmitted as a graphics character and 80 characters creating one row of graphics dots on the page. The dpi resolution selected determines the horizontal spacing between the dots.

Second, since there is no physical printhead involved, each graphics string output must be prefaced with position instructions explaining where on the page the dot image is to appear. However, as mentioned, this is precisely the element that makes it possible for the aspect of the output image to match the screen image faithfully.

The LaserJet Screen Print Utility

The utility functions in the LJGraph unit provide three modes for transferring your screen image to paper: Landscape, Portrait, and Grayscale. The first two modes, Landscape and Portrait, provide a fast monochrome output in 75 and 100 dpi resolutions. The third mode, Grayscale, translates screen colors into either four (CGA Low Resolution) or 16 (EGA/VGA) shades of gray (see Table 17-3).

Table 17-3: LaserJet Graphic Screen Dump Modes

MODE	APPROXIMATE DATA	RESOLUTION	TIME
LANDSCAPE	50,000 bytes	75 DPI	~1 minute
PORTRAIT	40,000 bytes	100 DPI	~1 minute
GRAYSCALE	600,000 bytes	300 DPI	~6 minutes

As you will note, the Grayscale mode requires a fair amount of time—slightly more than six minutes—to output some 600,000 bytes of information describing a color screen. The image produced is effectively the same resolution and size as in Landscape mode except that each pixel has been mapped to a 16-bit (4x4) gray dot image. The practice and options in gray scaling will be discussed further in this chapter (see *Sixteen- and Four-Tone Gray Scale Palettes*).

The same screen in either Landscape or Portrait mode requires slightly more than one minute. These times will vary, of course, depending on CPU speeds and other machine capabilities but the values given above provide a general rule for time requirements. Three other considerations should be kept in mind.

If you do not have a laserjet immediately available, the screen dump output can be redirected to a disk file and then sent directly from disk to a laserjet at a later time using the DOS PRINT command.

Multiple copies of a screen image can be printed without requiring multiple transmission times. Adding a multicopy command to the output print image will be discussed later in this chapter.

Do not attempt to use the Grayscale mode with CGA monochrome graphics. There is simply no point, the results will be a very pale image and the Landscape mode will produce much more satisfactory results in about $1/6$ the time.

LaserJet Instruction Codes

Table 17-4 shows a sample series of laserjet graphic output instructions with each command sequence appearing on a separate line and with comments. In actual practice, the command sequences are not separated by any CR/LF sequences unless they happen to appear as graphics dot commands.

Table 17-4: An Example of LaserJet Output Instructions

^{1}BE	reset
^{1}B&l1H	select paper feed from tray
^{1}B&l0O	reset 0 origin for printer cursor position
^{1}B*p0X	cursor position, 0 dots horizontal
^{1}B*p0Y	cursor position, 0 dots vertical
^{1}B*t300R	300 dpi resolution
^{1}B&a1228.8h1180.8V	cursor position, horizontal & vertical decipoints
^{1}B*r1A	start graphics at current cursor
^{1}B*b23W 0F FF FF FF FF FF FF FF FF FF FF FF FF FF FF FF FF FF FF FF FF FF F8	transfer 23 bytes graphic data
^{1}B*rB	end graphics
^{1}B&a1228.8h1183.2V	position cursor, horizontal & vertical decipoints
^{1}B*r1A	start graphics at current cursor
^{1}B*b23W 01 F0 20 20 20 20 20 20 20 20 20 20 20 20 20 20 20 20 20 20 20 27 80	transfer 23 bytes graphic data
^{1}B*rB	end graphics
.	
.	*(graphics instructions continue)*
.	
^{1}B*rB 0C	end graphics + form feed (0Ch)
^{1}B&l0	reset 0 origin printer cursor position *(default)*
^{1}B(8U	primary symbol set Roman-8 *(default)*
^{1}B(s0p10h12vsb3T	reset primary font values *(defaults)*
^{1}B&l1H	select paper feed from tray *(default)*

(end of printer instructions)

Each command sequence begins with the Escape character (^{1}B) followed by a series of ASCII characters that define the command and any parameters included in the command. For example, the sequence ^{1}B*t300R, sets 300 dpi resolution with the parameter *300* sent as a plain-text ASCII sequence and never as a code or value sequence as was used with the dot-matrix codes.

The DeciPoint Position Instructions

The laserjet supports three separate print cursor position modes: row, dot, and decipoint. For this application, only the decipoint coordinate system will be used.

First, a bit of explanation. Printers (meaning people rather than devices) have traditionally used a pica and point system to measure type sizes with six picas equalling one inch and 12 points equalling a pica. There are 72 points to the inch and the dot-matrix printer standard also provides for spacing in $1/72$ inch increments. But the laserjet uses a dot size of $1/300$ of an inch, requiring a finer position increment than a mere point size and the laserjet's dot coordinate system provides this spacing in $1/300$ inch steps.

An even finer degree of positioning, however, is provided by the decipoint coordinates. A decipoint is $1/10$ of a point or $1/720$ of an inch and, to carry precision one degree further, the decipoint measurements also allow a decimal fraction (as 1234.5 decipoints) for a precision of $1/7200$ of an inch.

And the decipoint.decimal is the position coordinate system that will be used to control the graphics print positions, which should be sufficient positioning to satisfy even the most finicky programmer.

One other bit of information: the 0,0 coordinate is a position roughly $1/2$ inch down from the top of the page and $1/2$ inch from the left. All decipoint measurements are made from this coordinate location.

Using 300 dpi resolution, each dot is nominally 0.0033... inches in diameter and, converting this measurement to decipoints, yields a basic vertical increment of 2.4 decipoints. For 150 dpi, this increment would be doubled to 4.8; at 100 dpi, becoming 7.2 decipoints and; at 75 dpi, the vertical increment becomes 9.6 decipoints.

These basic printer scan line increments are adjusted according to the screen pixel aspect ratios to ensure that the proportions of the final print image match the screen appearance.

Note also that the printer cursor position command consists of a single instruction preface followed by two values: the x and y coordinates. Since the 'h' character identifying the preceding as a horizontal decipoint position coordinate is lowercase, the instruction preface does not have to be repeated. The second coordinate is ended with a capital "V" indicating that the current command sequence is being terminated.

If you will look at the next to the last command sequence in Table 17-4, the sequence begins with a single instruction preface ($^1B(s)$) followed by a series of values and lowercase instruction indicators with the final instruction indicator in uppercase as a terminator. This format is used frequently when several commands sharing the same instruction preface sequence are being sent.

Additional information and explanation on the laserjet printer control sequences can be found in the *LaserJet series II Printer User's Manual*, Appendix A or in the *LaserJet series II Printer Technical Reference Manual*—both available from Hewlett-Packard.

Writing Graphics Characters to the LaserJet

Before the graphics data is transmitted, the printer cursor position is set using the horizontal and vertical decipoint coordinates, then the ^{1}B*r1A sequence confirms that graphics output will begin at the cursor setting.

The command sequence, ^{1}B*b##W, tells the printer to treat the next ## characters as graphics characters. Just as the 300 dpi resolution figure was sent as plain text instead of using code characters (as was done with the dot-matrix), the number of data characters to be transmitted will also be sent as plain-text ASCII. That is, if 80 graphics characters will follow, then the ## markers will read an ASCII "80" instead of the "P" character which would have been used with the dot-matrix. See Figure 17-4 for examples.

As before, the information is transmitted in the form of 8-bit characters and for the laserjet, these bit-images are calculated precisely the same as for the dot-matrix images, except for the direction and order of screen pixels read for each mode.

While the transmit graphics data command explicitly stated how many bytes (characters) of graphics data would be sent, an end graphics command string is still sent after the data transfer is complete. Granted, this appears redundant, but it is safe and adds little overhead to the data transmitted.

When all of the graphics data has been sent, the final end graphics command will be followed by the character 0Ch, the standard form feed character, instructing the laserjet to eject the page. The four code sequences following the form feed character are simply housekeeping sequences to reset the laserjet to default values.

Sixteen and Four Tone Grayscale Palettes

In addition to the direct mapping modes (Landscape and Portrait), the Grayscale mode maps each screen pixel on output to a gray 4x4 dot image, the gray value being determined by the palette color number of the screen pixel. This is not a true grayscale conversion (see *True-Color Grayscale Palettes*), but simply an arbitrary mapping providing 16 grays for EGA/VGA color screens and four grays for CGA low-resolution color screens.

This grayscale conversion is accomplished by setting an output resolution of 300 dpi, then scanning each screen pixel four times and outputting 16 dots (four per line on four lines) for each screen pixel. The resulting print image is the same size and aspect as created by the Landscape mode except that the screen colors are now approximated as shades of gray.

There are flaws in this particular method of gray-scaling.

Because this is an arbitrary gray mapping, the darker colors are assigned the lightest grays and White is printed as an almost solid black. The gray palette result for LightGray is out of order, being one dot lighter than the gray palette result assigned to DarkGray (assuming the default EGA/VGA color palette). This light to dark scaling was arbitrarily chosen as 'normal' since it leaves the screen background printed as white.

An option is provided to invert the gray-scale results such that the background will be printed as black and the White will be plotted as white on the page. This inversion, however, will not correct the minor discrepancy between the gray tones assigned to the LightGray and DarkGray default palette entries.

If new colors are assigned to the EGA/VGA palette, the grayscale values will not change to accommodate these colors. If the palette color entry number two is assigned a bright green, it will still be grayscaled according to the palette entry number and not the assigned color value.

The shades of gray provided may not be easily distinguished from each other and two adjacent shades of gray may be almost exactly the same in appearance, depending on the output device and the state of the ink (toner) cartridge used.

These are, however, the closest approximation to 16 shades of gray that it is possible to create within the limitations of the laserjet and the requirement of mapping an entire 640x350 (or larger) graphics screen.

Figure 17-4 shows the gray bit-maps assigned to each palette entry.

LJGraph Unit

The LJGraph unit contains the LaserJet Graphics driver functions and begins by declaring three constants and one global variable.

```
const
   PORTRAIT  = 0;
   LANDSCAPE = 1;
   GRAYSCALE = 2;
var
   Negative  : boolean;
```

The constants PORTRAIT, LANDSCAPE, and GRAYSCALE are provided as a convenience in selecting the desired mode when calling the LJGraph function. The Boolean variable Negative is used as a flag by the Gray-Scale function to select normal or inverse grayscale mapping.

The LJGraph function is called with one parameter, *Mode*, selecting Portrait, Landscape, or Grayscale output orientation and resolution. Since your calling program may not provide x and y screen limits and a screen aspect ratio, these are declared as local variables along with the real variables *XPrn*, *YPrn*, and *PrStep*.

```
procedure LJGraph( Mode: integer );
   var
      i, j, k, m, p, q, MaxX, MaxY : integer;
      xasp, yasp : word;
      XPrn, YPrn, PrStep, AspR : real;
```

Figure 17-4: Calculating Bit-Image Characters for the LaserJet

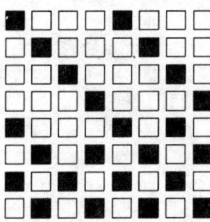

In PORTRAIT mode, the eight horizontal sets of pixels would be read as 88h, 44h, 22h, 11h, 8Ah, 55h, AAh and 55h. As with the dot-matrix, each set of eight pixels is transmitted as a single graphics character and each set would be transmitted on a separate line.

In LANDSCAPE mode, the pixels would be read as eight vertical sets as 15h, 2Ah, 45h, 8Ah, 15h, 22h, 45h and 8Ah. Again, each eight pixels are transmitted as a single graphics character and each vertical set shown here would be transmitted on a separate line.

Also, two character strings, *GrEnds* and *GrInit*, are defined.

The argument *ESC* is the Escape character (in hexadecimal format). The Escape character (or any control character) can be entered directly by using the Turbo Pascal editor's Control-Prefix entry (usually *Alt-P*), then entering the [key.

```
const
   ESC = #$1B;
   GrEnds = ESC + '*rB';
   GrInit = ESC + 'E' + ESC + '&l1H' + ESC + '&l0' +
           ESC + '*p0X' + ESC + '*p0Y' + ESC + '*t';
```

The *GrInit* character string breaks down into several commands as shown in Figure 17-5. The final portion of the string, ¹B*t*, is the preface to the set resolution command which will be completed before the sequence is transmitted.

Now, the LJGraph function checks the screen aspect ratio, then restores the viewport settings to the full screen.

```
begin
   PutImage( 0, PromptPos, ScrnImage^, CopyPut );
```

```
MaxX := GetMaxX + 1;
MaxY := GetMaxY + 1;
GetAspectRatio( xasp, yasp );
AspR := xasp / yasp;
SetViewPort( 0, 0, MaxX, MaxY, False );
```

Figure 17-5: Patterns for 16-level Grayscale Palette

Palette = 0 0 0 0 (0)   0 0 0 1 (1)   0 0 1 0 (2)   0 0 1 1 (3)

Gray-scale bit patterns (four scan lines) — scan 0, scan 1, scan 2, scan 3

Palette = 0 1 0 0 (4)   0 1 0 1 (5)   0 1 1 0 (6)   0 1 1 1 (7)

Gray-scale bit patterns (four scan lines) — scan 0, scan 1, scan 2, scan 3

Palette = 0 0 0 0 (8)   0 0 0 1 (9)   0 0 1 0 (A)   0 0 1 1 (B)

Gray-scale bit patterns (four scan lines) — scan 0, scan 1, scan 2, scan 3

Palette = 0 0 0 0 (C)   0 0 0 1 (D)   0 0 1 0 (E)   0 0 1 1 (F)

Gray-scale bit patterns (four scan lines) — scan 0, scan 1, scan 2, scan 3

The case command uses the *Mode* argument to select the desired output operation.

```
case Mode of
    PORTRAIT:
        begin
```

In Portrait mode, the output x/y coordinates are set using initial *decipoint* values.

```
XPrn := 690.0;
YPrn := 500.0;
```

The GrInit string is sent to the printer with the sequence '100' appended, selecting 100 dpi resolution.

```
write( Lst, GrInit, '100R' );
```

Now the *PrStep* variable is set to match the printer aspect ratio to the screen aspect ratio.

```
PrStep := 7.2 / AspR;
```

So far, this has all been setup and initialization for the printer and for values used while the graphics loops execute. Now it's time to read the video screen and send the output information to the printer.

Because this is Portrait mode, the loop begins at the top of the screen, sends a printer cursor position command, then increments the *YPrn* coordinate by the value in *PrStep*.

```
for j := 0 to MaxY do
begin
   write( Lst, ESC,'&a',
            XPrn:Fmt( XPrn ):1, 'h',
            YPrn:Fmt( YPrn ):1, 'V' );
   YPrn := YPrn + PrStep;
```

Notice that two parameters are used for the x coordinate and two for the y coordinate. The parameter provided by *format(XPrn)* is a width statement specifying how many places will be created in the %–*.1f* number string. C is notorious for formatting floating-point numbers in all number-to-string conversions. Since any leading or trailing spaces would confuse the laserjet, the format function has been created to return an integer value, setting the string format to exclude leading or trailing blanks.

Next, commands are sent to start graphics at the printer cursor and to specify the number of graphics characters that will follow. Happily, C is not fanatical about formatting integers with extra spaces, so no width parameter is required.

```
write( Lst, ESC, '*r1A', ESC, '*b',
         MaxX div 8, 'W' );
```

Now the printer is expecting a string of *MaxX/8* graphics characters and two loops (the first from *0* to *MaxX/8* and the second from *0* to *7*), to read a series of screen pixels, creating a graphics character describing each eight pixels and sending the final character to the printer.

```pascal
        for i := 0 to MaxX div 8 do
        begin
           m := 0;
           for k := 0 to 7 do
           begin
              m := m SHL 1;
              if GetPixel( i*8+k, j ) <> 0
                 then inc( m );
           end;
           write( Lst, char( m ) );
        end;
```

When these two loops are completed and the current row of pixels has been mapped to the printer, the *graph_ends* string is sent and the loop continues with the next row of pixels.

```pascal
        write( Lst, GrEnds );
     end;
  end;
```

In the Landscape mode, the initial setup is much the same except that a resolution of 75 dpi is selected and the printer line spacing is adjusted accordingly.

```pascal
  LANDSCAPE:
     begin
        XPrn := 1000.0;
        YPrn := 1000.0;
        PrStep := 9.6 * AspR;
        write( Lst, GrInit, '75R' );
```

The main loop, however, runs from screen left to screen right and the graphics strings will be created by reading a column of screen pixels instead of a row. Since *MaxY* may not be an even multiple of eight (EGA supports a vertical resolution of 350 pixels), *MaxY+4* is used to set the number of graphics characters that will be sent; otherwise, a few rows at the bottom of the screen may not be mapped to the printer.

```pascal
        for j := 0 to MaxX-1 do
        begin
           write( Lst, ESC, '&a',
                  XPrn:Fmt( XPrn ):1, 'h',
                  YPrn:Fmt( YPrn ):1, 'V' );
           YPrn := YPrn + PrStep;
           write( Lst, ESC, '*r1A', ESC, '*b',
                  (MaxY+4) div 8, 'W' );
```

The loop reading the screen pixels, however, does not require the addition to the *MaxY* variable, the <= specification is sufficient to ensure that all of the screen is read. Now, the loop proceeds as previously explained except that the horizontal pixel positions read are at *MaxX–j*, where *j* is looping from *0* to *MaxX*. This inversion is necessary; otherwise, the printed result would be a mirror image of the screen.

```
for i := 0 to MaxY div 8 do
begin
    m := 0;
    for k := 0 to 7 do
    begin
        m := m SHL 1;
        if GetPixel(MaxX-j-1,i*8+k) <> 0
            then inc( m );
    end;
    write( Lst, char( m ) );
end;
write( Lst, GrEnds );
end;
end;
```

The third mode is the Grayscale mode. This operates almost exactly the same as the Landscape mode except that a resolution of 300 dpi is used and each screen pixel is mapped to a 4x4 grayscale image.

```
GRAYSCALE:
begin
    XPrn := 1000.0;
    YPrn := 1000.0;
    PrStep := 2.4 * AspR;
    write( Lst, GrInit, '300R' );
```

The grayscale mapping is accomplished by adding a loop to read each screen pixel four times for four separate print lines.

```
for j := 0 to MaxX do
for p := 0 to 3 do
begin
    write( Lst, Esc, '&a',
            XPrn:Fmt( XPrn ):1, 'h',
            YPrn:Fmt( YPrn ):1, 'V' );
    YPrn := YPrn + PrStep;
```

Because only two screen pixels are read for each graphics character output to the printer, the length of the graphics string is specified as *MaxY/2* instead of *(MaxY+4)/8*.

```
write( Lst, ESC, '*r1A', ESC, '*b',
            MaxY div 2, 'W' );
for i := 0 to MaxY div 2 do
begin
    m := 0;
```

And *k* is looped from *0* to *1* while *m* is shifted left four places, then OR'd with the integer value returned by the SetGrayScale function for the current screen pixel.

```
               for k := 0 to 1 do
               begin
                  m := m SHL 4;
                  m := m OR SetGrayScale( p,
                       GetPixel( MaxX-j, i*2+k ) );
               end;
               write( Lst, char( m ) );
            end;
            write( Lst, GrEnds );
         end;
      end;
   end;   { case }
```

The final housekeeping, sending a form feed command and resetting the printer to its default state, is reserved until the switch statement is ended, instead of duplicating this instruction set for each of the three modes.

```
   write( Lst, #$0C, ESC, '&l0', ESC, '(8U',
          ESC, '(sp10h12vsb3T', ESC, '&l1H' );
end;
```

Selecting Multiple Copies on Output

One convenient option has not been provided in the LJ_Graph utility: the provision to print multiple copies of a screen image. This provision can be very simple. Before sending the final command set (the sequence beginning with *#$0C*), include the following command line:

```
write( Lst, ESC, '&l%dX', NumberOfCopies );
```

The parameter *Number_Of_Copies* can be any value from *1* to *99* and the laserjet will print the specified quantity from a single download.

The Fmt Function

The Fmt function accepts a double value, returning an integer value to specify the number of integer places for a numerical string. The integer variable *Width* begins with a value of *6* providing for four integer places, one decimal character, and one place following the decimal.

If the value of *MsgPos* is less than 1,000, *width* is decremented, then *MsgPos* is tested again against values of 100 and 10. The final value for *Width* is returned to the calling function.

```
function Fmt( MsgPos : real ): integer;
   var
      Width : integer;
   begin
      Width := 6;
      if( MsgPos < 1000.0 ) then dec( Width );
      if( MsgPos < 100.0 )  then dec( Width );
      if( MsgPos < 10.0 )   then dec( Width );
      Fmt := Width;
   end;
```

The SetGrayScale Function

The SetGrayScale function is called with two parameters: *ScanLine*, that specifies which of the four scan lines is being created for the current pixel; and *GPixel*, the color palette number read from the current screen pixel.

```
function SetGrayScale( ScanLine, GPixel : integer ):
integer;
   var
       Gray : integer;
   begin
```

The local variable *gray* is initially set to zero. When SetGrayScale is finished, the value in *gray* will be returned to the calling function.

```
       Gray := 0;
```

Provision is made here for a four-step gray scale for use with CGA low-resolution color modes (see Figure 17-6). Since *GPixel* for CGA modes can only have values from *0* to *3*, only two tests are required for each *ScanLine* and, if *GPixel* AND'd with the test value provides a true Boolean result, the variable *gray* is OR'd with the appropriate bit map value.

Notice that the values OR'd with *gray* for each case total 15. If both tests for each case are True, then the returned *gray* value will have all bits set and the plotted value will be a black square. If only one of the tests returns TRUE, one of the two gray-shade values will be returned; if neither returns TRUE, the plotted value will be a blank square for the tested pixel.

```
         if ( GraphDriver = CGA ) and
            ( GraphMode <> CGAHI ) then
         begin
            case ScanLine of
               0: begin
                     if GPixel AND 1 <> 0 then
                        Gray := Gray OR  9;
                     if GPixel AND 2 <> 0 then
                        Gray := Gray OR  6;
```

```
                    end;
            1:  begin
                    if GPixel AND 1 <> 0 then
                        Gray := Gray OR  4;
                    if GPixel AND 2 <> 0 then
                        Gray := Gray OR 11;
                end;
            2:  begin
                    if GPixel AND 1 <> 0 then
                        Gray := Gray OR  2;
                    if GPixel AND 2 <> 0 then
                        Gray := Gray OR 13;
                end;
            3:  begin
                    if GPixel AND 1 <> 0 then
                        Gray := Gray OR  9;
                    if GPixel AND 2 <> 0 then
                        Gray := Gray OR  6;
                end;
        end; { case }
    end else
```

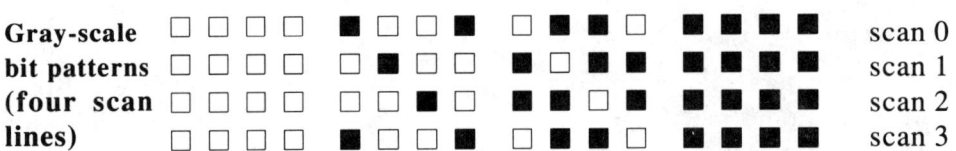

Figure 17-6: Bit Patterns for 4-Level Grayscale Palette

If the GraphDriver is not CGA, the 16-shade grayscale is created. Again, notice that the sum of the values for each test, except *case 3*, is 15. Since one dot in the gray-scale pattern is not used by any of the 16 gray shades, *case 3* omits the value 8, for a total of 7 (bits 4, 2, and 1).

In each test, only one bit in *GPixel* is used. Look back at Figure 17-5 and notice that the gray-scale palettes for 1, 2, 4, and 8 are the critical dot patterns used here and all of the other dot patterns are a combination of these four, allowing a very simple decision tree to create 16 progressive dot patterns.

```
        begin
            case ScanLine of
                0:  begin
                        if GPixel AND 4 <> 0 then
                            Gray := Gray OR  5;
                        if GPixel AND 8 <> 0 then
```

```
                    Gray := Gray OR 10;
              end;
         1: begin
              if GPixel AND 1 <> 0 then
                 Gray := Gray OR  2;
              if GPixel AND 2 <> 0 then
                 Gray := Gray OR  8;
              if GPixel AND 8 <> 0 then
                 Gray := Gray OR  5;
              end;
         2: begin
              if GPixel AND 4 <> 0 then
                 Gray := Gray OR  5;
              if GPixel AND 8 <> 0 then
                 Gray := Gray OR 10;
              end;
         3: begin
              if GPixel AND 2 <> 0 then
                 Gray := Gray OR  2;
              if GPixel AND 8 <> 0 then
                 Gray := Gray OR  5;
              end;
       end; { case }
end;
```

Next, if the flag variable *Negative* has been set, the bit pattern in *gray* is XOR'd with 0Fh to invert the results. This changes the default gray-scale that begins with the lightest pattern for a palette entry of 0 and proceeds to return the darkest pattern for a palette entry of 15, to a gray-scale that returns a dark gray-scale pattern for low palette colors and a blank gray-scale pattern for White (palette entry 15).

```
     if Negative then Gray := Gray XOR $0F;
```

Finally, the value in *gray* is returned to the calling function.

```
     SetGrayScale := Gray;
end;
```

The PrintPause Function

The PrintPause function is a simple utility to write a screen prompt and wait for a key response to select one of three output modes supported by LJGraph.

```
procedure PrintPause;
   var
      Ch   : char;
      Done : boolean;
   begin
      DetectGraph( GraphDriver, GraphMode );
```

```pascal
        Done := False;
        Negative := Invert;
        while not Done do
        begin
           PromptLine( 'Enter <P>ortrait, <L>andscape, ' +
              '<G>rayscale — any other key to exit ...' );
           while KeyPressed do Ch := ReadKey;
           Ch := ReadKey;
           PutImage( 0, PromptPos, ScrnImage, CopyPut );
           case upcase( Ch ) of
              'P' : LJGraph( PORTRAIT );
              'L' : LJGraph( LANDSCAPE );
              'G' : LJGraph( GRAYSCALE );
              else Done := True;
           end; { case }
           dispose( ScrnImage );
        end;
   end;
```

If you would like to use this prompt utility in another application, several approaches can be used without overwriting the existing screen.

One method would be to use the GetImage function to save the area of the screen that the prompt will overwrite, then use PutImage to restore the original screen before calling LJGraph or exiting. Another approach is to switch active video pages, write the prompt information on the alternate page and return to the original screen.

The PromptLine Function

The PromptLine function should already be familiar. PromptLine is called with a message string, draws a box at the bottom of the screen, centers the message in the box, and returns to the calling function for further action.

```pascal
procedure PromptLine( Msg : string );
   var
      ChrHt, MaxX, MaxY : integer;
   begin
      MaxX := GetMaxX;
      MaxY := GetMaxY;
      SetColor( BLACK );
      SetTextStyle( DefaultFont, HorizDir, 1 );
      SetTextJustify( CenterText, TopText );
      ChrHt := TextHeight( 'H' );
      PromptPos := MaxY - ( ChrHt + 4 );
      GetMem( ScrnImage,
              ImageSize( 0, PromptPos, MaxX, MaxY ) );
      GetImage( 0, PromptPos, MaxX, MaxY, ScrnImage^ );
      Bar( 0, PromptPos, MaxX, MaxY );
```

```
            Rectangle( 0, PromptPos, MaxX, MaxY );
            OutTextXY( MaxX div 2, MaxY - ( ChrHt + 2 ), Msg );
      end;
end.
```

More on Colors and Color Mapping

A caveat is in order here. Color, like beauty, is largely in the eye of the beholder. We may well differ in our perceptions of color and color values. You are perfectly free to rewrite or adapt the following color translation suggestions to better fit your own chromatic perceptions.

True-Color Gray Scale Palettes

In the GraySCALE option used in LJ_Graph, the gray-scale palette was mapped according to the palette item numbers assigned to the screen pixels, and not by the actual screen colors. But since the default palette colors are already arranged more or less in order of intensity, this is a minor discrepancy in most cases. If you need a more accurate color to gray-scale mapping, there are several possible approaches.

One approach would be to read the palette color values (not the palette item numbers), order the color values assigned to the palette entries, and create a color-to-gray-scale translation map. The drawback to this approach, unfortunately, is that these color values do not reflect actual color (visual) intensities and a secondary translation table would have to be manually prepared to provide some basis for ordering. An easier approach is to decipher the palette color values and create an intensity value for each color, then order the color-to-gray mapping according to these intensities.

To attempt this, however, some basis is necessary to say which color is more intense than another. Of the three primary colors (red, blue, and green), the human eye perceives green most strongly, red next, and blue the least. A gray-scale formula reflecting the perception of the human eye yields: *gray = 0.30 * R + 0.59 * G + 0.11 * B.*

But the EGA/VGA color palette values have two flags for each color, primary **R**ed and secondary **r**ed, primary **G**reen, and secondary **g**reen and primary **B**lue and secondary **b**lue, so a formula is needed that can calculate a gray value from six flags (colors) instead of only three.

If the secondary colors are arbitrarily assigned $1/3$ of the base value and the primary colors are assigned $2/3$, then a new formula yields: *gray = 0.30 * (r + 2 * R) / 3 + 0.59 * (g + 2 * G) / 3 + 0.11 * (b + 2 * B) / 3.*

Figure 17-7 shows gray-scale percentages generated using this formula. The default palette EGA/VGA colors are labeled with the actual color values appearing in the left column.

Figure 17-7: True Color Grayscale Conversion

VALUE	r	R	g	G	b	B	%	EGA COLOR
0	0	0	0	0	0	0	0	Black
8	0	0	1	0	0	0	37	
1	0	0	0	0	0	1	73	Blue
32	1	0	0	0	0	0	100	
9	0	0	1	0	0	1	110	
40	1	0	1	0	0	0	137	
33	1	0	0	0	0	1	173	
16	0	1	0	0	0	0	197	
4	0	0	0	1	0	0	200	Red
41	1	0	1	0	0	1	210	
24	0	1	1	0	0	0	233	
12	0	0	1	1	0	0	237	
17	0	1	0	0	0	1	270	
5	0	0	0	1	0	1	273	Magenta
48	1	1	0	0	0	0	297	
36	1	0	0	1	0	0	300	
25	0	1	1	0	0	1	307	
13	0	0	1	1	0	1	310	
56	1	1	1	0	0	0	333	DarkGray
44	1	0	1	1	0	0	337	
49	1	1	0	0	0	1	370	
37	1	0	0	1	0	1	373	
2	0	0	0	0	1	0	393	Green
20	0	1	0	1	0	0	397	Brown
57	1	1	1	0	0	1	407	LightBlue
45	1	0	1	1	0	1	410	
10	0	0	1	0	1	0	430	
28	0	1	1	1	0	0	433	
3	0	0	0	0	1	1	467	Cyan
21	0	1	0	1	0	1	470	
34	1	0	0	0	1	0	493	
52	1	1	0	1	0	0	497	
11	0	0	1	0	1	1	503	
29	0	1	1	1	0	1	507	
42	1	0	1	0	1	0	530	
60	1	1	1	1	0	0	533	LightRed
35	1	0	0	0	1	1	567	
53	1	1	0	1	0	1	570	
18	0	1	0	0	1	0	590	
6	0	0	0	1	1	0	593	
43	1	0	1	0	1	1	603	
61	1	1	1	1	0	1	607	LightMagenta
26	0	1	1	0	1	0	627	
14	0	0	1	1	1	0	630	
19	0	1	0	0	1	1	663	
7	0	0	0	1	1	1	667	LightGray
50	1	1	0	0	1	0	690	
38	1	0	0	1	1	0	693	
27	0	1	1	0	1	1	700	
15	0	0	1	1	1	1	703	
58	1	1	1	0	1	0	727	LightGreen
46	1	0	1	1	1	0	730	
51	1	1	0	0	1	1	763	
39	1	0	0	1	1	1	767	
22	0	1	0	1	1	0	790	
59	1	1	1	0	1	1	800	LightCyan
47	1	0	1	1	1	1	803	
30	0	1	1	1	1	0	827	
23	0	1	0	1	1	1	863	
54	1	1	0	1	1	0	890	
31	0	1	1	1	1	1	900	
62	1	1	1	1	1	0	927	Yellow
55	1	1	0	1	1	1	963	
63	1	1	1	1	1	1	1000	White

Examining the gray-scale order, notice that the sequence of gray values does not match the sequence generated by the color values, nor the sequence of grays generated by the default conversion in the SetGrayScale function. Here the gray sequence is strictly according to perception intensity and DarkGray falls midway in the low intensity colors between Magenta and Cyan, just as might be expected of an average gray tone. Similarly, the LightGray color falls between the LightMagenta and LightGreen shades and, you might also note, the LightBlue appears just slightly lighter than Brown.

As mentioned earlier, there is no hard and fast rule saying that this is the only gray-scale conversion formula possible and, if this does not suit your application or perceptions, please feel free to experiment with the conversion formula. One hint: the simplest method of experimentation would be to use a good spreadsheet, create your formula, apply it to the rRgGbB color bits and have the spreadsheet sort the results for your examination.

If all else fails, see Chapter 18.

EpGraph.PAS / EpGraph.TPU

```pascal
              {==================================}
              {   graphics output driver for     }
              {   dot matrix (Epson) printers    }
              {==================================}
unit EPGRAPH;

INTERFACE

uses Graph, Printer;

const
   PORTRAIT  = 0;
   LANDSCAPE = 1;
   ESC = #$1B;

procedure PrintGraph( Mode, Direction : integer );

IMPLEMENTATION

procedure PrintGraph;
   var
      i, j, k, m, Msb, Lsb, MaxX, MaxY : integer;
   begin
      MaxX := GetMaxX;
      MaxY := GetMaxY;
      SetViewPort( 0, 0, MaxX, MaxY, False );
      write( Lst, ESC,'A',#$07 );
                              { sets Line spacing to 7/72 inch }
      case Direction of
         PORTRAIT: begin
            Lsb := MaxX AND $00FF;      { MaxX modulo 256 }
            Msb := MaxX SHR 8;          { (int) MaxX / 256 }
            for j := 0 to MaxY div 8 do
            begin
               write( Lst, ESC, char( Mode ),
                      char( Lsb ), char( Msb ) );
```

```pascal
            for i := 0 to MaxX do
            begin
               m := 0;
               for k := 0 to 7 do
               begin
                  m := m SHL 1;
                                    { shift m left one bit   }
                  if GetPixel( i, j*8+k ) <> 0
                     then inc( m );
                                    { if pixel on, bit on    }
               end;
               write( Lst, char( m ) );
            end;
            write( Lst, #$0D, #$0A );
                           { use CR/LF codes vs. \n flag }
         end;
      end;
      LANDSCAPE: begin
         Lsb := MaxY AND $00FF;       {   MaxY modulo 256 }
         Msb := MaxY SHR 8;           {   (int) MaxY / 256 }
         j := 0;
         repeat
            write( Lst, ESC, '*', char( Mode ),
                   char( Lsb ), char( Msb ) );
            for i := MaxY downto 0 do
            begin
               m := 0;
               for k := 0 to 7 do
               begin
                  m := m SHL 1;
                                    { shift m left one bit }
                  if GetPixel( j+k, i ) <> 0
                     then inc( m );
                                    { if pixel on, set bit }
               end;
               write( Lst, char( m ) );
            end;
            write( Lst, #$0D, #$0A );
                           { use CR/LF codes vs writeln }
            inc( j, 8 );
         until j >= MaxX-1;
      end;
   end; { case }
   write( Lst, #$0C );       { form feed to advance paper }
end;

{ end EP-GRAPH.PAS }

end.
```

LjGraph.PAS / LjGraph.TPU

```
{==============================}
{     graphics output driver   }
{     for laserjet printers    }
{==============================}

unit LJGRAPH;

INTERFACE

const
    PORTRAIT  = 0;              { definitions for PrintGraph }
    LANDSCAPE = 1;              { image orientation          }
    GRAYSCALE = 2;              { and color to gray scale    }
var
    ScrnImage : pointer;
    PromptPos : integer;
    Negative  : boolean;        { flag for gray scale order  }
    GraphDriver, GraphMode : integer;

procedure PrintPause( Invert : boolean );

IMPLEMENTATION

uses GRAPH, PRINTER, CRT;

procedure PromptLine( Msg : string );
    var
        ChrHt, MaxX, MaxY : integer;
    begin
        MaxX := GetMaxX;
        MaxY := GetMaxY;
        SetColor( BLACK );
        SetTextStyle( DefaultFont, HorizDir, 1 );
        SetTextJustify( CenterText, TopText );
        ChrHt := TextHeight( 'H' );           { get text height }
        PromptPos := MaxY - ( ChrHt + 4 );
        GetMem( ScrnImage,
                ImageSize( 0, PromptPos, MaxX, MaxY ) );
        GetImage( 0, PromptPos, MaxX, MaxY, ScrnImage^ );
        Bar( 0, PromptPos, MaxX, MaxY );
        Rectangle( 0, PromptPos, MaxX, MaxY );
        OutTextXY( MaxX div 2, MaxY - ( ChrHt + 2 ), Msg );
    end;

function Fmt( MsgPos : real ): integer;
    var
        Width : integer;
    begin
        Width := 6;
```

```pascal
              if( MsgPos < 1000.0 ) then dec( Width );
              if( MsgPos < 100.0 )  then dec( Width );
              if( MsgPos < 10.0 )   then dec( Width );
              Fmt := Width;
           end;
    function SetGrayScale( ScanLine, GPixel : integer ):
                integer;
       var
          Gray : integer;
       begin
          Gray := 0;
          if ( GraphDriver = CGA ) and
             ( GraphMode <> CGAHI ) then
             begin
                case ScanLine of
                   0: begin
                         if GPixel AND 1 <> 0 then
                             Gray := Gray OR  9;        { bits 1.1. }
                         if GPixel AND 2 <> 0 then
                             Gray := Gray OR  6;        { bits .1.1 }
                      end;
                   1: begin
                         if GPixel AND 1 <> 0 then
                             Gray := Gray OR  4;        { bits ...1 }
                         if GPixel AND 2 <> 0 then
                             Gray := Gray OR 11;        { bits 111. }
                      end;
                   2: begin
                         if GPixel AND 1 <> 0 then
                             Gray := Gray OR  2;        { bits 1... }
                         if GPixel AND 2 <> 0 then
                             Gray := Gray OR 13;        { bits .111 }
                      end;
                   3: begin
                         if GPixel AND 1 <> 0 then
                             Gray := Gray OR  9;        { bits .1.1 }
                         if GPixel AND 2 <> 0 then
                             Gray := Gray OR  6;        { bits 1.1. }
                      end;
                end; { case }
             end else
             begin
                case ScanLine of
                   0: begin
                         if GPixel AND 4 <> 0 then
                             Gray := Gray OR  5;        { bits .1.1 }
                         if GPixel AND 8 <> 0 then
```

```
                        Gray := Gray OR 10;        { bits 1.1. }
                end;
            1: begin
                   if GPixel AND 1 <> 0 then
                        Gray := Gray OR  2;        { bits ..1. }
                   if GPixel AND 2 <> 0 then
                        Gray := Gray OR  8;        { bits 1... }
                   if GPixel AND 8 <> 0 then
                        Gray := Gray OR  5;        { bits .1.1 }
                end;
            2: begin
                   if GPixel AND 4 <> 0 then
                        Gray := Gray OR  5;        { bits .1.1 }
                   if GPixel AND 8 <> 0 then
                        Gray := Gray OR 10;        { bits 1.1. }
                end;
            3: begin
                   if GPixel AND 2 <> 0 then
                        Gray := Gray OR  2;        { bits ..1. }
                   if GPixel AND 8 <> 0 then
                        Gray := Gray OR  5;        { bits .1.1 }
                end;
          end; { case }
      end;
      if Negative then Gray := Gray XOR $0F;
                                    { bit-inverts gray scale }
      SetGrayScale := Gray;
   end;

procedure LJGraphic( Mode: integer );
   const
      ESC = #$1B;
      GrEnds = ESC + '*rB';
      GrInit = ESC + 'E' + ESC + '&l1H' + ESC + '&l0' +
               ESC + '*p0X' + ESC + '*p0Y' + ESC + '*t';
   var
      i, j, k, p, q, MaxX, MaxY : integer;
      xasp, yasp : word;
      XPrn, YPrn, PrStep, AspR : real;
      m : integer;
   begin
      PutImage( 0, PromptPos, ScrnImage^, CopyPut );
      MaxX := GetMaxX + 1;
      MaxY := GetMaxY + 1;
      GetAspectRatio( xasp, yasp );
      AspR := xasp / yasp;
      SetViewPort( 0, 0, MaxX, MaxY, False );
      case Mode of
```

```pascal
        PORTRAIT:
          begin
             XPrn := 690.0;
                        { initial page print positions }
             YPrn := 500.0;
             PrStep := 7.2 / AspR;
                        { adjust to match screen image }
             write( Lst, GrInit, '100R' );
                        { select 100 DPI resolution }
             for j := 0 to MaxY do
             begin
                write( Lst, ESC,'&a',
                       XPrn:Fmt( XPrn ):1, 'h',
                       YPrn:Fmt( YPrn ):1, 'V' );
                YPrn := YPrn + PrStep;
                write( Lst, ESC, '*r1A', ESC, '*b',
                       MaxX div 8, 'W' );
                for i := 0 to MaxX div 8 do
                begin
                   m := 0;
                   for k := 0 to 7 do
                   begin
                      m := m SHL 1;
                                 { shift m left one bit }
                      if GetPixel( i*8+k, j ) <> 0
                         then inc( m );
                                 { if pixel on, bit on }
                   end;
                   write( Lst, char( m ) );
                end;
                write( Lst, GrEnds );
             end;
          end;
        LANDSCAPE:
          begin
             XPrn := 1000.0;
                        { initial page print positions }
             YPrn := 1000.0;
             PrStep := 9.6 * AspR;
                        { adjust to match screen image }
             write( Lst, GrInit, '75R' );
                        { select 75 DPI resolution }
             for j := 0 to MaxX-1 do
             begin
                write( Lst, ESC, '&a',
                       XPrn:Fmt( XPrn ):1, 'h',
                       YPrn:Fmt( YPrn ):1, 'V' );
                YPrn := YPrn + PrStep;
```

```
            write( Lst, ESC, '*r1A', ESC, '*b',
                   (MaxY+4) div 8, 'W' );
            for i := 0 to MaxY div 8 do
            begin
               m := 0;
               for k := 0 to 7 do
               begin
                  m := m SHL 1;
                              { shift m left one bit }
                  if GetPixel(MaxX-j-1,i*8+k) <> 0
                     then inc( m );
                              { if pixel on, bit on  }
               end;
               write( Lst, char( m ) );
            end;
            write( Lst, GrEnds );
         end;
      end;
GRAYSCALE:
   begin
      XPrn := 1000.0;
                  { initial page print positions }
      YPrn := 1000.0;
      PrStep := 2.4 * AspR;
                  { adjust to match screen image }
      write( Lst, GrInit, '300R' );
                  { select 300 DPI resolution }
      for j := 0 to MaxX do
      for p := 0 to 3 do
      begin
         write( Lst, Esc, '&a',
                XPrn:Fmt( XPrn ):1, 'h',
                YPrn:Fmt( YPrn ):1, 'V' );
         YPrn := YPrn + PrStep;
         write( Lst, ESC, '*r1A', ESC, '*b',
                MaxY div 2, 'W' );
         for i := 0 to MaxY div 2 do
         begin
            m := 0;
            for k := 0 to 1 do
            begin
               m := m SHL 4;
                           { shift m left four bits }
               m := m OR SetGrayScale( p,
                     GetPixel( MaxX-j, i*2+k ) );
            end;
            write( Lst, char( m ) );
         end;
```

```pascal
                    write( Lst, GrEnds );
                end;
            end;
        end;   { case }
        write( Lst, #$0C, ESC, '&l0', ESC, '(8U',
               ESC, '(sp10h12vsb3T', ESC, '&l1H' );
                                          { close operations }
    end;
procedure PrintPause;
    var
        Ch : char;
        Done : boolean;
    begin
        DetectGraph( GraphDriver, GraphMode );
        Done := False;
        Negative := Invert;
        while not Done do
        begin
            PromptLine( 'Enter <P>ortrait, <L>andscape, ' +
                ' <G>rayscale — any other key to exit ...' );
            while KeyPressed do Ch := ReadKey;
            Ch := ReadKey;
            PutImage( 0, PromptPos, ScrnImage, CopyPut );
            case upcase( Ch ) of
                'P' : LJGraphic( PORTRAIT );
                'L' : LJGraphic( LANDSCAPE );
                'G' : LJGraphic( GRAYSCALE );
                else Done := True;
            end; { case }
            dispose( ScrnImage );
        end;
    end;
end.
```

CHAPTER 18

Graphics Plotter Output

In Chapter 17 I showed how a graphics screen could be output to a printer (either dot-matrix or laserjet). A great deal of the demo programs in this book, however, have been using colors, while the printer outputs have only been black-on-white or at best, gray-scaled. So, what about color output devices?

Aside from cameras, which do not depend on programming, only two types of devices are currently available for recording color images from computer screens: color printers and color plotters. Alternatively, of course, you can use a graphics screen capture utility and then use a graphics utility such as PC Paintbrush, Corel Draw, or Harvard Graphics to prepare color separations for printing.

Color Printers

Previously, color printers, which use multicolored ribbons to create color images, had been relatively limited in resolution and in the range of colors that can be created. Since several different models are available (though none are common) and since no standard presently exists for these devices, I am not going to cover them in much detail. I should say though that the dot-matrix driver can be easily modified for color recognition (see the gray-scale options in Chapter 16 and the Match_Color procedure in the PLOTTER unit in this chapter) and plotting—within its limited reproduction capabilities.

More recently, Hewlett-Packard has introduced the Color Jet printer which offers superior color capabilities—and is certainly faster than a color plotter—but these also are not yet common. Still, if your requirements include large numbers of color prints, this may be an alternative to consider.

Color Plotters

More commonly available color output devices are color plotters such as the Hewlett-Packard ColorPro which uses an eight-pen carousel (seven colors plus black). Alternatively, a monocolor plotter can be used if provision is made to swap pen colors as appropriate (or the color plotter's color range can be extended with provision for swapping pen carousels). The initial assumption here will be a plotter with an eight-pen carousel using, by virtue of being an industry standard, the HP Graphics Language instruction set.

Caveat

The color plotter was not designed nor intended to be used as a bit-mapped output device, but it comes closer to fitting this application than does anything else presently available. With a certain amount of care and accommodation, it is capable of providing hard copy color reproduction, but it does so with two principal drawbacks: slow operation (sometimes very slow) and limited color correspondence.

If you are already familiar with plotter operation, you may skip this explanation, but for those who are not, here's how a plotter works.

Plotter Operation

Plotters use special pens (hard-nib, fiber-tip, or roller-ball) to draw images directly on a sheet of paper or transparent film. Some plotters move the pen along two axes while the paper remains fixed on a flat platen (flatbed). Others move the pen along one axis and the paper along the second axis (gritwheel). The simplest plotters can use only one pen at a time, requiring manual assistance to change drawing colors and others hold 3, 4, 6, or 8 pens (usually in a carousel) and select pens according to software instructions.

Because the plotter is a mechanical device, physically moving a drawing pen across a sheet of paper and raising and lowering the pen to draw a single line at a time, the plotter is slower than other graphics output devices.

Likewise, plotter resolutions vary, ranging from resolutions of 0.00008 inch to a more common resolution of 0.004 inch with repeatability (accuracy of registration on subsequent plots) usually falling in the +\–0.004 inch range.

In operation, the plotter is designed to draw a line between two points specified by coordinate pairs (from xstart/ystart to xend/yend). This line is drawn simultaneously by moving the pen along both axes (or by moving both pen and paper simultaneously) and the resulting line is a direct (analog) output as opposed to the stepped-pixel (digital) line created on a CRT (or a laserjet).

The Hewlett-Packard Graphics Language (HPGL) provides an instruction set for communicating with the plotter to create images directly (not by recreating screen images) and, *for most applications*, is both faster and smoother than using a plotter screen dump. For more information on HP plotter capabilities and the HPGL instruction set, refer to the *HP ColorPro Graphics Plotter Programming Manual*, available from Hewlett-Packard.

Plotting The CRT

It isn't always practical to program an image directly. To map a CRT image to a plotter, individual screen pixels are recreated as a series of short lines, using one pen (drawing color) at a time and repeating the operation for each color used in the reproduction. Thus, for an EGA/VGA screen filled with an essentially random color dot pattern, a complete screen output in full color can require four to six hours (and this using a relatively *fast* plotter).

This is, however, the worst case example. For more common displays, by drawing adjacent pixels of a single color as a single continuous line, a full screen display can be recreated, in color, in only 30 to 45 minutes.

The PLOTTER utility was tested during development using the screen image generated by the COLORCUB demo program. The first working version of the PLOTTER utility required two hours, nine minutes, and 33 seconds to complete. With refinements, the same image can now be completed in a mere 32 minutes.

Plotter Colors

The second drawback mentioned in using a color plotter to copy a screen image, was a limited color palette on the plotter. Using the ColorPro plotter, 10 pen colors are available (yellow, orange, red, red-violet, violet, blue, aqua, green, brown, and black) and pen colors can be combined to yield some additional hues.

Because the pen carousel can only hold eight pens, the yellow, red-violet, red, green, blue, violet, brown and black pens were chosen for demonstration and should be inserted in the carousel in this order to match the instructions in the PLOTTER utility. The principal colors and color combinations are shown in Table 18-1.

Several of the possible color combinations are not particularly useful in emulating EGA/VGA palette colors. Quite a few of these combinations result in muddy hues and others do not match hues in the EGA/VGA default color palette.

Table 18-1: Pen Color Combinations Using Plotter

PEN[1] COLORS	YELLOW	RED/VIOLET	RED	GREEN	BLUE	VIOLET	BROWN	BLACK
Yellow	Yellow							
Red/Violet	*	LtMagenta			Resulting Colors			
Red	LtRed	*	Red					
Green	LtGreen	*	*	Green				
Blue	*Green*	*Blue*	*	*Cyan*	LtBlue			
Violet	*	*	*	*Blue*	*Blue*	Magenta		
Brown	*Brown*	*Violet*	*Rust*	*	*Grey*	*	Brown	
Black	**Black**	**Black**	**Black**	**Black**	**Black**	**Black**	**Black**	**Black**

1. Bold color names are approximations of default EGA/VGA palette. *Italic color names* are hues which do not correspond to any named colors in the palette. Asterisks indicate unnamed (or unnameable) color combinations.

Also, I have not been able to create good plotter equivalents for all colors. In the PLOTTER utility, the EGA/VGA default palette is mapped as shown in Table 18-2.

Table 18-2: Mapping EGA/VGA Colors to Plotter Colors

EGA/VGA COLORS	PEN COLORS	EGA/VGA COLORS	PEN COLORS
Yellow	yellow	LightBlue	blue
LightRed	yellow, red	Blue	blue, violet
LightGreen	yellow, green	DarkGray	blue, brown
LightMagenta	red-violet	LightGray	blue, brown
Red	red	Magenta	violet
Green	green	Brown	brown
Cyan	green, blue	White	black
LightCyan	green, blue		

As you can see, the Cyan and LightCyan, and the DarkGray and LightGray hues are identical. If you like, yellow can be added to the two lighter colors, but this will not greatly differentiate them. Also, the LightMagenta (red-violet) and Red (red) do not appear clearly separated.

White (on the screen) is mapped to black on paper while the screen background (Black) is not mapped at all. You can change this and experiment with your own color combinations, you may well find a better set of colors to fit a specific application.

Ideally, better color combinations could be created if a better initial set of pen colors—beginning with lighter primary colors—was available. With the currently available pen colors, however, the hues shown are the best possible. The present order of pen colors is chosen so the lightest colors are drawn first and the light pens do not become contaminated by darker inks picked up from the paper.

Selecting The Plotter Serial Interface

The HP ColorPro plotter (and many others) uses a serial interface for communication. On the ColorPro, a dip switch on the back of the unit (between the power and RS-232C connectors) is used to select the serial baud rate, stop bits, and parity information. The dip switch settings are shown in Table 18-3.

Table 18-3: HP Color Pro Switch Settings

BAUD RATE	1 STOP BIT				2 STOP BITS			
	B1	B2	B3	B4	B1	B2	B3	B4
75	-	-	-	-	1	0	0	0
110	-	-	-	-	0	1	0	0
150	1	1	0	0	-	-	-	-
200	0	0	1	0	-	-	-	-
300	1	0	1	0	1	1	0	1
600	0	1	1	0	0	0	1	1
1200	1	1	1	0	1	0	1	1
2400	0	0	0	1	0	1	1	1
4800	1	0	0	1	1	1	1	1
9600	0	1	0	1	0	0	0	0

PARITY	S1	S2	
none	0	0	(Space parity)
none	0	1	(Mark parity)
even	1	0	
odd	1	1	

And a Serial Curiosity

For reasons that I cannot explain all HP serial devices use a non-standard RS-232C serial port connection. Unfortunately, this small factor *is not* explained in any of the HP manuals, but is left to your powers of deductive reasoning. If you have purchased your serial cables from HP, then they should work fine with HP devices, but not with any other serial equipment such as modems, and standard dot-matrix devices.

One clue is provided, however, an unexplained diagram for a dummy modem appearing in an appendix in the user's manual.

And the special serial interface cabling required does correspond to the familiar "dummy" or null-modem cable. If you do not look forward to manufacturing a null-modem cable, a simple null-modem connector can be purchased at your local computer or electronic supply store. See Figure 18-1 for a detail of the cable.

Figure 18-1: RS-232C Dummy (Null) Modem

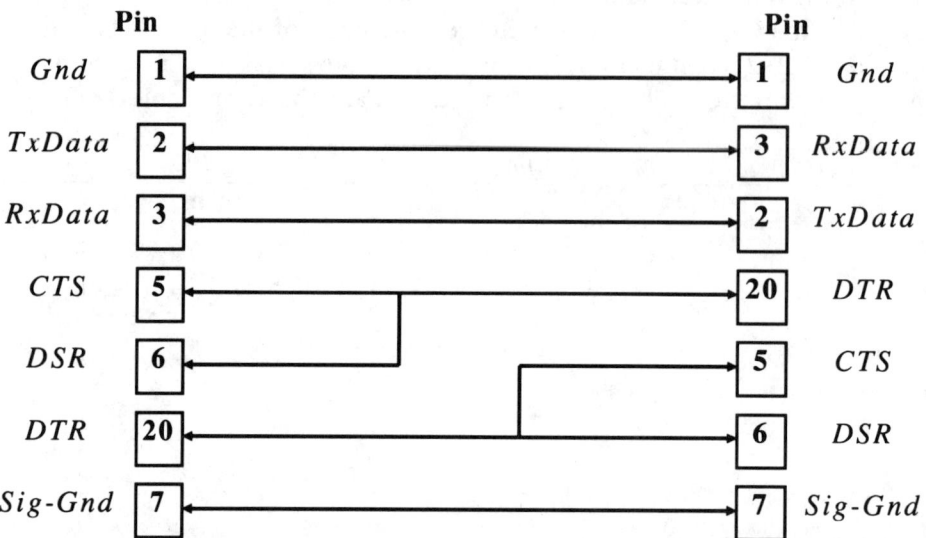

Using The PLOTTER Utility

To use the Plotter unit, the CallPlotter procedure following accepts a port argument and four screen coordinates to specify the area that will be output to the plotter.

```
procedure CallPlotter( SelectPort : word;
       XStart, YStart, XEnd, YEnd : integer );
begin
   if InitPort( SelectPort ) AND InitComm  0 then
   begin
      InitPlotter;
      PlotScreen( XStart, YStart, XEnd, YEnd );
      ClosePlotter;
   end;
end;
```

No provisions are included to test errors in the port or screen coordinates passed as arguments. This procedure is not included in the Plotter unit.

Communicating With The Serial Port

While Turbo Pascal provides predefined access for the standard ports (*LPT1*, *LPT2*, and *LPT3* for printer ports—parallel or PRN—and *stdin*, *COM1*, and *COM2* for serial ports), these do not allow you to direct communications to COM3 or COM4.

If you are like me, you probably already have the COM1 port (and maybe COM2) in use. While DOS will allow for the redirecting of your output to any of the ports, it is an awkward method of handling output.

Instead of worrying about these predefined output streams, the PLOTTER utility uses ROM BIOS calls to communicate directly with the serial port selected and definitions are provided for COM1, COM2, COM3, and COM4.

Before communications can be opened, the desired serial port must be initialized with the desired baud rate, parity, stop bits and word len (see Table 18-4). Normal settings for the ColorPro plotter are: 9600, none, 8 bits = 11100011 (E3h).

The InitPort function is called with an argument that selects the desired port and returns an unsigned integer showing the port status. The *InitComm* parameter is defined in the PLOTTER unit as *E3*h (see Table 18-4).

```
function InitPort( ActivePort : word ): word;
  begin
       Port := ActivePort;
       Regs.AX := InitComm;
       Regs.DX := ActivePort;
       Intr( $14, Regs );
       InitPort := Regs.AX;
  end;
```

Table 18-4: Serial Port Initialization Parameter Values

	BAUD RATE	PARITY	STOP BITS	WORD LEN
BITS	7,6,5,	4, 3	2,	1, 0
	000 = 110	00 = Space	0 = 1 Bit	00 = N/A
	001 = 150	01 = Odd	1 = 2 Bits	01 = N/A
	010 = 300	10 = Mark		10 = 7 Bits
	011 = 600	11 = Even		11 = 8 Bits
	100 = 1200			
	101 = 2400			
	110 = 4800			
	111 = 9600			

Initializing The Plotter

The InitPlotter procedure is used to set up values in order to map the screen to the plotter and to initialize the plotter for operation. Prior to initialization, the assumption is that the plotter has been turned on and loaded—operations that can only be executed manually from the plotter control panel.

When using the plotter, unlike the EPGraph and LJGraph utilities, no provisions are required to match the screen aspect to the device. The four parameters *XPlot1*, *YPlot1*, *XPlot2* and *YPlot2*, defined in the PLOTTER unit, match the active plot area to the physical screen proportions, while the *HStep* and *VStep* variables calculated in InitPlotter (using the *MaxX* and *MaxY* variables read from the system) adjust the plotter increments to match the screen aspect ratio within the plotting area.

```
procedure InitPlotter;
   var
      Buf1, Buf2 : string;
   begin
      MaxX := GetMaxX;
      MaxY := GetMaxY;
      HStep := XPlot2 / MaxX;
      VStep := YPlot2 / MaxY;
```

The WritePort procedure is first called to set the plotter to hardwire handshaking using the Escape-'P3' sequence. Several other handshaking methods and protocols are supported if needed, including XOn/XOff, ENQuiry/ACKnowledge and software checking handshakes (see the *HP ColorPro Programming Manual* for details).

```
      WritePort( ESC+'P3;' );
```

Next, the 'IN;' instruction is sent to set the plotter to its default conditions, cancelling any coordinate rotations, scaling, or other settings.

```
      WritePort( 'IN;' );
```

Finally, the 'SC' (scale) instruction is passed with the four predefined parameters setting up the P1 and P2 coordinate locations that define the corners of the active plotting area.

```
      str( XPlot1, Buf1 );
      str( YPlot1, Buf2 );
      Buf1 := 'SC '+ Buf1 + ', ' + Buf2 + ', ';
      str( XPlot2, Buf2 );
      Buf1 := Buf1 + Buf2 + ', ';
      str( YPlot2, Buf2 );
      Buf1 := Buf1 + Buf2 + '; ' + #$0D + #$0A;
      WritePort( Buf1 )
   end;
```

By default, the plotter expects all measurements to be in plotter units. A plotter unit (pu) is defined (for the ColorPro) as 0.025 mm or 0.00098 inches (40 pu = 1 mm or 1016 pu = 1 inch). Remember, however, that the plotter is only accurate to 0.004 inches or about four plotter units.

Plotting The Screen

The PlotScreen procedure is called with four parameters that select the screen area to be mapped to the plotter. The PlotScreen procedure begins by selecting a pen from the carousel, then reading the graphics screen by rows and columns, looking for pixels matching the pen selection. (The screen is read by column from left to right, each column being read from bottom to top.)

```
procedure PlotScreen( XStart, YStart, XEnd, YEnd: integer
);
    var
        x, y, Pen : integer;
        PenStat, Retrace : boolean;
        Buf1, Buf2 : string;
    begin
        XPlot1 := 0;
        YPlot1 := 0;
        XPlot2 := 10250;
        YPlot2 := 7479;
        for Pen := 1 to 8 do
        begin
            SelectPen( Pen );
            for x := 1 to MaxX do
            begin
                PenStat := FALSE;
                Retrace := TRUE;
                for y := MaxY downto 0 do
                begin
```

As long as the pen is up (*PenStat* = FALSE), PlotScreen begins by looking for a screen pixel that matches the current pen color (or which the current pen color is used to plot). When found, a plot absolute ('PA') command is sent with the plotter coordinates corresponding to the pixel coordinates, followed by a pen down ('PD') instruction. If the *Retrace* flag is TRUE, a brief delay is executed to allow time for the pen to move from its previous position.

The *Retrace* flag is reset at the beginning of each column scanned. The *YRef* variable is updated with the y-axis plot coordinates, with each pen up instruction and the delay is calculated according to the distance the pen is required to move on retrace. Finally, the pen status flag (*PenStat*) is set to TRUE.

```
                    if not PenStat and
                        MatchColor( Pen, GetPixel(x,y) ) then
                    begin
                        str( x * HStep :9:3, Buf1 );
                        str( ( MaxY - y ) * VStep :9:3, Buf2 );
                        WritePort( 'PA' + Buf1 + ',' + Buf2 +
                                    ';PD;' + #$0D + #$0A );
                        if Retrace then
                        begin
                            delay( round( abs( YRef -
                                    ( y * VStep ) ) ) div 10 );
                            Retrace := FALSE;
```

```
            end;
            PenStat := TRUE;
         end;
```

Now the scan continues, but this time it seeks a pixel that does not require the current pen color.

```
         if PenStat and
            not MatchColor( Pen, GetPixel(x,y) )
         then begin
            YRef := round( y * VStep );
            str( x * HStep :9:3, Buf1 );
            str( ( MaxY - ( y + 1 ) ) *
                    VStep :9:3, Buf2 );
            WritePort( 'PA' + Buf1 + ',' + Buf2 +
                       ';PD;' + #$0D + #$0A );
            PenStat := FALSE;
         end;
      end;
```

When found, the immediately preceding pixel location (which presumably, *did* use the current pen color) is used to send a second set of plotter coordinates, again using the plot absolute ('PA') instruction, but ending with a pen up ('PU') instruction and setting *PenStat* to FALSE. With this last instruction set completed, a line is drawn from the previous coordinate position to the present position. Note also that the *YRef* variable has received the plotter y-axis position that may or may not be used subsequently to provide a retrace delay.

If, on the current scan, no pixel is found that does not use the present pen color (the line extends to the top of the screen), instructions are provided to complete the line at this point.

```
      if PenStat then
      begin
         YRef := round( y * VStep );
         str( x * HStep :9:3, Buf1 );
         str( ( MaxY - ( y + 1 ) ) *
                 VStep :9:3, Buf2 );
         WritePort( 'PA' + Buf1 + ',' + Buf2 +
                    ';PD;' + #$0D + #$0A );
         PenStat := FALSE;
      end;
   end;
```

Finally, when the graphics screen has been completely scanned, the *SelectPen(0)* instruction returns the current pen to the carousel. The initial loop then proceeds to select the next pen in order and another scan begins.

```
      SelectPen( 0 );
   end;
end;
```

The SelectPen Procedure

The SelectPen procedure is called with one argument that indicates the desired pen number or with a zero argument that instructs the plotter to return the present pen (if any) to the carousel.

```
procedure SelectPen( Pen : integer );
   var
      Buffer : string;
   begin
      str( Pen:1, Buffer );
      WritePort( 'SP' + Buffer + ';' );
      if Pen <> 0 then delay( 5000 );
   end;
```

If a fresh pen is being selected from the carousel, a five-second delay is provided to allow time for the pickup. No delay is provided when a pen is being returned to the holder.

The MatchColor Function

The MatchColor function is called, with the current pen number an pixel value, and decides which screen pixel colors are plotted v pen color. If the pixel color (palette entry) matches the test current pen number, MatchColor returns TRUE; otherw turns FALSE.

```
function MatchColor( Pen, SColor: integer
   var
      Result : boolean;
   begin
      Result := False;
      case Pen of
         1: case SColor of
               Yellow, LightRed, LightGreen
                  Result := TRUE;
            end;
         2: if SColor = LightMagenta then Result
         3: case SColor of
               LightRed, Red : Result := TRUE;
            end;
         4: case SColor of
               LightCyan, Cyan,
               LightGreen, Green : Result := TRUE;
            end;
         5: case SColor of
               LightCyan, Cyan,
               LightBlue, Blue,
               LightGray, DarkGray : Result := TRUE;
```

```
              end;
        6 : case SColor of
                Magenta, Blue : Result := TRUE;
            end;
        7 : case SColor of
                Brown, LightGray, DarkGray :
                    Result := TRUE;
            end;
        8 : if SColor = White then Result := TRUE;
      end; { case }
      MatchColor := Result;
  end;
```

For a CGA system, a new MatchColor function would be required using both the palette entry and the palette (Mode) selection. Remember, the color values here refer to only the EGA/VGA default palette entries, not to the actual color values assigned to the palette.

The WritePort Procedure

The WritePort procedure accepts a character or format string with optional arguments for output to the active serial port.

```
procedure WritePort( WorkStr: string );
  var
     i : integer;
  begin
```

In outputting the final string to a serial port, special handling is required. In this instance, the string (*WorkStr*) is sent to the plotter one character at a time, with the Ready function called before each character is sent, to be sure that the plotter is ready to accept additional input.

```
        for i := 0 to ord( WorkStr[0] ) do
        begin
            while not Ready do ;
```

Once Ready returns TRUE, the AH register is given the argument 01h (function 1—write to serial port) and the AL register takes the character value.

```
            Regs.AH := $01;
            Regs.AL := ord( WorkStr[i] );
{========== alternate ==========}
{   Regs.AX := $0100 + str[i];      }
{===============================}
```

The DX register receives the *port* argument.

```
            Regs.DX := port;
```

Then Intr calls the ROM BIOS interrupt 14h—BIOS serial port services.

```
      Intr( $14, Regs );
   end;
end;
```

The Ready Function

Because the plotter has only a small buffer for input, the Ready function is used to test the selected serial port before information is sent.

```
function Ready: boolean;
   var
      Result : word;
   begin
      Regs.AX := $0300;
      Regs.DX := Port;
      Intr( $14, Regs );
      delay( 5 );
      Result := Regs.AX;
      Ready := Result AND $0010 <> 0;
   end;
```

Interrupt 14h, Function 03h asks the serial port and the device connected to the port for status information. The AH register returns the serial port status; the AL register returns information from the device connected to the port (such as a modem or, in this case, a serial plotter). The meaning of the bit flags returned are shown in Table 18-5.

Table 18-5: Serial Port Status Bytes

BIT	AH REGISTER	BIT	AL REGISTER
7	Timed-out	7	Receive line signal detected
6	Tx shift register empty	6	Ring indicator
5	Tx hold register empty	5	Data-set ready (DSR)
4	Break detected	4	Clear to send (CTS)
3	Framing error	3	Detect change in receive line signal
2	Parity error	2	Trailing edge ring indicator
1	Overrun error	1	Change in DSR status
0	Data ready	0	Change in CTS status

In this instance, only one bit is tested: the CTS (Clear To Send) status flag. If you have any trouble with a plotter not responding correctly, you might change the test conditions to check *60B0h*, which tests the serial port tx shift and hold registers and the DSR, CTS, and receive line signals.

The ClosePlotter Procedure

When the screen plot is completed, the ClosePlotter function is called to set the pen position to the P1 location and to return the current pen to the carousel.

```pascal
procedure ClosePlotter;
   begin
      WritePort( 'PA0,0;SP0;' + #$0D + #$0A );
   end;
```

Plotter.PAS / Plotter.TPU

```pascal
                   {================================}
                   {    Unit for direct control     }
                   {       of serial plotter        }
                   {================================}
unit Plotter;

INTERFACE

const
   COM1 = $0000;                  { def port for COM1 device }
   COM2 = $0001;                  { def port for COM2 device }
   InitComm = $00A3;              { initialization parameter }

function InitPort( ActivePort : word ) : word;

procedure InitPlotter;

procedure PlotScreen( PortNum : word );

procedure ClosePlotter;

IMPLEMENTATION

uses GRAPH, DOS, CRT;

var
   HStep, VStep : real;
   XPlot1, YPlot1, XPlot2, YPlot2,
   MaxX, MaxY, Port, YRef: integer;
   Regs : Registers;

function InitPort( ActivePort : word ) : word;
   begin
      Port := ActivePort;
      Regs.AX := InitComm;        { initialization parameter }
      Regs.DX := ActivePort;      { which port to open       }
      Intr( $14, Regs );
      InitPort := Regs.AX;
   end;

function Ready: boolean;
```

```pascal
      var
         Result : word;
      begin
         Regs.AX := $0300;
         Regs.DX := Port;
         Intr( $14, Regs );
         delay( 5 );
         Result := Regs.AX;
         Ready := Result AND $0010 <> 0;
      end;
   procedure WritePort( WorkStr: string );
      var
         i : integer;
      begin
         for i := 0 to ord(WorkStr[0]) do
            begin                       { output string to plotter }
               while not Ready do ;    { wait for buffer space     }
               Regs.AH := $01;
               Regs.AL := ord( WorkStr[i] );
         {========== alternate ==========}
         {   Regs.AX := $0100 + str[i];       }
         {===============================}
               Regs.DX := port;
               Intr( $14, Regs );
            end;
      end;

   procedure InitPlotter;
      var
         Buf1, Buf2 : string;
      begin
         MaxX := GetMaxX;
         MaxY := GetMaxY;
         HStep := XPlot2 / MaxX;
         VStep := YPlot2 / MaxY;
         WritePort( '[P3;' );    { EscP3 - initiate handshake }
         WritePort( 'IN;' );     { initialize plotter          }
         str( XPlot1, Buf1 );
         str( YPlot1, Buf2 );
         Buf1 := 'SC '+ Buf1 + ', ' + Buf2 + ', ';
         str( XPlot2, Buf2 );
         Buf1 := Buf1 + Buf2 + ', ';
         str( YPlot2, Buf2 );
         Buf1 := Buf1 + Buf2 + '; ' + #$0D + #$0A;
         WritePort( Buf1 )        { set scaling / plot window }
      end;
   procedure ClosePlotter;
      begin
```

```pascal
            writeport( 'PA0,0;SP0;' + #$0D + #$0A );
      end;
procedure SelectPen( Pen : integer );
      var
            Buffer : string;
      begin
            str( Pen:1, Buffer );
            writeport( 'SP' + Buffer + ';' );
                                          { select pen from carousel }
            if Pen <> 0 then delay( 5000 );
                                          { allow time for pickup    }
      end;
function MatchColor( Pen, SColor: integer ): boolean;
      var
            Result : boolean;
      begin
            Result := False;
            {======= pen colors to video colors =======}
            {     Pen Colors      Order    Video Palette       }
            {     Yellow          1        14, 12, 10          }
            {     Red-Violet      2        13                  }
            {     Red             3        12, 4               }
            {     Green           4        11, 10, 3, 2        }
            {     Blue            5        11, 9, 8, 7, 3, 1   }
            {     Violet          6        5, 1                }
            {     Brown           7        6, 8, 7             }
            {     Black           8        15 ( White )        }
            {==========================================}
            case Pen of
               1: case SColor of
                     Yellow, LightRed, LightGreen :
                        Result := TRUE;
                  end;
               2: if SColor = LightMagenta then Result := TRUE;
               3: case SColor of
                     LightRed, Red : Result := TRUE;
                  end;
               4: case SColor of
                     LightCyan, Cyan,
                     LightGreen, Green : Result := TRUE;
                  end;
               5: case SColor of
                     LightCyan, Cyan,
                     LightBlue, Blue,
                     LightGray, DarkGray : Result := TRUE;
```

```pascal
                    end;
                6:  case SColor of
                        Magenta, Blue : Result := TRUE;
                    end;
                7:  case SColor of
                        Brown, LightGray, DarkGray :
                            Result := TRUE;
                    end;
                8:  if SColor = White then Result := TRUE;
            end; { case }
            MatchColor := Result;
        end;
procedure PlotScreen;
    var
        x, y, Pen : integer;
        PenStat, Retrace : boolean;
        Buf1, Buf2 : string;
    begin
        XPlot1 := 0;
        YPlot1 := 0;                { plotter origin points    }
        XPlot2 := 10250;            { max x-axis plotter units }
        YPlot2 := 7479;             { max y-axis plotter units }
        for Pen := 1 to 8 do
        begin
            SelectPen( Pen );
            for x := 1 to MaxX do
            begin
                PenStat := FALSE;
                Retrace := TRUE;
                for y := MaxY downto 0 do
                begin
                    if not PenStat and
                        MatchColor( Pen, GetPixel(x,y) ) then
                    begin
                        str( x * HStep :9:3, Buf1 );
                        str( ( MaxY - y ) * VStep :9:3, Buf2 );
                        WritePort( 'PA' + Buf1 + ',' + Buf2 +
                                    ';PD;' + #$0D + #$0A );
                        if Retrace then
                        begin    { allow time for pen to retrace }
                            delay( round( abs( YRef -
                                    ( y * VStep ) ) ) div 10 );
                            Retrace := FALSE;
                        end;
                        PenStat := TRUE;
                    end;
                    if PenStat and
                        not MatchColor( Pen, GetPixel(x,y) )
```

```pascal
              then begin
                 YRef := round( y * VStep );
                 str( x * HStep :9:3, Buf1 );
                 str( ( MaxY - ( y + 1 ) ) *
                        VStep :9:3, Buf2 );
                 WritePort( 'PA' + Buf1 + ',' + Buf2 +
                            ';PD;' + #$0D + #$0A );
                 PenStat := FALSE;
              end;
           end;
           if PenStat then
           begin         { if the Pen's still at screen end }
              YRef := round( y * VStep );
              str( x * HStep :9:3, Buf1 );
              str( ( MaxY - ( y + 1 ) ) *
                     VStep :9:3, Buf2 );
              WritePort( 'PA' + Buf1 + ',' + Buf2 +
                         ';PD;' + #$0D + #$0A );
              PenStat := FALSE;
           end;
        end;
        SelectPen( 0 );
     end;
  end;
{ end of Plotter unit }
end.
```

CHAPTER 19

The Turbo Font Editor

The Font Editor is a utility designed to create or to edit stroked fonts for use with Turbo Pascal, Turbo C, or Turbo Prolog using BGI graphics displays. The Font Editor utility consists of the editor program FE.EXE, and nine character fonts: EURO.CHR, GOTH.CHR, LCOM.CHR, LITT.CHR, SANS.CHR, SCRI.CHR, SIMP.CHR, TRIP.CHR, and TSCR.CHR.

Also available from Borland, are a .BIN-to-.BGI conversion utility (DFONT.EXE, DFONT.C, and FONT.H), a .BGI Driver Toolkit (see Appendix D), and a new video driver, VGA256.BGI (see Appendix E).

A minor bug in Turbo Pascal 5.5 appears when an attempt is made to load any external font whose source file is larger than 16K—such as the Triplex (TRIP.CHR—16,699 bytes), Italic (TSCR.CHR—16,933 bytes), or Gothic (GOTH.CHR—18,151 bytes) fonts. If necessary, the GOTH.CHR font distributed with Turbo Pascal, which lacks the extended ASCII characters (size 8,560 bytes), can be used.

Alternatively, any of these three problem fonts can be edited using FE.EXE to remove unnecessary characters—such as the box characters, B0h..DFh, or the math characters, E0h..FEh—and thus reduce the size of the font. The following instructions apply to Font Editor revision 1.0.

Introduction to Stroked Fonts

Stroked fonts define characters as line sequence instructions (strokes) showing the outline composing the specific characters (see also Chapter 16, *Turtle Graphics*, for another illustration of a stroked font creation). The standard text font displayed by your computer is a bitmap font with each character defined as a matrix of dots.

The advantage found in stroked fonts is that the characters can be arbitrarily scaled in size and in proportions without loss of resolution. Bitmap fonts can be enlarged, but only in simple multiples of the grid size for they suffer degradation of appearance as they're enlarged.

For example: if a bitmap font is enlarged four times, each dot in the original grid becomes a 4x4 pixel square in the enlargement, resulting in a jagged, stepped appearance (see Figure 19-1).

Figure 19-1: Bit-Mapped vs. Stroked Fonts

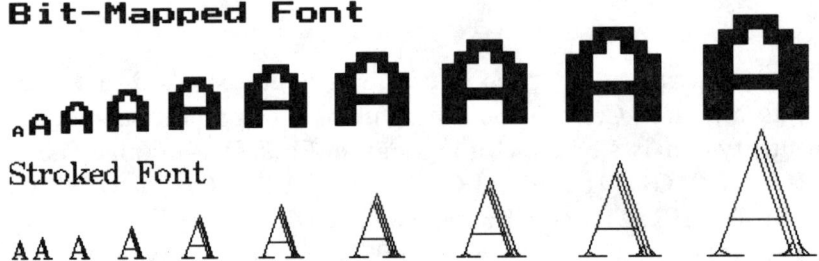

Stroked fonts are not converted to dot patterns (pixels) until the desired font size and output device resolution are known. A stroked font can be sized without suffering in appearance. Also, stroked fonts can be output to devices with quite different resolution (such as 120 dpi dot-matrix printers or 300 dpi laserjet printers), without loss of stroke resolution.

Furthermore, the Font Editor can be used to create non-alphabetic or symbol fonts for specialized displays and applications. For example, in Chapter 9, bit images were created for use with the line graph display and, in Chapter 15, another type of bit images was created for icons. Using FE, these same images could be created as a stroked symbol font, much more conveniently that writing bit-by-bit instructions. The resulting symbols can be used, not only in the line graph display, but in a variety of applications and in any size desired (see Figure 19-2).

Also, several new stroked fonts are available (see Table 19-1).

Table 19-1: Stroked Fonts

FILENAME	FONT	NAME	VALUE
EURO.CHR	European (large)	-	-
GOTH.CHR	Gothic	GothicFont	4
LCOM.CHR	Text (Roman)	-	-
LITT.CHR	Small	SmallFont	2
SANS.CHR	SansSerif	SansSerifFont	3
SCRI.CHR	Script	-	-
SIMP.CHR	Simplex	-	-
TRIP.CHR	Triplex	TriplexFont	1
TSCR.CHR	Text (Italic)	-	-

Figure 19-2: Special Symbol Font Characters (Runic Alphabet)

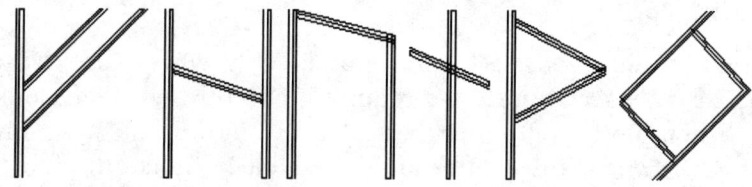

System Requirements

The Font Editor is compatible with most systems, but does impose a few minimum requirements.

Computer Requirements

Font Editor (FE.EXE) runs on IBM PCs, PC/XTs, PC/ATs, and most compatibles. You must also copy the appropriate .BGI driver (this will be EGAVGA.BGI in most cases) to the same directory as FE.EXE or provide a path in your AUTOEXEC.BAT file to the directory containing the .BGI files.

Mouse Requirements

Font Editor requires a mouse supporting the Microsoft External Mouse Driver Interface (MM protocol). This includes the Microsoft, Mouse Systems, and Logitech bus or serial mice.

If you are using another hardware mouse type, consult your mouse manual for installation instructions. The mouse driver (MOUSE.COM or MOUSE.SYS) must be installed in memory before calling FE. Normally, the mouse is loaded as a DOS device driver by definition in your CONFIG.SYS file (DEVICE = MOUSE.SYS) or in your AUTOEXEC.BAT (MOUSE<cr> or MOUSE 2<cr>), depending on the port used.

Graphics Requirements

Font Editor also requires an Enhanced Graphics Adapter (EGA) or compatible and a color display. The graphics adapter card must have a minimum of 128K RAM installed.

Plotter Requirements

(Optional) Font Editor supports hardcopy output to one of the following Hewlett-Packard or compatible plotters:

- HP 7470
- HP 7475 (8 1/2 x 11 paper only)
- HP 7440 (ColorPro)

There are two considerations to keep in mind. First, when using a plotter and a serial mouse, two serial ports are required, one for the plotter and one for the mouse. When plotter output is requested, FE will prompt you for the port (COM1 or COM2) for the plotter and will then initialize the indicated serial port (see Chapter 18 for details on serial port initialization). Be sure that you indicate the correct port for the plotter or you may find the mouse no longer responds. After the plotter port is selected, FE will ask for initialization parameters, assuming 9600 baud, Even parity, 7 bits, and 1 stop bit. If other settings are desired, the serial port should be initialized using the DOS Mode command before calling Font Editor.

Second, the most common problem interfacing between an HP plotter and a non-HP computer is in the connecting cable. If you experience any problems in this area, Hewlett-Packard supplies a standard cable for this application, part number HP 17255D, or you can use straight-through RS-232C cabling together with a dummy (null) modem—see Chapter 18.

General Capabilities

Font Editor edits Borland stroked fonts (files with the .CHR extension shipped with Turbo C and Turbo Pascal or fonts supplied with the Font Editor). You can read in fonts, edit individual characters, preview characters on screen or on a plotter, and save the resulting font back to disk.

Font Editor Display

The Font Editor screen is divided into four major areas that are explained momentarily. Because each screen area reacts slightly differently with the mouse, mouse usage will be covered first.

Mouse Conventions

The left and right mouse buttons are treated identically.

Two major operations are performed using the mouse with Font Editor. The first is a *click*, a quick press-and-release of the mouse button when the graphics cursor is positioned on an object to select that object. The second is a *drag*, a press-hold-and-move operation used to slide objects or to define an area. When the drag operation is being used, the object sticks to the mouse cursor, moving with the cursor until the button is released.

Area Definition Using The Mouse

The mouse can be used to define an area within the work screen. The location where a mouse button is depressed marks one corner and the diagonally opposite corner is defined when the button is released.

If you define the starting corner erroneously, the error cannot be changed except by starting over (defining a new rectangle). The second corner, however, can be changed by moving the mouse before releasing the mouse button.

Using The Mouse in The Character Window

When the mouse is used in the Character (Edit) window, you will notice that the mouse moves in discreet steps, moving only between indicated intersection points where strokes can start and stop. The spacing of the grid points depends on the *Zoom* option and also on the size of the font being edited. For example, if you select LITT.CHR (SmallFont), the grid points will be widely spaced (a 12x10 point grid), while selecting SANS.CHR (SansSerifFont) will show a tightly spaced grid (a 44x33 point grid).

Escape From Plotter Output

Pressing any mouse button during a plotter output terminates the graphics plotter dump. This may, however, require you to hold the mouse button down for several seconds until the button status is recognized. Also, plotting will not halt immediately, but will continue until the drawing commands in its internal buffer are completed.

The Font Editor Menu

When using Font Editor, a series of menus are displayed as a line of text across the top of the screen for selection by mouse click.

Some items in the menu, such as *Load* and *Save,* perform a single function and, when the function is completed, display the same menu. Other items, such as *Edit,* display a new menu. All menus except the initial menu contain the item *Exit* which will return you to the previous menu.

The *Quit* item in the main menu returns to DOS. If changes have been made to the current font, a *Save* prompt will appear before exiting.

Selecting A Character For Editing

When FE is first called, a menu shows all of the .CHR fonts in the current directory. The first step is to use the mouse to select a font for editing. After selection, the display will shift to the edit screen. The font directory can also be called by selecting *Load* from the menu options across the top of the screen.

At the right of the edit screen a large rectangular area shows a 256-character display (using the extended ASCII character set, not the font currently being edited). Clicking on any character within this box selects this character for edit, displaying the current font's equivalent character in the Edit Window as a series of strokes and below the selection box as it would appear on screen with a size definition of 1. Characters can also be selected for edit by keyboard entry.

Within the selection window, the displayed characters appear in green if the current font contains a stroked character definition or in red if no stroked image has been defined for this character. The characters 00h (null), 20h (space), and FFh appear as blanks, but can be selected and defined as font characters.

The currently selected character is highlighted in the window (as bright green or bright red).

The Character Window

The character window is the large rectangular area on the left half of the screen (see Figure 19-3) where character editing takes place. The Font Editor will display the strokes comprising a selected character. An existing character can be edited or a new character can be created using the mouse to delete elements or to add new lines in this window.

Figure 19-3: Edit Window Display

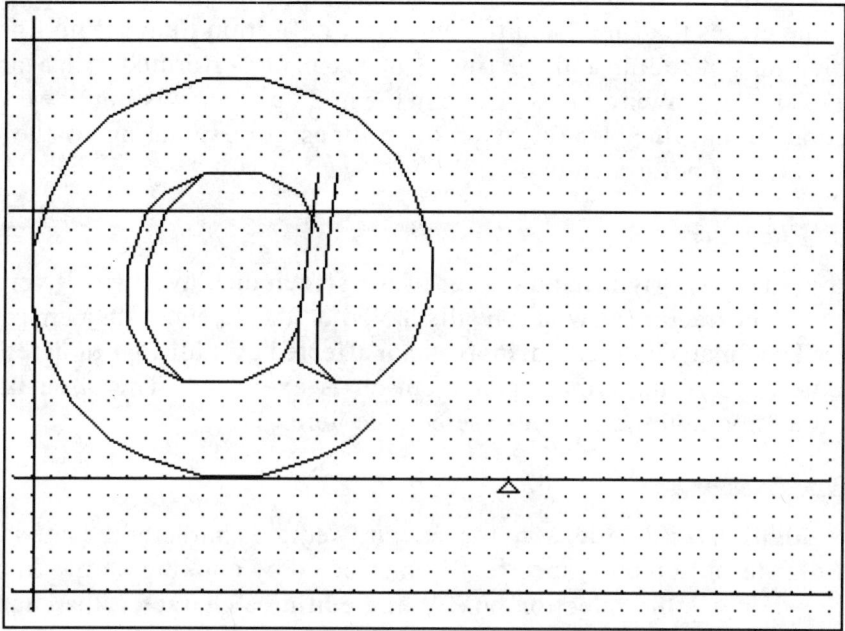

The vertical line along the left side of the grid shows the left edge of the character. Four horizontal lines, beginning at the top, show the height of a capital character (A, B etc.), the height of a lowercase character (a, c etc.), the baseline and the descender depth (as for g, j, or y).

Character Width and Spacing

Notice the small triangle to the right of the baseline. This marker shows the beginning position for the next character (the intercharacter spacing). The character width can be changed by dragging the triangle to a new position.

Kerning, the practice used by typesetters where intercharacter spacing is adjusted to allow specific character pairs to fit together—is not supported, though character widths can be adjusted to create tightly or loosely spaced fonts as required.

Editing a Character

Character strokes are added or deleted by moving the mouse cursor to the desired starting point, pressing the button, and dragging to the desired end point. If no stroke previously connected these points, then a new stroke is added; if one did exist, then it is deleted.

Curves are not supported. Instead, curves and bends are created as a series of strokes as shown in Figure 19-3. Drawing a line where there was none before will add a stroke to the character definition. Drawing a line on top of an existing line erases that line from the character definition (leaving no line).

Combinations of adding and deleting strokes can be performed with a single line. For example, drawing a new stroke in the middle of an existing line erases that portion of the line, leaving two other lines corresponding to the end portions that were not drawn over.

The Small Character

The area in the lower right-hand corner of the screen displays a small version of the current character (as would be displayed on the screen with a character size of 1). The Small Character display is not affected by additions or deletions in the Edit window until the Update option is exercised. This area is for information only; nothing is mouse selectable here.

The Update Selector Box

Changes, additions or deletions, to the currently edited character are not added to the stroke definition until specifically instructed by clicking on the *Update* option shown above the selection box. While editing a character, the changes made to a character are saved in an edit buffer. To make the edits permanent, the mouse is used to select the *Update* option, writing the edit buffer to the actual character.

Clicking on the current character in the selection box will bring up a prompt asking if the strokes are to be added (or subtracted) from the current character. Clicking on a new character will display the same prompt before the new selection is displayed in the edit window.

The edit actions on characters affect the edit image only, *not* the character stroke data. For example, suppose several lines are added to a character, but the character is not updated. Now, if the *Edit* option is selected from the menu and used to move the character, only the information in the character buffer will be affected; the new lines added to the character image will not be moved. This applies to all of the edit functions, including move, flip, flop, reverse, shift, cut, and copy.

Editing Tools

This section gives a brief description of the Font Editor tools, see the *Command Reference* section for detailed descriptions of these commands.

Single Strokes

Single strokes can be added or deleted from a character image by moving the mouse cursor into the character window and performing a drag operation between the grid points where the stroke should be added or deleted. As the mouse is dragged, a line appears between the start point and the mouse cursor. This is a process known as *rubber banding* because the line appears to stretch or to shrink when following the cursor.

Drawing over an existing stroke deletes the line and drawing over a portion of an existing line deletes only a portion of the line. Also, if the mouse cursor is moved outside the character window while rubber banding a line, the stroke will be canceled.

Groups of Strokes

Because many characters share the same stroke groups, groups of strokes can be manipulated as a single object using the Edit and Clipboard commands. For example, the strokes defining the left-hand part of a "c" will probably be the same as those in the lefthand part of a "d."

The tools available in the Clipboard menu allow selection of a group of strokes from a character to be used again in that character or in another character. Cut and Copy move a group of characters into a holding buffer (the Clipboard). Cut removes the strokes from the current character, while Copy leaves the originals undisturbed.

Strokes are selected for Clipboard by rubber banding a rectangle around the strokes. Both end points of a given stroke must be completely inside the rectangle in order to be selected for a Cut or Copy.

The strokes in Clipboard are pasted into a character by selecting the *Paste* option which adds the contents to the character window. The strokes can be moved using a drag operation. Paste does not empty Clipboard; the next paste operation will find the same strokes. Cut and Copy always change the contents of the Clipboard. Delete operates like Cut, except that the deleted strokes are not placed in Clipboard, but are discarded. Move is similar to a combined Cut and Paste operation, except that the contents of Clipboard are not altered.

The contents of the Clipboard buffer can also be rotated using the commands under Edit and Flip to flip the contents upside down (horizontal axis) or right and left (vertical axis).

Whole Characters

Special techniques are provided for manipulating whole characters.

- CopyChar (Edit menu) allows you to copy from one character within a single font to another, duplicating the selected character strokes as a

new character. For example, after creating a "c," the "c" could be copied to "d" and edited to create the new character without repeating the strokes used for the "c."
- Flip (Edit menu) allows you to flip a character upside down, right/left, or both.
- Shift (Edit menu) allows you to move a whole character right, left, up, or down. For example, the characters, b, d, p, and q are usually just flipped versions of one another. You can draw one and use CopyChar and Flip to make the other three.

Whole Fonts

The commands under Global allow you to perform operations on the entire font. These are primarily concerned with intercharacter spacing and usually, will be used as a part of the final editing process of a font.

- LeftSpace will move every character in the font so that its left-most part is the specified distance from the left margin (the dark solid vertical line in the character window).
- RghtSpace will set the character spacing marker of every character in the font to the distance specified to the right of the right-most stroke of each character.
- BaseLine will shift every character up or down by the same amount so that the base line corresponds to zero.
- Copy allows selection of another font, copying characters from it into the current work font. Many characters, such as the graphic characters, will not change from one font to another and Copy saves the trouble of recreating these.

Font Editor Command Reference

In this section, the Font Editor menu commands and functions are described in detail.

Load   Loads an existing font file into Font Editor. A large rectangle will be drawn on the screen. There are two mouse sensitive areas within this rectangle: the file selector area and the file prompt line.

Clicking on the file prompt line will allow you to enter a new filename for loading and may include a new path. If the path or filename does not exist, you will be warned. If you confirm that the file does not exist, the file will be created and will become the default output file when the font is saved.

The file selector area contains a list of all of the files with the extension .CHR on the current drive/directory. As the mouse cursor is moved over these, the filenames will appear on the file prompt line. Clicking on one of these names will select the current file for load.

Show The tools under Show simply show the appearance of the selected font but, do not operate on or change the font.

Font Shows all of the currently defined characters on the monitor and is useful for a quick check of the intercharacter spacing. Overlapping characters or gaps between characters will indicate errors in intercharacter spacing.

String Allows you to type a string of characters for display. Sometimes it is important to see two special characters together to determine the proper appearance and spacing. When a line becomes full, display will continue on the next line or the Enter key can be used to force a new line. When the bottom of the screen is reached, the display does not scroll. The Escape key is used to exit the String mode.

Plotter Draws the current font on an HP plotter. See the section on *Optional Hardware* or Chapter 18 for a discussion of connecting the plotter.

When you select this tool, you will be asked if the plotter is COM1 or COM2. Font Editor must have the serial port on the PC configured to be able to communicate with the plotter. You may either let FE set the serial port to 9600 baud, Even parity, 7 data bits, and 1 stop bit (in which case the DIP switches on your plotter must be set for this configuration) or you may select NO to make FE skip this step. If FE does not initialize the plotter's serial port, you must issue the DOS Mode command prior to starting FE to match your plotter's switch settings. If you're using a serial mouse, be careful not to choose the serial port to which your mouse is connected.

Finally, you'll be asked to confirm plot. Have the paper loaded and the plotter ready before selecting YES. If you start plotting and want to stop before the plot is complete, press and hold a mouse button until the screen clears.

Your plotter output will be labeled with the name of the file from which it came, and the page number. In the case of multiple page plots, FE will stop at the end of each page to allow you to load a new piece of paper.

Exit Returns you to the main menu.

Global These commands operate on an entire font, unlike most commands which operate on a single character or stroke.

LeftSpace Adjusts the space between the left-most stroke of a character and the vertical guide line shown in the character window. Typically, this should be set to zero for all fonts so that an application that mixes fonts will maintain character spacing between font changes.

RghtSpace   Adjusts the character-width mark of all the characters to the set value. The character width value set for each character is the number selected from submenu, plus the right-most stroke of the character. This choice will therefore, provide uniform intercharacter spacing for a proportionally spaced font.

Typically, this choice is issued for the entire font for proportional spacing, then selected characters, such as the numeric characters and the graphics character symbols which require the same total widths for column lineup, are adjusted individually.

BaseLine   Adjusts each character in the font up or down by the same amount. This option is exercised for an entire font so that all fonts refer to the same baseline value. An application switching fonts will not have the baseline of the new font shifted up or down from the previous font.

Copy   Selects characters from a different font file. The source font file is selected as under the *Load* option. When *Copy* is selected, you will see two character selector boxes on the screen: the left box corresponding to the source font selected, the right box corresponding to the working font.

Characters are copied individually by clicking on the character desired from the source character box, then clicking on the destination character in the right-hand character box. To quit, select Done in the menu area.

Exit   Returns to the main menu.

Edit   Provides tools for editing whole characters or groups of strokes. The Clipboard functions under this heading are of particular importance.

CopyChar   Allows intra-font copying of characters by selecting source and destination characters within the working font. If a character already exists where you selected the destination character, then you will be asked if that character should be replaced.

Flip   Allows flipping either the current character or the contents of Clipboard. Characters are flipped within the space that they occupy. For example, if a character only occupies the lower portion of the character cell, then the results, after flipping it vertically, will only occupy the lower portion of the character cell. The *Shift* option can be used to change positions.

The results of flipping the Clipboard will not be visible until it is pasted into the Edit window.

Shift   Moves a character one dot in any direction. It does not modify the inter-character spacing.

ShowAlso   Superimposes another character over the character currently being edited. The superimposed character's strokes and width marker are shown in RED where strokes match the edit character or in GREEN where they do not coincide.

The superimposed character will remain in the edit window until Update is executed or a new edit character is selected.

Clipboard   Contains all the tools for working on groups of strokes. The *Cut*, *Copy* and *Paste* options work by reading and writing a buffer area called the Clipboard. *Move* and *Delete* do not use the Clipboard.

Strokes are selected from the current character by rubber banding a rectangle around them. One corner of the rectangle is defined by the location where you press a mouse button, the diagonally opposite corner is defined by the position where the mouse button is released.

Remember, both end points of a stroke must lie completely within the rectangle in order to be selected.

For the *Move* and *Paste* options, when a region has been defined, the strokes contained in the region are copied within the window, to the right of the character width marker. The upper-left corner of the strokes will be attached to the mouse cursor, while a mouse button is pressed and will stay attached until the button is released.

Cut   Removes the selected strokes from the current character, placing them in the Clipboard. The previous contents of Clipboard are lost.

Copy   Copies the selected strokes from the current character to the clipboard without changing the current character. The previous contents of Clipboard are lost.

Paste   Copies the contents of the Clipboard to the current character. The contents of the Clipboard are not changed.

Move   Moves the selected strokes to a new location. This is the equivalent of a *Cut* and *Paste* operation except that the contents (if any) of the Clipboard are not changed.

Delete   cuts the selected strokes from the current character. This is equivalent to a **Cut** except that the contents of the Clipboard are not changed.

Exit   Returns to the Edit menu.

Exit   Returns to the Main menu.

Save   Writes the current font data to an output file. Save works like the Load command, drawing a large rectangle on the screen that contains two mouse sensitive areas: the file selector area and the file prompt line.

Clicking on the file prompt line allows entry of a new filename and may include a new path. You will be warned if the filename entered does not exist. If you confirm that the file does not exist, the file will be created.

The file selector area contains a list of all of the files on the current drive/directory with the extension .CHR. As the mouse cursor is moved over this list, each filename will show on the file prompt line. Clicking on one of these names will select the current destination file.

The options under Window control how the character editing window displays. These options do not change the characters, only the way that they are displayed.

The default values shown are set automatically when a font file is loaded. If Font Editor is called without selecting an initial font file (for example, by bypassing Load) these values must be set.

Zoom Out   Reduces the magnification used to display the character in the Edit window. Magnification is automatically set to show all characters in the character window as large as possible when the font file is loaded.

Zoom In   Increases the magnification used to display the character in the Edit window. Magnification is automatically set to show all characters in the character window as large as possible when the font file is loaded.

Magnification may be increased so that characters are larger than the window—parts of characters that would be outside the window are clipped to the window limits. This is useful while working on lowercase letters or the strokes that make up the serifs of a serif font.

Origin   Allows positioning the origin guide line anywhere within the character editing window.

While, for most fonts, this is drawn underneath the baseline guideline and won't be visible, it is still movable. Move the origin guideline towards the top of the window and zoom in to work on descending strokes or move the origin guideline to the bottom of the window to work on uppercase letters.

d-ht   Sets the descender height guideline in the character editing window. This has no effect on the character, character edits, or display of the character in the window. It is simply for your convenience.

b-ht   Sets the base line height guideline in the character editing window. This has no effect on the character, character edits, or display of the character in the window. It is simply for your convenience.

x-ht   Positions the x-height guide line (lowercase height) in the character editing window. This has no effect on the character, character edits, or display of the character in the window. It is simply for your convenience.

c-ht   Positions the character height guide line (uppercase height) in the character editing window. This has no effect on the character, character edits, or display of the character in the window. It is simply for your convenience.

ShowMovs   Shows each *move, draw, draw, ...* sequence in a different color so that some notion of how the character is being stroked can be gained. The sequence of colors shows the order in which strokes are generated.

This option defaults to OFF. Turning this option on may produce disquieting results when drawing in the character editing window. Its use is not recommended.

Grid   Shows the grid of points in the character editing on which stokes can begin and end. This option defaults ON.

Exit   Returns to the Main menu.

Quit   Returns to DOS; you will be asked if you want to save any edits.

Beginning a New Font from Scratch

Here are a few considerations for the user who wishes to start a new font from scratch. To begin a new font, start Font Editor and select a new font filename. The screen will show a character window with no characters defined (all character choices will be displayed in red). The four global parameters for the font are determined automatically by the font editor when a file is loaded or saved. These parameters are the Base Height, the Capital Height, the Descender Height, and the Lowercase Height (or x Height). The values for these are determined by examining the characters that a typographer would use to determine the same information.

Capital Height   This value is determined by examining the E Ligature character (144 decimal). This is the tallest of the European characters. If this character is undefined, the capital M is used as the capital height. If neither of these characters is defined, the value will default to 40 (of a maximum +/−64).

Base Height   This value is determined by examining the E Ligature or the Capital M. This value is used as the origin for the other three dimensions. If neither of these characters is defined, the value will default to 0 (of a maximum of +/−64).

Descender Height   This value is determined by examining the lowercase 'q' letter. If the lowercase 'q' is undefined, the value will default to −7 (of a maximum of +/−64).

Lowercase Height (or x Height) This value is determined be examining the lowercase 'x' letter. If the lowercase 'x' is undefined, the value will default to the Capital Height divided by two.

To define the size and placement of the characters in the font, it is best to define the 'M,' 'q,' 'x,' and E Ligature (if desired) as the first characters. The next time the font is loaded, the character dimensions will be used to define the size and placement of the character window for the font.

If you are defining a special symbol font, these parameters may not be relevant, but in most cases, as a minimum, the Base Height should be defined.

Using Custom Fonts

The original fonts supplied with Turbo Pascal (or Turbo C) are built-in the BGI Graphics library. Unlike the original fonts, however, user-created fonts (and the five new fonts supplied with the Turbo Font Editor) cannot be referenced directly, but must first be installed in the internal font table.

The InstallUserFont function is supplied for this purpose and returns a font ID number that can be used subsequently with SetTextStyle to identify the font.

The NEWFONTS.PAS demo program (at the end of this chapter) installs the five new fonts supplied with the Turbo Font Editor and prints a brief message to the screen with each font (see Figure 19-4).

Identifying The Fonts

The four original stroked fonts are identified by constant names in the GRAPH unit. For convenience and to provide compatibility, the new fonts are also identified by font names but, since no library constants exist for these, values must be assigned by calling the InstallUserFont procedure.

```
     LargeFont,                        (* EURO.CHR *)
     RomanFont,                        (* LCOM.CHR *)
     SimplexFont,                      (* SIMP.CHR *)
     ItalicFont,                       (* TSCR.CHR *)
     ScriptFont : integer;             (* SCRI.CHR *)
```

Figure 19-4: New Graphics Character Fonts

9 ABCDEFGHIJKL Large
8 ABCDEFGHIJKL Roman
7 *ABCDEFGHIJKL Italic*
6 ABCDEFGHIJKL Simplex
5 ABCDEFGHIJKL Script

An Install_Font Utility

Now, because the possibility always exists that the .CHR file required for a particular font may not even exist, a simple InstallFont function can be used.

InstallFont is called with the path and filename for the desired font and returns an integer identifying the entry in the internal font table. If the .CHR file for a specified font is not found, InstallFont can display a message and, instead of returning a negative error code, returns a zero value which provides a simpler Boolean test than the graphics error code.

```
function InstallFont( FontName : string ): integer;
   var
      Result : integer;
   begin
      Result := InstallUserFont( FontName );
      if Result <= 0 then { report error };
      InstallFont := Result;
   end;
```

Loading Several Fonts

If more than one font is required, the simplest route is to assign all the fonts needed at one time. The returned integer values are assigned to the font variable names (LargeFont, RomanFont, etc.). This does not require any excessive memory expenditure, only the font names are installed and the font information itself is loaded into memory only when the font is actually assigned using the SetTextStyle function.

```
   procedure LoadFonts;
   begin
      LargeFont   = Install_Font( "EURO.CHR" );
      RomanFont   = Install_Font( "LCOM.CHR" );
      ItalicFont  = Install_Font( "TSCR.CHR" );
```

```
    ScriptFont  = Install_Font( "SCRI.CHR" );
    SimplexFont = Install_Font( "SIMP.CHR" );
end;
```

Short and simple, that's it. Between the Turbo Font Editor and the preceding utility procedures, there's a world of possibilities for special displays and graphics features.

BGI Stroke File Format

The structure of Borland .CHR (stroked font) file follows, beginning at offset 00h with a header:

```
        HeaderSize      equ     080h
        DataSize        equ     (size of font file)
        descr           equ     "Triplex font"
        fname           equ     "TRIP"
        MajorVersion    equ     1
        MinorVersion    equ     0
        db      'PK',8,8
        db      'BGI ',descr,' V'
        db      MajorVersion + '0'
        db      (MinorVersion / 10) + '0', (MinorVersion mod 10) + '0'
        db      ' - 19 October 1987', 0Dh, 0Ah
        db      0,1Ah                           ; null & ctrl-Z = end
        dw      HeaderSize                      ; size of header
        db      fname                           ; font name
        dw      DataSize                        ; font file size
        db      MajorVersion,MinorVersion       ; version #'s
        db      1,0                             ; minimal version #'s
        db      (HeaderSize - $) DUP (0)        ; pad out to header size
```

The data for the file begins at offset 80h:

```
    80h         '+'     flags stroke file type
    81h-82h             number chars in font file (n)
    83h                 undefined
    84h                 ASCII value of first char in file
    85h..86h            offset to stroke definitions (8+3n)
    87h                 scan flag (normally 0)
    88h                 distance from origin to top of capital
    89h                 distance from origin to baseline
    90h                 distance from origin to bottom descender
    91h..95h            undefined
    96h                 offsets to individual character definitions
    96h + 2n            width table (one word per character)
    96h + 3n            start of character definitions
```

The individual character definitions consist of a variable number of words describing the operations required to render each character. Each word consists of an (x,y) coordinate pair and a two-bit op-code, encoded as shown—see Tables 19-2 and 19-3.

Table 19-2: Encoded Op-codes

COORDINATE	OP-CODE	ENCODED OP-CODE
Bit #	7	6..5..4..3..2..1..0
Byte 1	Op1	<7-bit Signed X Coord>
Bit #	7	6..5..4..3..2..1..0
Byte 2	Op2	<7-bit Signed Y Coord>

Table 19-3: Op-codes

Op1	Op2	MEANING
0	0	End of character definition
1	0	Move the pointer to (x,y)
1	1	Draw from current pointer to (x,y)

NEWFONTS.PAS — New Turbo .CHR Alphabets

```
uses GRAPH, CRT;

var
    GraphDriver, GraphMode, MaxColors, ErrorCode,
    LargeFont, RomanFont, GothicFont,
    SimplexFont, ItalicFont, ScriptFont : integer;

procedure Initialize;
    begin
        GraphDriver := DETECT;
        InitGraph( GraphDriver, GraphMode, '\TP\BGI' );
        ErrorCode := GraphResult;
        if ErrorCode <> grOk then
            ReportError( 'Initialize', ErrorCode );
    end;

procedure Pause;
    var
        Ch : char;
    begin
        while KeyPressed do Ch := ReadKey;
        Ch := ReadKey;
    end;

function InstallFont( FontName : string ): integer;
    var
        FontNumber : integer;
```

```pascal
   begin
      FontNumber := InstallUserFont( FontName );
      if FontNumber < 0 then
      begin
         writeln('Font Error — Graphics System Error: ',
                  GraphErrorMsg( FontNumber ) );
         halt( 1 );
      end else InstallFont := FontNumber;
   end;
procedure Display_Alphabet( Font, VPos : integer;
                            Name : string );
   var
      X : integer;
      Temp : string;
   begin
      X := 5;
      str( Font, Temp );
      SetTextStyle( Font, HorizDir, 4 );
      OutTextXY( X, VPos, Temp+' ABCDEFGHIJKL '+Name );
   end;
procedure LoadFonts;
   begin
      ItalicFont   := InstallFont( 'TSCR.CHR' );
      LargeFont    := InstallFont( 'EURO.CHR' );
      RomanFont    := InstallFont( 'LCOM.CHR' );
      ScriptFont   := InstallFont( 'SCRI.CHR' );
      SimplexFont  := InstallFont( 'SIMP.CHR' );
      GothicFont   := InstallFont( 'GOTH.CHR' );
   end;
begin
   LoadFonts;
   Initialize;                              { set graphics mode }
   ClearDevice;
   SetColor( White );
   SetTextJustify( LeftText, TopText );
   Display_Alphabet(  9,  20, 'Large',   LargeFont   );
   Display_Alphabet(  8,  80, 'Roman',   RomanFont   );
   Display_Alphabet(  7, 120, 'Italic',  ItalicFont  );
   Display_Alphabet(  6, 160, 'Simplex', SimplexFont );
   Display_Alphabet(  5, 200, 'Script',  ScriptFont  );
   Display_Alphabet(  4, 240, 'Gothic',  GothicFont  );
   Pause;
   CloseGraph;                              { restore text mode }
end.
```

CHAPTER 20

On The Shores of Fractal Seas

The shores of the Fractal Seas comprise a strange and wonderful land. This is a realm charted, not by explorers with canoes and native guides but mapped and sounded by mathematicians. It is travelled via the repetitious labors of a computer chip and drawn in bits of light and shadow on computer screens.

These strange lands are neither imaginary nor fantasy. They are very real. So real, in fact, that the fractal universe appears to form the very root and basis of our own, more familiar, universe.

To be less poetic and more accurate, the same equations in which we find these strange worlds also govern commonplace elements of our universe ranging from the crystal structures of minerals (and snow flakes and proteins) to the delicate tracery of a fern and the complex labyrinth of our circulatory structures.

In this chapter I will offer directions for entry to a few of these fascinating realms. (I will not attempt to provide a detailed explanation for either the mathematics behind these excursions nor their relevance to the larger physical universe.) I will offer a few suggestions at the end as to where you can find guidebooks and additional information.

Caveat emptor[1], many of these realms remain unknown land and I offer no surety against your entrapment in a maze of wonderment nor warranty for your eventual sane and sound return to the mundane cosmos. Hic draconis![2]

The Fractal Universe

The now-ubiquitous term *fractal* was first coined by Benoit B. Mandelbrot to denote the fact that, in reality, the dimension of a surface (in the mundane world) or of an equation (in the mathematic world) was often determined by how it was measured. To use a physical example, if you measure the coastline of the state of Maine using a yardstick which is ten miles in length, you will arrive at a certain numerical result.

But, if you now repeat your survey a second time—this time using a one mile unit of measure—you will derive a second result, one which is fractionally larger than the first. I am assuming, of course, that your results are not affected by variations due to tidal changes.

A third survey, using a mere $1/10$ mile yardstick, will yield a third, still greater, result while a fourth survey—now reducing the incremental measurement to a true 36" yard—yields a fourth figure greater than its predecessors.

In like fashion, as you continue to decrease the size of our unit of measure, your survey includes smaller and smaller irregularities as you sum the length of this irregular boundary and, predictably, L_1 is less than L_2 is less than L_3 ... L_{n-1} is less than L_n.

No matter how small your increment of measure becomes—even when you reach the point of tracing the irregularities of individual bits of sand—we can also say that L_n is less than twice L_1 ... thus the length has not increased without bounds.

The mathematics behind the preceding statement are left as an exercise to the interested reader or may be found in the references cited at the end of this chapter. For those less patient, this assertion is easily proven and may simply be provisionally accepted as valid. However, please remember this figure of magnitude—2—because this will be used further in testing fractal explorations.

The Mandelbrot Set

The Mandelbrot set is probably the most famous fractal landscape currently explored and has been featured (usually in full color) in scholarly journals,

---

1   (Latin) Let the buyer beware.
2   (Latin) Here there be dragons.

Scientific American, and *Time* as well as countless less prestigious publications. While Benoit Mandelbrot was not the first to discover this fascinating land—its shores had previously been sighted by mathematicians Robert Brooks and J. Peter Matelski—Mandelbrot was the first to make a detailed exploration and is indelibly appended to the maps of this realm.

The Mandelbrot set is an equation lying in the realm of numbers between –2.0 and +0.5 longitude and –1.25 and +1.25 latitude and is dominated by a large fractal sea with bays, inlets and tributaries as shown in Figure 20-1. While the realm of numbers certainly extends far beyond this region, the landscape of the equation beyond these limits is visually rather uninteresting.

As with many lands, the most interesting regions are those immediately surrounding the sea, offering seemingly irregular terrain and, most certainly, fitting my earlier description of the difficulties in precisely measuring the coastline of Maine.

In this case, no attempt will be made to measure a coastline. Instead, the coastline is a mathematical artifice created by recursively examining a relatively simple equation: $Z_{n+1} = Z_n^2 + C$, where C is the value of each point (the longitude and latitude of the point) and Z_1 is zero for each point (an initial value).

In this landscape, however, while longitude is measured in real numbers, the latitude lies along the imaginary axis and, therefore, all latitudinal values are denoted by the letter *i* which, to mathematicians, indicates the square root of minus 1—an *imaginary* number. Some term other than imaginary might have been better chosen to describe such numbers and would have saved countless students from confusion between the denotative and connotative meanings of the word. The time for such decisions, however, is long past and the term is firmly entrenched in the language of mathematics and, of course, bothers mathematicians not at all, but then, we're all a bit strange anyway.

To mathematicians, imaginary numbers are not numbers which do not exist but are simply numbers which have the strange property that, when squared, they produce negative results. If this bothers you and seems to go against all that is rational and real, I suggest you leave now; things will get stranger before we're done.

In conventional terms, if a positive number is squared (multiplied by itself), the result is a positive number. In like fashion, if a negative number is squared, the result is also a positive number. Thus, both 2^2 and -2^2 yield 4.

With imaginary numbers, however, $2i^2$ or $-2i^2$ both yield the result –4 while the square root of –4 is an imaginary number with the value +/–2*i*.

And using imaginary numbers for the axis of latitude is no less real than the Mandelbrot set itself. Please remember, each time the value for the latitude is squared, the results will be negative, regardless of the sign of the original value, but will no longer be imaginary. At the same time, an imaginary number multiplied by a real number always produces an imaginary result. Now, with this brief excursion into the theory of mathematics out of the way, I'll return to the formula used to explore the Mandelbrot set (or, more properly, the formula which *is* the Mandelbrot set).

Beginning at an arbitrary position within the set, using the point coordinates -0.6 and $0.4i$ for my example, the first value calculated is:

1) $Z_0 = (0)^2 - 0.6 + 0.4i$
   $= -0.6 + 0.4i$

In the second step, reiteratively, the result of the first calculation becomes the first term of the equation while the original point coordinates remain as the constant term in the equation.

2) $Z_1 = (-0.6 + 0.4i)^2 - 0.6 + 0.4i$
   $= 0.36 - 0.48i - 0.16 - 0.6 + 0.4i$
   $= -0.4 - 0.08i$

I will also calculate a distance between the current position, $-0.4 - 0.08i$ and the graph zero point, yielding the result $0.407921561...$ and, as long as this distance is not equal to or greater than 2.0 I will continue the calculations recursively, producing the third term as:

3) $Z_2 = (-0.4 - 0.08i)^2 - 0.6 + 0.4i$

again, calculating the resulting distance as: $0.178283369...$, which is still much less than 2.0 (but don't assume that the distance is always getting smaller).

Two End-Points

With the recursive formula used for the Mandelbrot set, each calculated point will tend to one of two end-points. First, after X-number of recursions, the distance result will exceed 2.0 and, after this point, the distance will continue to increase indefinitely. Second, after an X-number of recursions, the distance result will still be less than 2.0 and can be expected to continue to remain less than 2.0.

In the second instance, when distance never reaches nor exceeds 2.0—and I've chosen 100 recursions as a practical limit—the point can be said to lie within the fractal sea, the broad blank areas which form the dominate feature of the Mandelbrot set. In this case, I can say that the point has a fractal dimension which is less than 2 and, arbitrarily, this point is assigned a sea level color value (i.e., is part of the fractal sea).

It's the first instance, when distance eventually exceeds 2.0, that determines the features of the landscape surrounding the fractal sea and which makes the

Mandelbrot set most interesting. Each time the recursive distance reaches the breakpoint, the "altitude" of the landscape is determined by the number of recursions required to reach this point. For example, if the breakpoint is reached on the third recursion, the altitude is 3 and the point is plotted in the corresponding color. In other terms, the altitude is a measure of how fast each point, excepting those at sea level, approaches infinity.

The results are a complex map of colors showing the contours of a fractal landscape.

However, there's also more. If you will examine Figure 20-1 or 20-2 (or, better yet, your own color version), you will find that the fractal sea has many bays and tributaries along its shores. And, if you magnify (recalculate) any of these areas (as done in Figure 20-2), you will also find that all areas of the fractal sea are contiguous. There are no isolated areas and, as any area is enlarged, you will also find that the same principal features shown in Figure 20-1 repeat themselves in smaller and smaller scale throughout the Mandelbrot set, but also always remain joined together with the larger scale features.

Figure 20-1: The Mandelbrot Set

Approximate area shown in Figure 20-2 (next page).

Figure 20-2: Magnification of the Mandelbrot Set

Implementing The Mandelbrot Set

The program MANDEL.PAS provides a basic implementation of the Mandelbrot set and shows the entire area from longitude −2.0 to +0.5 and latitude −1.25 to +1.25. Viewing smaller areas of the set (and in greater detail) can be provided simply by changing the XOrg and XMax and YOrg and YMax values. The rest of the mapping procedure will adjust to accommodate the values chosen though, if desired at higher magnifications, you may also increase the Limit value beyond 100.

Warning, plotting the Mandelbrot set is slow at the best of times and increasing the value of Limit can increase the plotting times. Also, a math co-processor can assist in reducing calculation times.

MANDEL.PAS is brief and fairly straightforward but does use two subprocedures, beginning with the Calculate procedure which is used to provide the reiterative calculation for the complex expression: $(x + y)^2$.

```
procedure Calculate( XPos, YPos: real;
                 var XIter, YIter: real );
var   XTemp, YTemp: real;
```

```
begin
   XTemp := sqr( XIter ) - sqr( YIter ) + XPos;
   YTemp := 2 * ( XIter * YIter ) + YPos;
   XIter := XTemp;
   YIter := YTemp;
end;
```

Within the Calculate subprocedure, XTemp and YTemp are used to store results until both values have been calculated because both variable arguments are used in calculating each result and the original values must be available for each. Since XIter and YIter are provided as variable parameters, they return the resulting products to the calling procedure.

The second subprocedure, Distance, is a function returning a real value for the absolute distance from the arbitrary zero point (X-axis = 0, Y-axis = 0).

```
function Distance( XVal, YVal: real ): real;
begin
   if ( XVal <> 0.0 ) AND ( YVal <> 0.0 )
      then Distance := sqrt( sqr(XVal) + sqr(YVal) )
      else if XVal = 0.0 then Distance := abs( YVal )
                         else Distance := abs( XVal );
end;
```

Distance is calculated quite simply according to the Pythagorean theorem— that the sum of the squares of two sides of a right triangle is equal to the square of the hypotenuse and, therefore, the hypotenuse or distance is equal to the square root of the sum of the two squares.

The Henon Curve

In addition to fractal landscapes, a variety of other curious entities inhabit the mathematic universe and one of these is the Henon curve, an example of a wondrous mathematic creature known as a *strange attractor*.

Like the Mandelbrot set, the Henon attractor also uses a simple recursive formula and, at first glance, appears to be plotting a series of scattered dots. As the process continues, however, you will see that these scattered points actual form a complex curve as shown in Figure 20-3, rather as if some strange force continually impelled these seemingly random points to gather together in a coherent pattern. Hence, the name *strange attractor*.

The Henon Curve is like the Mandelbrot set in that any portion of it can be magnified to show greater detail. What may appear to be a single thread, under magnification, becomes a skein of threads and/or loops and curves as shown in Figure 20-4. The formula for the Henon Attractor is expressed as:

$X = Y + 1 - 1.4 * X^2$
$Y = 0.3 * X$

Warning, as magnification increases, it may be necessary to increase the number of reiterations in order to plot enough points for the details to become clear.

Figure 20-3: The Henon Attractor

The Henon attractor shows how a simple recursive formula—producing what initially appears as a scatter of points—actually creates a complex line full of folds and delicate tracery.

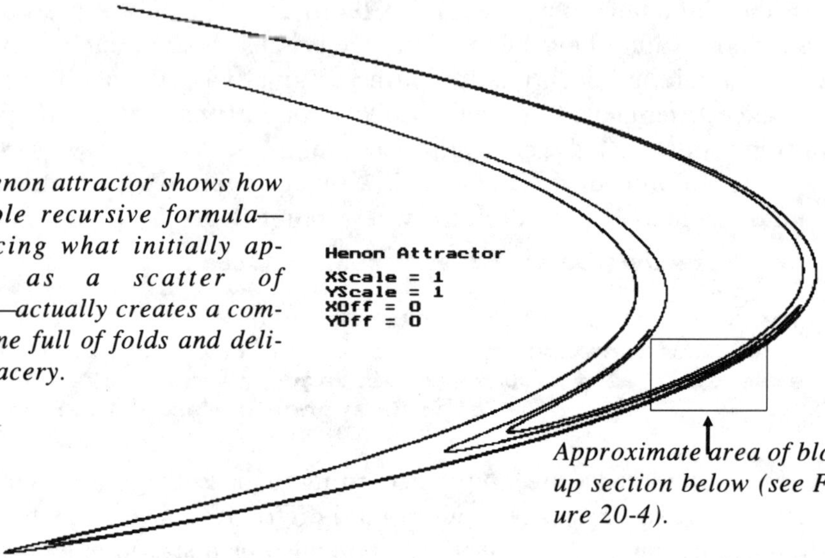

Henon Attractor
XScale = 1
YScale = 1
XOff = 0
YOff = 0

Approximate area of blow-up section below (see Figure 20-4).

The Malthusian Curve

Some years ago, while playing with the Henon Attractor, I began looking at other recursive formulas and investigating their properties in a similar manner. There are quite a variety of recursive formulas, many of which are worth looking at and one of the formulas I tried was the Malthusian Growth formula which, supposedly, calculates the growth of a population through successive generations, and is expressed as:

$$P_{n+1} = R * P_n * (1 - P_n)$$

where R is the rate of growth for successive generations of the population.

For practical purposes of calculating population growth, I suspect this formula is rather an over simplification. However, mathematically, it is also interesting because the Malthusian Curve is another strange attractor—or, more correctly, a family of strange attractors.

Figure 20-4: The Henon Attractor

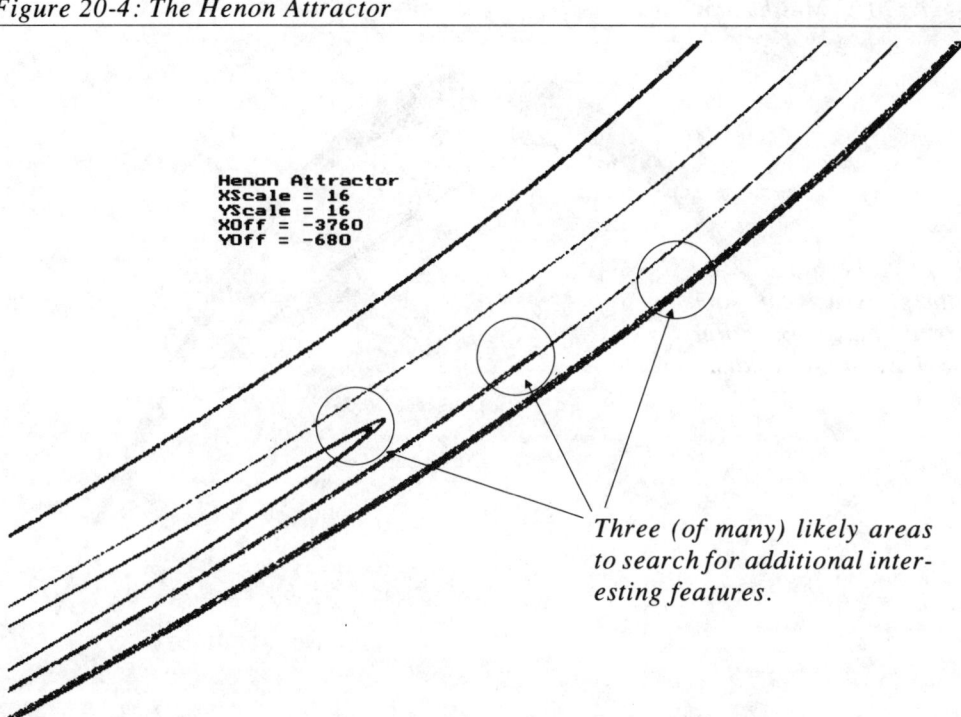

Three (of many) likely areas to search for additional interesting features.

Leaving the practical aspects aside[3], by plotting changes in R for values in the range 2.3 to 3.8 and calculating several thousand generations at each value, a series of curves are produced with each value of R creating a single, complex curve after (approximately) the first seven generations.

The values plotted for the first few generations calculated at each R can be seen in Figure 20-5 as a series of strokes beginning at the lower-left corner and show the initial generations before the values enter the proximity of the strange attractor. Once the proximity of the strange attractor is reached, however, all subsequent points—for each given value of R—will appear somewhere along the curve defined by the attractor.

Figure 20-6 provides a second view of the same set of attractors, primarily because differing views reveal details that may have been hidden earlier.

As with the previous examples, the Malthusian Curve is best understood by watching its generation (preferably on a high-resolution, color monitor) rather than by examining a black-and-white reproduction of the end result.

---

3   These are being investigated by at least one qualified professor at Chiang Mai University and are certainly beyond my explanation.

Figure 20-5: Malthusian Flux

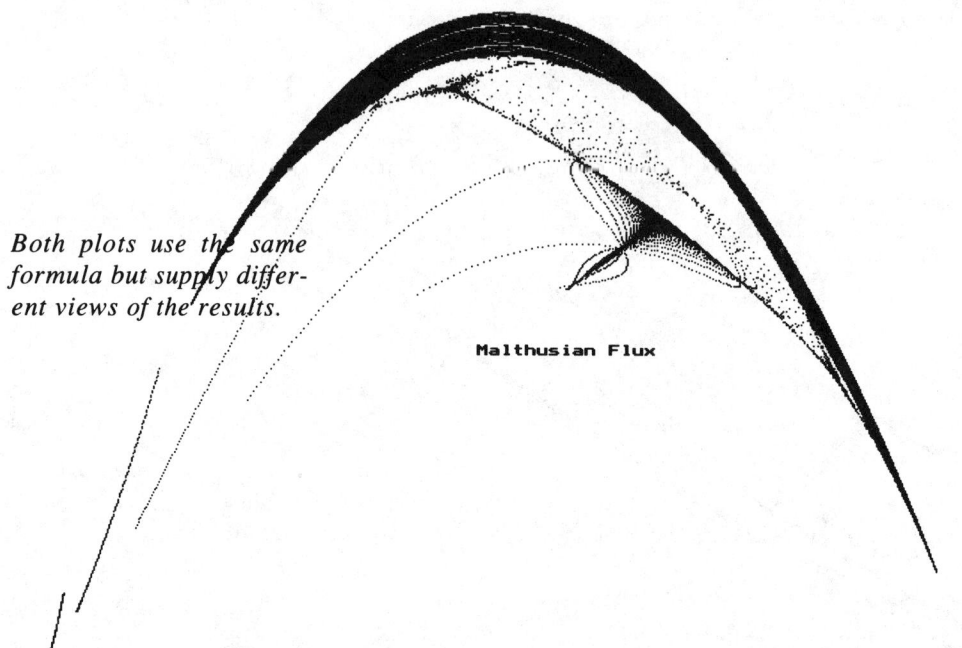

Both plots use the same formula but supply different views of the results.

Both graphs are created by plotting populations at different rates of growth. Several catastrophic discontinuities are obvious even on the scale used here while other features become visible only as the scale increases or when a different view is selected.

Figure 20-6: Malthusian Flux

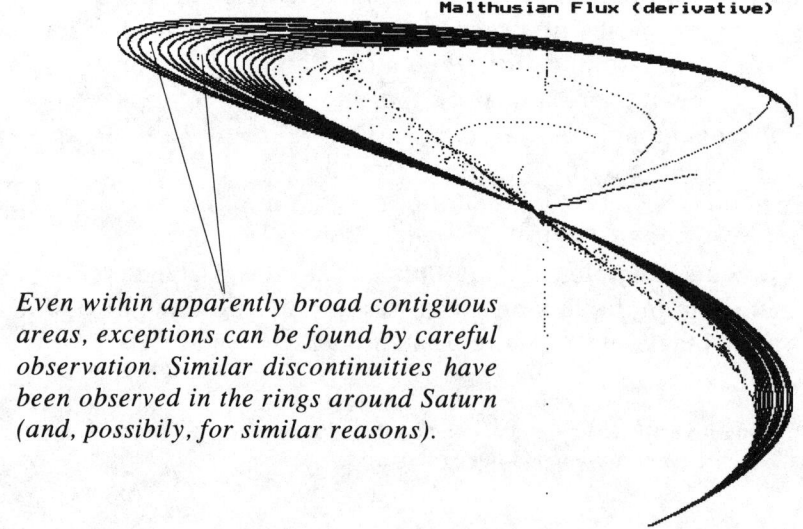

Even within apparently broad contiguous areas, exceptions can be found by careful observation. Similar discontinuities have been observed in the rings around Saturn (and, possibily, for similar reasons).

You should also notice that there are several points (values of R) where the strange attractor quite suddenly changes form and shape. And, within the final series of attractors, the group forming the broad, sweeping curve, several further discontinuities can be observed where specific values of R do not create continuous curves but only a few selected points.

In these latter cases, one possibility is that these regions may be artifacts of the machine, products of the calculations interacting with the limitations of the CPU and the algorithms used.

This brings me to my final excursion in the world of the mathematically strange.

Hic Draconis

The Dragon Curve is an interesting fractal pattern that begins as a straight line but, in each successive generation, exhibits a fractal dimension equal to the square root of 2. For example, after any two generations, the dimension (length) of the line is precisely doubled though the absolute distance between the begin and end points always remains constant.

Figure 20-7 shows a Dragon Curve in the 1st, 2nd, 3rd, and 13th generations as created by the algorithm in DRAGON.PAS, but there are two points which you should realize about each of the figures shown.

First, the Dragon Curve is composed entirely of line segments, all of which are individually equal in length and always meet at 90 degree angles. Second, the Dragon Curve is always a single continuous line that does not, at any point, cross itself (though vertices may and do coincide).

With these two cautions firmly in mind, you may enjoy attempting to trace the length of the curve. On the other hand, if you would like a less taxing approach, simply modify the source program (DRAGON.PAS) to provide a brief time delay after each segment in drawn and then watch how it's done.

Arabesque

The Dragon Curve algorithm, with one minor change, also generates a second interesting pattern that I've titled Arabesque. To produce this second fractal pattern, simply comment out the instruction:

```
Sign := Sign * -1;
```

and adjust the y-axis position as necessary.

Figure 20-7: The Dragon Curve

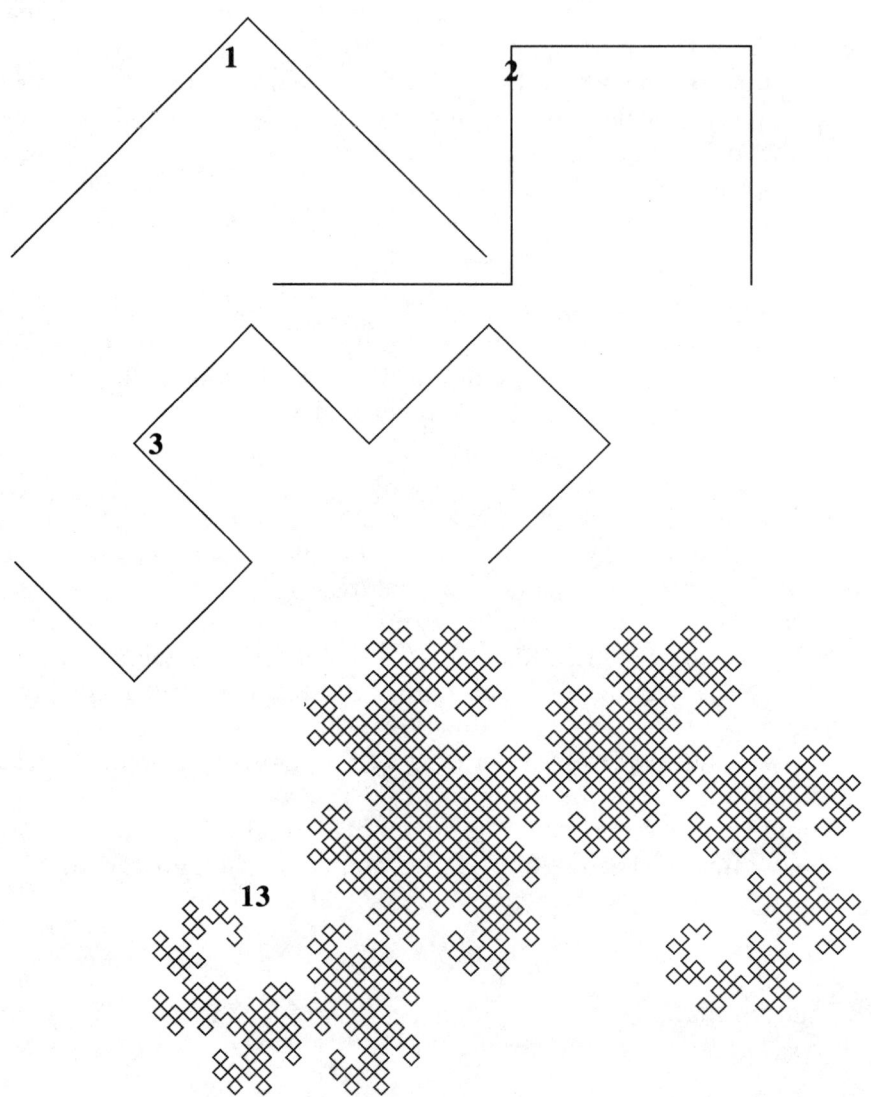

Summary

The subject of fractals is entirely too extensive to be covered in any detail in a single chapter or even in a single book. Here, I've only been able to provide a brief glimpse into a fascinating world filled with strange and wonderful detail. However, a variety of sources are available to provide at least a few maps and suggestions for further exploration, some of which are:

Mandelbrot Explorer

The Mandelbrot Explorer is a software program together with a series of stored Mandelbrot images that can be used to explore different areas within the Mandelbrot set. Requires MSDOS 2.0 or later and EGA or VGA. Available from:

> Peter Garrison
> 1613 Altivo Way
> Los Angeles, CA 90026
> (213) 665-1397

Chaos -- Making A New Science

Chaos, by James Gleick is available from Penguin Books and provides an execellent introduction and guide, not only to the world of fractal mathematics, but also to the science of chaotic systems and chaotic behavior. It explains how these mathematic entities have very real effects in the physical universe. Complete with numerous color plates, this volume is highly recommended and contains an extensive bibliography.

Chaos

Chaos, edited by Arun V. Holden, published by Princeton University Press, is an international collection of mathematical and technical papers dealing with chaotic systems, strange attractors, and fractal dimensions. While fascinating and informative—a fair knowledge of mathematics is required—this volume is not recommended for the casually curious. It will be greatly appreciated by those with the appropriate background and a modicum of patience.

Fractal Programming in Turbo Pascal

Fractal Programming by Roger T. Stevens is available from M&T Books and includes extensive program examples covering everything from the Mandelbrot set to strange attractors and fractal curves. This volume includes extensive background and notes and is recommended for anyone interested in exploring this marvelous realm.

The Science of Fractal Images

Fractal Images, edited by Peitgen and Saupe is published by Springer-Verlag and contains extensive color illustrations as well as notes and explanations from a variety of sources. This volume falls somewhere between a "coffee table" edition and an illustrated textbook but is well worth looking at.

```pascal
{ ======================== }
{          MANDEL.PAS      }
{ ======================== }
program Mandelbrot;

uses Crt, Graph;

var
   GraphDriver, GraphMode, ErrorCode: integer;

procedure Initialize;
begin
   GraphDriver := DETECT;
   initgraph( GraphDriver, GraphMode, '' );
   ErrorCode := graphresult;
   if ErrorCode <> grOk then
   begin
      writeln(' Graphics System Error: ',
              grapherrormsg( ErrorCode ) );
      halt( 1 );
   end;
end;

procedure Pause;
var
   Ch : char;
begin
   while KeyPressed do Ch := ReadKey;
   Ch := ReadKey;
end;

function Distance( XVal, YVal: real ): real;
begin
   if ( XVal <> 0.0 ) AND ( YVal <> 0.0 )
      then Distance := sqrt( sqr(XVal) + sqr(YVal) )
      else if XVal = 0.0 then Distance := abs( YVal )
                         else Distance := abs( XVal );
end;

procedure Calculate( XPos, YPos: real;
                     var XIter, YIter: real );
var
   XTemp, YTemp: real;
begin
   XTemp := sqr( XIter ) - sqr( YIter ) + XPos;
   YTemp := 2 * ( XIter * YIter ) + YPos;
   XIter := XTemp;
   YIter := YTemp;
```

```pascal
    end;
var
   XSize, YSize, Limit, i, j, Steps : integer;
   XStep, YStep, XPos, YPos, XOrg, YOrg,
   XMax, YMax, XIter, YIter : real;
   Done : boolean;
begin
   Initialize;
   XSize := GetMaxX;                   { physical screen size }
   YSize := GetMaxY;                   { physical screen size }
   Limit := 100;                       { reiteration limit   }
   {            -1.25          }
   {              ^            }
   {              |            }
   {   -2.0  <- - + - -> +0.5  }
   {              |            }
   {              v            }
   {            +1.25          }
   XOrg := -2.0;      XMax := 0.5;    { X area of Mandelbrot }
   YOrg := -1.25;     YMax := 1.25;   { Y area of Mandelbrot }
   XStep := ( XMax - XOrg ) / XSize;
   YStep := ( YMax - YOrg ) / YSize;
   for i := 0 to XSize do
      for j := 0 to YSize do
      begin
         XPos := XOrg + i * XStep;
                        { initialize value for position }
         YPos := YOrg + j * YStep;
         XIter := 0.0;    { zero the beginning values        }
         YIter := 0.0;
         Steps := 0;      { zero step value                  }
         Done := FALSE;
         repeat
            Calculate( XPos, YPos, XIter, YIter );
            inc( Steps );
            if Distance( XIter, YIter ) >= 2.0
               then Done := TRUE;
            if Steps = Limit then Done := TRUE;
            if KeyPressed then       { break out of loops }
            begin
               i := XSize;
               j := YSize;
               Done := TRUE;
            end;
         until Done;
         if Steps < Limit then PutPixel( i, j, Steps );
   end;
```

```pascal
      Pause;
      CloseGraph;
end.

                    {========================}
                    {         HENON.PAS      }
                    {========================}
program Henon_Attractor;

uses Graph, Crt;

var
   GraphDriver, GraphMode, MaxColors, ErrorCode,
   MaxX, MaxY, XScale, YScale, XOff, YOff : integer;

function I2S( X: integer ): string;
var
   TempStr : string;
begin
   str( X, TempStr );
   I2S := TempStr;
end;

procedure Initialize;
begin
   GraphDriver := DETECT;
   initgraph( GraphDriver, GraphMode, '' );
   ErrorCode := graphresult;
   if ErrorCode <> grOk then
   begin
      writeln(' Graphics System Error: ',
               grapherrormsg( ErrorCode ) );
      halt( 1 );
   end;
   MaxX := GetMaxX;
   MaxY := GetMaxY;
end;

procedure StrangeAttractor;
var
   a, i, Color: integer;
   XPos, YPos : integer;
   Xold, Xnew, Yold, Ynew,
   Xmax, Xmin, Ymax, Ymin: real;
begin
   {          Henon Attractor             }
   {   x := y + 1 - ( 1.4 * x * x )       }
   {   y := 0.3 * x                       }

   Xold := 0;   Xnew := 0;   Yold := 0;   Ynew := 0;
```

```pascal
      Xmax := 0;    Xmin := 0;    Ymax := 0; Ymin := 0;
      for Color := 1 to 15 do
         for i := 1 to $7FFF do
         begin
            Xnew := Yold + 1 - ( 1.4 * Xold * Xold );
            Ynew := 0.3 * Xold;
            XPos := trunc( ( XNew * MaxX/3 * XScale )
                         + MaxX/2 + XOff );
            YPos := trunc( ( YNew * MaxY * YScale )
                         + MaxY/2 + YOff );
            if ( XPos >= 0 ) AND ( XPos <= MaxX ) AND
               ( YPos >= 0 ) AND ( YPos <= MaxY ) then
                  putpixel( XPos, YPos, Color );
            Yold := Ynew;
            Xold := Xnew;
         end;
      outtextxy( 10, 10, 'Henon Attractor' );
      outtextxy( 10, 20, 'XScale = '+I2S( XScale ) );
      outtextxy( 10, 30, 'YScale = '+I2S( YScale ) );
      outtextxy( 10, 40, 'XOff = '+I2S( XOff ) );
      outtextxy( 10, 50, 'YOff = '+I2S( YOff ) );
end;

procedure Pause;                       { see previous example }

begin
   Initialize;
   cleardevice;
   XScale := 1;                        { values to adjust scale }
   YScale := 1;
   XOff := 0;                          { and screen position    }
   YOff := 0;
   StrangeAttractor;
   Pause;
   closegraph;
end.


               {========================}
               {      MALTHUS1.PAS      }
               {========================}
program Malthus_1;

uses Graph, Crt;

var
   GraphDriver, GraphMode, MaxColors, MaxX, MaxY, MaxGen,
ErrorCode : integer;

procedure Initialize;
begin
```

```pascal
    GraphDriver := DETECT;
    initgraph( GraphDriver, GraphMode, '' );
    ErrorCode := graphresult;
    if ErrorCode <> grOk then
    begin
        writeln(' Graphics System Error: ',
                graperrormsg( ErrorCode ) );
        halt( 1 );
    end;
    MaxX := GetMaxX;
    MaxY := GetMaxY;
end;

procedure StrangeAttractor;
var
    i, j, k, l, Color, Count, X, Y: integer;
    PopOld, PopNew, Rate: real;
begin
    {                                          }
    {     Malthusean Population Growth         }
    {         Pn+1 = R * ( Pn - Pn^2 )         }
    {                                          }
    PopNew := 0.0;
    Rate := 2.3;
    Color := BLACK;
    for j := 1 to 151 do
    begin
        inc( Color );
        if Color >= WHITE then Color := BLUE;
        Count := 0;
        Rate := Rate + 0.01;              { increment Rate    }
        PopOld := 0.01;                   { reset Population  }
        for i := 1 to MaxGen do
        begin
            PopNew := Rate * ( PopOld * ( 1 - PopOld ) );
            X := trunc( PopOld * MaxX );
            Y := trunc( MaxY - ( PopNew * MaxY ) );
            putpixel(  X, Y, Color );
            if PopOld = PopNew then inc( Count )
                               else Count := 0;
            if Count > 10 then i := MaxGen;
                                          { stagnant - break out }
            PopOld := PopNew;
        end;
    end;
    outtextxy( 10, 10, 'Malthusian Flux' );
end;

procedure Pause;                          { see previous examples }
```

```pascal
begin
   Initialize;
   cleardevice;
   MaxGen := $7FFF;
   StrangeAttractor;
   Pause;
   closegraph;
end.
```

```
{=======================}
{       MALTHUS2.PAS    }
{=======================}
```

```pascal
program Malthus_2;

uses Graph, Crt;

var
   GraphDriver, GraphMode,
   MaxColors, MaxX, MaxY, ErrorCode : integer;

procedure Initialize;
begin
   GraphDriver := DETECT;
   initgraph( GraphDriver, GraphMode, '' );
   ErrorCode := graphresult;
   if ErrorCode <> grOk then
   begin
      writeln(' Graphics System Error: ',
               grapherrormsg( ErrorCode ) );
      halt( 1 );
   end;
   MaxX := GetMaxX;
   MaxY := GetMaxY;
end;

procedure StrangeAttractor;
var
   i, j, k, l, Color, Count: integer;
   PopOld, PopNew, X, Y, Rate: real;
begin
   PopOld := 0.0;
   PopNew := 0.0;
   Rate := 2.3;
   Y := 0;
   for j := 1 to 15 do
   begin
      inc( Color );
      if Color > WHITE then Color := BLUE;
      for k := 1 to 10 do
      begin
```

```
         Count  := 0;
         Rate   := Rate + 0.01;
         PopOld := 0.01;
         for  i := 1 to 10000 do
         begin
            PopNew := Rate * ( PopOld * ( 1 - PopOld ) );
            X := PopNew - PopOld;
            putpixel( trunc((X*MaxX/2)+MaxX/2),
                      trunc((MaxY/2)-(Y*MaxY/2)), Color);
            if PopOld = PopNew then inc( Count )
                               else Count := 0;
            if Count > 100 then i := 10000;
            PopOld := PopNew;
            Y := X;
         end;
      end;
   end;
   outtextxy( 10, 10, 'Malthusian Flux' );
end;

procedure Pause;                     { see previous examples }

begin
   Initialize;
   cleardevice;
   StrangeAttractor;
   Pause;
   closegraph;
end.

                {=========================}
                {       DRAGON.PAS        }
                {=========================}

program Dragon_Curve;

uses Crt, Graph;

var
   GraphDriver, GraphMode, ErrorCode: integer;
   XAxis, YAxis : array[1..4098] of integer;
   Step, Sign: integer;

procedure Initialize;
begin
   GraphDriver := DETECT;
   initgraph( GraphDriver, GraphMode, '' );
   ErrorCode := graphresult;
   if ErrorCode <> grOk then
   begin
      writeln(' Graphics System Error: ',
```

```
                        grapherrormsg( ErrorCode ) );
         halt( 1 );
      end;
   end;
end;

procedure Pause;                              { see previous examples }
procedure Generate_Dragon( color: integer );
var
   i, j, dx, dy: integer;
begin
   j := Step div 2;
   setcolor( color );
   i := 1;
   repeat
      dx := xaxis[Step+i] - xaxis[i];
      dy := yaxis[Step+i] - yaxis[i];
      Sign := Sign * -1;
      xaxis[i+j] :=  xaxis[i] +
                     ( dx + ( dy * sign ) ) div 2;
      yaxis[i+j] :=  yaxis[i] +
                     ( dy - ( dx * sign ) ) div 2;
      if color <> 0 then
      begin
         line( xaxis[i], yaxis[i],
               xaxis[i+j], yaxis[i+j] );
         line( xaxis[i+j], yaxis[i+j],
               xaxis[i+Step], yaxis[i+Step] );
      end;
      inc( i, Step );
   until i >= 4096;
end;

var
   i: integer;
begin
   Step := 4096;
   sign := -1;
   Initialize;
   xaxis[1] := GetMaxX div 4;
   xaxis[4097] := 3 * GetMaxX div 4;
   yaxis[1] := 2 * GetMaxY div 3;
   yaxis[4097] := yaxis[1];
   setcolor( BLUE );
   line( xaxis[1], yaxis[1], xaxis[4097], yaxis[4097] );
   delay( 1000 );
   for i := 1 to 12 do
   begin
      clearviewport;
      OutTextXY( 1, 10, 'Fractal Dragon Curve' );
```

```
         Generate_Dragon( i );
         Step := Step div 2;
         delay( 1000 );
      end;
      Pause;
      closegraph;
end.
```

APPENDIX A

The BGI Driver Toolkit

Creating Device Drivers for the Borland Graphics Interface

The BGI Driver Toolkit is available at no charge on an "as is" basis to users of Turbo Pascal, Turbo C, and Turbo Prolog and may be downloaded from Borland International's languages forum on the CompuServe network. The BGI Driver Toolkit also includes a .BIN-to-.BGI conversion utility (DFONT.EXE, DFONT.C, and FONT.H) and a "debug" driver.

Also available from Borland, via CompuServe, are the Turbo Font Editor (see Chapter 17) with nine graphics character fonts: EURO.CHR, GOTH.CHR, LCOM.CHR, LITT.CHR, SANS.CHR, SCRI.CHR, SIMP.CHR, TRIP.CHR, and TSCR.CHR; and a new VGA 256-color .BGI driver (see Appendix E). Future revisions and updates will be available on Borland's CompuServe forum.

The BGI Driver Toolkit

Copyright (c) 1988 Borland International
Revision 1
September 15, 1988

This information and the accompanying program files are supplied at no charge to registered users of Borland's Turbo Pascal, Turbo C, and Turbo Prolog products.

Introduction

The Borland Graphics Interface (BGI) is a fast, compact, and device-independent software package for graphics development built into the Turbo Pascal, Turbo C, and Turbo Prolog language products. Device independence is achieved via loadable device-specific drivers called from a common kernel. This document describes basic BGI functionality, as well as the steps necessary to create new device drivers. Accompanying this document are files containing sample code (see Table D-1) and other pertinent information.

Table A-1: Sample Code Files

FILENAME	FILE DESCRIPTION
BH.C	BGI loader header building program source
BH.EXE	BGI loader header building program
DEVICE.INC	Structure and macro definition file
DEBVECT.ASM	Vector table for sample (DEBUG) driver
DEBUG.C	Main module for sample driver
MAKEFILE	Build file
BUILD.BAT	Batch file for MAKE-phobics
TEST.C	C program demonstrating how to register and load a new device driver
DFONT.EXE	.BIN-to-.BGI conversion utility
DFONT.C	C source code for the conversion utility
FONT.H	Header file used by DFONT

BGI Run-time Architecture

Programs produced by Borland languages create graphics via two entities acting in concert; the generic BGI kernel and a device-specific driver. Typically, an application built with a Borland compiler will include several device driver files on the distribution disk (extension .BGI) so that the program can run on various types of screens and printers. Graphics requests (for example, draw line, and draw bar) are sent by the application to the BGI kernel, which in turn makes requests of the device driver to actually manipulate the hardware.

A BGI device driver is a binary image; that is, a sequence of bytes without symbols or other linking information. The driver begins with a short header, followed by a vector table containing the entry points to the functions inside. The balance of the driver comprises the code and data required to manipulate the target graphics hardware.

All code and data references in the driver must be near (i.e., small model, offset only), and the entire driver, both code and data, must fit within 64K. In use, the device driver can count on its being loaded on a paragraph boundary.

The BGI kernel uses a register-based calling convention to communicate with the device driver (described in detail below).

BGI Graphics Model

When considering the functions listed below, keep in mind that BGI performs most drawing operations using an implicit drawing or tracing color (COLOR), fill color (FILLCOLOR), and pattern (FILLPATTERN). For example, the PieSlice call accepts no pattern or color information, but instead uses the previously set COLOR value to trace the edge of the slice, and the previously set FILLCOLOR and FILLPATTERN values for the interior.

For efficiency, many operations take place at the position of the CP. For example, the Line routine accepts only a single (x,y) coordinate pair, using the CP as the starting point of the line and the passed coordinate pair as the ending point. Many functions (Line, to name one) affect CP, and the MOVE function can be used to explicitly adjust CP. The BGI coordinate system places the origin (pixel 0,0) at the upper left-hand corner of the screen.

Header Section

The device header section, which must be at the beginning of the device driver, is built using macro BGI defined in file DEVICE.INC. The BGI macro takes the name of the device driver to be built as an argument. For example, a driver named DEBUG would begin as shown here:

```
CSEG    SEGMENT PARA PUBLIC 'CODE'     ; any segment naming may be used
        ASSUME   DS:CSEG, CS:CSEG       ; cs=ds
        CODESEG
        INCLUDE DEVICE.INC              ; include the device.inc file
        BGI            DEBUG            ; declare the device header section
```

The device header section declares a special entry point known as EMULATE. If the action of a device driver vector is not supported by the hardware of a device, the vector entry should contain the entry EMULATE. This will be patched at load-time to contain a jump to the kernel's emulation routine. These routines will emulate the action of the vector by breaking down the request into simpler primitives. For example, if the hardware has functionality to draw polygons, the polygon vector will contain the address of the routine to dispatch the polygon data to the hardware and would appear as follows:

```
        dw      offset    POLYGON       ; Vector to the Polygon Routine
```

If, as is often the case, the hardware doesn't have the functionality to display polygons, the vector would instead contain the EMULATE vector:

```
        dw                EMULATE       ; Polygon functions must be emulated
```

The kernel has emulation support for the following vectors:

Table A-2: Vector Emulation Support

VECTOR	DESCRIPTION
POLYGON	Rendering polygons
BARFILL	Filling rectangles
PATBAR	Pattern filling of rectangles
ARC	Elliptical arc rendering
PIESLICE	Elliptical pie slices
FILLEDELLIPSE	Filled ellipses
SYMBOLS	Line marking symbols
FILLSTYLE	Solid filling styles
TSTYLE	Text drawing styles
TEXT	Hardware text rendering
TEXTSIZ	Scaling of hardware text

The Driver Status Table

BGI requires that each driver contain a Driver Status Table (DST) to determine the basic characteristics of the device which the driver addresses. As an example, the DST for a CGA display is shown here:

```
STATUS   STRUC
STAT        DB      0           ; Current Device Status (0 = No Errors)
DEVTYP      DB      0           ; Device Type Identifier (must be 0)
XRES        DW      639         ; Device Full Resolution in X Direction
YRES        DW      199         ; Device Full Resolution in Y Direction
XEFRES      DW      639         ; Device Effective X Resolution
YEFRES      DW      199         ; Device Effective Y Resolution
XINCH       DW      9000        ; Device X Size in inches*1000
YINCH       DW      7000        ; Device Y Size in inches*1000
ASPEC       DW      4500        ; Aspect Ratio = (y_size/x_size) * 10000
            DB      8h
            DB      8h          ; for compatibility, use these values
            DB      90h
            DB      90h
STATUS   ENDS
```

The BGI interface provides a system for reporting errors to the BGI kernel and to the higher level code developed using Borland's language packages. This is done using the STAT field of the Driver Status Table. This field should be filled in by the driver code if an error is detected during the execution of the device installation (INSTALL). The following error codes are predefined in the header file GRAPHICS.H for Turbo C and in the Graphics unit for Turbo Pascal.

Table A-3: BGI Error Codes

FUNCTION	ERROR	COMMENT
grOk	= 0	Normal operation, no errors
grNoInitGraph	= –1	
grNotDetected	= –2	
grFileNotFound	= –3	
grInvalidDriver	= –4	
grNoLoadMem	= –5	
grNoScanMem	= –6	
grNoFloodMem	= –7	
grFontNotFound	= –8	
grNoFontMem	= –9	
grInvalidMode	= –10	
grError	= –11	Generic driver error
grIOerror	= –12	
grInvalidFont	= –13	
grInvalidFontNum	= –14	
grInvalidDeviceNum	= –15	

The next field in the Device Status Table, DEVTYP, describes the class of the device which the driver controls; for screen devices this value is always 0.

The next four fields, XRES, YRES, XEFRES, and YEFRES contain the number of pixels available to BGI on this device in the horizontal and vertical dimensions, minus one. For screen devices, XRES=XEFRES and YRES=YEFRES. The XINCH and YINCH fields are the number of inches horizontally and vertically into which the device's pixels are mapped, times 1,000. These fields in conjunction with XRES and YRES permit device resolution (DPI, or dots per inch) calculation.

$$\text{Horizontal resolution (DPI)} = (\text{XRES}+1) / (\text{XINCH}/1000)$$
$$\text{Vertical resolution (DPI)} = (\text{YRES}+1) / (\text{YINCH}/1000)$$

The ASPEC (aspect ratio) field is effectively a multiplier/divisor pair (the divisor is always 10,000) which is applied to Y coordinate values to produce aspect-ratio adjusted images (for example, round circles). For example, an ASPEC field of 4,500 implies that the application will have to transform Y coordinates by the ratio: 4,500/10,000 when drawing circles to that device if it expects them to be round. Individual monitor variations may require an additional adjustment by the application.

The Device Driver Vector Table

The device driver routines are accessed via a vector table. This table is at the beginning of the driver and contains 16-bit offsets to subroutines and configuration tables within the driver. The format of the vector table is shown below.

```
VECTOR_TABLE:
        DW      INSTALL         ; Driver initialization and installation
        DW      INIT            ; Initialize device for output
        DW      CLEAR           ; Clear graphics device; get fresh screen
        DW      POST            ; Exit from graphics mode, unload plotter, etc.
        DW      MOVE            ; Move Current Pointer (CP) to (X,Y)
        DW      DRAW            ; Draw line from (CP) to (X,Y)
        DW      VECT            ; Draw line from (X0,Y0) to (X1,Y1)
        DW      POLY            ; Define polygon
        DW      BAR             ; Filled rectangle from (CP) to (X,Y)
        DW      PATBAR          ; Patterned rectangle from (X,Y) to (X1,Y1)
        DW      ARC             ; Define arc
        DW      PIESLICE        ; Define an elliptical pie slice
        DW      FILLEDELLIPSE   ; Draw a filled ellipse
        DW      PALETTE         ; Load a palette entry
        DW      ALLPALETTE      ; Load the full palette
        DW      COLOR           ; Set current drawing color/background
        DW      FILLSTYLE       ; Filling control and style
        DW      LINESTYLE       ; Line drawing style control
        DW      TEXTSTYLE       ; Hardware font control
        DW      TEXT            ; Hardware draw text at (CP)
        DW      TEXTSIZ         ; Hardware font size query
        DW      FLOODFILL       ; Fill a bounded region
        DW      GETPIX          ; Read a pixel from (X,Y)
        DW      PUTPIX          ; Write a pixel to (X,Y)
        DW      BITMAPUTIL      ; Bitmap size query function
        DW      SAVEBITMAP      ; BITBLT from screen to system memory
        DW      RESTOREBITMAP   ; BITBLT from system memory to screen
        DW      SETCLIP         ; Define a clipping rectangle
        DW      COLOR_QUERY     ; Color Table Information Query
        DW      RESERVED        ; Reserved for Borland's use (0)
        DW      SYMBOL          ; Draw a graphics symbol
;
;       32 additional vectors are reserved for Borland's future use.
;
        DW      RESERVED        ; Reserved for Borland's use (1)
        DW      RESERVED        ; Reserved for Borland's use (2)
        DW      RESERVED        ; Reserved for Borland's use (3)
            .
            .
            .
        DW      RESERVED        ; Reserved for Borland's use (30)
        DW      RESERVED        ; Reserved for Borland's use (31)
        DW      RESERVED        ; Reserved for Borland's use (32)
```

```
;
;           Any vectors following this block may be used by
;           independent device driver developers as they see fit.
;
```

Vector Descriptions

The following information describes the input, output, and use of each of the functions accessed through the device vector table.

    DW offset INSTALL ; device driver installation

The kernel calls the INSTALL vector to prepare the device driver for use. A function code is passed in AL. The following function codes are defined:

Install Device

  —>Install Device: AL = 00
  Input: CL = Mode Number for device
            CH = Auto-Detect maximum device number
  Return: ES:BX —> Device Status Table
            (see STATUS structure, preceding)

The Install Device function is intended to inform the driver of the operating parameters that will be used. The device should not be switched to graphics mode (see INIT). On input, CL contains the mode in which the device will operate, and CH contains the maximum device number which will be used. An example of the use of the maximum device number is a graphics board with four modes, the last two of which require extended hardware. The Auto-Detect routine would check for the additional hardware, and if it is not present, would set the Maximum Device Number to limit entering the modes requiring the additional hardware.

The return value from the Install Device function is a pointer to a Device Status Table (described earlier).

Mode Query

  —>Mode Query: AL = 001h
  Input: Nothing
  Return: CX number of modes supported by device

The Mode Query function is used to inquire the maximum number of modes supported by this device driver. This value is effected by the setting of the Auto-Detect Maximum Device Number as set in the Install Device function described above.

Mode Names

—>Mode Names:	AL = 002h	
Input:	CX	The mode number for the query
Return:	ES:BX —> a Pascal string containing the name	

The Mode Names function is used to inquire the ASCII form of the mode number present in CX. The return value in ES:BX points to a Pascal string describing the given mode.

A Pascal, or _length_, string is a string in which the first byte of data is the number of characters in the string, followed by the string data itself. To ease access to these strings from C, the strings should be followed by a zero byte, although this zero byte should not be included in the string length. The following is an example of this format:

```
NAME:          db      16, '1280 x 1024 Mode', 0
```

INIT

DW	offset	INIT	; Initialize device for output
Input:	ES:BX		—> Device Information Table
Return:	Nothing		

This vector is used to change an already INSTALLed device from text mode to graphics mode. This vector should also initialize any default palettes and drawing mode information as required. The input to this vector is a device information table (DIT). The format of the DIT is shown below and contains the background color and an initialization flag. If the device requires additional information at INIT-time, these values can be appended to the DIT. There in no return value for this function. If an error occurs during device initialization, the STAT field of the Device Status Table should be loaded with the appropriate error value.

```
; ************* Device Information Table definition **************
struct  DIT
        DB      0               ; Background color for initializing screen
        DB      0               ; Init flag; 0A5h = don't init;
                                ;   anything else = init
        DB      64 dup 0        ; Reserved for Borland's future use
                                ; additional user information here
DIT     ends
```

CLEAR

 DW offset CLEAR ; Clear the graphics device
 Input: Nothing
 Return: Nothing

This vector is used to clear the graphics device to a known state. In the case of a CRT device, the screen is cleared. In the case of a printer or plotter, the paper is advanced, and pens are returned to station.

POST

 DW offset POST ; Exit from graphics mode
 Input: Nothing
 Return: Nothing

This routine is used to close the graphics system. In the case of graphics screens or printers, the mode should be returned to text mode. For plotters, the paper should be unloaded and the pens should return to station.

MOVE

 DW offset MOVE ; Move the current drawing pointer
 Input: AX the new CP x coordinate
     BX the new CP y coordinate
 Return: Nothing

Sets the Driver's current pointer to (AX,BX). This function is used prior to any of the TEXT, Arc, SYMBOL, DRAW, FloodFill, Bar, or PieSlice routines to set the position where drawing is to take place.

DRAW

 DW offset DRAW ; Draw a line from the (CP) to (X,Y)
 Input: AX the ending x coordinate for the line
     BX the ending y coordinate for the line
 Return: Nothing

Draws a line from the to (X,Y). The current LineSTYLE setting is used. The current pointer is updated to the line's endpoint.

VECT

 DW VECT ; Draw line from (X1,Y1) to (X2,Y2)
 Input: AX X1; The beginning X coordinate for the line

	BX	Y1; The beginning Y coordinate for the line
	CX	X2; The ending X coordinate for the line
	DX	Y2; The ending Y coordinate for the line
Return:	Nothing	

Draws a line from the (X1,Y1) to (X2,Y2). The current LineSTYLE setting is used to draw the line. CP is *not* changed by this vector.

POLY

	DW	POLY	; Define polygon.
Input:	ES:BX		—> polygon
	CX = number of points in polygon		
	AX = 6		outline polygon in current color
	AX = 7		outline and fill polygon in current color, fill color and fill pattern
	AX = 8		fill polygon in current fill color and fill pattern
Return:	Nothing		

The polygon entry point is usually EMULATEd. Users with hardware capable of accepting polygon data in a single operation should contact Borland's technical support department for more information.

BAR

	DW	BAR	; fill and outline rectangle (CP),(X,Y)
Input:		AX	X — right edge of rectangle
		BX	Y — bottom edge of rectangle
		CX	3D = width of 3D Bar (ht = .75 * wdt); 0 = no 3D effect
		DX	3D Bar top flag; if CX <> 0 and DX = 0, draw a top
Return:	Nothing		

Fills and outlines a bar (rectangle), using the current COLOR, FILLCOLOR, and FILLPATERN. The current pointer defines the upper, left corner of the Rectangle and (X,Y) is lower, right. An optional 3-D shadow effect (intended for business graphics programs) is obtained by making CX nonzero. DX then serves as a flag indicating whether a top should be drawn on the bar.

PATBAR

	DW	PATBAR	; fill Rectangle (X1,Y1), (X2,Y2)
Input:		AX	X1 — the rectangle's left coordinate
		BX	Y1 — the rectangle's top coordinate
		CX	X2 — the rectangle's right coordinate
		DX	Y2 — the rectangle's bottom coordinate
Return:		Nothing	

Fills (but doesn't outline) the indicated Rectangle with the current fill pattern and fill color.

ARC

	DW	ARC	; Draw an elliptical arc
Input:		AX	Starting angle of the arc in degrees (0..360)
		BX	Ending angle of the arc in degrees (0..360)
		CX	X radius of the elliptical arc
		DX	Y radius of the elliptical arc
Return:		Nothing	

Arc draws an elliptical arc using the CP as the center point of the arc, from the given start angle to the given end angle. To get circular arcs, the application (not the driver) must adjust the Y radius as follows: *YRAD := XRAD * (ASPEC / 10000)* where ASPEC is the aspect value stored in the DST.

PIESLICE

	DW	PIESLICE	; Draw an elliptical pie slice
Input:		AX	Starting angle of the slice in degrees (0..360)
		BX	Ending angle of the slice in degrees (0..360)
		CX	X radius of the elliptical slice
		DX	Y radius of the elliptical slice
Return:		Nothing	

PieSlice draws a filled elliptical pie slice (or wedge) using CP as the center of the slice, from the given start angle to the given end angle. The current FILLPATTERN and FILLCOLOR is used to fill the slice and it is outlined in the current COLOR. To get circular pie slices the application (not the driver) must adjust the Y radius as follows: *YRAD := XRAD * ASPEC / 10000* where ASPEC is the aspect value stored in the driver's DST.

FILLED_ELLIPSE

DW	FILLED_ELLIPSE	; Draw a filled ellipse at CP
Input:	AX	X Radius of the ellipse
	BX	Y Radius of the ellipse
Return:	Nothing	

This vector is used to draw a filled Ellipse. The center point of the Ellipse is assumed to be at the current pointer. The AX Register contains the X Radius of the Ellipse, and the BX Register contains the Y Radius of the Ellipse.

PALETTE

DW	PALETTE	; Load a color entry into the palette
Input:	AX	Index number and function code for load
	BX	Color value to load into the palette
Return:	Nothing	

The PALETTE vector is used to load single entries into the palette. The register AX contains the function code for the load action and the index of the color table entry to be loaded. The upper two bits of AX determine the action to be taken. The table below tabulates the actions. If the control bits are 00, the color table index in (AX AND 03FFFh) is loaded with the value in BX. If the control bits are 10, the color table index in (AX AND 03FFFh) is loaded with the RGB value in (Red=BX, Green=CX, and Blue=DX). If the control bits are 11, the color table entry for the background is loaded with the value in BX.

Table A-4: Register AX Actions

CONTROL BITS	COLOR VALUE AND INDEX
00	Register BX contains color, AX is index
01	Not used
10	Red=BX, Green=CX, Blue=DX, AX is index
11	Register BX contains color for background

ALLPALETTE

DW	ALLPALETTE	; Load the full palette
Input:	ES:BX	—> array of palette entries
Return:	Nothing	

The ALLPALETTE routine loads the entire palette in one driver call. The register pair ES:BX points to the table of values to be loaded into the palette. The number of entries is determined by the color entries in the Driver Status Table. The background color is not explicitly loaded with this command.

COLOR

DW	COLOR	; Load the current drawing color
Input:	AL	Index number of the current drawing color
	AH	Index number of the fill color
Return:	Nothing	

The COLOR vector is used to determine the current drawing color. The value in AL is the index into the palette of the new current drawing color. The value in the AH register is the color index of the new fill color. All primitives are drawn with the current drawing color until the color is changed.

The fill color is used for the interior color for the Bar, polygon, pie slice, and FloodFill primitives.

FILLSTYLE

DW	FILLSTYLE	; Set the filling pattern
Input:	AL	Primary fill pattern number
	ES:BX	If the pattern number is 0FFh, this points to user define pattern mask.
Return:	Nothing	

Sets the fill pattern for drawing. The fill pattern is used to fill all bounded regions (Bar, POLY, and PieSlice). The numbers for the pre-defined fill patterns are as follows:

Table A-5: Predefined Fill Patterns

CODE	DESCRIPTION	8-BYTE FILL PATTERN
0	No Fill	000h, 000h, 000h, 000h, 000h, 000h, 000h, 000h
1	Solid Fill	0FFh, 0FFh, 0FFh, 0FFh, 0FFh, 0FFh, 0FFh, 0FFh
2	Line Fill	0FFh, 0FFh, 000h, 000h, 0FFh, 0FFh, 000h, 000h
3	Lt Slash Fill	001h, 002h, 004h, 008h, 010h, 020h, 040h, 080h
4	Slash Fill	0E0h, 0C1h, 083h, 007h, 00Eh, 01Ch, 038h, 070h
5	Backslash Fill	0F0h, 078h, 03Ch, 01Eh, 00Fh, 087h, 0C3h, 0E1h
6	Lt Bkslash Fill	0A5h, 0D2h, 069h, 0B4h, 05Ah, 02Dh, 096h, 04Bh
7	Hatch Fill	0FFh, 088h, 088h, 088h, 0FFh, 088h, 088h, 088h
8	XHatch Fill	081h, 042h, 024h, 018h, 018h, 024h, 042h, 081h
9	Interleave Fill	0CCh, 033h, 0CCh, 033h, 0CCh, 033h, 0CCh, 033h
10	Wide Dot Fill	080h, 000h, 008h, 000h, 080h, 000h, 008h, 000h
11	Close Dot Fill	088h, 000h, 022h, 000h, 088h, 000h, 022h, 000h
0FFh	User-defined fill pattern	

In the case of a user-defined fill pattern, the register pair ES:BX point to 8 bytes of data arranged as a 8x8 bit pattern to be used for the fill pattern.

LINESTYLE

DW	LineSTYLE	; Set the line drawing pattern
Input:	AL	Line pattern number
	BX	User defined line drawing pattern
	CX	Line width for drawing
Return:	Nothing	

Sets the current line drawing style and the width of the line. The line width is either one pixel or three pixels in width. The following table defines the default line styles:

Table A-6: Default Line Styles

CODE	DESCRIPTION	16-BIT PATTERN	HEXADECIMAL
AL = 0	Solid Line Style	1111111111111111b	FFFFh
AL = 1	Dotted Line	1100110011001100b	CCCCh
AL = 2	Center Line	1111110001111000b	FC78h
AL = 3	Dashed line	1111100011111000b	F8F8h
AL = 4	User-defined line style		

If the value in AL is four, the user is defining a line style in the BX register. If the value in AL is not four, then the value in register BX is ignored.

TEXTSTYLE

DW	TEXTSTYLE	; Hardware text style control
Input:	AL	Hardware font number
	AH	Hardware font orientation
		0 = Normal, 1 = 90°, 2 = Down
	BX	Desired X character size *
	CX	Desired Y character size *
Return:	BX	Closest X character size available *
	CX	Closest Y character size available *
		* in graphics units

The TEXTSTYLE vector is used to define the attributes of the hardware font for output. The parameters which are affected are the selection of which hardware font to be used, the orientation of the font for output, the desired height and width of the font output. All subsequent text will be drawn using these attributes.

If the desired size is not supported by the current device, the closest available match to the desired size should be used. The return value from this function give the dimensions of the font (in pixels) which will actually used.

For example, if the desired font is 8x10 pixels, and the device supports 8x8 and 16x16 fonts, the closest match will be the 8x8. The output of the function will be BX = 8, and CX = 8.

TEXT

DW	TEXT	; Hardware text output at (CP)
Input:	ES:BX	—> ASCII text of the string
	CX	The length (in characters) of the string
	AL	Horizontal justification point
		0 = Left, 1 = Center, 2 = Right
	AH	Vertical justification point
		0 = Bottom, 1 = Center, 2 = Top
Return:	BX	The width of the string in graphics units
	CX	The height of the string in graphics units

This function is used to send hardware text to the output device. The text is output to the device beginning at the (CP). The placement of the text with respect to the (CP) is determined by the two bytes in AX. The value in AL is the horizontal justification flag. If the value is 0, the (CP) defines the left-most edge of the text string, if the value is 1, the (CP) defines the center of the text string, and if the value is 2, the (CP) defines the right-most edge of the text string. The value in AH is the vertical justification flag. If the value is 0, the (CP) defines the bottom edge of the text string, if the value is 1, the (CP) defines the center of the text string, and if the value is 2, the (CP) defines the top edge of the text string. The following table demonstrates the justification point placement:

Table A-7: Justification Point Placement

	LEFT	CENTER	RIGHT
TOP	AL=0, AH=2	AL=1, AH=2	AL=2, AH=2
CENTER	AL=0, AH=1	AL=1, AH=1	AL=2, AH=1
BOTTOM	AL=0, AH=0	AL=1, AH=0	AL=2, AH=0

TEXTSIZ

DW	TEXTSIZ	; Determine the height and width of text
		; strings in graphics units
Input:	ES:BX	—> ASCII text of the string
	CX	The length (in characters) of the string
Return:	BX	The width of the string in graphics units
	CX	The height of the string in graphics units

This function is used to determine the actual physical length and width of a text string. The current text attributes (set by TEXTSTYLE) are used to determine the actual dimensions of a string without displaying it. The application can thereby determine how a specific string will fit and reduce or increase the font size as required. There is *no* graphics output for this vector. If an error occurs during length calculation, the STAT field of the Device Status Record should be marked with the device error code.

FLOODFILL

DW	FLOODFILL	; Fill a bounded region using a flood fill
Input:	AX	The x coordinate for the seed point
	BX	The y coordinate for the seed point
	CL	The boundary color for the Flood Fill
Return:	Nothing	(Errors returned in Device Status STAT field)

This function is called to fill a bounded region on bitmap devices. The (X,Y) input coordinate is used as the seed point for the flood fill. (CP) becomes the seed point. The current FILLPATTERN is used to flood the region.

GETPIXEL

DW	GETPIXEL	; Read a pixel from the graphics screen
Input:	AX	The x coordinate for the seed point
	BX	The y coordinate for the seed point
Return:	DL	The color index of the screen pixel read

GetPixel reads the color index value of a single pixel from the graphics screen. The color index value is returned in the DL register.

PUTPIXEL

DW	PUTPIXEL	; Write a pixel to the graphics screen
Input:	AX	The x coordinate for the seed point
	BX	The y coordinate for the seed point
	DL	The color index of the pixel
Return:	Nothing	

PutPixel writes a single pixel with the the color index value contained in the DL register.

BITMAPUTIL

DW	BITMAPUTIL;	Bitmap Utilities Function Table
Input:	Nothing	
Return:	ES:BX	—> BitMap Utility Table

The BITMAPUTIL vector loads a pointer into ES:BX which is the base of a table defining special case entry points used for pixel manipulation. These functions are currently only called by the ellipse emulation routines that are in the BGI kernel. If the device driver does not use emulation for ellipses, this entry does not have to be implemented. This entry was provided since some hardware requires additional commands to enter and exit pixel mode, thus adding overhead to the GETPIXEL and SETPIXEL vectors. This overhead affected the drawing speed of the Ellipse emulation routines. These entry points are provided so that the Ellipse emulation routines can enter pixel mode and remain in pixel mode, for the duration of the Ellipse rendering process.

The format of the BITMAPUTIL table is as follows:

```
DW    offset  GOTOGRAPHIC
                      ; Enter pixel mode on the graphics hardware
DW    offset  EXITGRAPHIC
                      ; Leave pixel mode on the graphics hardware
DW    offset  PUTPIXEL
                      ; Write a pixel to the graphics hardware
DW    offset  GETPIXEL
                      ; Read a pixel from the graphics hardware
DW    offset  GETPIXBYTE
                      ; Return a word containing the pixel depth
DW    offset  SET_DRAW_PAGE
                      ; Select page in which to draw primitives
DW    offset  SET_VISUAL_PAGE
                      ; Set the page to be displayed
DW    offset  SET_WRITE_MODE
                      ; XOR Line Drawing Control
```

The parameters of these functions are as follows:

GOTOGRAPHIC   ; Enter pixel mode on the graphics hardware

This function is used to enter the special Pixel Graphics mode:

EXITGRAPHIC   ; Leave pixel mode on the graphics hardware

This function is used to leave the special Pixel Graphics mode:

PUTPIXEL   ; Write a pixel to the graphics hardware

This function has the same format as the PutPixel entry described previously:

  GETPIXEL   ; Read a pixel from the graphics hardware

This function has the same format as the GetPixel entry described previously:

  GETPIXBYTE   ; Return a word containing the pixel depth

This function returns the number of bits per pixel (color depth) of the graphics hardware in the AX register:

  SET_DRAW_PAGE ; Select alternate output graphics pages (if any)

This function takes the desired page number in the AL register and selects alternate graphics pages for output of graphics primitives:

  SET_VISUAL_PAGE ; Select the visible alternate graphics pages (if any)

This function takes the desired page number in the AL register and selects alternate graphics for displaying on the screen:

  SET_WRITE_MODE ; XOR Line drawing mode control

XOR Mode is selected if the value in AX is one, and disabled if the value in AX is zero.

SAVEBITMAP

DW	SAVEBITMAP	; Write from screen to system memory
Input:	ES:BX	—> write buffer in system memory
	SI	Starting X coordinate of screen block
	DI	Starting Y coordinate of screen block
	CX	Ending X coordinate of screen block
	DX	Ending Y coordinate of screen block
Return:	Nothing	

The SAVEBITMAP routine is a block copy routine that copies screen pixels from a defined Rectangle as specified by (SI,DI)–(CX,DX) to the system memory.

RESTOREBITMAP

DW	RESTOREBITMAP	; Write system memory to the screen
Input:	ES:BX	—> buffer in system memory
	SI	Starting X coordinate of screen block
	DI	Starting Y coordinate of screen block
	CX	Ending X coordinate of screen block

	DX	Ending Y coordinate of screen block
	AL	Write mode for block writing
Return:	Nothing	

The RESTOREBITMAP vector is used to load screen pixels from the system memory. The routine reads a stream of bytes from the system memory into the Rectangle defined by (SI,DI)–(CX,DX). The value in the AL register defines the mode that is used for the write. The following table defines the values of the available write modes:

Table A-8: Write Mode Values

PIXEL OPERATION	CODE
OVERWRITE MODE	0
LOGICAL **XOR**	1
LOGICAL **OR**	2
LOGICAL **AND**	3
COMPLEMENT	4

SETCLIP

	DW	SETCLIP	; Define a clipping Rectangle
Input:	AX	Upper Left X coordinate of clipping rectangle	
	BX	Upper Left Y coordinate of clipping rectangle	
	CX	Lower Right X coordinate clipping rectangle	
	DX	Lower Right Y coordinate clipping rectangle	
Return:	Nothing		

The SETCLIP vector defines a rectangular clipping region on the screen. The registers (AX,BX)–(CX,DX) define the clipping region.

COLOR_QUERY

    DW   offset   COLOR_QUERY ; Device Color Information Query

This vector is used to inquire the color capabilities of a given piece of hardware. A function code is passed into the driver in AL. The following function codes are defined:

	—>	Color Table Size	AL = 000h
Input:	None:		
Return:	BX	The size of the color lookup table	
	CX	The maximum color number allowed	

The COLOR TABLE SIZE query is used to determine the maximum number of colors supported by the hardware. The value returned in the BX register is the number of color entries in the color lookup table. The value returned in the CX register is the highest number for a color value. This value is usually the value in BX minus one, however, there can be exceptions.

```
—>      Default Color Table    AL = 001h
Input:   Nothing
Return:  ES:BX              —> default color table for the device
```

The DEFAULT COLOR TABLE function is used to determine the color table values for the default (power-up) color table. The format of this table is a byte containing the number of valid entries, followed by the given number of bytes of color information.

SYMBOL

```
DW       SYMBOL      ; Draw a graphics symbol at (CP)
Input:   AL          Code number of symbol (see below)
Return:  Nothing
```

This vector is used to write a symbol (or marker—an indicator for representing points on a line graph) to the output device. The symbol is written at the current pointer.

Table A-9: Vector Symbols

SYMBOL NUMBER	DESCRIPTION
0	Filled square
1	Plus sign
2	Eight-pointed star
3	An unfilled square
4	An 'X' character
5	A filled triangle
6	An hourglass
7	Six pointed star
8	Square with an 'X' inside
9	Shadowed cross
10	Vertical Line
11	Horizontal Line

Device Driver Construction Particulars

The source code for a sample, albeit unusual, BGI device driver is included with this Toolkit to assist developers in creating their own. The demonstration driver is provided in two files, DEBVECT.ASM and DEBUG.C. This Debug driver doesn't actually draw graphics, but instead simply sends descriptive messages to the console screen (via DOS function call 9) upon receiving commands. Instead of simply playing back commands, your own driver would be structured similarly, but would access control ports and screen memory to perform each function.

Cookbook

1. Compile or assemble the files required.
2. Link the files together, making sure that the device vector table is the first module within the link.
3. Run EXE2BIN on the resulting .EXE or .COM file to produce a .BIN file. There should be no relocation fixups required.
4. Run program BH (provided with the toolkit) on the .BIN file to produce the .BGI file.

The resulting driver is now ready for testing. Examine the file TEST.C for an example of installing, loading, and calling a newly-created device driver.

Examples

```
; To call any BGI function from assembly language include the structure below and
; use the CALLBGI macro.
;
CALLBGI  MACRO   P
         MOV            SI,$&P            ; Put opcode in (SI)
         CALL           CS:DWORD PTR BGI_ADD; BGI_ADD points to driver
         ENDM
;
; e.g., to draw a line from (10,15) to (200,300):
         MOV            AX, 10
         MOV            BX, 15
         MOV            CX, 200
         MOV            DX, 300
         CALLBGI        VECT

; To index any item in the status table include the status table structures below and
; use the BGISTAT macro.
;
BGISTAT  MACRO   P                          ; get ES:<SI> —> BGI STATUS
         LES            SI, CS:DWORD PTR STABLE; get location of status to SI
         ADD            SI, $&P           ; offset to correct location
         ENDM
;
; e.g., to obtain the aspect ratio of a device:
;
         BGISTAT ASPEC
         MOV            AX, ES:[SI]       ; (AX) = Y/X *10000
```

APPENDIX B

A VGA 256-color .BGI Driver

In addition to the Font Editor utility and the custom .BGI package, Borland has provided a new VGA driver (VGA256.BGI) which supports the full VGA color resolution with a 256 hue palette employing the Hue-Saturation-Intensity (HSI) color model.

Available from Borland's languages forum on CompuServe, the VGA utility package consists of five programs: the VGA256.BGI driver, the HSI.EXE and HSI.PAS color hue demonstration, and VGADEMO.EXE and VGADEMO.PAS.

The VGADEMO is the principal demonstration (and does work on non-VGA systems without the full range of 256 colors). The VGADEMO program includes demonstrations of several graphics functions which are new to Turbo Pascal version 5.0 (or Turbo C version 2.0), including the SetAspectRatio, FillEllipse, Sector, and SetWriteMode functions. The 256 Color and SetRGBPalette demos will only execute correctly on systems with VGA or compatible video cards. On an EGA system, for example, these two demo segments execute, but are restricted to the EGAVGA default palette of 16 colors.

Of particular interest to the programmer, in the HSI or VGADEMO programs, are the VGASetAllPalette procedure and the DetectVGA256 function. The source codes for both demo programs are written in Turbo Pascal but C programmers should have little difficulty converting them if necessary.

APPENDIX C

The Graphic Character Fonts

Ten graphics character fonts are shown following. Fonts 0..4 are graphics character fonts distributed with Turbo C, Turbo Pascal, and Turbo Prolog. Fonts 5..9 are provided with the Turbo Font Editor (see Chapter 19).

The following font illustrations were captured directly from a 640x480 VGA display with the font sizes as shown for each example.

The exact appearance of each font will vary depending on screen resolution and character magnification. For example, note characters B0h..B2h which show some distortion toward the bottom of the character where the stroke instructions "slip" slightly as they are mapped to the pixel image. This is normal and expected and is usually not visually apparent on the screen.

Also, the overall appearance of the characters on screen is generally smoother—due to the tendency of illuminated pixels to visually melt together—than they appear on paper.

A minor bug in Turbo Pascal 5.5 appears when an attempt is made to load any external font whose source file is larger than 16K, such as the Triplex (TRIP.CHR—16,699 bytes), Italic (TSCR.CHR—16,933 bytes) or Gothic (GOTH.CHR—18,151 bytes) fonts. If necessary, the GOTH.CHR font distributed with Turbo Pascal, which lacks the extended ASCII characters (only 8,560 bytes) can be used.

Alternatively, any of these three problem fonts can be edited using FE.EXE to remove unnecessary characters, such as the box characters, B0h..DFh, or the math characters, E0h..FEh—and thus reduce the size of the font.

Table C-1: Graphics Character Fonts

FONT	FONT NAME	TYPE	FILENAME
0	DefaultFont[1]	Bit-mapped	—none—
1	TriplexFont[1]	Stroked	TRIP.CHR
2	SmallFont[1]	Stroked	LITT.CHR
3	SansSerifFont[1]	Stroked	SANS.CHR
4	GothicFont[1]	Stroked	GOTH.CHR
5	ScriptFont[2]	Stroked	SCRI.CHR
6	SimplexFont[2]	Stroked	SIMP.CHR
7	ItalicFont[2]	Stroked	TSCR.CHR
8	RomanFont[2]	Stroked	LCOM.CHR
9	LargeFont[2]	Stroked	EURO.CHR

1. The versions of fonts 1..4 shown here are the expanded versions of the original distribution fonts provided with the Turbo Font Editor utility.
2. Font numbers and font titles for fonts 5..9 are not predefined. The font numbers shown were arbitrarily assigned by InstallUserFont in the order each font was assigned to the internal font table while preparing these illustrations. The font names are equally arbitrary but are intended as descriptive mnemonics.

Appendix C: The Graphic Character Fonts 503

Font Number: 0—DefaultFont—Bit-mapped
Source File: GRAPH unit—Size = 3

Font Number: 1—TriplexFont—Stroked
Source File: TRIP.CHR — Size = 3

	0	1	2	3	4	5	6	7	8	9	A	B	C	D	E	F
0																
1																
2		!	"	#	$	%	&	'	(	)	*	+	,	−	.	/
3	0	1	2	3	4	5	6	7	8	9	:	;	<	=	>	?
4	@	A	B	C	D	E	F	G	H	I	J	K	L	M	N	O
5	P	Q	R	S	T	U	V	W	X	Y	Z	[	\	]	^	_
6	`	a	b	c	d	e	f	g	h	i	j	k	l	m	n	o
7	p	q	r	s	t	u	v	w	x	y	z	{	|	}	~	△
8	Ç	ü	é	â	ä	à	å	ç	ê	ë	è	ï	î	ì	Ä	Å
9	É	æ	Æ	ô	ö	ò	û	ù	ÿ	Ö	Ü	ø	£	Ø	₧	ƒ
A	á	í	ó	ú	ñ	Ñ	ª	º	¿	⌐	¬	½	¼	¡	«	»
B	░	▓	▒	│	┤	╡	╢	╖	╕	╣	║	╗	╝	╜	╛	┐
C	└	┴	┬	├	─	┼	╞	╟	╚	╔	╩	╦	╠	═	╬	╧
D	╨	╤	╥	╙	╘	╒	╓	╫	╪	┘	┌	█	▄	▌	▐	▀
E	α	β	Γ	π	Σ	σ	µ	γ	Φ	θ	Ω	δ	∞	ø	∈	∩
F	≡	±	≥	≤	⌠	⌡	÷	≈	°	·	·	√	n	²	■	

Appendix C: The Graphic Character Fonts 505

Font Number: 2—SmallFont—Stroked
Source File: LITT.CHR—Size = 8

	0	1	2	3	4	5	6	7	8	9	A	B	C	D	E	F
0																
1																
2		!		#	$	%	&	'	(	)	*	+	,	-	.	/
3	0	1	2	3	4	5	6	7	8	9	:	;	<	=	>	?
4	@	A	B	C	D	E	F	G	H	I	J	K	L	M	N	O
5	P	Q	R	S	T	U	V	W	X	Y	Z	[	\	]	^	_
6	`	a	b	c	d	e	f	g	h	i	j	k	l	m	n	o
7	p	q	r	s	t	u	v	w	x	y	z	{	|	}	~	△
8	Ç	ü	é	â	ä	à	å	ç	ê	ë	è	ï	î	ì	Ä	Å
9	É	æ	Æ	ô	ö	ò	û	ù	ÿ	Ö	Ü	ø	£	Ø	₧	ƒ
A	á	í	ó	ú	ñ	Ñ	ª	º	¿	⌐	¬	½	¼	¡	«	»
B	▦	▦	▨	│	┤	╡	╢	╖	╕	╣	║	╗	╝	╜	╛	┐
C	└	┴	┬	├	─	┼	╞	╟	╚	╔	╩	╦	╠	═	╬	╧
D	╨	╤	╥	╙	╘	╒	╓	╫	╪	┘	┌	█	▄	▌	▐	▀
E	α	β	Γ	π	Σ	σ	µ	γ	Φ	θ	Ω	δ	∞	ø	ε	∩
F	≡	±	≥	≤	⌠	⌡	÷	≈	°	·	·	√	ⁿ	²	■	

Font Number: 3—SansSerifFont—Stroked
Source File: SANS.CHR—Size = 3

	0	1	2	3	4	5	6	7	8	9	A	B	C	D	E	F
0																
1																
2		!	"	#	$	%	&	'	(	)	*	+	,	−	.	/
3	0	1	2	3	4	5	6	7	8	9	:	;	<	=	>	?
4	@	A	B	C	D	E	F	G	H	I	J	K	L	M	N	O
5	P	Q	R	S	T	U	V	W	X	Y	Z	[	\	]	^	_
6	`	a	b	c	d	e	f	g	h	i	j	k	l	m	n	o
7	p	q	r	s	t	u	v	w	x	y	z	{	|	}	~	△
8	Ç	ü	é	â	ä	à	å	ç	ê	ë	è	ï	î	ì	Ä	Å
9	É	æ	Æ	ô	ö	ò	û	ù	ÿ	Ö	Ü	ø	£	Ø	₧	ƒ
A	á	í	ó	ú	ñ	Ñ	ª	º	¿	⌐	¬	½	¼	¡	«	»
B	░	▒	▓	│	┤	╡	╢	╖	╕	╣	║	╗	╝	╜	╛	┐
C	└	┴	┬	├	─	┼	╞	╟	╚	╔	╩	╦	╠	═	╬	╧
D	╨	╤	╥	╙	╘	╒	╓	╫	╪	┘	┌	█	▄	▌	▐	▀
E	α	β	Γ	π	Σ	σ	µ	τ	Φ	Θ	Ω	δ	∞	ø	∈	∩
F	≡	±	≥	≤	⌠	⌡	÷	≈	°	·	·	√	ⁿ	²	■	

Appendix C: The Graphic Character Fonts 507

Font Number: 4—GothicFont—Stroked
Source File: GOTH.CHR—Size = 3

Font Number: 5—ScriptFont ²—Stroked
Source File: SCRI.CHR—Size = 3

Font Number: 6—SimplexFont ^{2}—Stroked
Source File: SIMP.CHR—Size = 3

	0	1	2	3	4	5	6	7	8	9	A	B	C	D	E	F
0																
1																
2		!	"	#	$	%	&	'	(	)	*	+	,	−	.	/
3	0	1	2	3	4	5	6	7	8	9	:	;	<	=	>	?
4	@	A	B	C	D	E	F	G	H	I	J	K	L	M	N	O
5	P	Q	R	S	T	U	V	W	X	Y	Z	[	\	]	^	_
6	`	a	b	c	d	e	f	g	h	i	j	k	l	m	n	o
7	p	q	r	s	t	u	v	w	x	y	z	{	|	}	~	△
8	Ç	ü	é	â	ä	à	å	ç	ê	ë	è	ï	î	ì	Ä	Å
9	É	œ	Æ	ô	ö	ò	û	ù	ÿ	Ö	Ü	ø	£	Ø	₧	ƒ
A	á	í	ó	ú	ñ	Ñ	ª	º	¿	⌐	¬	½	¼	¡	«	»
B	▒	▓	▒	│	┤	╡	╢	╖	╕	╣	║	╗	╝	╜	╛	┐
C	└	┴	┬	├	─	┼	╞	╟	╚	╔	╩	╦	╠	═	╬	╧
D	╨	╤	╥	╙	╘	╒	╓	╫	╪	┘	┌	█	▄	▌	▐	▀
E	α	β	Γ	π	Σ	σ	µ	τ	Φ	Θ	Ω	δ	∞	ø	∈	∩
F	≡	±	≥	≤	⌠	⌡	÷	≈	°	·	·	√	ⁿ	²	■	

Font Number: 7—ItalicFont ^{2}—Stroked
Source File: TSCR.CHR—Size = 3

	0	1	2	3	4	5	6	7	8	9	A	B	C	D	E	F
0																
1																
2		!	"	#	$	%	&	'	(	)	*	+	,	-	.	/
3	0	1	2	3	4	5	6	7	8	9	:	;	<	=	>	?
4	@	A	B	C	D	E	F	G	H	I	J	K	L	M	N	O
5	P	Q	R	S	T	U	V	W	X	Y	Z	[	\	]	^	_
6	'	a	b	c	d	e	f	g	h	i	j	k	l	m	n	o
7	p	q	r	s	t	u	v	w	x	y	z	{	|	}	~	△
8	Ç	ü	é	â	ä	à	å	ç	ê	ë	è	ï	î	ì	Ä	Å
9	É	œ	Æ	ô	ö	ò	û	ù	ÿ	Ö	Ü	ø	£	Ø	₧	ƒ
A	á	í	ó	ú	ñ	Ñ	ª	º	¿	⌐	¬	½	¼	¡	«	»
B	▓	▓	▓	│	┤	┤	┤	┐	┐	╡	║	╖	╜	╛	╛	┐
C	└	┴	┬	├	─	┼	┝	╟	╚	╔	╩	╦	╠	═	╬	╧
D	╨	╤	╥	╙	╘	╒	╓	╫	╪	┘	┌	█	▄	▌	▐	▀
E	α	β	Γ	π	Σ	σ	μ	γ	Φ	θ	Ω	δ	∞	ø	∈	∩
F	≡	±	≥	≤	⌠	⌡	÷	≈	°	∙	·	√	ⁿ	²	■	

Appendix C: The Graphic Character Fonts 511

Font Number: 8—RomanFont—Stroked
Source File: LCOM.CHR—Size = 3

Font Number: 9—LargeFont—Stroked
Source File: EURO.CHR—Size = 1

Index

A
Active Viewport, 23
AddBar, 111
ALLPALETTE, 488
AndPut, 57
Arabesque, 465
Arc, 49
    Aspect Ratio, 47
    and the BGI, 487
    GetArcCoords, 48
    Line Style, 48
    line styles, 41
ArcCoordsType, 50
ArcTan, 193
Arrow Cursor, 229
Aspect Ratio, 46
    EGA/VGA, 47
ATT-400, 6
    palletes, 34
ATT.BGI, 70
ATTDriverProc, 70

B
background colors, 31
Bar, 44, 101
    and the BGI, 486
    line styles, 41
Bar3D, 44, 101, 111
    line styles, 41
BarGraph, 100
BGILINK.MAK, 69
BITMAPUTIL, 493
Borland Graphics Interface (BGI), 474-498
    ALLPALETTE, 488
    BITMAPUTIL, 492-493
    construction, 496-497
    Driver Toolkit, 501
    GETPIXBYTE, 493
    linking, 7
    run-time architecture, 478
    stroke font format, 452
BottomText, 62

business graphs, 89
Button, 272
    ButtonHit, 284
    Done, 279
    DoubleClick, 285
    Draw, 280
    Erase, 284
    Init, 278
    SetOutline, 279
Button object type, 277

C

Cartesian coordinate system, 191, 351
CenterText, 62
CGA, 6, 207
    CGA.BGI, 70
    color, 206
    color palette, 207
    color values, 33
    CGADriverProc, 70
    high resolution, 208
    palettes, 34
Chaos, 467
charsize, 62
Check Cursor, 231
CHR linking, 7
Circle, 49
    Aspect Ratio, 47
    coordinate rotation, 184
    Line Style, 48
    line styles, 41
CLEAR, BGI, 484
ClearDevice, 23-24
ClearImages, 150
ClearViewPort, 23-24
Clipboard
    Font Editor, 443, 447
ClipFlag, 24-25
CloseDotFill, 138
CloseGraph, 16, 151
ClrScr, 24
COLCUBE.C, 211
COLOR, BGI, 488
Color Graphics Adapter, 6
Color Printers, 347
Color Values, 33
    RrGgBg color values, 209
COLORS.PAS, 212
COLOR_QUERY, BGI, 495-496
concatenating strings, 80
constructor methods, 273, 278
CopyPut, 43, 57
CP, 23
    HorizDir, 60
    LeftText, 60
    LineRel, 41
    OutText, OutTextXY, 60
    TextWidth, 60
creating driver units, 69
creating font units, 69
Cross Cursor, 231
current position (CP), 23
cursors, 229-232
custom fonts, 450

D

default graphics values, 14
DefaultFont, 61, 85, 503
    SetUserCharSize, 63
descenders, 449
destructor methods, 279
DETECT, 10
DetectGraph, 6, 9, 11
Device Information Table (BGI), 484
Directions, 61
Directories, 8
Dispose, 83, 305
dot referencing, 280
dotmatrix, 384-385
dragon curves, 465

DRAW, BGI, 485
DrawPieGraphs, 90
DrawPoly, 44
    line styles, 41
    SetWriteMode, 43
DriverPath, 11
drivers
    Driver Status Table (BGI), 480
    external, 68
    Graphic, 70
    linked, 69
    user-designed, 72
dummy modem, 438

E
EGA, 6
    Aspect Ratio, 47
EGA Yellows, 210
EGA/VGA
    color values, 33
    Default Palette, 208-209
    color relations cube, 211
    EGAMono, 27
    EGAVGA.BGI, 70
    EGAVGADriverProc, 70
    manipulating color/hue, 210
    RrGgBb color system, 206
    RrGgBg Color Values, 209
Ellipse, 49
    Aspect Ratio, 47
    coordinate rotation, 184
    GetArcCoords, 48
    Line Style, 48
    line styles, 41
emulation support (BGI), 479
Enhanced Graphics Adapter, 6
Erase Block, 84
EraseStr, 81
error codes (BGI), 481
error functions, 11-12
EURO.CHR, 437, 451, 512

EventRec (data structure), 228
explicit referencing, 280
external drivers, 68

F
FileImage.Pas, 178
Fill Patterns, 53
FillColor, 30
FILLED_Ellipse (BGI), 487
FillEllipse, 50
FillPatternType, 54
FillPlane, 107, 111
FillPoly, 46, 107, 137, 138
    GraphResult, 46
FillSettingsType, 54
FILLSTYLE (BGI), 489
FloodFill, 46, 52, 108, 137
    BGI, 492
    PieSlice, 51
Fmt function, 402
font editing tools, 442
Font Editor, 435, 443-450
    area definitions, 439
    and characters, 440-441
    Command Reference, 444
    computer requirements, 437
    display, 439
    graphics requirements, 438
    mouse conventions, 437-439
    Plotter requirements, 438
font ID number, 450
Fonts, 61, 450
    custom, 450
    external, 68
    graph unit fonts, 61
    graphic, 71
fractal, 456
Fractal Programming in Turbo Pascal, 467
FX-85 graphics modes, 384

G

GCursor (mouse cursor), 228
GenMouse implementation, 236
GenMouse object, 234
GetArcCoords, 48, 50, 93
GetAspectRatio, 47
GetBackground, 160
GetBkColor, 32
GetColor, 31
GetDefaultPalette, 33
GetDriverName, 11
GetFillPattern, 54
GetFillSettings, 54
GetGraphMode, 13, 15
GetImage, 24, 55, 83, 85, 102, 115
   data compression, 179
GetLineSettings, 42
GetMaxColor, 29
GetMaxMode, 14
GetMaxX, 37
GetMaxY, 37
GetMem, 115, 142
GetModeName, 11, 14
GetModeRange, 13, 14-15
GetPalette, 32
GetPaletteSize, 33
GetPixel, 40
   BGI, 492
GetTextSettings, 59, 64
GetViewSettings, 23, 25
GetX/GetY, 38, 85
Glove Cursor, 232
GOTH.CHR, 71, 437
GothicFont, 61
GothicFontProc, 71
GRAPH.TPU, 11
GraphDefaults, 14
GraphErrorMsg, 11, 12
graphic control objects, 272
graphic error codes, 10
Graphic User Interface, 4
GraphicMouse, 227
GraphicMouse object, 234
graphics buffer, 54
graphics error messages, 12
graphics mode functions, 13
Graphics Pages, 25
GraphResult, 11, 12, 16, 24
   FillPoly, 46
   SetTextJustify, 62
gray scale palettes and printers, 394-395
grInvalidMode, 15
GUI, 4
GWrite, 85
GWriteLn, 86
GWriteXY, 85

H

Henon attractor, 461
HERC.BGI, 70
HercDriverProc, 70
Hercules Monochrome Graphics Adapter, 6
Hewlett-Packard Graphics Language, 419
HorizDir
   OutText, 60
HP Color Pro switch settings, 421
HPGL, 419
Hypot, 193

I

Ibeam Cursor, 232
IBM8415
   SetPalette, 35
IBM-8514, 6, 29, 208
   DetectGraph, 35
   GetPalette, 35
   SetAllPalette, 35
   VGA compatibility, 35
IBM8514.BGI, 70

IBM8514DriverProc, 70
IBM-8514 Video, 34
Icons, 330-333
Image Copy Options, 57
image files, 178
image manipulation, 55
image options, 56
image rotation, 183
    video aspect correction, 186
ImageSize, 55, 115, 142, 181
IMB8514
    FloodFill, 35
IMPLEMENTATION, 235
INIT (BGI), 484
InitGraph, 9, 10, 14, 15, 16
InitializeColors, 214
Install_Font, 451
InstallUserDriver, 72
InstallUserFont, 73, 450
integer-string conversion, 79
INTERFACE, 228
ItalicFont, 510

J
justification, 62

L
Landscape mode
    Dot-Matrix, 385
    Laserjet, 392
LARGE_Font, 450
LargeFont, 512
Laserjet printer, 391
    DeciPoint, 394
    graphics characters, 395
    graphic screen dump modes, 392
LCOM.CHR, 437, 451, 511
LeftText, 62
    OutText, 60
Line, 40
    line styles, 41

SetWriteMode, 43
line drawing functions, 40
    viewport, 40
line graph, 112
line styles, 41
    predefined, 42
    widths, 42
LineSTYLE, 489
    bit patterns, 490
LineGraph, 115
LinePattern, 41
LineRel, 41
    line styles, 41
    SetWriteMode, 43
LineSettingsType, 42
LineTo, 40
    line styles, 41
    SetWriteMode, 43
linked drivers, 69
linking graphics drivers, 68
linking graphics fonts, 68
LITT.CHR, 71, 437, 505
LJGraph unit, 396
LoadFonts, 451

M
Make utility, 69
Malthusian attractor, 462
Mandelbrot Explorer, 467
Mandelbrot Set, 456
MCGA, 6
MCGA palettes, 34
monochrome display
    graph labels, 102
morphological animation, 151
mouse
    ConditionalHide, 244
    EventHandler method, 243
    GetPosition, 238
    Hardware text cursor, 246
    Initialize (graphic mouse), 245

Initialize (text mouse), 245
QueryBtnDn method, 239
QueryBtnUp method, 240
ReadMove method, 241
Reset method, 237
SetAccel method, 242
SetCursor (graphic), 244
SetCursor (text), 246
SetLimits method, 240
SetPosition, 239
SetRatio method, 242
Show method, 237
Software text cursor, 246
TestMouse method, 237
mouse access, 276
Mouse Cursor, 229
mouse driver types, 226
mouse unit, 226
MouseHandler, 236
MousePtr
    Button operations, 247
MousePtr utility, 247
MOV, 43
MOVE (BGI), 485
MoveImage, 145
MoveRel, 38
MoveTo, 38
Multi Color Graphics Array, 6
Multi-Sync, 6
MultiBarGraph, 100
multiple graphics/video pages, 25

N
New, 303
non-standard RS232 serial port, 421
NoSound, 150
NotPut, 57
null (dummy) modem, 422, 438

O
object-oriented programming, 77
object types, 277
OrPut, 57
OutText, 59-60, 79
    LeftText, 62
OutTextXY, 59, 60, 79

P
palettes
    BGI, 488
    color number, 30
    palette.colors[], 216
    PaletteType, 30, 32
    predefined, 39
    size, 29
PATBar, 486
PC-3270, 6
PC3720.BGI, 70
PC3720DriverProc, 70
pen color combinations, 420
pie graphs, 91
    exploded, 95
PieSlice, 51, 93
    BGI, 487
    Aspect Ratio, 47
    GetArcCoords, 48
    Line Style, 48
    line styles, 41
pixel images, 55
plotters, 418
    ClosePlotter, 430
    Create, 274
    Draw, 274
    Erase, 275
    Init, 273
    Initialization, 423
    MatchColor, 427
    Move, 274
    plotter colors, 419
    plotter utility, 422
    Ready, 429
    RestoreViewPort, 274

SelectPen, 427
serial port, 445
SetColor, 275
SetLoc, 275
WritePort, 428
Point object type, 273
PointType, 45, 137
polar coordinates, 191
POLY (BGI), 486
polygons, 44
Portrait mode for printers, 385
Position (data structure), 228
PositionImage, 149
POST (BGI), 485
predefined colors, 34
predefined palettes, 34
printers
    Dot-Matrix, 384-385, 386-387
    Laserjet, 391-392, 402-403, 407
    Print_Pause, 405
    PrintGraph, 387
PutImage, 24, 56, 83, 85, 102, 115
    CopyPut, 139
    OrPut, 139
    XOrPut, 83, 143
PutPixel, 39
    BGI, 492
    predefined palettes, 39
Pythagorean Theorem, 194

R
RadioButton, 272
    ButtonHit, 289
    Draw, 288
    Erase, 289
    Init, 287, 288
    object type, 286
RCos, 153
ReadImage, 181
real-string conversion, 79
rectangle, 43

line styles, 41
SetWriteMode, 43
RegisterBGIDriver, 70
RegisterBGIFont, 61, 71
reset (mouse), 230
RESTOREBITMAP (BGI), 494-495
RestoreCrt, 15
RestoreCrtMode, 16
RGBI color system, 207
RightText, 62
ROMAN_Font, 450
RomanFont, 511
RrGgBb color system, 206
RrGgBg color system, 209
RSin, 153

S
SANS.CHR, 71, 437, 506
sans serif font, 61, 506
    SansSerifFontProc, 71
SAVEBITMAP (BGI), 494
SaveImage, 142
screen coordinates, 191
Screen Mask, 229
SCRI.CHR, 437, 452, 508
SCRIPT_Font, 450
ScriptFont, 508
ScrollBar, 273
    Done, 293
    Draw, 294
    GetPercent, 297
    Init, 291
    object type, 290
    ScrollHit, 295
    SetThumbPad, 295
sector, 51
Serial Port Status Bytes, 429
SetActivePage, 23, 25, 26, 27, 134
SetAllPalette, 30-31, 34, 207
SetBkColor, 31, 207
SETCLIP (BGI), 495

SetColor, 30
SetFillPattern, 52
SetFillStyle, 53
SetGraphBufSize, 55
SetGraphMode, 10, 14, 15, 16
SetLineStyle, 41
SetPalette, 30-31, 34, 207
SetRBGPalette, 35
SetTextJustify, 59, 62
    GraphResult, 62
SetTextStyle, 11, 59, 61, 450
SetUserCharSize, 59, 62, 63
SetViewPort, 23, 24
SetVisualPage, 23, 25, 26, 27, 134
SetWriteMode, 43, 161
ShowLabels, 109
SIMP.CHR, 437, 452, 509
SIMPLEX_Font, 450
SimplexFont, 509
SizeOf, 45
SmallFont, 61
SmallFontProc, 71
smart linking, 67
stroked fonts, 436
SYMBOL (BGI), 496
symbol fonts, 436

T
TALIC_Font, 450
TEXT (BGI), 491
text, 61-62
    settings information, 64
TEXTSIZ (BGI), 491
TEXTSTYLE (BGI), 490
TextHeight, 59, 64
TextMouse, 227
TextMouse object, 235
TextSettingsType, 64
TextWidth, 59, 64, 85
The Science of Fractal Images, 468
three-dimensional graphs, 103

TopText, 62
TRIP.CHR, 71, 437, 504
TriplexFont, 61, 504
TriplexFontProc, 71
TSCR.CHR, 437, 451, 510
Turbo Font Editor, 1
TurnLeft, TurnRight, 361
Turtle
    Back, 358
    Clear, 355
    Delay, 356
    DrawStr, 358
    Forwd, 357
    Heading, 362
    Hide, 356
    Home, 356
    Init, 355
    NoWrap, 356
    PenDown, 362
    PenUp, 362
    SetHeading, 361
    SetPenColor, 361
    SetPosition, 357
    Show, 356
turtle drawing, 361
turtle graphic commands, 355
turtle graphics, 351
turtle information, 362
turtle movements, 356
TurtleWrite, 363
TWindow, 355

U
user-designed drivers and fonts, 72
UserBitLn, 41
UserFill, 53
using custom fonts, 450
using linked drivers, 69
using linked fonts, 69
using units, 7

utilities
    BINOBJ utility, 68
    Plotter utility, 422

V

variable graphics adapter, 6
variable outputs, 79
VECT (BGI), 485
vector calculations, 190
    BGI descriptions, 483
VGA, 6
    Aspect Ratio, 47
VGA256, 208
video adapter types, 5
video aspect ratio, 46
video modes, 6-8
    identifying, 8
video pages, 25
video signal cues, 207
viewport, 14, 25, 96
    FloodFill, 52
ViewPortType, 25
VueMeter, 273
    Close, 300
    Done, 299
    Draw, 299
    Init, 298, 299
    Open, 300
    Select, 300
VueMeter object type, 298

W

WhereT, 362
Wrap, 356

X

xasp, 47
XCor, 362
XOR, 43
XOrPut, 43, 57

Y

yasp, 47
YCor, 362

Disk to Accompany
Graphics Programming in Turbo Pascal® 5.5

The Pascal source files listed in **Graphics Programming in Turbo Pascal 5.5** by Ben Ezzell are available on one 5 1/4" disk.

Equipment you will need:

Hardware: IBM® Personal Computer, or 100% IBM PC-compatible computer; DOS 2.0 or higher.

Memory: 640 K

Available by mail only. Use the postage-paid card below.

Please send me_____(quantity) Disks to accompany *Graphics Programming in Turbo Pascal 5.5* by Ben Ezzell, at $19.95 each.   ISBN 0-201-57024-6

____ Check enclosed (include your state sales tax; Addison-Wesley will pay postage and handling)

____ Charge to my Visa card #_____ Exp. date:_____

____ Charge to my MasterCard #_____ Exp. date:_____

                                                    Four digits above your name:_____

____ Charge to my American Express card #_____ Exp. date:_____

YOUR SIGNATURE:_____

Name:_____ Title:_____

Company (if applicable):_____

Address:_____

City:_____ State:_____ Zip:_____